VACCINE A

VACCINE A

THE COVERT GOVERNMENT EXPERIMENT THAT'S KILLING OUR SOLDIERS

and Why GI's Are Only the First Victims

GARY MATSUMOTO

BASIC
BOOKS

A MEMBER OF THE PERSEUS BOOKS GROUP

NEW YORK

Published by Basic Books,
A Member of the Perseus Books Group

Basic Books are available at special discounts for bulk purchases in the
United States by corporations, institutions, and other organizations. For
more information, please contact the Special Markets Department at the
Perseus Books Group, 11 Cambridge Center, Cambridge MA 02142, or
call (617) 252-5298, (800) 255-1514 or e-mail
special.markets@perseusbooks.com.

A CIP catalog record for this book is available from the Library of Congress.
ISBN 0-465-04400-X

04 05 06 / 10 9 8 7 6 5 4 3 2 1

For the men and women in the armed forces of the United States and the United Kingdom ...

and for my daughter Helen

Contents

Introduction

This is a book that the U.S. Department of Defense does not want you to read. It is about human medical experimentation—not that undertaken by the Japanese and Nazi doctors of World War II more than sixty years ago, but human experimentation being conducted on U.S. citizens by U.S. doctors and scientists working for the U.S. military. You may be familiar with some of the more shameful medical episodes in American history—the Tuskegee syphilis trials conducted by the U.S. Public Health Service or the Cold War LSD experiments conducted by the CIA. But this book is not about the past, except as the past is also prologue to our present and future. The unethical experiments detailed in this book are ongoing, with little prospect of being self-limiting. Why? Because they have been shielded from scrutiny and public accountability by national security concerns.

The victims of this story are the young men and women who volunteered for the U.S. armed forces, fully recognizing that they might be asked to risk their lives in battle and found themselves, without their knowledge or permission, the subjects of dangerous medical experimentation. Clinical evidence now exists that military doctors in both the United States and Britain have been testing a new anthrax vaccine on soldiers who weren't told they were getting an unlicensed immunization, let alone one that contains a substance shown in peer-reviewed scientific literature to be capable of causing incurable if not fatal disease. The justification for this secret experimentation was intelligence that Saddam Hussein had biological weapons that he might use if the war went against him. While Saddam had plans, if not an ongoing program, to develop a nuclear weapon, and certainly once had and indeed used chemical weapons, a sad irony of this story is that after years of U.N. inspections and now a war that has put Saddam Hussein behind bars, no samples of Iraqi dried anthrax have yet been discovered.

Following its stellar performance in the first Gulf War, the Afghan invasion and second war against Iraq, our nation's military establishment reached a level of popularity unseen since the years following World War II, in the process acquiring—the Abu Ghraib prison scandal aside—a patina of infallibility. This book will argue that the military has used public goodwill to shut off debate on a matter of vital interest to all Americans. I will show what can happen when the military is allowed to fend off criticism with national security claims and by equating criticism with disloyalty. Like any institution, the Department of Defense is as flawed and fallible as the humans who fill its ranks, and so the public must not assume that the DOD will always act honorably and with integrity because humans do not. Some will say that such talk is un-American. But I maintain that dissent against the abuse of power is one of this country's proudest traditions. It is a privilege that Americans have given their lives for, and one that we neglect at our own peril.

In 1990, when the United States launched Operation Desert Shield and then Desert Storm, I was an NBC correspondent covering the war from Saudi Arabia. Although the term was not yet used, I would become an embedded journalist for the ground offensive. Like the soldiers I covered, I was fully warned about the risk that the other side might employ biological or chemical warfare weapons. I had my protective gear and pills to take in the event of a nerve agent gas attack.

Fortunately, we won that war rather quickly. The air assault took little more than a month and the ground war ended in just four days. The Iraqi troops were simply no match for U.S. military power, and the "Mother of All Battles" that Saddam Hussein had threatened never materialized. As a result, American casualties were phenomenally low in comparison to those suffered in any other war in U.S. history. Sadly, many of the casualties that did occur were the result of friendly fire—we mistakenly hurt our own. But Saddam never put his dreaded biological and chemical weapons into play.

A little more than a year or so after war's end, reports began to emerge about a strange malady afflicting returning veterans. The symptoms were often vague, many subjective, but remarkably consistent—aching joints and muscles, rashes, fatigue, weight loss, weight gain, hair loss, sore gums, diarrhea, nausea, swelling of hands and feet, short-term memory loss and headaches. Of course, taken individually, these symptoms could each be attributed to a myriad of possible causes. Yet even grouped together they still did not add up to a recognizable disease, according to military doctors.

When people are scared, or in pain, as these GIs clearly were, when everyone is wondering who will be the next to be robbed of his or her meaningful life by crippling illness, rumors invariably abound. Because I am not, by temperament or training, the type of person to be caught up in idle rumor, my attention was caught not by the rumors themselves but by the military response to one of them, that a nerve agent might be the source of these complaints. Around 1997, the CIA and the military suggested a scenario that seemed to confirm these suspicions. It allowed for possible injury to about 100,000 troops, by remarkable coincidence almost precisely the number of Gulf War veterans who were registered as ill at the time.

The scenario went as follows: A U.S. Army engineering battalion inadvertently released a plume of nerve agent when it blew up an Iraqi ammunition dump at a place called Khamisiyah stocked with chemical munitions. If you read between the lines the subtext was clear: it was really Saddam's fault; he should not have been storing nerve agent. All this sounded quite plausible, except to those of us the military had trained to identify a chemical attack. The consequences we had been taught to look for in no way matched the symptoms the sick GIs were experiencing.

The military's own scientific literature—research with nerve agents tested on both animals and humans and published decades earlier—also undermined the idea that nerve agents released into the open air could cause the symptoms Gulf War veterans were reporting. Eventually, the military's own epidemiologists published data that further discredited the nerve agent theory, and angry senators censured both the Army and the CIA for releasing highly speculative, spurious information. The GAO has recently published a report saying there was no sound basis for the Khamisiyah theory.

But by that time, I had other reasons to see the nerve agent explanation as untenable. I strongly suspected that Gulf War Syndrome was not caused by something that had happened in Kuwait or Iraq. Why? Because soldiers from most of the countries in the anti-Iraq coalition did not suffer from this malady.

No Arab soldiers or civilians, on either side, got sick. Nor did any journalists get sick, embedded or otherwise. Of all those who had been on the ground during the war, only soldiers from the United States, Great Britain, Canada and Australia were experiencing symptoms. Also telling was that GIs who had never left these shores were complaining of the same symptoms as those who had been deployed to the Gulf.

The more I thought about the nerve agent explanation, the more I wondered why the CIA and the Army would have propagated an explanation that would in time surely come to be revealed as bogus and thereby subject them to justly deserved ridicule. What were they hiding that was so uncomfortable that they put out such a manifestly unsupportable explanation? Or were they hiding nothing? Was I just missing something?

My own first reaction was to assume that I had indeed missed something.

I am someone who had three uncles who served proudly in the U.S. Army—two of them were sergeants and the third retired a lieutenant colonel. My dad was a buck private too young to see combat in World War II, but he went through boot camp and did his tour of duty in Tennessee at the end of the war. I looked up to these men, in part, because they had served in the Army. As a young Japanese-American growing up in the 1950s, I played war, as young boys invariably do, even when the neighborhood kids taunted me about being a Jap. But I knew—even if they didn't—that one of the most decorated combat units in U.S. history was a band of "Buddha-heads" made up of Hawaiians of Japanese descent and volunteers out of the relocation camps for Japanese-Americans on the mainland—all American-born—who fought with valor in Europe. Still later, I learned about those colorful characters in the Pacific—guys like my cigar-chomping Uncle Thomas—who served in military intelligence as a translator. I heard less from my Uncle George, who served on the front lines in Korea as a sergeant in the Army Signal Corps; Uncle George lost so many of his friends in that war that he never wanted to talk about it. From his reticence I gathered that war was not quite the bloodless affair I saw on my favorite '60s TV show, *Combat*, though as a young boy I could not even begin to conceive its true carnage. It was my Uncle Shug—a lieutenant colonel in the military police who served as an Army criminal investigator in occupied Japan and then in Germany—who used to tell me with conviction that in the Army there was only one color: olive green.

With a 1-A classification and a low draft number, I was a prime candidate for the rice paddies of Vietnam, but President Nixon ended the draft just as I was about to be called up. Instead, I spent two years in a mandatory Army ROTC program at a religious college I attended outside of Chicago—a college that graduated at least one speechwriter for the current Bush administration. I come from a Midwest Republican family whose members are "born again" Christians. While I don't claim to be exactly like my family in dogma or politics (who is?), I am proud of my heritage, particularly of my family's service in the Army. As a TV journalist I sought out assignments involving the military whenever I could, and won awards for my reporting.

I have gone on at some length about myself because what I am about to relate in this book is more than a controversial story. It is an almost unbelievable story. All told it took me six years to pull all the pieces together. But once I felt I knew what had happened and why, I had only one goal in mind—to draw attention to the secret activities of a few (not all) U.S. military doctors, who, I came to realize, have been medically experimenting on troops for the past fifty years, almost without pause. There is clinical evidence that their most recent experiment led to an unknown number of formerly healthy young men and women—possibly tens of thousands of them—having their lives destroyed by illness. Some have even died.

This book will show that shortly after the war ended, the U.S. government, in response to the catastrophic nature of Gulf War illness, spent well in excess of $100 million on studies to learn what the illness was and what had caused it. These studies came to the conclusion that no single disease could account for all the medical problems experienced by sick Gulf War veterans. The degree of illness from one to the next veteran varied enormously—from aches and pains to death. U.S. military doctors used these studies to justify treating Gulf War veterans complaining of these symptoms as if they were suffering from nothing more than psychosomatic illnesses due to stress, denying them modern medical treatment.

I will then tell you about a researcher and her husband, a physician, and finally other scientists at Tulane University, who identified the symptoms experienced by Gulf War veterans in their study as autoimmune. What is autoimmune disease? It is the damage that occurs when the immune system mistakenly identifies the body's own tissues as foreign matter and then attacks it. Lupus, rheumatoid arthritis and multiple sclerosis—diseases that the anthrax vaccine manufacturer openly associates with its vaccine—are all au-toimmune. Upon examination by civilian doctors, some veterans—said to be suffering from an indefinable syndrome—were diagnosed with autoimmune diseases. Most important, I will show that Tulane helped establish one of the most important and painful pieces of information—that these illnesses were iatrogenic, that is, induced by medical treatment.

By developing an assay—a test to determine whether an individual has antibodies to a particular substance in his or her blood—scientists from Tulane University Medical School established what they say is a "marker" for Gulf War Syndrome. This marker identifies whether a GI had been injected with a substance called "squalene" (pronounced SKWAY-leen). Those who had a so-called Gulf War illness consistently tested positive for antibodies to squalene in their blood; healthy Gulf War veterans do not have these antibodies. The Tulane scientists then tested their next hypothesis—that squalene had been introduced into these veterans through the anthrax vaccine the veterans had been given. The licensed anthrax vaccine, they knew, did not contain squalene, which explains why hundreds of thousands of soldiers did not get sick. To test the connection between Gulf War illness and a possible, unlicensed, experimental anthrax vaccine secretly given to an unknown number of military personnel, Tulane tested the blood of four Air Force reservists scheduled to get their anthrax vaccine. Before the vaccination, their blood did not contain the antibodies. Afterward, it did. All four had been injected with anthrax vaccine confirmed by the FDA to contain squalene.

Squalene is what is called an adjuvant. Adjuvants stimulate the immune system to respond—which is what a vaccine has to do to build up immunity. My book will show why the military doctors felt they needed an immuno-stimulant so desperately just as the Gulf War began—their licensed vaccine was not going to be effective quickly enough. It can take weeks to develop im-munity with a good vaccine; with the licensed anthrax vaccine, a not-so-good vaccine, it can take months. When military doctors started vaccinating troops less than ten days before the United States would be at war, it was almost pointless to use the old vaccine. Using the Army's newest anthrax vaccines was the logical thing to do. At the time, Army scientists believed that they could generate more immunity in less time with just one shot of the new vac-cine. Had Saddam launched an attack with anthrax resulting in mass casual-ties, not using this new vaccine would have been seen, in retrospect, as a near dereliction of duty. There was little downside to such a decision. Army scientists thought their new vaccine was safe. Sadly, as the clinical evidence now attests, U.S. and British military personnel paid a terrible price for this mistake, a mistake that might not have been made had the Army scientists been more familiar with the literature on oil-based adjuvants.

Rather than defend their actions as a hard judgment call, to this day, military doctors deny having used an experimental anthrax vaccine and deny that the anthrax vaccine given any veteran had squalene in it.

In 1999, I published an article in *Vanity Fair* magazine in which I laid out for the first time anywhere a connection between squalene, the anthrax vaccine and Gulf War illness. Counterattacks began almost immediately. One Army officer declared that I was "reckless, irresponsible and wrong." The Air Force Surgeon General at the time, who made it clear that he shared an equally dim view of the article, insisted there was no squalene in anthrax vaccine; there never had been, he insisted, nor would there ever be. In *Vanity Fair* I identified two lots of vaccine that correlated with a positive antibody response to the oil. In response to that article, the FDA ran tests on those lots of vaccine and three others and found squalene in all five.

The military's new response: squalene is a naturally occurring substance that the anthrax bacterium probably makes. This of course does not explain why with few exceptions only military personnel inoculated with anthrax vaccine confirmed by the FDA to contain squalene have tested positive for the antibodies. Later, I would discover peer-reviewed data that bacteria, and specifically *B. anthracis,* do not make squalene—contrary to the assertions made by military scientists. The Army and the FDA had little excuse for propagating a demonstrably inaccurate theory on the provenance of squalene in anthrax vaccine. The evidence had been published decades before and was available in just about any well-stocked medical library. Still, here and there, one scientist or another will note in the scientific literature, or before Congress, that the anthrax vaccination cannot be ruled out as a cause of Gulf War Syndrome.

But as I've said earlier, this is not a book about the past, but about the present and the future. There is now evidence that squalene—first injected into U.S. GIs because there was a perceived need for a vaccine that would provide effective immunity quicker—is still being given to GIs today when there is no verifiable battlefield threat from anthrax. Troops given anthrax vaccine for Operation Iraqi Freedom have now tested positive for anti-squalene antibodies.

More than a hundred U.S. troops who deployed to Iraq in 2003 developed pneumonia; at least two of them died. Many of these cases were "aseptic," which means they did not result from bacterial infection. An NBC News cameraman, Craig White, developed a transient pneumonia after anthrax vaccination. Later, he tested positive for antibodies to squalene, which has, in the past, correlated with vaccine lots subsequently proven by the FDA to contain this oil. In February 2004, the previous Army Surgeon General, Lt. General James Peake, conceded that some of these pneumonias may be a consequence of autoimmunity. Unknown to most members of the American public, the Secretary of the Army now possesses a patent for a new anthrax vaccine that allows for its formulation with squalene.

If that isn't frightening enough, the Bush administration has just ordered 75 million doses of the new, as yet unlicensed anthrax vaccine—enough to inoculate 25 million unwitting civilians—and has announced its intention to give it to all of us, license or no license, in the event of a broad-based anthrax threat. Of greater concern is the fact that with funding from the NIH, scientists have formulated vaccines for flu, human papilloma virus (to prevent cervical cancer), malaria, HIV and herpes that also contain squalene.

Scientists will tell you that there is no such thing as a 100 percent safe vaccine. This is true. While vaccines are imperfect—and for an unfortunate few, vaccination has caused permanent injury—vaccines remain one of the most successful public health innovations in the past 200 years. Along with sanitation and antibiotics, vaccines have saved countless lives. But with anthrax lots proven to contain squalene, the systemic reactions are now running 35 percent or higher, compared to what it was before the Army started using squalene additives—less than 1 percent. The General Accounting Office's research shows that the rate of adverse reactions among Air Force Guard and Reserve pilots and crew—perhaps less than coincidentally immunized during the time that the FDA has confirmed the presence of squalene in specific lots of anthrax vaccine—is running around 84 percent.

What's more, the updated pharmaceutical insert—stuffed into boxes of anthrax vaccine after the FDA reported that it found squalene in some (but not all) anthrax vaccine lots—reports a wide range of autoimmune diseases now associated with anthrax immunization, including lupus, multiple sclerosis and arthritis.

Before you say that all this is impossible in this country—impossible after what happened at Tuskegee and after the horrible Cold War experiments with radiation on handicapped children and LSD on unsuspecting GIs—let me explain why it is more than possible. In this country, actions that have put the public at risk are generally challenged in litigation. Subpoenas force the production of relevant documents, truthful testimony is compelled under oath, reporters cover the proceedings and the media reports the sworn charges, defenses and countercharges. Just the threat of litigation now causes most organizations to anticipate vulnerabilities in the event of a suit and make changes that have the practical consequence of safeguarding the public.

But military physicians, and even the pharmaceutical companies who produce drugs and vaccines for military use, are shielded by law from medical malpractice suits. These physicians do not even bother to carry malpractice insurance. They do not need to. GIs, who have no right to refuse inoculations they see as dangerous, have no right to their own medical records when they find their lives ruined by illness. They are without recourse before the injury and after it.

The outrage that followed public awareness of the extent of medical experimentation once conducted in prisons and institutions for the mentally retarded, as well as elsewhere, successfully led to changes in the law requiring informed consent when an unproven drug or technique will be tested on human subjects. Today, there is only one venue where physicians can still test experimental drugs on humans without informed consent, and with impunity—the U.S. military. Existing safety regulations require informed consent for experimentation on military personnel. But subsequent memorandums of agreement have created loopholes in those regulations, allowing for the *therapeutic use* of investigational drugs without informed consent as long as such experimentation is undertaken strictly to protect the health of troops, if not their lives. Without strict oversight, there is always a risk that someone will interpret the rules too loosely and go too far. During the Gulf War, the FDA granted a waiver of informed consent for the use of selected investigational new drugs. Although the Army's new anthrax vaccine was not among them, Tulane's data raises this question: Did military doctors slip something extra past the FDA, specifically an unlicensed anthrax vaccine that contained squalene? The clinical evidence supports this conclusion.

In the years that followed publication of my *Vanity Fair* article, I have traveled across the country and as far away as the Ural Mountains in Russia and to Stockholm, Sweden, in search of the facts. I have interviewed research scientists and the military physicians who inoculated soldiers with this "new and improved" anthrax vaccine—a vaccine so hush-hush that they were told to destroy all the vials after use and not to record the vaccine in the GI's medical records unless specifically asked to do so by the GI. I have spoken with countless GIs who keep wondering why they can't get straight answers to their questions.

In 1994 the Senate Veterans Affairs Committee recommended that the Feres Doctrine—a 1950 Supreme Court decision that ruled military personnel cannot sue the Department of Defense for monetary damages over negligence—should not apply in the case of military personnel harmed by inappropriate medical experimentation when informed consent has not been obtained. Congress has never acted on that recommendation. There is now evidence that we are paying the price for this failure.

This book begins as a story of unexplained illness. But it is ultimately a story of betrayal, betrayal of the thousands of young men and women who signed up for military service, willing to risk their lives in battle, only to be secretly used in medical research. When I wrote this book, I had them in mind. This book is an IOU. I owe the soldiers of the 10th Mountain Division and the 24th Mechanized Infantry Division, who hauled my sorry behind, and those of my journalist colleagues, across the Iraqi desert in vehicles already overstuffed with soldiers who could have used the extra space. This book is for the 101st Airborne Blackhawk pilots and crew who hunkered down with us hacks when the sandstorms blew in, and shared their water. This book is for the men and women of Dover Air Force Base, some of whom I have gotten to know personally over the years, who are among those who have borne the brunt of the Army's campaign—in concert with the FDA and National Institutes of Health—to test a new anthrax vaccine.

This book is for my Army veteran uncles and my dad, none of whom approve of the conduct by Army doctors and scientists that I describe in the pages that follow. This book is also for my daughter and for the children of my friends. I do not want to happen to them what has happened to the men and women who have worn the uniform of this great republic and that of the United Kingdom. They are all someone's children too. I have met some of their parents, and have seen with my own eyes their anguish for their injured sons and daughters.

The great mystery in this story, a mystery that I cannot completely solve, is why the scientists developing these vaccines are covering up their mistake and continuing to advocate the use of a new vaccine that will have such devastating consequences on their own people. There is some evidence that the corrupting influence of money has played a role in this. President Eisenhower long ago warned us of the dangers of an emerging military-industrial complex. Most of us believed that the danger involved only those highly visible contractors who produced gazillion-dollar planes, missiles and nuclear submarines. Let everyone be especially vigilant over companies making military vaccines that are intended for sale to the large and lucrative U.S. civilian market.

For those who read this book and say that our republic is not as great as I still maintain it is, I would argue that there are few nations on earth, at any time in human history, where someone could have written a book as openly critical of a government's national security policies as this one is, and then actually see it in print. Even in Britain, where I lived for more than a decade, I could not have gotten many of the documents that provide the foundation for this book. Britain has an Official Secrets Act; America has a Freedom of Information Act. As imperfect as that act is, this book is a testament to its value, and to the remarkable degree of freedom that we enjoy in this country. There are those who will argue—especially in times such as these—that I got my hands on too much information. To them I say that a measure of this nation's greatness is its openness and tolerance for dissent. Our democracy was born of such stuff, and I thank God for that.

As for the military doctors and scientists who allegedly perpetrated this experiment, there is a blurry line between what is legal and what is illegal in these matters. Although I have focused primarily on the scientific rather than legal aspects of this case, what limited reading I have done on the laws and regulations governing human experimentation in America leads me to conclude that a line was crossed. These were transgressions undoubtedly done with the best of intentions. Some officers were simply obeying orders given in good faith and with the welfare of troops uppermost in their minds. Others probably knew that they went too far, but it was a trade-off aimed at saving people. I am convinced that those who took the decision to test these vaccines on military personnel thought it would protect far more people than it would hurt. But that is the problem with public health risk/benefit calculations; with experimentation there are always unknown variables and the resulting damage can be irreversible. The scientists injecting squalene into humans assumed that it was safe. Many of them worked for the National Institutes of Health; and who would dispute the judgments of the NIH? But it was an assumption for which too many of our finest men and women have paid too high a price. Herein lies the moral conundrum at the heart of this book. The military doctors and scientists who run these experiments want to protect people; in exposing these doctors and scientists, so do I.

Whether or not such experiments should be allowed to continue is a matter for rigorous public debate. What is not debatable, I think, is the issue of accountability. Those who perform these experiments must be held responsible for their consequences. Those who are harmed must be helped.

An old Latin expression, *quis custodiet ipsos custodes*, asks the question: "Who shall keep watch over the guards?" American democracy is based on a system of checks and balances. All actions taken in the name of our republic must be subject to oversight and scrutiny by other branches of government. As I will show in this book, Gulf War illness is evidence this system is failing us. Where this oversight fails, it becomes the responsibility of the press to expose these actions to direct public scrutiny. The process can be painful, but it is only by doing so that we force accountability on those who act in our name. If individuals shielded under the rubric of national defense can continue to operate outside these rules, the consequences will be far worse than an epidemic of autoimmune disease. We will have lost an essential guarantee of personal freedom.

VACCINE A

HE THAT TROUBLETH HIS OWN HOUSE SHALL INHERIT THE WIND.

—Proverbs Chapter 11, Verse 29—

Chapter One

Footprints in the Snow

Thursday, April 5, 1979, Berezovsk, Soviet Union

It started with a cough. Boris Georgievich Romanov trudged along the pavement and coughed again—a shallow involuntary hack to clear his throat.[1] He had been doing that a lot today. In Berezovsk, a small town near the westernmost fringe of Siberia, winter always arrives early and leaves late. Now it was spring, but a "weak" snow, as the Russians say, had dusted the trees and coated the streets in fresh powder. Romanov was a burly man, nearly six feet tall with wavy brown hair and the faintest wisp of gray at his temples. The geometry of his face was all right angles. The sides of his head met his scalp at a near perfect ninety degrees, and he had the squarest of jaws. A human head could hardly have been more rectangular had it been molded from clay pressed into all four corners of a box. It gave Romanov a stolid look, accentuated by a pair of black horn-rimmed glasses. In the only photograph I could find of him, he did not look happy to be in front of a lens. His lips were thin and sagged down at the corners as if he had spent his entire life frowning. If one's appearance says anything about one's soul, Romanov's, at age forty, gave the impression that somewhere inside of him was a reservoir of pent-up anger that no one with good sense would dare disturb. In a dark suit, wearing a tie thickly knotted in the '70s style, he looked as though he had been mass produced on one of the Soviet Union's assembly lines—a model proletarian in a wool suit whose life had narrowed down to little more than duty and routine. Any hint of panache or youthful ideals had been purged from his appearance, and were it not for that persistent cough, any trace of his undistinguished life might have vanished like footprints in melting snow.

A cough was hardly unusual for this time of year; he probably thought nothing of it. Catching something, in fact, was almost inevitable. Romanov had just returned from Gorodok Devyatnadtçat and Tridtsat-Dva, Compounds 19 and 32, a Soviet army base at the southeastern edge of nearby Sverdlovsk, a city of more than a million people on the banks of the Iset River. He was a reservist, and every five years, Romanov took the diesel-chugging avtobus (pronounced ahv-toh-boose) down the Berezovsky Tract, the two-lane black-top connecting his town with Sverdlovsk, for duty. For the past month, he had been cooped up with hundreds of other reservists, inhaling a miasma of germs, smoke from cheap cigarettes and fumes emanating from the nether regions of his barrack mates' trousers after meals of stringy beef and cabbage.

Compounds 19 and 32 were two reasons why Sverdlovsk was still closed to foreigners. It was a city of peerless Soviet pedigree, named after Yakov Mikhailovich Sverdlov, the goateed and pince-nez–wearing Bolshevik who helped Vladimir Lenin organize the October Revolution and then, along with Lenin, arranged the executions, in this very city, of the last Czar and Czarina, Nicholas II and Alexandra, and their five children. But it was the city's military connections that made it off-limits to non-Soviet citizens. In the early days of the "Great Patriotic War," when the Wehrmacht laid siege to Leningrad and Guderian's panzers swept toward the gates of Moscow, Stalin moved entire factories out of the Nazi-occupied territories to Sverdlovsk. It was the logical place to retrench. Blessed with rich veins of iron ore and an ice-free river that could power water mills through the winter, Ekaterinburg, the city's prerevolutionary name, had been a center of Russian industry since the reign of Czar Peter the Great. The Ural Mountains also provided a natural line of defense, shielding Sverdlovsk from the arctic winters that helped defeat Napoleon's armies and then Hitler's. Here, far from distant battlefronts, and protected from temperatures that could literally freeze a man's blood, Stalin's reconstituted factories built the T-34 tanks and the Katusha rockets—the missile launchers that looked like organ pipes mounted on truck beds—that were instrumental in defeating German armies that numbered more than three million men. After the war, Sverdlovsk's factories continued to make weapons—tanks, munitions and new generations of missiles. Unknown to most people living in this city, Soviet army scientists and technicians were also hard at work on another weapon, one that did not roll off any assembly line.

Despite his thick coat, Romanov shivered; his chill came from within. A light wind brushed his face, blowing the snow in long wisps across the streets of Berezovsk to the curbs, where it collected in gently sloping drifts. The continuing snow, in fact, was one of the top stories of the day. On the front page of *Vercherny Sverdlovsk*, the Evening Sverdlovsk, the headline read: "Lish Soidut Snega" (The Snow Is Not Going Anywhere). Local farms were still covered in a "thick layer of snow," the story lamented, and the soil would be "saturated with moisture"—bad for the spring planting. Pervaya, one of the Soviet Union's two television channels, scheduled a documentary about Ethiopia at 4:10 in the afternoon. No one knows if Romanov read the paper that day, or watched TV. Most likely he was too sick to care about the spring planting or Ethiopians.

By Friday, the temperature outside hovered around 33 degrees Fahrenheit, mild for the Urals at this time of year, but Romanov perspired and shivered in turn. His coughing erupted now in convulsive staccato fits. It takes more energy to cough than most people realize, and it steadily weakened him. He felt short of breath. He gulped air but couldn't fill his lungs. His neck felt stiff, too. When he took his temperature it was 39° C (in Fahrenheit this is over 102°), but it was his headache that finally drove him to see a doctor. This was no ordinary throb. It was pain so bad that he could barely open his eyes. If he did, it felt as though his eyes might pop clear of their sockets from the pressure. Romanov's doctor prescribed a pain reliever called Analgin and told him to stay in bed.

Sometime over the weekend—his medical records don't specify when—Romanov would have felt better, maybe even well enough to convince him that he was finally recovering.

That's when he crashed.

Monday, April 9th

When the dark green ambulance pulled up in front of Romanov's house, he was slipping in and out of consciousness. His fever had climbed higher; his cough had become a near gasp—a labored wheeze that left him sounding as if he was struggling for every molecule of air. The pain in his head and neck was so severe it nauseated him. His blackouts were almost merciful.

The paramedics had arrived in an old UAZ. The Russians pronounce it "Ooh-ahz"—an Ul'anovsk Avtobus Zavod, nicknamed, without affection, the "kozlik." A kozlik is a small goat, a skittish animal that jumps around a lot, which tells you a lot about the vehicle's suspension. In the rear compartment of an UAZ, you felt every defect in the road. Hitting a pothole could launch stretcher and patient toward the ceiling; then they would crash back down, sending IV poles and other gear toppling to the floor in a jangling heap. The UAZ bearing the feverish Romanov sped toward Sverdlovsk, where emergency rooms were overflowing. Area clinics were doing little more than dispensing aspirin and antibiotics, which was not enough. Something awful was happening there.

When Romanov arrived, he was barely conscious. A nurse doing triage instructed the paramedics to take him directly to intensive care. Because of his headaches, the ICU physician asked the hospital's neurosurgeons to examine him. By now, Romanov could barely move his neck, a sign that he might have meningitis—an infection that causes inflammation of the membranes, called the meninges, surrounding the brain and spinal cord. Romanov also couldn't straighten his elevated leg while lying prone. The physicians treating Romanov called this the "Kürnick symptom," something they had seen before with meningitis. To confirm the diagnosis, one of the doctors performed a spinal tap. Feeling the vertebrae protruding from Romanov's back, the doctor looked for a good space between the bones, then inserted a special needle that could make even soldiers like Romanov queasy at the sight of it—a three-inch shaft with a canula inside, a thin rod that prevented tissue from clogging the extra-wide needle as it penetrated the fibers surrounding the spinal column. The doctor applied steady pressure, but not too much. He didn't want to hit a nerve. Suddenly, he felt the resistance give way. He was through. He pulled out the canula and attached a syringe to it. When the fluid started to drain into the tube he took a good look and blinked. Normal spinal fluid is opalescent, almost clear. Romanov's had a pinkish tinge. There was blood in it.

Meningitis doesn't cause hemorrhaging into spinal fluid. The blood could be from an aneurysm—a ruptured artery, possibly at the base of his brain. That would explain the bloody fluid, but not the cough . . . or the fever. So an aneurysm didn't make sense either. What was wrong with this man? Unable to diagnose Romanov's disease, his doctors treated his symptoms. Until they knew what was wrong with him, it was all they could do. For his low blood pressure, they hooked him up to an IV drip containing electrolytes and poly-gleukin, a protein solution that acts as a blood substitute. To ease his pain, they gave him more Analgin. They did not know what was wrong yet, but they fully expected Romanov to recover.

For reasons left unexplained in his medical records, none of the doctors thought to culture his blood.

Tuesday, April 10th, Hospital 40, Sverdlovsk

On the morning of April 10th, he stopped breathing and flatlined.

"Doktor . . . Srotchno! Urgent!" someone in the ICU shouted as Romanov's cardiac monitor started beeping an alarm. Nurses rushed to his bedside. One of the neurosurgeons arrived first and started to administer mouth-to-mouth resuscitation. He pinched Romanov's nose, placed his mouth over Romanov's, and blew. Romanov's chest rose, but only slightly, and then subsided quickly as very little air appeared to be getting into his lungs. The surgeon blew again, harder this time. Again the chest expanded, but not to the extent the surgeon expected to see. Romanov was a strapping fellow, barrel-chested. The surgeon blew again. Romanov's trunk barely budged. Something was very strange about this. His lungs wouldn't inflate. Once more, the surgeon placed his mouth over the patient's and blew as hard as he could. Romanov's chest elevated slightly, but no higher than the previous times.

He was dead.

Romanov's doctors were not yet aware that other people in Sverdlovsk were cycling through the same symptoms—the coughing jags, high fevers, headaches and shortness of breath—all with unexpectedly catastrophic results. After appearing to recover, they suddenly died. A pattern was emerging, but its outlines were still too vague to apprehend, in part because the entries on death certificates appeared to be unrelated. "Sepsis" was a common notation, as were "bacterial pneumonia" and "infectious pneumonia." Some doctors in town began to talk of a new and frighteningly virulent strain of hemorrhagic influenza, but they were just guessing.

Apparently, Hospital 40's neurosurgeons knew nothing about this. Whatever the disease was, it was filling victims' lungs with fluid and leaving dark hemorrhages on their skin . . . ugly purple blotches that looked like someone spilt red wine on their chests, except the stain had spread *under* their skin.

Some invisible contagion was stalking the city, and it was unbelievably lethal. Dmitri Vinogradov's neighbors remember him as a "big, healthy" man, but whatever killed him literally stopped him in his tracks.[2] He fell down unconscious, mid-stride, in the street—a trail of footprints in the snow, ending in a shallow depression where his body lay. Like the chalk silhouette at a murder scene after the body had been removed, the outline of Vinogradov's ebbing life remained on the ground for all to see—until its contours were slowly trampled into obscurity by passersby. Vinogradov was no isolated case. There were whispers of people slumping over dead in the city's trolley cars and collapsing while waiting in line for treatment at a clinic.

How much was true and how much was exaggeration was impossible to tell, but doctors in nearby hospitals were growing more and more alarmed; bodies were stacking up and there were more visits from the police. Not a word of these deaths appeared in the city's newspapers; the TV and radio were silent about them. Many people knew nothing of the drama unfolding in the city's southeastern sector. They stood in lines at the stores. They went to work. They attended the opera. One of the finest opera companies outside of Moscow was in Sverdlovsk—the Akademichesky Teatr Opera e Balleta imeni Lunacharskogo, the Academy Theater and Ballet, named for a Bolshevik minister, Lunacharsky. It had just performed *Rigoletto* to a packed house; *La Traviata* was on for the 12th. Teenagers were listening to Alla Pugaheva, a husky-voiced Russian pop singer who sounded a bit like Dusty Springfield; the edgy rock band Mashina Vremeny (Time Machine); and bootleg records by the Euro-dance band Boney M—four Caribbean session singers, working in Germany.[3] Boney M's "Rasputin" was an international hit, and big in Sverdlovsk. Somewhere in the city, booming from some vodka-sodden dorm room or student apartment that Friday night, you would have heard Boney M's souped-up balalaika, backed by a thumping disco beat: *"Rah, Rah, Rahspoo-teen, lover of the Russian queen . . . there was a cat that really was gone!"*

If people just a few miles from the outbreak were oblivious to it, Moscow was not. Word had reached the Soviet Union's highest-ranking public health officials nearly a thousand miles away. They dispatched a team of physicians from the capital to help treat the sick and dying, including a Soviet Deputy Minister of Health, Dr. Pyotr Sergeevich Burgasov, and Dr. Vladimir Niko-

layevich Nikiforov, a top infectious disease specialist from Moscow's presti-
gious Botkin Hospital.[4] They set up shop in Hospital 40, the city's largest.
Hospital 40 had some of Sverdlovsk's best medical facilities and was close to
the affected area.

There were other signs that this was no ordinary epidemic—the police for
instance. That some people die from disease is a demographic certainty, but
when this happens there is rarely any reason to involve the police. When
Dmitry Vinogradov died at Hospital 20, paramedics returned his body home
for the wake, but the police showed up and took his body away.[5] A truck took
Anna Komina's body directly from Hospital 20 to the cemetery without telling
her family.[6] On a tip from hospital staff, Komina's son, Yuriy, and his wife
Tatyana showed up for the burial but were not allowed inside the gate; the police were there. Mikhail Markov was buried in a special coffin, bought by the
city, not his family, and guarded by the police.[7]

Most of the victims were buried in the Vostochniy cemetery, at the edge of
town, and in the same secluded section.[8] Something else was odd about these
hasty burials under police escort. The coffins and gravesites were doused in
chlorinated lime.[9]

On the day Romanov died, not a word of these deaths appeared in the
Vercherny Sverdlovsk. On the newspaper's front page was an item about an
emergency evacuation of Crestview, Florida—a train derailment had spilled
toxic chemicals onto the tracks and a deadly plume of chlorine, phenyl and
acetone threatened to drift over the town. Elsewhere on the front page were
the paper's obligatory tributes to the city's working men and women—photographs of people standing next to imposing machines, gripping wrenches and
wearing hard hats. At a local ceramics factory, workers were sick and dying—
an alarming number of them—but the *Vercherny Sverdlovsk* didn't report that.
TV news didn't report it either. The radio played Prokofiev.

Romanov's death mystified the surgeons. They were always troubled at losing a patient, but this was easier to take when there was some sign of its in-
evitability. The doctors knew all too well the limitations of their craft. In this
case, though, there was no such sign—death seemed entirely avoidable. Romanov's illness, though undiagnosed, struck them as curable and the treatment they prescribed was correspondingly routine—the Russian equivalent of
Tylenol.[10] His blood pressure was low, but the IV solution of glucose and electrolytes should have taken care of that.[11] The one thing that threw them was

Romanov's pink-tinged CSF—the blood in his cerebrospinal fluid.[12] Had disease caused that, or some injury to the brain?

If Romanov's case had been routine, the attending doctors would have waited a day to do an autopsy. But his death so mystified them that they wanted one done right away.[13] The pathologist on duty was Dr. David Mihailovich Fliegel, a competent man, but this particular autopsy, they felt, required an especially gifted interpreter of flesh and bone.[14] An autopsy was a kind of narrative that unfolded on a slab of stone, but the body divulges its secrets only to those who have truly mastered its peculiar language. Each organ, artery or piece of cartilage could tell such a person a story. Done properly, this would be a final revelation, not of Romanov's life, but of his death. A well-placed scalpel stroke might yield an unalterable truth about his final hours on earth. A less precise cut, or a less precise eye, might leave them forever in the dark. No, this autopsy called for the best pathologist in Sverdlovsk, a doctor who seemed to know the body's every nuance.

"Get Faina," they said.

The neurosurgeons wanted Dr. Faina Afanasyevna Abramova. No one would touch Romanov until she arrived.

April 10th, mid-morning

Boris Georgievich Romanov would tell her what she needed to know. Though he would never utter another word, his body might still impart some secret to those who could decipher it. Dr. Faina Afanasyevna Abramova gazed into the eyes that could no longer gaze back and felt something in the presence of death that few people outside of her profession would understand. It was only natural to be repelled by death; some pathologists never grow entirely accustomed to it. But Abramova was at ease . . . as if she were in the presence of an old companion.

Having retired just a year earlier from her post as associate professor of pathology at the Sverdlovsky Gosudarstveny Medicinsky Institut, Dr. Abramova continued to work half days at Hospital 40, doing what she did better than anyone else. She would talk to the dead; they would yield their secrets to her—tell her stories that no one else could hear quite so well.

This affinity with death could not reside in a less likely place. Faina was a vessel overflowing with life. She came from a tiny village called Rasdolya—a drab outpost of Stalinist collectivism that in the 1930s had fewer than twenty buildings and a single horse-drawn plough.[15] Her real first name was Afanasia. But Russians often prefer to use shorter versions of given names—diminutives that mothers and fathers, brothers and sisters use as terms of endearment. Thus a Mikhail becomes "Misha" . . . Alexandr is "Sasha" and Dmitri, "Mitya." Afanasia's family called her "Fai," and as she grew older, "Fai" evolved into "Faina." Both names suited her. "Fai" especially had a whimsical ring to it that captured the young girl's spirit. She stood five-three in bare feet and was cheerful to the core. She had ice-blue eyes, brown hair that lightened to amber blond in the summer, and an extra-wide mouth and big round cheeks that caught the sun and the wind year round, so they always seemed to glow. When she grinned, which was often, it drew every inch of her face into the act.

Today, Faina wasn't smiling. A group of neurosurgeons huddled round the mortuary table in the basement of Hospital 40; it looked as though the whole department had shown up. Romanov was broad-shouldered, muscular and hirsute. A man of such strength, she thought, should not have succumbed so quickly to death.[16] It puzzled her. Faina had survived the "Great Patriotic War," saw death harvest the souls of her countrymen with bullets and disease and starvation. As a teenager, she daydreamed of being a pilot—captivated, like many young girls at the time, by the news that three Soviet women, already celebrated aviatrixes, had just set a world record by flying a Russian twin-engine bomber more than four thousand miles nonstop from Moscow to Siberia. The names Raskova, Osipenko and Grizodubova became as renowned in the Soviet Union as the name Earhart was in the West, but Fai was destined for more earthly pursuits. She was so short that her feet would never reach the foot pedals in an airplane cockpit. So after school one day, she found a job in a pathology lab . . . and her life's work.

For the next forty years, she would study diseases and the way they killed. In the hospital mortuary, she would dictate her observations to students or physicians, who in the Soviet Union were ordered to attend the autopsy of any patient who died in their care. Faina spoke to the living, but in her mind she also conversed with the dead. She still yearned to stymie death. She knew his smell—the sickly sweet odor of an unwashed body and its effluent, the sting of formaldehyde and chloramine in her nostrils, and the gases that would sometimes seep from a rotting cavity when she inserted a scalpel. She knew death's touch—cold and unyielding—and she knew his lack of compassion, saw it in the tears of agonized young mothers and in the faces of their babies who had barely known life before death had introduced himself. Those who lay silent on the mortuary's marble slabs—today, a forty-year-old man named Boris Georgievich Romanov—would teach her more about death's dark arts than they ever could in life.

In that snowy April of 1979, death wielded his scythe in a manner that stymied doctors across the city; even Faina had never seen anything quite like it. She heard the reports of people keeling over in the streets, in open fields, on trams and in the waiting rooms of clinics. Always the symptoms were the same—high fever (as high as 104° F), coughing, vomiting and difficulty breathing.[17] Sometimes, in the late stages of the illness, people sounded as if they were choking. It looked like pneumonia, but it wasn't. And then there was the false recovery. The patients seemed to get better. Then, when the worst seemed to be over, purple blotches would appear on patients' chests, on their abdomens and under their arms. Their ears and lips turned blue. That's when the rending chest pains would come—pain so severe that paramedics thought their patient was going into cardiac arrest. But emergency IV's of epinephrine had no effect. The sick would slip into unconsciousness and soon after they would die.

The doctors from Moscow were now in charge. The team leader, Dr. Vladimir Nikolayevich Nikiforov, feared the outbreak of some deadly new disease—it looked like pneumonia but was unlike any he had seen before. Patients were hemorrhaging badly. Livid bruises appeared all over their bodies, mostly on their chests. The disease didn't respond well to antibiotics either. Was it viral? Hemorrhagic fever was not unknown in the Soviet Union, but it affected the brain, not the lungs. Had some strain mutated into something that also caused pulmonary disease? Was it contagious?

Romanov's case was strange. Initially, the surgeons suspected he had meningitis, then maybe an aneurysm. No one considered the possibility that a pulmonary disease killed him. His symptoms, as far as the doctors could tell, were mainly neurological.

"Tell me Boris Georgievich, what killed you?" Abramova asked without speaking. *"It wasn't an aneurysm, was it?"* According to his chart, Boris Georgievich Romanov had sickened just five days ago. Paramedics had rushed him to Hospital 40 the day before, on April 9th, and in less than twelve hours he was dead. Abramova shook her head. *"No, Boris,"* she thought, *"an*

aneurysm did not do this to you." Dr. David Mikhailovich Fliegel would per-form this autopsy, but Abramova, called in as a consultant, was the senior pathologist; she was in charge.[18] She looked at the hemorrhaging on Boris's chest then motioned to her assistant.

"Sasha . . . start with his head."

Sasha switched on a small electrical saw. It was circular, attached to a grip the size of a flashlight; rotating at high speed, it whined like the drill in a den-tist's office. He started an inch above the bridge of Romanov's nose, at the center of his skull, where the forehead protruded farthest. The whine of the saw changed pitch as it bit into the bone. Sasha always thought that cutting bone sounded similar to cutting a piece of hardwood like mahogany. It was tough on the ears. As he drew the whirring saw across Romanov's right tem-ple, he eased off the pressure. The skull was thinner here and Sasha didn't want to tear into the brain. He cut past the earlobe; a fine spray of shredded flesh and clotted blood splattered his goggles. When he had cut down to the bulge at the back of the skull, he stopped to turn Romanov on his side. Dr. Fliegel held Romanov in this position while Sasha drew the saw across the back of the head then up the left side. Sasha's skill showed that day in the mortuary. He had circumnavigated Romanov's skull without rending the sheer brain membranes, and the seam he had cut met perfectly above the brow; he wasn't off by so much as a millimeter. Sasha set down the saw and reached for a metal rod with one end flattened like a chisel. He inserted the flat end into the red seam circumscribing Romanov's scalp and pried off the top of his head.

———

Abramova's eyes grew wide, but she made no sound. Even before Dr. Fliegel took over from Sasha to do the more delicate work of removing the brain enve-lope called the dura, she could see something was wrong. You could see it plainly through the diaphanous membranes. Romanov's brain was the wrong color. Once Fliegel peeled back the dura, there was no mistaking it. The hemi-spheres of Romanov's brain glistened with a film of blood, dark red from lack of oxygen. Pooled in his cranial fissures was edema that had the look and consis-tency of blackberry jelly. A sickening goop filled the crenellations of Romanov's brain—the folds, still white, like little islands in an archipelago, erupting from the surface of a dark wine sea. Abramova's pulse quickened; she had seen this before, somewhere long ago . . . in the museum at her old medical school. One of her professors had asked her to fetch a special brain specimen for his lecture. What was it called again, a cap? Yes, yes . . . a "cardinal's cap." She was sure of it. *"Bozhe moy! [My god!] How did this happen, Boris?"* . . . once again, thinking the words without saying them. Abramova's expression revealed nothing. She closed a door to her mind. *"Who did this to you?"* A bulb flashed. Sasha was taking photographs. Beneath the dura, which is attached to the underside of the skull, was a softer membrane called the arachnoidea mater—a delicate filigree of tissue, resembling a spider's web, on which the brain is cushioned.[19] Beneath this was another thin membrane, the pia, hard to see because it clings to the surface of the brain like plastic wrap, making it glisten. Fliegel peeled away both of these layers, then scraped some of the congealed, jelly-like blood from the brain fissures and put it into a glass tube filled with a liquid mixed with nutrients to culture whatever germs it contained.

"Sasha, you can stop taking photographs," said Abramova. "Do the chest now." She moved closer. Sasha reached for a scalpel, plunged it into Boris's chest above the sternum and began to slice downward in one motion toward the navel. He cut two more incisions from each shoulder that met at the sternum to form a "Y," then pulled back the flesh. "Sasha . . . cut here," she said, pointing to the ribs. Sasha sawed through the ribs to expose the lungs. They were swollen with blood. "Massive infection," she said to the doctors observing the procedure. Something splashed from his lung cavities. *"Bozhe moy!"* said another doctor. The two lateral cavities in Romanov's chest were flooded with liquid—more than enough in each to fill a quart-sized milk carton. The liquid in Romanov's lungs, amber-colored plasma denatured of its red blood cells, had seeped out and squeezed the lobes of each lung into the top third of the chest cavity. The trachea, the tube through which air passes to the lungs, is reinforced by rings of cartilage the shape of horseshoes, which preserves its shape. The lungs, however, are more elastic and can expand and contract like balloons. In Romanov, there was no space left for them to do this. "No wonder he couldn't breathe," said a neurosurgeon. Streaked across the surface of the pleural sacs—the membranous sleeves that envelop the lungs—were globs of yellowish exudate of the same gooey consistency as mucous. Romanov's chest was a septic mess. "Look here and here," said Abramova, pointing into the mediastinum—the space in the chest demarcated in front and back by the sternum and the spine, and on either side by the lung cavities. This was where the ancients believed the human soul resided. The heart is found in this space, tucked under a lobe of the left lung. So are the trachea or windpipe, and the fleshy tubes called bronchi that branch off the windpipe to convey air into each lung—and entwining these tubes, a network of lymphatic vessels that look like tiny vines bulging with nodules the size of peas. All of these structures were grossly inflamed, crimson in some places, almost black in others. There was dead tissue everywhere. Using a big ladle, Sasha scooped out some of the amber-colored fluid mixed with runny, semi-gelatinous lumps and poured it into a bowl filled with disinfectant. Some of it he put it a tube filled with liquid nutrient. "I'm afraid this isn't pneumonia," Abramova said.

The autopsy room fell silent. The neurosurgeons, Dr. Fliegel, and Sasha all turned to Abramova, waiting for her to say something more. She paused, but not to be theatrical. She wanted to be accurate in what she said next, and didn't want to scare anyone without being absolutely sure.

"It looks very much like anthrax," she said quietly.

Sasha almost dropped his ladle. The neurosurgeons recoiled. Fliegel's expression turned to stone. No one except Sasha wore a mask, and instantly they regretted it. Except Abramova . . . she was unfazed; her eyes shone with conviction. "Yes, I think it is anthrax," she said.

"What do we do now?" It was the voice of the neurosurgeon who had tried to revive Romanov with mouth-to-mouth resuscitation. His eyes were wide. "What do I do?" he asked.

"The only thing you can do now is drink alcohol," said Abramova. She wasn't joking, and she didn't mean vodka. She meant raw alcohol. "Drink about 25 to 50 grams," she said.[20] "Swish it around in your mouth . . . then swallow."

The neurosurgeons had heard enough. They adjourned to the sink, rinsed their hands in alcohol and left the room.

Wednesday, April 11th

The next morning the lab reports for Romanov's autopsy arrived in Dr. Abramova's office. Just as she thought, pneumonia didn't kill him. It was *Siberskaya yazva*, or "Siberian ulcer" as the Russians call it. Anthrax.

Romanov had yielded up his secret, but he had told Abramova more than she expected. Anthrax was an animal disease that had jumped species to infect man eons ago. The organism grew in soil, and you could find it in many parts of Sverdlovskaya—the regional administrative area that the Soviets called an "oblast." Livestock contracted it when feeding. Anthrax spores are naturally sticky. When a grazing cow or sheep scraped contaminated ground with its muzzle, spores would cling to the animal's nose or lips, which it would then lick, ingesting the spores. From time to time there would be a small outbreak among animals, an "epizootic," in the outlying villages. But it was April and snow still covered the ground. The livestock hadn't started grazing in the pastures yet. Animals were an unlikely source of this outbreak. What's more, if animal anthrax had jumped species to man, it was almost always as a nonfatal infection of the skin—cutaneous anthrax, or *kozhnaya*—that could be easily cured with antibiotics.

Boris Georgievich Romanov did not have *kozhnaya*. He'd had little chance of surviving the type of anthrax that really took his life—at least not in its late stages when his lips had turned blue. His blood flow had slowed to a trickle, initiating a cascade of failing systems. Damaged capillaries leaked plasma, flooding body cavities, leaving behind a concentrated sludge of blood cells—a proteinaceous ooze in capillaries and vessels on which rapacious bacteria fed before eating through more tissue. Lungs collapsed; tissues died. Inside his intestines, Abramova saw large scabby carbuncles where dead tissue had started to rot. Without blood to transport it, Romanov's body was starved of oxygen. Lack of oxygen turned his skin blue. Although he could still breathe, he had, in fact, slowly asphyxiated.

Just five days after he first started to cough and three weeks shy of his forty-first birthday, Romanov died from an overwhelming toxic shock that stopped his heart. No, Abramova knew exactly what had killed him. She had suspected it the minute she saw the ugly hemorrhage that had spread across his chest.

Sometime after April 12th

To be absolutely sure, Abramova had to do another autopsy. By this time there was no shortage of corpses in Hospital 40. One awaited her on the mortuary table now. It was another suspicious case, and one that especially interested an infectious disease specialist from Moscow named Dr. Olga Yampolskaya. For the past ten hours, from the time he was admitted to the time he died, she had tried to save this patient, a worker from a local ceramics factory.[21] But his prognosis was bad from the moment paramedics wheeled him through the emergency room doors. The man's entire body had a bluish tinge. His gray eyes stared out, unblinking, from their sockets. When Yampolskaya shone a light into them, nothing happened. His pupils should have narrowed when she flashed the light into his eyes, but they remained dilated. She ordered an IV drip with the antibiotic cephalosporin—the maximum dosage. It made no difference. She put him on a ventilator, but his lungs wouldn't inflate. It was not until she saw X-rays of his lungs that she realized all her work had been in vain—nothing could save him.

"And what will you tell us today, young man," Abramova thought as she gazed down at his corpse. Would she see it again? It was so rare. She had spotted it first with Romanov. Now she looked out for it again. Sasha pried off the top of his skull. The answer was plain, but just to be sure, she carefully cut through the translucent membranes that sheathed the hemispheres of the man's brain. She peeled them away, and now everyone could see.

It wasn't there. There was no cardinal's cap.

Sasha opened the chest next . . . and it was then that Abramova knew. It couldn't be anything else. Its livid reality was inescapable. Just as the X-rays showed, something had squeezed the man's lungs into a mere strip, no more than two inches wide, at the very top of the pleural sacs. She knew the moment she sliced into the sacs and the fluid came splashing out. "One . . . two" . . . she carefully ladled out the fluid, watching the level rise in the bowl as she counted . . . *"This is unbelievable,"* she thought . . . "four . . . five" . . . till finally she scooped out the dregs. In all, Abramova had removed more than half a gallon of liquid from each cavity—a toxic soup of viscid plasma, teeming with anthrax bacteria. She drew in her breath and held it for a moment, exhaling slowly, savoring the simple and vital act that this unfortunate man, even on a ventilator, could not perform in the final hours before his death.

She surveyed his eviscerated trunk. There was the same catastrophic damage in the chest . . . the ugly lesions, necrotic tissues and lumpy mucus-like edema clinging everywhere. When she examined the tissues in the abdomen, they seemed, at first glance, less severely damaged. This was the best evidence yet of how the anthrax got into the victims. The extent of destruction in the corpse's mediastinum told her that here was where the spores had been the longest . . . where they had the most time to germinate, corrupt and defile. This was the likely "portal of entry" for these tiny seeds of death that had blossomed into living cells: eating, secreting and multiplying in the body's moist dark recesses, then spreading with the help of the body's own fluids—a deadly bacterial bloom transported through its host on warm currents of lymph and blood. *"This is no ordinary anthrax,"* she thought. *"It looks like* legochnaya"*—pulmonary anthrax. Abramova couldn't be sure, and she dared not voice her suspicions. But that is what the evidence suggested. Somehow Romanov and this man, and God knows how many others, had inhaled a fatal dose of anthrax spores. How did this happen? Dozens of people had died from the same symptoms. She glanced at the other corpses awaiting autopsy. They had the same hemorrhaging on the trunk, and their ears and lips were blue. She was stunned. Never in the history of Mother Russia had anyone seen such an outbreak; never anywhere in the world as far as she knew. Where had this come from? Had *she* breathed in these spores? Had her children?

Dr. Pyotr Sergeevich Burgasov had arrived unannounced at Hospital 40, and then left as suddenly as he came. This, too, she found odd. A bear of a man whose appetites were made plain by his considerable girth, Burgasov could be as loud as he was large. He was not shy. Under normal circumstances, he was hard to miss; if you didn't see him coming, his booming voice would alert you to his approach. But these days he was silent. His comings and goings were a mystery, and no one dared question him about it. Burgasov had been a general in the Red Army and now worked as an epidemiologist for the Soviet Ministry of Health in Moscow; he was a trusted bureaucrat, an insider. The ministry had dispatched him to Sverdlovsk to find the source of the epidemic. Abramova heard the rumors: The Army did secret work at Compound 19; even the taxi drivers were whispering about it now. What was the Army doing there? What had Burgasov heard?

Abramova picked up more tidbits from the ambulance drivers. They always seemed to know the latest; it was through them that Abramova first began to grasp the barest outlines of what was happening in her city, and it did not look good. Hospital 40 with its 500 beds was the city's largest. When the emergency room was full at Hospital 24, the drivers took patients to Hospital 40, bringing news with them. Now they just bypassed the smaller hospitals, which were overwhelmed, and came here directly. This morning the drivers overheard Margarita Ivanova Ilyenko, a doctor at Hospital 24, talking to her staff. Margarita Ivanova said dozens of patients had already died there; dozens more, on the verge of death, showed up every day. What about Hospital 20?

Some of the bodies from Hospital 20 had been transferred here for autopsy. How many had died at Hospital 20?

The signs were ominous. Abramova walked past the hospital pharmacy . . . it was dispensing tetracycline, an antibiotic, to the staff. When a patient died of anthrax, the police, not the family, took custody of the body. Public health workers were disinfecting the streets and rounding up dogs. Dogs? What was that about?

April 14th

Abramova's autopsy reports had disappeared. Not every report, only those coded with the numbers 022. Any patient diagnosed with anthrax had the code 022 entered into his or her chart. She had expected something like this to happen.

She checked the door to her office. No damage. There was no sign of a break-in. Whoever took her reports had a key. *"How dare they,"* she thought. *"This is my work."* But even thinking that was dangerous right now. As she had done so many times before, she closed her mind, refusing to think about why certain things happened. Her face became a mask.

She checked a file cabinet near her office. In one of the drawers she had stashed some of her handwritten notes. They were still there. If the reports were truly gone, at least she had these, and her precious specimens. Dr. Nikiforov, the head of the Moscow team, had given her permission to keep specimens from the outbreak, and she carefully preserved the most interesting ones, including Romanov's. Abramova had not labeled them, so only she knew which was which.

In 1979, this was a risky thing to do. Nixon and Brezhnev had pursued détente not long before, but that was for diplomats in places like Geneva. This was Sverdlovsk, a closed military city deep in the Soviet Union. The American U2 pilot, Francis Gary Powers, had been shot down on May 1, 1960, just a few miles away, while trying to photograph what was going on here. The mere perception of impropriety could have dire consequences. Abramova had only to look at the city's train yards to know that. Sverdlovsk was the gateway to the Soviet Gulag—the main transit point for prisoners being sent by rail into Siberian exile. If Abramova wasn't careful, she could wind up joining them.

Dr. Nikolay Babich told her to say nothing on the telephone about the outbreak, let alone the specimens.[22] Babich, head of the Sverdlovsk Oblast Sanitary Epidemiological Station, was a cautious man. "You will get no reward for this, Faina . . . only *reschotka*," he warned. *Reschotka* meant bars in Russian, as in prison bars. Babich held up his arms and crossed them to mimic the bars on a jail cell.

Could it have been the Komitet Gosudarstvennoy Bez-opnanosti, the KGB, that took her reports? There was no way to find that out without asking questions, and asking questions could draw unwanted attention. No, as long as she had her specimens, she would keep quiet.

Her mind drifted to the jars in the hospital's pathology museum. Inside those jars were the organs that she had removed from the anthrax victims—their spleens and livers, adrenal glands, intestines, stomachs, lungs and brains. Some of the brains were fixed in blocks of paraffin. As a precaution, she had put these specimens in the museum where they were indistinguishable from those taken from patients who had died of other causes. Side by side, who could tell the difference? Not even she could without her handwritten notes.

Abramova glanced at the corner cabinet near the autopsy room and breathed deeply. Her tissue samples were still there, undisturbed. So were her specimens on the museum shelves, hidden right out in the open.

That morning, the *Vercherny Sverdlovsk* reported an outbreak of "Siberian ulcer." The Health Ministry had passed out leaflets too. She had seen one of them the day before when an ambulance driver dropped it off at the hospital. It warned people not to eat contaminated meat or to touch stray animals.

"*Contaminated meat?*" she thought. "*Stray animals?*" No wonder they were rounding up dogs. Abramova shook her head. The contours of an official explanation were becoming clear. Bad meat and mangy dogs were the culprits. It was absurd. Her autopsy data made it clear how the anthrax spores got into these victims—they were inhaled. Besides, *kisechnaya*, stomach anthrax, was even rarer than the pulmonary form. It sometimes occurred in rural Africa when villagers ran short of fuel to cook their meat. There was no shortage of cooking fuel in Sverdlovsk. If roasting a joint or frying a sausage didn't kill all of the spores, the acid in someone's stomach would kill those that survived the kitchen stove.

Dr. Abramova looked at the row of organs on the pathology museum shelf, curing in jars of formaldehyde. Several jars contained the brains of recently autopsied victims. They were mostly grayish white, with two exceptions. Two of the specimens were dark red, almost black, as if they had been scorched.

The one on the right was Romanov's. Romanov had had lesions in his GI tract, but Hospital 40's pathologists did not find anthrax-contaminated meat there. Though dead, Boris did, indeed, tell a story. What remained of him might still have the last word.

Monday, October 29, 1979, Brussels, Belgium

The telex in the secure communications room at NATO headquarters in Brussels began to clatter. The U.S. Defense Intelligence Agency began transmitting a message that required the highest clearances to the U.S. military commander at NATO.

TOP SECRET
PAGE 001
TOR: 291946Z OCT 79

FM SSD DIA
R 270220Z OCT 79

SUBJ: DIA DEFENSE INTELLIGENCE AGENCY NOTICE (DIR) (0)

USSR: POSSIBLE ACCIDENT

A SOVIET ÉMIGRÉ REPORTED BEING TOLD BY THREE CLOSE FRIENDS ON SEPARATE OCCASIONS DURING MAY 1979 OF AN ACCIDENT AT A BIO-LOGICAL WARFARE (BW) INSTITUTE IN SVERDLOVSK THAT RESULTS IN 40 TO 60 DEATHS. OTHER SOURCES ALSO HAVE HEARD RUMORS OF SUCH AN ACCIDENT. THE SPECIFIC NATURE OF THE ACCIDENT IS UNDETER-MINED. THE ALLEGED NUMBER OF DEATHS HAS VARIED FROM 40 TO 300. SOVIET INTELLIGENCE REPORT OF A QUARANTINE IMPOSED BY THE MILITARY IN SVERDLOVSK IN MID-APRIL TENDS TO SUPPORT RUMORS OF A DISEASE-RELATED OUTBREAK.

ALTHOUGH A TOXIN CANNOT BE RULED OUT AS THE CAUSATIVE AGENT, TWO REPORTS OF THE ACCIDENT SUGGESTED A DISEASE THAT ALSO AFFECTS CATTLE, AND ONE SOURCE IDENTIFIED THE BACTERIAL AGENT ANTHRAX AS A POSSIBLE CAUSE.[23]

The contents of this telex—anthrax, an accident at a biological warfare (BW) institute in Sverdlovsk and some large number of deaths—might have been news to the SACEUR (Supreme Allied Commander Europe), the four-star general who had just resumed command the previous June, but it wasn't news to a certain O-6 back in Maryland. Colonel Richard O. Spertzel knew all about Sverdlovsk.[24] Spertzel was executive officer of the Medical Research and Development Command at Fort Detrick, the Army's chief biodefense lab. As XO of this particular command, it was Spertzel's job to know about it. In fact, if that telex from the Defense Intelligence Agency was anything to go by, Spertzel knew a lot more about Sverdlovsk than the SACEUR did.

The new SACEUR, General Bernard Rogers, would have had America's highest security clearances, but the details about Sverdlovsk, the really deep voodoo, was S.I., "Special Intelligence." S.I. was strictly need-to-know stuff, and Rogers didn't need to know. The S.I. on Sverdlovsk was all medical, which would have meant nothing to an infantry officer like Rogers.

But it did mean something to Dick Spertzel, a Ph.D. in microbiology from Notre Dame who first arrived at Fort Detrick in the late 1950s, when the Army was still making anthrax weapons there. He didn't buy anything the Soviets were saying about Sverdlovsk. Less than a week into the outbreak, the Soviet government was already saying it was due to contaminated meat. This seemed plausible enough. Cattle in villages a few kilometers to the south of Sverdlovsk had died of "Siberian ulcer." Diseased animals, butchered after dying so the meat would not have gone to waste, could have been the vector for the outbreak. The moment Dick Spertzel heard this explanation, he thought it was bullshit. Diplomacy would never be his forte. When he heard about Moscow's contaminated meat story, he scoffed, not because he was a knee-jerk cold warrior, but because an outbreak of gastrointestinal anthrax, large or small, was almost unheard of. Besides, it happened in Sverdlovsk; U.S. intelligence had had its eye on Sverdlovsk for decades as a possible biological warfare site.

I met with Spertzel in his home outside of Frederick, Maryland, an easy commute from Fort Detrick. Colonel Spertzel is heavier now than he was in 1979, but not a lot. His hair is white and his eyesight is a little dimmer. But he still recalls with exquisite clarity his years of head-butting with the Iraqis, when he was the U.N.'s chief biological weapons inspector. And he still criss-crosses the country teaching courses funded by the Justice Department to an assortment of FBI agents, firefighters and paramedics—the people who'd be the first to respond to any bioterrorist attack.

He sips his coffee. It's black . . . no milk, no sugar. Having been on the receiving end of some of Spertzel's blunt talk in the past, I am not surprised. He's strictly a no-frills guy. He takes another sip and says, "We had the autopsy results, you know."

I am not sure I heard him correctly. I put down my cup. "What you mean? What autopsy reports?"

"That doctor . . . what's her name?"

"Abramova?"

"Yeah, that's her," he says. "We had her autopsy data."

I am stunned. As far as I knew—as far as anyone has known for the past twenty-five years—the KGB had confiscated Abramova's reports during the outbreak. She hadn't published anything about it until it was safe to do so in the 1990s . . . after Gorbachev made bywords out of *glasnost* (openness) and *perestroika* (restructuring), and an inebriated Yeltsin really loosened things up, starting with his own hips, taking off his jacket at a public rally and boogying to a decadent backbeat.

"When did you have them?" I ask.

"That fall," says Spertzel. "In 1979 . . . it couldn't have been more than three months after the outbreak."

This is extraordinary. For fourteen years after the incident, the question of whether the anthrax victims in Sverdlovsk had died from contaminated sausages—or from inhaling spores that had somehow escaped a military installation—had been vigorously and inconclusively debated. Spertzel was saying the Army knew what had happened almost from the beginning.

"I remember going to another building on post to read about it," he says. "I think it was the Armed Forced Medical Intelligence Center, but I can't be sure because it's been so long . . . but I think I read the stuff at AFMIC. They weren't the original autopsy reports in Russian. They were summaries of those reports in English."

"And what did they tell you?"

"Hell, it was inhalation anthrax," says Spertzel. "Couldn't have been anything else. I remember thinking that at the time . . . that it *had* to be inhalation. We didn't have the photos, but the pathology described in those summaries was classic. Most of the victims had edema in their lungs and 'mediastinitis' . . . that's hemorrhaging, tissue necrosis and edema in the cavity be-tween the lungs. Awful stuff. I've seen it in monkeys."

"Why didn't you tell anybody?" I ask. "All that time people wasted arguing about the outbreak being caused by bad meat kept biodefense funding out of your hands."

"Couldn't say anything," he says. "Where do you think those summaries came from?"

"A spook?" I venture, somewhat timidly.

"Course it was," says Spertzel. "Had to be somebody inside the KGB. We *couldn't* say anything. We'd have blown the guy's cover. He would've been sent to the Gulag, or worse, and that source of intel would have dried up."

"Do you remember how the Army responded to all this?"

"Sure," says Spertzel. "We decided we had to get back into a defensive pos-ture with anthrax. After Nixon killed the BW program in 1969, a lot of the de-fensive work stopped too. The budget must've been cut in half, at least. I was one of the biggest advocates for getting back into defensive work."

"Do you remember who you talked to about it?"

"No, not really," says Spertzel, "it was so long ago. I would've talked to Dick Barquist, the Commander of USAMRIID (the United States Army Medical Research Institute of Infectious Diseases at Fort Detrick), about it . . . but he's dead now, so you can't ask him about it. But even though I don't remem-ber specific conversations, I remember what the general feeling was at the time."

"And what was that?"

"Well, we all knew the first thing we needed to do. We needed to make a new anthrax vaccine."

Chapter Two

The Weakest Vaccine
Ever Made

The reason the Army needed a new vaccine was that the one it had did not work. In a deliberate rejection of the history of anthrax immunization through the 1950s, the Army tried to do something that had never been done before: make an anthrax vaccine that contained no anthrax. All previous vaccines were for livestock. These veterinary vaccines contained living organisms that had been sufficiently weakened to make an animal immune to anthrax without killing it—most of the time. Therein lay the problem. There had never been an anthrax vaccine that did not kill some of the animals some of the time. It was too risky to make such a vaccine for humans. So the Army came up with its novel approach.

It seemed like a good idea at the time. Bad bacteria—that is, bacteria that can kill you like anthrax, cholera and tetanus (good bacteria live in your body all the time and can be very helpful)—harm you by secreting poisonous toxins. These toxins are proteins. Army scientists said to themselves, why not take one of the three proteins in the anthrax toxin and make a vaccine from it? This is what they did, choosing the protein called protective antigen, which by itself is harmless. This had been done before for diphtheria and tetanus, and it had worked. Why not then for anthrax? The Army succeeded, but the result was arguably the weakest vaccine the FDA has ever licensed. That is why, when the FDA approved the vaccine in 1970, the agency stipulated that it must be given in a six-shot series to confer protection. The design was safe. The problem was that no matter how many shots were given, six or sixty, there was evidence that people would not be effectively immunized against anthrax; and the Army knew it.

Some of Fort Detrick's top anthrax experts started contesting the new design as early as 1962; by 1966 they flatly condemned it as scientifically unsupportable. The minimalist approach—limiting the vaccine's active ingredient to one of the germ's secretions—was more controversial than anyone outside of Fort Detrick seems to understand even to this day. Because this secretion was not even part of the organism, there was nothing in the vaccine to promote an immune response to the germ itself. The germ could still grow in the body after vaccination.

It is clear from the Army's published papers and internal memoranda over the past half-century that it succeeded in getting the FDA to license this product even though its shortcomings were well known. If not for Sverdlovsk, the vaccine's ineffectiveness might never have been an issue. But at the end of 1979, it was.

A Brief History of Anthrax Vaccination

The central fact the Army resisted was this: To immunize, one must first infect. Immunization is in essence a deliberate and controlled infection; thus the chief ingredient of any classic vaccine is the germ itself. The vaccine activates the body's immune system, in effect teaching it to recognize the germ and fight it in the future. Most vaccines contain live organisms that have been weakened by heat or chemicals, a process called "attenuation," which bring on a mild case of whatever disease the vaccine is meant to protect against. For most people, this is a balancing act—a mild infection that is enough to promote immunity but not enough to make you really sick. This was the principle behind the world's first anthrax vaccine, created by the patriarch of modern immunology—France's Louis Pasteur. A mistake, however, can exact a terrible price. If the weakening process fails for some reason, you could be injected with an infectious dose of fully virulent microbes. Depending on the organism, an improperly made "living" vaccine could do more than just make you sick. This was the issue preoccupying military scientists trying to devise an an-thrax vaccine for humans. They knew that Pasteur's vaccine had killed.

——

When Pasteur first announced, in 1881, that he had discovered a way to im-munize livestock against anthrax, some members of the French Academy greeted the news with derision. No one was more skeptical than the es-teemed veterinarian Hippolyte Rossignol, editor of *The Veterinary Press*. "Mi-crobiolatry is the fashion," he griped in an editorial. "It reigns undisputed; it is a doctrine which must not even be discussed, especially when its Pontiff, the learned Monsieur Pasteur, has pronounced the sacramental words, 'I have spoken.'"[1] Even a scientist as eminent as Pasteur could not escape at-tack when challenging a scientific orthodoxy. Rossignol not only mocked Pas-teur's preposterous notion that germs caused disease, he challenged Pasteur to prove that he had indeed fashioned a successful anthrax vaccine. All Pas-teur had to do was perform an experiment under the scrutinizing gaze of the press. Rossignol offered his own farm at Pouilly-le-Fort near the town of Melun, southeast of Paris, as an arena for what he expected would be Pas-teur's comeuppance.

Pasteur vs. Rossignol turned into a high-stakes celebrity grudge match pit-ting a man already acknowledged as one the world's great scientists against a challenger who was decidedly less well known. If the test failed, Pasteur would be ruined. Newspaper reporters rushed from the capital to witness the event. Even the *London Times* dispatched to the scene its flamboyant Paris correspondent, Henri de Blowitz, known to some of his contemporaries as "Blowitz-own-Tromp."[2]

Ever the showman, Pasteur announced that he would inject the vaccinated animals with three times the lethal dose of anthrax. A month after the first vaccination, Pasteur injected twenty-four sheep, one goat and six cows with fully virulent germs.[3] He did the same to corresponding groups of unvacci-nated animals. By prearrangement, he would check on them in two days. At 2 P.M. on June 2, 1881, as the press looked on, Pasteur entered the farmyard with his two colleagues, Charles Chamberland and Emile Roux. They were greeted by all twenty-four vaccinated sheep and one goat, bleating and in good health.[4] The six immunized cows were healthy too.[5] Laid in a row were twenty-one unvaccinated sheep stiff with rigor mortis.[6] Two of the surviving untreated sheep, as if on cue, died in front of the assembled spectators.[7] Another staggered on the verge of death (it succumbed later that day). Although the four untreated cows, a less susceptible species, survived the killer doses of anthrax, they were clearly sick whereas the six vaccinated cows were not.[8] Pasteur had triumphed.

"Inoculate me with your vaccines, Monsieur Pasteur, just as you have done to those sheep you have saved so wonderfully. Then I will submit to the injection of the murderous virus. All men must be convinced of this marvelous discovery!" exclaimed one of Pasteur's exuberantly repentant critics.[9] Blowitz wired the news to London: "The experiment at Pouilly le Fort is a perfect, unprecedented success."[10] *The London Times,* which seldom went overboard praising anything French, declared Pasteur "one of the scientific glories of France."[11] Rossignol's plan had backfired. Instead of ignominy, he had orchestrated his rival's elevation to superstardom; the experiment at Pouilly-le-Fort earned Pasteur international acclaim and France's Grand Cordon of the Legion of Honor.

If Pasteur was already brash, the public relations bonanza at Pouilly-le-Fort made him more so.[12] Wanting to capitalize on his success, he hastily mixed up big batches of vaccine in his laboratory on Rue d'Ulm in Paris and then left for the countryside to inoculate livestock. Upon returning to Paris, Pasteur started receiving letters from towns across France. Instead of outpourings of gratitude, they were filled with invective. In their haste, he and his staff had been sloppy. Some batches of vaccine were still fully virulent; they killed sheep instead of protecting them.

Did the fault lie with Pasteur's preparation, or with those who administered it—perhaps improperly? Germany's Robert Koch stepped in to provide the answer. Koch was the other man in the world who, along with Pasteur, could lay claim to having proved the germ theory of disease, and in addition to being Pasteur's great competitor Koch was also his most ardent critic. It was Koch, in fact, who had definitively demonstrated the causal link between the microbe *Bacillus anthracis* and "MilzbrandKrankheit"—the livestock disease anthrax.[13] While there was undoubtedly an element of Franco-Prussian chauvinism in their rivalry, by all accounts these two titans of nineteenth-century science were by temperament inclined to dislike each other anyway— Koch, a taciturn and punctilious clinician, Pasteur an effusive man whose vocabulary did not include the word "humble." For Pasteur, an attack from someone like Rossignol was a fleabite in comparison to being savaged by Robert Koch. So it was a source of acute embarrassment when Koch procured a sample of the acclaimed French anthrax vaccine and confirmed that its key ingredient, Pasteur's attenuated anthrax microbes, did in fact kill the animals they were supposed to protect.[14]

Pasteur's scientific reputation survived this bad batch of vaccine as well as Koch's denunciations, because, when properly made, the vaccine worked. For the next fifty years it was used widely in Europe and South America.[15] But because the Pasteur vaccine was made from living (albeit weakened) organisms, some animals of feeble disposition succumbed to a full-blown anthrax infection brought on by the immunizations themselves. This was the cost of "herd immunity." To preserve the health of the herd, a livestock farmer might lose an animal or two. But on balance, the benefits outweighed the risks, at least for animals.

Later attempts to improve on Pasteur's "duplex" vaccine were mainly for convenience. *Duplex* referred to the fact that it was a two-stage immunization—one shot of weakened or "attenuated" germs, followed by a second shot of more lethal ones. Once an animal's immune system had been primed with an initial dose, it could tolerate the second shot of more virulent microbes. Pasteur attenuated his microbes by cooking them. The second stage of the vaccine came from cultures heated to the same temperature as the first but for less time, which left the germs in a more robust state. This process was delicate and time consuming—a bit like making a soufflé. As a result, Pasteur's vaccine could vary from batch to batch. It had other shortcomings, too. Its potency declined over time, inadequately attenuated organisms could kill (as Pasteur had discovered, to his embarrassment), and each animal required two shots, which meant it took a long time to fully inoculate a herd.[16] To make anthrax immunization faster and less cumbersome, a South African scientist named Max Sterne found a variant of the germ that could be injected without attenuation; because of its peculiarities, it caused infection but not full-blown illness. Sterne's wholespore vaccine, introduced in 1939, became the industry standard—"the world's most potent weapon against anthrax."[17] But the dose required to achieve 100 percent immunity in guinea pigs often resulted in a certain number of animals dying from the vaccination.[18]

If there was ever a non-military demand for a human anthrax vaccine, it would have been in Pasteur's time, when outbreaks of "woolsorter's disease" were fairly common among textile workers who handled animal hides contaminated with spores. But by 1939, possibly because vaccination had drastically reduced the incidence in animals, human anthrax was almost unheard of in Europe and the United States. No one bothered developing a human anthrax vaccine; there was no need for one.

That would soon change.

The First Anthrax Weapon

Beginning in 1932 and continuing until the end of World War II, Japan's Kwantung Army maintained a vast network of secret bases in China to develop biological weapons. Under the cover of benign names like the Water Purification Bureau, and then more forbiddingly designated entities like Unit 731 and Unit 100, the Japanese conducted experiments on Chinese civilians and Allied POWs in remote Manchurian outposts like Beiyinhe, Ping Fan and Changchun. Later, when they grew bolder, they ran experiments in Nanking—a large provincial capital. The names of the doctors who created this infernal gulag—Ishii, Kitano and Wakamatsu—mean little to most Americans, but these men committed atrocities that surely earned them a place in infamy alongside Dr. Josef Mengele, the Auschwitz doctor known as the "Angel of Death." One of the Japanese Army's favorite pathogens was anthrax. Under the direction of Ishii Shiro, a professor of immunology at the Tokyo Army Medical School who rose to the rank of lieutenant general during the war, Japanese scientists tested the effectiveness of prototype anthrax bombs using Chinese prisoners tied to stakes in the ground. Exploding specially designed biological munitions, the Japanese raked these prisoners with anthrax-contaminated shrapnel.[19] The prisoners, called "maruta" or logs in Japanese Army records to conceal these activities, were left to die in agony from their untreated wounds and disease. Some of these experiments were gratuitously diabolical: According to testimony from a Japanese prisoner at the 1949 Soviet war-crimes trial in Khabarovsk, Ishii personally supervised the distribution of anthrax-laced chocolate candy to unsuspecting Chinese children.[20]

The British also developed anthrax weapons during the war, but by entirely different means. One such weapon even went into mass production—a cattle cake. Five million of them, the size of dog biscuits, were made from linseed meal and anthrax spores.[21] The British plan called for dropping these delicacies onto German pastures where unsuspecting cattle would literally eat themselves into a grave. There was something Monty Python-esque in all this. Anthrax, as Britain planned to use it, wasn't an antipersonnel weapon; it was antibovine.[22] Still, as ludicrous as anthrax bonbons and cattle biscuits sound, they turned biological weapons into a tool of modern warfare. By the war's end, several nations were experimenting with anthrax weapons, including the Soviet Union, Britain, Canada and the United States.[23] Biodefense became a strategic imperative. If there was still no commercial need for a human anthrax vaccine, there was now a military one.

The risk/benefit ratio with the existing anthrax vaccine had now acquired a new variable: human life. The potential toxicity of a "living" anthrax vaccine was no longer a matter of losing one or two sheep. *People* could die. At the end of World War II, Army generals had the perfect example of this risk fresh in their minds.

The Harm in Good Intentions

In 1939, a Japanese physician named Ryoichi Naito aroused suspicion when he showed up unannounced at New York's Rockefeller Institute seeking samples of yellow fever virus, allegedly for the purpose of making a vaccine.[24] Although this sounded plausible—an Institute scientist, Max Theiler, had recently developed a yellow fever vaccine—Institute officials were skeptical of Naito's motives. Naito was a faculty member of the Army Medical College in Tokyo, and yellow fever was a tropical virus found in the rain forests of Africa and South America—but not, as far as anyone knew, in Japan. The virus is debilitating and can be fatal; it causes high fever, headaches, bleeding from mucous membranes, black vomit, signs of pulmonary, liver or kidney failure, and shock.[25] Between five and twenty percent of infected patients can die from it.[26] When the Institute's director, Wilbur Sawyer, refused Naito's request, a stranger stopped one of Sawyer's lab technicians on the street a few days later and offered him $3,000 to procure the virus for a "scientific project in Japan"; the lab tech rejected the bribe and reported the incident to the authorities.[27]

Three years later, America was at war with Japan. Fearing a possible biological warfare attack with yellow fever, the Army ordered the vaccination of U.S. troops in 1942 with an experimental yellow fever vaccine. The Army's response to this perceived threat inadvertently caused far more harm than the threat itself. No soldier ever got yellow fever from a biological weapon, but many got hepatitis from the yellow fever vaccine. It caused the largest epidemic of physician-induced viral hepatitis in recorded history. Of the 141 yellow fever vaccine lots supplied to the Army, seven were made with human sera contaminated with the hepatitis B virus.[28] Tests indicated that up to 330,000 U.S. military personnel in the Western Defense Command (which included Army bases in six western states and Hawaii) were injected with contaminated vaccine during basic training; some 51,000 American troops were hospitalized with jaundice.[29] In World War II, the average strength of a U.S. Army infantry division was around 14,250 men.[30] Going by this figure, the Army lost nearly four whole divisions to a badly made vaccine. All of the soldiers recovered, but the lesson stuck. When the U.S. and British armies decided jointly to develop the world's first human anthrax vaccine, they understandably did not want any live anthrax bacilli in it.

Too Clever for Anyone's Good

Deciding to make a non-living anthrax vaccine was the easy part. The hard part was coming up with a way to do it. Strictly speaking, the licensed anthrax vaccine is not a vaccine; it is a kind of toxoid. A toxoid is an immunization that contains a poison secreted by certain bacteria (not all bacteria make poisons) but does not contain the germ itself. There were two such toxoids already in existence at the time—diphtheria and tetanus—but in the 1940s scientists did not yet know that *Bacillus anthracis* secreted such toxins. One option they rejected was an "inactivated" or "killed" vaccine—one made with dead germs. The problem was that the chemicals used to kill the microbe could change it in subtle ways that would prevent the immune system from recognizing the real thing. Live attenuated anthrax was a non-starter, too, and not only because germs could be insufficiently weakened and then sicken or kill soldiers.

There was also the issue of "reversion"—even properly weakened germs could revert to their fully virulent state. This can happen too easily with anthrax. A *Bacillus anthracis* colony the size of a shirt button can contain more than a 100 billion microbes; that population can double in just forty-eight minutes.[31] Twenty-four hours in "bacteria-time" is positively epochal—enough to spawn more generations than are recorded in the Old Testament's Book of Chronicles. Because of their light-speed reproduction and sensitivity to the slightest changes in their environment, bacteria evolve and mutate quickly. One mutation that occurs in attenuated germs is reversion to their fully virulent state. If such a reversion took place in a batch of live anthrax vaccine, it could do a lot worse than put soldiers in the hospital with jaundice.

That left the Army one other option. British and U.S. military scientists harked back to the founding days of immunology, to the early 1900s and a second-rank institution in the now defunct Austro-Hungarian Empire; they drew on the work of Oskar Bail and Alfred Pettersson—two "Privatdozents" or "outside lecturers" (they weren't even full faculty), working in relative obscurity at the Hygiene Institute at the German University in Prague. In an inspired experiment, Bail and Pettersson discovered that the edema fluid in animals dying from anthrax (the same gooey exudate that Dr. Abramova found in the chest of Boris Romanov) made an effective immunization.[32] Unlike Pasteur's vaccine, which relied on attenuated germ cells to immunize, there were no anthrax bacilli in Bail and Pettersson's edema fluid; it was sterile. Something else besides the germ had provoked a protective immune response. This fluid was, in effect, a cell-free vaccine. Scientists at both Porton Down in England and what was then "Camp" Detrick in Frederick, Maryland, set about trying to replicate this work.[33]

It would take another two generations before British and U.S. military scientists would be haunted by this decision.

———

From the beginning, in 1946, there was evidence suggesting that going down the same road as Bail and Pettersson was the wrong choice. Scientists at Camp Detrick ran experiments with the edema fluid from infected animals and verified that it could, indeed, protect against anthrax. But it also seemed to do as much damage as a dose of actual microbes; it left ugly lesions at the injection site much like those caused by injections with fully virulent anthrax.[34] A vaccine made from edema fluid also posed an insurmountable production problem. Scientists could only recover the fluid from living animals. Making large-scale quantities of vaccine would thus require legions of sick rabbits or some other animal, whose anthrax-infected flesh would exude toxic goop to be harvested by the bucketful. This was a public health nightmare waiting to happen. The military had to find some other way to get this stuff.

It was a British scientist, G. P. Gladstone, who first discovered how to produce the desirable agent from a toxic goop in a laboratory beaker. From that he isolated an immunizing protein that could protect animals without any risk of infecting them with the actual disease.[35] Gladstone called it "protective antigen"—"protective" because it conferred protection against anthrax, "antigen" because that is the term immunologists use to refer to any molecule to which the immune system reacts.

That was the good news. Now for the not-so-good news: Blood taken from animals injected with Gladstone's protective antigen did *not* contain protective antibodies. Gladstone really didn't know whether his "protective antigen" was a single protein that the organism secreted or many. To fully describe the immunizing material would have required technology that did not yet exist. But U.S. and British military leaders couldn't wait around for some technological breakthrough. Britain already had stockpiles of "Agent N," as it called anthrax, and the United States was about to commence production of anthrax weapons at Camp Detrick. The military thought it had to have a human vaccine quickly, if for no other reason than to protect workers who were making biological weapons. So protective antigen remained the best choice.

Wright Vaccine, Wrong Choice

Working closely with the British, two teams of Army scientists at Camp Detrick developed anthrax vaccines based on Gladstone's protective antigen. Dr. Alden K. Boor and his young protégé, Hugh Tresselt, were the first to succeed. In 1955 they announced that they made a cell-free (read: anthrax-free) anthrax vaccine that protected Rhesus macaques from a whopping dose of the strain used by both the U.S. and British armies to make weapons.[36] But the Army preferred the vaccine made by a second team at Camp Detrick, led by

Dr. George Wright. The Boor/Tresselt vaccine was made with serum, albeit from animals.[37] The Army couldn't risk that. Wright's recipe contained no serum—just some amino acids, some chemical salts and glucose, a sugar.[38] It was the state of the art in purity and safety. But it yielded only very small amounts of the antigen. The British tweaked Wright's recipe to produce enough antigen to make large-scale vaccine production feasible.[39] The United States and Britain started to make variations of the same vaccine.

As if to reassure the Army that it had made the right call, the year Boor and Tresselt announced the creation of the world's first protective antigen or "PA" vaccine, 1955, there was an outbreak of polio caused by Jonas Salk's live polio vaccine.[40] Here was yet another example of a "living vaccine" causing injury and death.

But before either Wright or his counterparts in Britain had time to congratulate themselves, another British scientist, Harry Smith, made a groundbreaking discovery that challenged the very basis of a vaccine made exclusively from one protein. Smith identified a second substance in Gladstone's original toxic goop; Smith called it "lethal factor."[41] Gladstone's protective antigen was not just one protein, after all. Without yet knowing how many proteins were really necessary to confer immunity, U.S. and British scientists had devised what was, for its time, a technologically advanced vaccine. But here was the first sign that it was not all that it was cracked up to be. Now Smith had proven there were at least two proteins that might confer immunity. Maybe there were even more.

There were. In the early '60s, Smith discovered a third substance, which he named "edema factor," in Gladstone's filtrate. By now, scientists working on anthrax for the U.S. and British armed forces realized their mistake, admitting that Gladstone's original material probably contained all three components of the anthrax toxin.[42] They began to doubt the wisdom of relying on just one protein, "protective antigen," as the magic bullet for anthrax. Harry Smith recommended adding edema factor to enhance the protectiveness of a chemical vaccine.[43] At least one group of Fort Detrick scientists, led by Ralph E. Lincoln, argued for vaccine that contained all three antigens.[44] What's more, Lincoln argued, it might be necessary to generate antibodies against the germ's cells *and* its spores, as well as to all three toxin proteins to get full immunity.[45] But by this time the Wright vaccine, a medically safe concoction because of its unmatched purity, had become bureaucratically safe as well. A position once rooted in a legitimate concern grew hidebound and unmovable. Lincoln was ignored. Whenever anyone needed protection from anthrax, they were given this single protein vaccine.

His view had some unlikely supporters—America's Cold War adversaries, the Soviet Union. Soviet scientists had achieved good results with a whole spore anthrax vaccine. They delivered it as a powdered aerosol dispersed in a room, where people simply breathed it in. In 1963, in the midst of one of the more arctic periods in the Cold War, the Soviet vaccine inspired lavish praise in the West; one U.S. analyst hailed it as an "achievement in bacteriology rivaling in brilliance the launching of the first Russian Sputnik."[46] An inhaled vaccine was indeed a clever innovation, but what made this particular vaccine truly effective was that it contained whole spores from not one but *two* different anthrax strains—and it was, by Soviet accounts, safe.[47] Volunteers were enveloped in a cloud of some 64 million viable spores and no one got sick.[48]

The Army really didn't need Moscow's help to convince anyone that a live spore vaccine was better, because its own case was overwhelming. In experiment after experiment, several boosters of the single protective antigen vaccine failed to ensure survival. The results were so dismal that Lincoln and his colleagues proposed a compromise—the Army should consider a shot of protective antigen followed by a single booster of live vaccine. According to Lincoln's experiments, vaccination with protective antigen increased an untreated guinea pig's resistance to anthrax "1000-fold." But following that with a booster of live vaccine increased the animal's resistance "100,000,000-fold."[49] One hundred million fold! Without this booster, the limited immunity conferred by protective antigen vaccine was also short-lived. In one experiment with cattle, the immunity generated by protective antigen lasted a month at best; then an immunized animal's resistance to anthrax "rapidly declined."[50] When exposed to anthrax three months later, nearly half the animals inoculated with protective antigen died.[51] All the animals injected with the Sterne whole-spore vaccine survived exposure to virulent spores three months after their injections.[52]

There was very little data on resistance in humans vaccinated with the Army's single protein vaccine, but what little there was didn't look good. If antibody levels were anything to go by, then the immunity in people vaccinated with protective antigen was transient too—"at 3 months . . . [antibody levels] are approaching or are at zero," one study reported.[53] Some of the top scientists at Detrick had seen enough. The theoretical foundation of the protective antigen vaccine, they concluded, was incorrect. There was "no experimental basis for selection or use of a single antigen for immunizing man, domestic, or experimental animals," wrote Fort Detrick's scientists.[54] "Indeed all evidence is contrary to this practice."[55]

Why did the Army ignore its own data and continue to develop a single-protein vaccine, especially when the Soviets said they had a whole-spore vaccine that was safe?[56] Perhaps because it had bigger worries at the time. Nukes, not germs, preoccupied the Joint Chiefs' strategic thinking. In the 1960s, nuclear anxiety was everywhere—air raid sirens, classroom "duck and cover" drills and TV shows interrupted by tests of the emergency broadcast system were commonplaces of American life. Stanley Kubrick ended his darkly hilarious film *Dr. Strangelove* with "Slim" Pickens astride a hydrogen bomb, waving his ten-gallon hat, shouting "Yahoooo!" as he fell to earth and the end of the world. In the hierarchy of weapons of mass destruction, strategic germ warfare (large-scale attacks on civilians) was overkill—a barbaric and futile anticlimax to a nuclear apocalypse. When President Nixon took the bold step in 1969 of unilaterally canceling U.S. production of such weapons, he was throwing a bone to the liberals, giving up a program that he didn't think necessary for national security. Congress agreed. Defensive research came to a virtual halt, too, as funding for biological warfare vaccines, antitoxins and detectors dwindled almost overnight.

Vietnam was another distraction. At the height of the Vietnam War, the Pentagon had more than half a million men deployed in Southeast Asia, where the most pressing medical threats to U.S. troops were diseases like malaria, dengue fever, Japanese encephalitis, cholera, hepatitis, plague and even syphilis and gonorrhea.[57] What a nineteen-year-old draftee could pick up in a Saigon bordello was a much bigger concern than anthrax. The vaccine the FDA finally approved in 1970, based largely on Wright's single-protein, protective-antigen formula, was the weakest vaccine ever licensed. It required the most injections to achieve immunity; it required boosters every year after that, and after all that rigmarole, it was still one of the FDA's least effective vaccines. Yet nobody seemed concerned.

Until Sverdlovsk.

The King of the Eight Ball

After the Sverdlovsk outbreak revealed to the military that the Soviets had never stopped their bioweapons research, the job of defending the nation against the threat of an anthrax weapon fell to USAMRIID, pronounced Yoo-SAM-rid, the United States Army Medical Research Institute of Infectious Diseases. For the job of overseeing the creation of a new anthrax vaccine, USAMRIID commander Col. Richard Barquist knew who he wanted on the job. He wanted Joe Jemski.[58]

Jemski was a former streetwise kid with a University of Pennsylvania Ph.D. His specialty,[59] from the time he started working for the Army in 1953, had been experiments to establish the lethal doses for agents like anthrax, tularemia and plague. In the netherworld of "black biology," he was best known for having established the lethal dose of anthrax that would kill monkeys—the animal "model" closest to man.[60] No one could predict the exact number of spores it would take to fatally infect any individual monkey. Some monkeys succumbed to just twelve spores; others survived thousands; the majority met death somewhere in between. Genes, nutritional status, age or any number of other factors might make a particular monkey more susceptible to infection and death, or more resistant.[61]

Jemski ran many of his experiments in the "Eight Ball"—a giant sphere that looked like something out of Jules Verne. It was two stories high and forty feet across, with portholes at its base and equator . . . its steel walls, an inch and a quarter thick, encompassed one million cubic liters of air. At the base of the sphere was a cylindrical chamber. Jemski called it the "bombardier's cabinet," because he would sometimes detonate a small bomb inside it to propel a payload of agent to the top of the sphere. A fan above the catwalk at the sphere's equator would whir to life, swirling the agent around the interior to ensure an even mix. The animals inside would then be blanketed in a fallout of lethal microbes. With non-lethal, "incapacitating" agents like Q-fever, Jemski had even run tests on human subjects—conscientious objectors who had volunteered for the Army's top-secret Operation Whitecoat. Having refused combat as draftees during the Vietnam War—often because of their religion—they risked their lives instead in human medical experiments.[62] They would sit in the Eight Ball wearing masks through which Jemski and his team pumped deadly aerosols of Q fever and tularemia. As chief of the Test Sphere Branch,

Jemski was the master of this macabre domain. He was the King of the Eight Ball.

Jemski knew anthrax spores. He certainly had killed enough monkeys with them. There was no one better qualified to find out precisely how deadly a given strain of the stuff was—or how much immunity a supposed immunization really conferred. Barquist asked Jemski to use that dark knowledge in a crash program to make a better anthrax vaccine. Throughout 1980 and 1981, Jemski tested six different anthrax vaccines to see which one worked best—the Army's licensed anthrax vaccine, a licensed veterinary vaccine with living spores, and four new prototypes developed in USAMRIID's Pathology Division by Jemski's colleague, Dr. Anna Johnson-Winegar.

On March 25, 1982, the King of the Eight Ball gave the last presentation of his Army career to the assembled scientific staff at Fort Detrick. What they heard was surely one of the most sobering valedictories ever given. Jemski would be briefing his colleagues on Fort Detrick's efforts to develop a new and improved anthrax vaccine.

Some people in this audience knew what Jemski knew going in. In the early '60s Army scientists ran an experiment with the "NH–6" strain, a proven mankiller. The "NH" stood for "New Hampshire." NH–6 came from the 1957 outbreak of anthrax at the Arms Textile Mill, on the banks of the Merrimack River in Manchester, New Hampshire. It killed four out of the nine mill workers it infected that year, the first known outbreak of inhalation anthrax in the twentieth century.[63] In the Army's subsequent experiments with the New Hampshire strain, in the 1960s, none of the guinea pigs vaccinated with the protective antigen vaccine survived exposure to it.[64] The strain killed ten out of ten. In a second experiment it killed five out of six. The implications couldn't be worse: in guinea pigs, the licensed human vaccine provided little or no protection against a strain that had previously killed humans.

Using the flat, emotionless language of science, Jemski informed his audience that USAMRIID's initial attempt to make a better anthrax vaccine had failed. In the process of testing these new vaccines—there were four of them—Jemski exposed vaccinated guinea pigs to virulent anthrax and got the same results that his predecessors got nearly two decades before. The single-protein vaccine did not work as well as the Sterne whole-spore vaccine. The four prototype replacements, also based on a single-protein design, failed badly. Two of them provided no protection at all.[65] Embedded in Jemski's dry recitation of data was this bleak message: in the face of a renewed biological weapons threat from America's most dangerous adversary, the country had, in effect, no defense at all.

His experiments with anthrax had persuaded him in what every experiment in the past had shown: it might be necessary to scrap the protective antigen vaccine the FDA had licensed just over a decade earlier. This was not the answer the Army wanted to hear. Rather than abandon a design that it had embraced back in the 1950s —a design that failed in test after test to protect guinea pigs from certain strains of virulent anthrax—the Army kept trying to make a single-protein vaccine work. Lincoln had shown that it would not; so now had Jemski. But the Army still kept running what was essentially the same experiment over and over. It would not. After Jemski's talk, complacency was replaced by a mood of urgency. But urgency did not bring with it greater wisdom.

———

By 1986, it was clear that the results were worse than even Jemski antici-pated. Jemski had retired, and a new generation of anthrax specialists at US-AMRIID, in yet another round of experiments, again exposed the shortcoming of the single-protein vaccine. Scientists Stephen Little and Gregory Knudson discovered that nine out of twenty-seven strains of anthrax they tested—a third of them—killed guinea pigs immunized with the licensed U.S. vaccine.[66] These strains had been isolated from much bigger animals—cows, goats, a buffalo. In microbiology, you can sometimes gauge the virulence of a strain by the size of the animal it kills. So it wasn't surprising that the Ames strain, extracted from a cow in Texas, was a killer. The Ames strain (later made notorious by its use in the 2001 anthrax letter attacks), exterminated the guinea pigs. All of them died.[67] But five of the deadliest anthrax strains in this experiment came from animals much smaller than cows—they came from hu-mans.[68] The man-killing strains wiped out two-thirds or more of the guinea pigs in each cohort exposed to them.

The evidence was not only stark, it was inescapable. Some anthrax strains could defeat the licensed vaccine. With Sterne, the Army got the opposite re-sults. The Sterne whole-spore vaccine provided near complete protection from all the isolates. In eight out of ten groups there were zero fatalities. The authors of this study, Little and Knudson, were as unequivocal in their conclusions as their data. The whole-spore vaccine was "superior," they wrote.[69]

The evidence kept piling up on both sides of the Atlantic. High antibody levels, or "titers," against protective antigen were virtually meaningless. The licensed British and American vaccines, which were virtually the same thing, generated high titers in guinea pigs, but when exposed to virulent strains like Ames and New Hampshire the animals died anyway.[70] Their survival rate was an abysmal 17 percent. Animals injected with the live spore vaccines fared much better, though it took time to build up immunity; if exposed to spores after three months, all the animals survived.[71] The U.S. vaccine elicited the highest number of antibodies to protective antigen of any vaccine, but animals injected with it had the lowest chance of survival. More than thirty years of work had achieved a preposterous result: a vaccine that generated antibodies in guinea pigs but provided almost no protection against disease.[72]

Throughout the mid-1980s, the U.S.-British tag team approach continued to support the U.S. findings from previous decades. But a different generation was in place now, with different training and far more sophisticated technology. By the '80s, scientists at Fort Detrick and Porton Down could not only purify proteins with ease, they could characterize epitopes—the infinitesimally small binding sites to which antibodies affix themselves on the surface of individual molecules. With such tools at their disposal, they continued to probe further and further into the ultra-fine structure of the anthrax germ on the assumption that a single snippet of DNA, or a single protein, could lead to a risk-free but effective immunization against anthrax. All they needed to do was find the *right* snippet.

The new generation of military scientists kept finding more parts of the microbe to which the immune system formed antibodies—specific regions on the surfaces of spores and of cells.[73] But the way these scientists thought about their discoveries could not have departed more radically from their predecessors. When Fort Detrick's "old school" researchers discovered antibodies to some new component of the germ, they recommended that it be added to the vaccine to improve its efficacy. The Army's younger anthrax specialists took the opposite view. Once they discovered an antibody reaction to some freshly scrutinized part of the germ, they would then isolate it from the rest of the spore or cell, and inject that alone. When this component failed to confer immunity or "extend the time to death," they would dismiss it as an antigen of "little consequence."[74] This was like taking a single piston out of your car's engine, and upon discovering that it alone couldn't power your car, declaring that pistons were of "little consequence" in getting your car started in the morning. In experiment after experiment, this was how Fort Detrick scientists proceeded until they convinced themselves that only protective antigen mattered.

Scientists at Porton Down, at least in the '80s, were more old school in their thinking, which is to say, more inclusive. When they discovered a new anthrax component that elicited antibodies, they suggested that it be included in a vaccine. The latest technologies enabled scientists to now purify the three known anthrax toxin components (protective antigen, lethal antigen and edema factor, discovered in the 1960s) to an unprecedented degree. Why not add all three to the vaccine now, as the Army's Ralph Lincoln had suggested long ago, and as the King of the Eight Ball had more recently urged? The British agreed with Lincoln and Jemski, recommending that even more antigens be added to the mix. Fort Detrick didn't listen. Its scientists would not acknowledge, in their published papers at least, that good protection from anthrax might arise from a comprehensive immune response to many components of the microbe. That was, in fact, how the immune system had evolved to respond to infectious organisms. Immunity was not the product of just one response to one part of a germ; it was the sum of *many* responses . . . to *many* parts. An antibody to a single protein, a single sequence of amino acids or a single molecule on the surface of a spore could not protect an animal all by itself; it was the aggregate of multiple responses that conferred immunity. That's what the data from the U.S. and British experiments in the '80s pointed to . . . just as it had done before.

But conceding this would be at odds with a way of thinking that had taken hold at Fort Detrick. The Army has never been an organization that rewarded subtlety, complexity or self-doubt. Its leaders, confident, serious men who prized straight talk, looked to their scientists for precise, definitive answers. That was what science was for. The formulations coming out of the laboratories were to be neat, not messy. Purity was the way to go.

Ambiguities were ignored. Ambiguities did not help calculate the throw weights of nuclear-tipped missiles or put satellites into space; they would not help defend troops against biological weapons. The vaccine Hugh Tresselt created in 1955 supposedly consisted of purified protective antigen, but it probably (so its creator told me in 2004) contained lethal factor and "other stuff too." Wright's vaccine, the one the Army adopted in 1969, was purer than Tresselt's, and it worked less well. "The more you took out of the vaccine," Tresselt says, meaning the more kinds of different, unidentified antigens expressed by the anthrax bacteria were filtered out, "the weaker it was." In the 1950s, as in the 1980s and even to this day, some people have found it simply inconceivable that purity could be a bad thing.

Moreover, the technology for producing a pure antigen vaccine was exquisitely refined. "Attenuated whole organisms and mixed antigen cocktails were considered Stone Age by officials at the FDA and the British Medicines Control Agency," says Jack Melling. In the '80s, Melling worked at Porton Down's Center for Applied Microbiological Research (CAMR) as one of Britain's top anthrax specialists. "There was a push to get simpler and cleaner vaccines to reduce reactogenicity," he says.[75] Reactogenicity, the reaction caused by the vaccine itself, might mean something as marginal as a sore arm, but even that, says Melling, was enough to persuade civilian health officials to try to "identify the one or two components that gave protection and purify them out."[76]

In the late '80s, this faith in purity reached its zenith in the creation of a series of prototype "second-generation" vaccines, including ones for anthrax. They were made from recombinant DNA—DNA that had been reengineered from the way nature had put it together. To achieve absolute purity, the Army went from work with single proteins to mere shards of DNA. Using "restriction endonucleases," a kind of enzyme knife, they could shear off a bit of DNA and insert it into another organism, cutting and pasting the very language of life into different combinations. This was heady stuff. In mastering the molecule, humanity could become the author of its biological destiny and would start by systematically dismantling its most implacable enemies: cancer and infectious disease. Even new and terrifying scourges like HIV might be defeated. Scientists would never dare inject HIV into anyone, but now they wouldn't even need to contemplate that possibility. The right DNA sequence extracted from the virus's genome might confer risk-free immunity. Suddenly, vaccines for incurable diseases like malaria and emerging global killers like HIV seemed plausible.

Too Many Shots, Too Little Time

In October 1987, the Central Intelligence Agency issued a secret report on Iraq's nascent biological weapons program that gave the Army's anthrax vaccine project some renewed urgency. If Baghdad had, in fact, produced biological weapons, the CIA report said it would most likely be "in spore form of *Bacillus anthracis* [anthrax] or cholerae."[77]

A subsequent background paper written by the Defense Intelligence Agency for I. Lewis "Scooter" Libby—undersecretary of defense for strategy and resources under Paul Wolfowitz and Dick Cheney before the first Gulf War—was more assured in its conclusions: "Iraq is assessed to have the BW agents anthrax and botulinum toxin."[78] That was bad enough, but of "major concern" to the DIA was the fact that Iraq might have the ability to deliver its biological agents in an aerosol made with "dust-like carriers" such as silica, "which could penetrate mask filters and permeable protective suits."[79] If a dusty anthrax could seep through the Army's gas masks and charcoal-lined chemical warfare suits, then an improved anthrax vaccine became even more critical.

By 1989, Secretary of Defense Richard B. Cheney began shifting the Pentagon's focus away from its long-anticipated showdown with the Soviet Union. Cheney wanted the Persian Gulf oil supply protected from a "robust regional threat" and made that mission one of the Defense Department's top priorities.[80] The only "robust" regional threat at the time was Iraq. Southwest Asia was Central Command's turf; its commander was Norman Schwarzkopf. Heeding Cheney's instructions, Chairman of the Joint Chiefs Colin Powell instructed Schwarzkopf to overhaul CENTCOM's war plan to focus on regional, non-Soviet threats to the oil supply. Schwarzkopf drew up contingency plans assuming an Iraqi incursion into Saudi Arabia with as many as twenty-two divisions.[81] As long as Saddam Hussein was fighting the Iran-Iraq War, he had been something of an ally—a nasty character but a convenient firewall against the spread of radical Islam. But by 1988, the war was over, and the Iranian military—exhausted by its long conflict with Baghdad—was no longer a credible threat. Syria was preoccupied with Israel. That left Iraq with a degree of leverage that it never had before . . . and that left Fort Detrick with a predicament. Friend or foe, biological weapons in the hands of a third-world dictator, especially one with a demonstrated disregard for international law, was bad news. Now the bad news had just gotten worse. The foe in CENT-COM's war games was not in doubt: it was Iraq, and Iraq had anthrax.

It wasn't just the licensed vaccine's inability to protect against certain strains that gave the generals heartburn, or the potential inability of the Army's chem/bio suits to protect against "dusty" anthrax; it was also a matter of combat logistics: the licensed vaccine required too many shots.[82] If all six shots weren't administered on schedule, immunity might not be achieved. This was a nightmare. The protective-antigen vaccine not only required that a soldier get his second shot on time; he also had to get a third, and a fourth, and a fifth, and a sixth shot on time. Miss one shot in this series and, in theory, you had to start over from the beginning. Could you imagine a division commander stopping 14,000 troops in the midst of a battle so they could roll up their sleeves to take a two-week booster? That wasn't going to happen. There was also the "time-to-immunity" issue. No one is protected right after vaccination. It takes time to build immunity; it does not happen overnight. Going by the conventional wisdom at the time, the estimated time-to-immunity with the licensed U.S. vaccine was somewhere around six months: after the fourth shot. The time-to-immunity with the licensed British vaccine was eight months, which was also after the fourth shot (the British dosing schedule was different, requiring fewer total shots with longer intervals between each booster).[83] An unvaccinated force deployed on short notice against an enemy with "dusty" anthrax, in theory, could be decimated. Saddam had a weapon against which U.S. troops were defenseless. And he was just crazy enough to use it.

The Army needed a new vaccine more than ever. The generals wanted one that produced more immunity in less time with just one shot. It was Fort Detrick's job to create it.

Chapter Three

The Greatest Story Never Told

For the past seventeen years, the Army has been working on a new anthrax vaccine that contains no anthrax, and is made with an ingredient that it does not want to name. That ingredient is called squalene. Squalene is an oil. Without it, the new vaccine will not work any better than the old one. In fact, for all intents and purposes, without squalene the new vaccine *is* the old one. What makes squalene so important is its proven ability to stimulate a strong response from the immune system. That is something the main ingredient of the new vaccine, the now ultra-purified protein secreted by the anthrax microbe—recombinant protective antigen—cannot do by itself. It is too weak.

Immunologists have a special name for substances used to boost feeble vaccines. They are called adjuvants. Adjuvants are arguably the most extensively researched pharmaceutical product in the last quarter century that you never heard of. I have used the word *adjuvant* three times in this paragraph so far and that is probably three times more than you have ever seen it in print. This is partly because the most effective adjuvants, those formulated with oils, are too dangerous for human use. That is squalene's other proven ability, causing incurable disease, which is why it is such a touchy subject with the Department of Defense.

The word *adjuvant* comes from a Latin word that means "to help." But with oil adjuvants like squalene, that term is misleading. Today, only one adjuvant—an aluminum salt called alum—is licensed for human use. All the oil adjuvants are so noxious that their use is restricted to experiments with animals, and even then, governments have written strict regulations to govern how they are used. The classic oil adjuvant, called Freund's Complete Adjuvant, is considered too inhumane to even inject into animals.[1] It does a terrific job of stimulating the immune system, though. Unfortunately, Freund's Complete Adjuvant can cause permanent organ damage and incurable disease. As early as the 1930s, these oil additives were notorious for inducing illness. By the 1950s, scientists knew these illnesses were specifically autoimmune. Today that is their chief use in research—inducing disease instead of preventing it. Scientists studying autoimmune disease cannot wait around for its spontaneous appearance in a lab animal; they inject it with Freund's Complete Adjuvant to reproduce autoimmunity on demand. Oil adjuvants made with squalene are equally effective at this job, and regrettably according to Dutch scientists, equally inhumane.[2]

Autoimmune diseases are chronic and progressively debilitating ailments; some, like multiple sclerosis and lupus, can be fatal. They occur when the immune system loses its ability to distinguish what is "self" from what is foreign. Under normal circumstances, your immune system ignores the constituents of your own body; immunologists call this "tolerance." But if tolerance is broken, the immune system turns relentlessly self-destructive, attacking the body it is supposed to defend.

Adjuvants can break tolerance. In 1956, Dr. Jules Freund, the Hungarian-born scientist who gave his name to the adjuvant he created, warned that animals injected with Freund's developed terrible conditions: allergic aspermatogenesis (stoppage of sperm production), experimental allergic encephalomyelitis (the animal version of multiple sclerosis) and allergic neuritis (inflammation of nerves that can lead to paralysis), and allergic uveitis (an inflammation in the eye that can cause blindness).[3] There was no reversing any of these conditions.

Scientists are still unsure why oil adjuvants do this. One theory is that oils have the ability to hyperactivate the immune system. "The cause is probably that when injecting these molecules, you create a chaos in the immune system," says Dr. Johnny C. Lorentzen, an immunologist with the Karolinska Institute, which awards the annual Nobel Prize for Medicine. He says these oils induce "an extremely powerful response," so powerful, in fact, that the immune system goes haywire and starts attacking things it would otherwise leave alone. Another possibility, which has not been explored very much, is that this harmful phenomenon actually has something to do with one of the greatest distinguishing characteristics of the immune system—its specificity. Over eons in time, this extraordinarily elegant and powerful system has evolved to respond very precisely to what it deems potentially harmful to the body. Our bodies contain all sorts of oily molecules. It could be that when an oil is injected, the immune system actually responds to it with a high degree of precision—just as it responds to everything else—but because the adjuvant resembles too closely those oils found in the body, the immune system begins attacking those, too. In immunology this is called a "cross reaction." Neither proposition—chaos or specificity—has been proven so far. But however oils do their damage, it is well known that they do.

Army scientists have been as aware as anyone else of the harm that injecting oils can do. The problem for military personnel is that these scientists learned this lesson by injecting oils into troops in experiments that in some cases they did not agree to participate in.[4] The central question in this book is whether such an experiment has been done again with the new anthrax vaccine and squalene.

Round One

Despite their dangers, oil adjuvants have come to exert an almost irresistible allure on researchers. If they could truly stimulate the immune system safely, oil additives could help defend mankind from diseases like malaria and HIV. For germs such as these, no one dared make a classic vaccine—the kind made from the germ itself—for fear of accidentally infecting someone with an incurable, if not fatal infection. By splicing off just a little bit of such a germ—not enough to make anyone sick—and combining that shard with an adjuvant, scientists hoped to protect people from lethal microbes. If they could do it for HIV, they reasoned, they could do it for any germ in creation.

The first time Army scientists succumbed to this allure was in 1951 at Fort Dix, New Jersey, in an experiment that involved 44,459 troops. More than 18,000 of them got injected without their informed consent with a newly for-mulated oil additive for vaccines. The Army thought it had something new and safe. The world's best additive that no one dared inject into humans, Freund's Complete Adjuvant, was more than just mineral oil. It also contained *Mycobacterium tuberculosis,* the germ that caused TB. The mycobacteria were dead, but scientists thought they still might be in some way responsible for the problems associated with this concoction. So they removed the mycobac-teria in hopes that the oil alone could do the trick; they called this new adju-vant "Freund's *In*complete Adjuvant." The incomplete adjuvant was just mineral oil in water, and a detergent to keep the oil evenly dispersed. Using it was a risky thing to do, but the Army considered the risks of not running this experiment even higher. This "incomplete" additive had been incorporated into an experimental flu vaccine. It was the flu that really worried the Army.

By all accounts, the great Spanish Flu pandemic of 1918 wasn't really Spanish at all. It was American. In fact, it was an Army flu. The first victim, the "index patient," was an Army private named Albert Gitchell who worked as a cook at the Army's Camp Funston on the vast Fort Riley military reservation in Kansas. It is believed that U.S. troops heading to Europe brought this flu with them. Before it was over, more than twenty million people had died of in-fluenza around the world—the deadliest natural disaster in world history. Army scientists wanted to prevent another global killer from emerging from an Army post where new recruits might become an unintended hatchery for some vicious new flu strain that once again could wipe out millions of people. Trying out a new oil additive on troops seemed like a relatively modest risk in comparison to the benefits of a better flu vaccine.

The Fort Dix experiment took place with the blessing of Fort Detrick. It was funded by the U.S. Army Medical Research and Development Command (USAMRDC), which would later oversee the development of the new anthrax vaccine and newer oil additives too. The Armed Forces Epidemiological Board (AFEB), which would sponsor a large number of the experiments conducted on military personnel, would later recommend injecting an experimental flu vaccine containing oil into every man and woman in the U.S. military without their informed consent. The risk of an outbreak of killer flu seemed too great to do otherwise. To run this experiment, the Army would contract none other than Jonas Salk. Salk had already tested Freund's Incomplete Adjuvant on medical students at the University of Pittsburgh under the sponsorship of the Armed Forces Epidemiological Board, and with funding from the Army Surgeon General.[5] Based on this study, Salk thought it was safe.[6]

Over the next two decades, the entire U.S. public health establishment—civilian and military—kept watch on what happened to the troops from Fort Dix. Everyone wanted in on the act. USAMRDC funded this study and its follow-ups.[7] The National Academy of Sciences, the Walter Reed Army Institute of Research (WRAIR) and the Walter Reed Army Medical Center (WRAMC) did the initial round of surveys. Then the list started to grow. The National Academy of Sciences and the National Research Council organized more studies at the request of the Veteran's Administration, the Army and the U.S. Public Health Service "in collaboration with the Armed Forces Epidemiological Board."[8] At the seventeen-year mark, academia got involved too. An AFEB scientist on the faculty of the University of Michigan School of Public Health organized yet another follow-up.[9] No one, it seemed, wanted to be left out of such an important experiment.

And an experiment that seemingly had no end. Twenty-one years after Salk first injected unsuspecting soldiers with a theoretically new and improved flu vaccine, the Fort Dix troops were under the microscope yet again. The list of sponsors included many of America's most respected public health institutions: the National Academy of Sciences-National Research Council, the American Cancer Society, the Veterans Administration, the Department of Defense, the U.S. Public Health Service and the Commission on Influenza of the Armed forces Epidemiological Board.[10] USAMRDC bankrolled this study, just as it did the first one.[11] What was remarkable about this twenty-one-year project—involving the military, civilian public health authorities and a major university—is that at no time during its execution did any of the scientists involved publicly discuss whether it was ethical to run a medical experiment on people without telling them. If these doctors had any concerns, they did not publish them.

Long before the last study was completed, AFEB proposed the adoption of an experimental flu vaccine with oil for everyone in the military. In 1963 and 1964, AFEB recommended injecting every man and woman in the armed forces with the new vaccine. The board also recommended that the Department of Defense also commence studies with oil added to tetanus and diphtheria toxoids, and polio vaccines.[12] Army doctors seemed determined to add oil to every vaccine they could.

Here is what they were not telling anyone. By 1964, the year when everyone in the military was supposed to get immunized with an oil-boosted influenza vaccine, the Army already knew the risks this vaccine presented for a very specific type of illness. AFEB's Colonel Abram S. Benenson had drawn up a list of diseases that investigators should watch out for in veterans injected with the oily flu vaccine at Fort Dix. Benenson's list read like the contents of a chapter on autoimmune disease in an immunology textbook. It included multiple sclerosis, myelitis, Guillain-Barré syndrome, uveitis, neurodermatitis circumscripta and disseminata, amyloidosis, lupus erythematosus, dematomyositis, scleroderma, chronic pericarditis, Raynaud's disease, rheumatoid arthritis, rheumatoid myositis and acute glomerulonephritis—all of them autoimmune diseases.[13]

The final study on the Fort Dix troopers included data that none of the previous ones had: autopsy results. The soldiers had grown older and many of them had died. Epidemiologists, mainly working for the National Research Council and the American Cancer Society, reported a "significant excess of deaths" in soldiers given the oil-boosted vaccine, which the investigators related to "ill-defined vascular lesions of the central nervous system."[14] They attributed this fact to the greater number of autopsies performed on the soldiers given the oil-boosted vaccine.[15] But there were hints of a problem with autoimmunity. Ten percent of the soldiers studied who were injected with the oil-boosted vaccine developed a "collagen disease," which is a term doctors used to use interchangeably with autoimmune disease. Still, the number of patients in this study was too low to extrapolate any reliable conclusions from that ten percent figure. Government and military doctors concluded that the oily flu vaccine was safe. Nevertheless, what the government then did not do was revealing. The FDA never licensed the vaccine, or the oil adjuvant, for human use.

The Fort Dix experiment was the first time Army doctors and scientists injected an oil-boosted vaccine into U.S. troops without informed consent; there is now clinical evidence that it was far from the last. For more than a half century, factions in military medicine and in the U.S. public health establishment have actively campaigned to get an oily vaccine additive licensed.

The Emperor's New Clothes

When scientists at Fort Detrick, following Joe Jemski's 1992 talk, reviewed the existing literature on the Wright vaccine, it didn't look good. Even with six shots, the vaccine did not protect very well. Guinea pigs vaccinated with the licensed human vaccine died when exposed to certain strains of anthrax. In 1986 the bad news got worse. In discovering that the licensed vaccine protected against the Army's old weapons strain, Vollum—from which the vaccine had been derived— Stephen Little and Gregory Knudson also discovered eight more anthrax strains for which the PA vaccine did not work.[16] Among them was the now notorious Ames strain that was mailed in the 2001 anthrax letter attacks. Like the Army's previous research, the data confirmed that a live spore vaccine provided better protection against more strains.[17] "The fact that the spore vaccine provided protection against all isolates tested suggests that other antigens may play a role in active immunity," they concluded.[18] Which would argue for a live anthrax vaccine, but Fort Detrick's scientists expressed an age-old concern about a problem with living vaccines that could be traced all the way back to Pasteur: "Since this vaccine is a live immunogen," they warned, "safety factors must be considered before its use." Little and Knudson did not rule out the possibility of resorting to a live spore vaccine, but that is not what they then chose to pursue.

When they, along with Fort Detrick scientists Bruce Ivins and Sue Welkos, began working on a new anthrax vaccine, they chose a design that was increasingly popular at the NIH—subunit plus adjuvant. "Subunit" refers to small fragments of a germ. For safety, NIH scientists were using subunits of lethal viruses like HIV to be the chief component of their new generation of genetically engineered vaccines. These ultra-pure vaccines, which reduced an immunization to mere molecules from a microbe, were safe, but at a price. They were weak. In some cases, they afforded no detectable level of protection at all. This is why the NIH wanted an adjuvant more robust than alum for its new vaccines.

The subunit that Little, Knudson, Ivins and Welkos chose for the Army's new anthrax vaccine was a little surprising. It was protective antigen—the same main ingredient in the vaccine they were trying to replace. Although all the data from both U.S. and British military experiments from the '60s forward indicated that more components of the anthrax microbe needed to be in any effective anthrax vaccine—a fact that even Little and Knudson acknowledge in their 1986 paper—Fort Detrick's newest generation of anthrax investigators did just the opposite. In fact, they did one better. With recombinant DNA technology, their new vaccine would eliminate every extra molecule of anthrax unrelated to protective antigen. It would be purest PA formulation ever made, and would hence be the weakest anthrax vaccine ever made. Remember, in immunology, purity equals weakness.

Yet when Fort Detrick's scientists traveled to England in 1989 to report on their new vaccine to the International Workshop on Anthrax, they had some startling results to announce: Fort Detrick had found what everyone had been looking for: a single-shot anthrax vaccine. In guinea pigs, the new anthrax vaccine produced complete protection against the Ames strain with just *one* dose.[19]

If this was completely at odds with everything Army scientists had found over the previous three decades, it was because the Fort Detrick team had added something new to the formula. It was a kind of trick, though not in the sense of something fraudulent or deceptive. The Army's scientists made no effort to conceal what they did. Quite the contrary, they reported this trick in great detail. It was an old trick. In the '80s, scientists at NIH had been promoting the use of oils in vaccines again. By now, there was a new crop of oily vaccine boosters hot off the lab bench. It was the oil emulsions that helped transform the Army's hapless protective antigen formula into a potent single-shot vaccine.

Dr. Bruce Ivins informed the workshop gathering in the old cathedral city of Winchester that he had added three different adjuvants to his one-shot wonders. One was called "Tri-Mix," another "DeTox," and a third was "SAF–1," which stood for Syntex Adjuvant Formula 1. They were all made with bacterial scraps from truly noxious microbes like *Salmonella typhimurium* and *Mycobacteria tuberculosis*. The British scientists from Porton Down tried a different tack—adding a preparation to the British anthrax vaccine made from the whooping cough germ, *Bordetella pertussis*. At Winchester, the Porton contingent called their approach "microbial supplementation." All of these adjuvants relied on bacteria, or portions of them, to stimulate the immune system.

The three additives used by Fort Detrick, however, differed from Porton Down's in one very significant way. The Fort Detrick additives were all emulsified in oil. The oils were only supposed to be "vehicles" that conveyed the bits of bacteria through the bloodstream. SAF-1, which provided less protection than the other two, contained the oil squal*ane*.[20] The adjuvants that helped provide complete protection from Ames in guinea pigs, Tri-Mix and DeTox, contained fragments of bacteria suspended in squal*ene*.[21]

Having invested decades in refining protective antigen to a singular purity, Ivins et al. were essentially polluting this new ultra-pure vaccine with extraneous antigens to make it work. That is what an adjuvant was—extra antigenic material for a vaccine that had been purified to such an extent that it could no longer do the job it was designed to do. Perhaps it was the importance of their apparent breakthrough that blinded these scientists to what they had done. Whatever it was, it prevented them from seeing the absurdity of their new creation, or its risks. A fully intact microbe presents dozens of different chemical binding sites an antibody can latch onto. Each of these sites is a separate target for a multi-front attack by the immune system. In pursuit of purity, Army scientists had removed all of the targets of the anthrax germ but one. Now they had a dubious product that they were determined to improve, and they did it by adding targets from germs *other* than *B. anthracis*. Instead of adding more antigenic material from the anthrax microbe—as Lincoln had suggested in the '60s and as Turnbull and Melling had done in the '80s—the Fort Detrick team incorporated pieces of completely different germs.

This was Rube Goldberg immunology. The Army's vaccine makers had devised a convoluted, expensive and time-consuming way to make a virtually identical product—protective antigen—and then added material that essentially diverted the immune system's attention away to antigens unrelated to anthrax. Fort Detrick's new, souped-up single protein vaccine, like the old one, did nothing to induce an immune response to the organism itself, which could still feed, secrete toxins and multiply inside a vaccinated host. There was also one more flaw in this design: oils are potentially toxic, and the Fort Detrick team knew it. In Bruce Ivins's frequently cited paper on the Army's pursuit of an improved human anthrax vaccine, he noted that oil adjuvants "*can provoke toxic, allergic, ulcerative, or lethal reactions.*"[22] This should have made him think twice before using an oil adjuvant, but many scientists at the time were convinced that squalene could be safely injected because it was already found in the body.[23] Neither he nor anyone

else who worked on this vaccine at Fort Detrick has published an explanation
for why they did this.

Round Two

Anyone even remotely familiar with oil additives for vaccines could have told
you that they were a big problem. For reasons science has yet to fully explain,
oils and other fatty substances found in the body, like cholesterol and
phosopholipids, are potent stimulants to the immune system. Try as they
might, scientists trying to harness this property have yet to come up with an
oil adjuvant safe enough to use in humans. Since the 1930s, the gold standard
has been the aforementioned Freund's Complete Adjuvant—an elixir banned
from human use because of its toxicity. When Freund's Incomplete Adjuvant,
a vaccine additive made chiefly from mineral oil, proved too risky as well, scientists tried changing the oil.

In the early 1970s, scientists at UCLA Medical Center, including one of
the most respected rheumatologists in the country at the time, Carl M. Pearson, started looking for a less toxic alternative to Freund's. They ran a series of
experiments with a variety of edible oils on the assumption that because they
were "metabolizable" the body could process them safely.[24] In other words, if
you could ingest them, you could inject them. Intuitively, this premise seems
somewhat dubious: your body could metabolize a cheeseburger, for instance,
but you couldn't liquefy it in a blender and inject the resulting slurry, and then
expect to feel well in the morning. Pearson's associates, Michael Whitehouse
and Frances W. Beck, injected more than a dozen of these metabolizable oils
into rats, including castor oil, coconut oil, olive oil, sesame seed oil, cotton-
seed oil, corn oil, wheat germ oil, safflower oil, cod liver oil, oleomargarine
and the commercial lubricating oil, silicone.[25] When these were mixed with
heat-killed *Mycobacteria tuberculosis*, the UCLA group got results it didn't expect. All of the oils were toxic; they all induced arthritis in rats with varying
degrees of severity.[26] The data changed Whitehouse's views on the safety of
metabolizable oils. "To summarize very simply, I think most oils are dangerous," he now says.[27] Based on their ability to cause arthritis, the researchers
assigned the oils "arthritis scores," ranging from (+), which was moderately
toxic, to (++++), which was guaranteed to cripple.[28] Of all the metabolizable

oils tested by Pearson's group, two were better than all the others at causing arthritis: squalene and squalane, the same emulsifying oils that Bruce Ivins used in his single-shot anthrax vaccines.[29]

Squalene and squalane scored (+++) and (++++) respectively.[30] Between these two oils, squalene is the one you could definitely eat. Olive oil contains squalene; in theory, you could drizzle it onto a salad along with a little vinegar and have no worries. Your body would metabolize it along with the arugula and endive without as much as a hiccup. Injecting squalene, though, was another story. To make sure it was the oils that did the damage, Beck, Whitehouse and Pearson tried injecting rats with squalene and squalane without mycobacteria in the formula. Rats injected with either squalene or squalane all developed experimental allergic encephalomyelitis—the same MS-like disease caused by Freund's. The injected animals were left hobbled, dragging their paralyzed hindquarters through the wood chips in their cages.[31] The UCLA team had found what it was looking for: oils that induced autoimmune disease, but with less inflammation. Between the two of them, squalene was less desirable for UCLA's purposes. "Squalene was more arthritogenic," Beck recalls, "but it also produced a greater inflammation."

Risk vs. Benefit

Given these oils' proven ability to induce autoimmune disease, the Army's decision to put either of them in its second generation anthrax vaccine only makes sense when you place it in the context of the times, and in this case, a specific location. When he canceled America's offensive biological warfare program, President Nixon also freed up some buildings for a more popular research effort. Arriving by helicopter at Fort Detrick's Blue and Grey Field in October 1971, President Nixon personally announced the creation of the Frederick Cancer Research Facility of the National Cancer Institute (NCI). Nixon had Fort Detrick allocate about sixty-eight acres and seventy of its buildings as a new research campus for NCI. It was a fateful decision that would have consequences that even a president as forward-thinking as Nixon could not have foreseen. It would set in motion a series of decisions that would lead to the use of a substance that would endanger the health of hundreds of thousands of U.S. troops.

It is unclear how squalene first came to the attention of Army scientists at Fort Detrick, but one possibility is through the National Cancer Institute, now on its doorstep. Eliyahu Yarkoni and Herbert Rapp of NCI published a paper in 1979 that stirred national and international interest in the alleged therapeutic benefits of squalene and squalane. When combined with fragments of a particular bacterium, squalene and squalane had an astonishing effect.[32] Yarkoni and Rapp reported complete tumor regression in mice injected with squal*ane*, and nearly complete regression (92 percent) in mice injected with squal*ene*.[33] When they injected these oils directly into mouse tumors, the tumors either shrank or disappeared completely. The more oil in the mixture, the better it worked. Based on these early experiments, oils looked like they might hold the keys to the kingdom—a cure for cancer. There was, however, a hitch.

Yarkoni and Rapp knew about the UCLA data; citing the Beck and Whitehouse paper, Yarkoni and Rapp reported that squalene and squalane both caused autoimmune disease in rats—a fact that you will not find mentioned in any Army paper concerning Fort Detrick's work with squalene emulsions in the new anthrax vaccine. Even Yarkoni and Rapp barely mentioned the problem with squalene and squalane; it was limited to a single sentence at the end of their short paper. Although causing debilitating and ultimately fatal neurological damage in animals was a big downside, their concern, after all, was cancer.

Several more factors emerged in the 1980s that would affect the direction of the Army's anthrax vaccine research. The first was HIV. After the discovery of the human immunodeficiency virus in 1984, the cause of Acquired Immune Deficiency Syndrome (AIDS), the National Institutes of Health would devote billions to develop a vaccine. That year, the Centers for Disease Control reported 7,699 AIDS cases with 3,665 dead.[34] By 1988, the number of diagnosed U.S. cases was 82,764 with 46,344 dead.[35] That was a jump of more than 1,000 percent in just four years. Mortality was 100 percent; for someone with AIDS, drugs could prolong life but not save it. Public health officials doing the math were horrified. No one dared make a whole virus vaccine, living or dead, from a germ like HIV. Vaccine researchers embraced gene-splicing as their only alternative—inserting HIV genes into non-lethal organisms like vaccinia. But the results were disappointing: these microbial hybrids barely elicited an immune response.[36] That's why a new adjuvant was essential to NIH. Because of Yarkoni and Rapp's work, squalene and squalane emulsions had by then established themselves as NIH's adjuvants of choice.

HIV was threatening to become the great plague of the twentieth century, worse even than the flu pandemic of 1918 that claimed more than 20 million lives. It was the public health *cause célèbre* of the 1980s. Rock Hudson had it; so did Liberace. When an Indiana school banned fourteen-year-old Ryan White from classes because he had HIV, Elton John and Michael Jackson became his friends and offered their support. Vice President George Bush called for mandatory HIV testing. No other disease made as many headlines or pushed as many political buttons. For NIH, that translated into wide-open government coffers. For researchers, it offered a shot at immortality. Any scientist who found a way to stop this new global scourge could reserve a seat in Stockholm for a Nobel Prize ceremony. A successful recombinant HIV vaccine would be just a start. The goal was to roll back *all* infectious diseases through immunization . . . if that were possible. But it wasn't going to happen without a more powerful vaccine booster. The FDA, stung by criticism from dying AIDS patients who wanted access to new drugs that could keep them alive even a few months longer, started to "fast-track" drugs through its licensing labyrinth, including experimental vaccines containing squalene. This was not without risks. The problem with the fast track was knowing when someone was playing it fast and loose.

Even NATO got on this bandwagon by sponsoring a conference in Cape Sounion, Greece, on vaccine adjuvants in the summer of 1988. The search for a new adjuvant was now a matter of national security. The U.S. Army sent a contingent from its Walter Reed Army Institute of Research led by Dr. Carl R. Alving, a proponent of vaccine boosters emulsified in squalene, in addition to his own favorite: liposomes. Liposomes are microscopic vesicles containing vaccine antigens. Think bath oil beads. Encapsulating bath oil in soluble beads makes it possible to transport measured doses of oil from the drugstore where you bought them to where you ultimately want to put them—in your bathtub. Alving's liposomes were made from cholesterol, another oily substance closely related to squalene.

The Soviets Again

If anyone in the military had been inclined to ask questions about squalene's toxicity in the late 1980s, something else happened around then that might have diverted them. In October 1989, a high-ranking Soviet biological weapons scientist defected to the West—the first one to do so. This was an extraordinary intelligence coup. At the invitation of a French pharmaceutical equipment maker, Dr. Vladimir Pasechnik of the Leningrad Institute of Ultra-Pure Biopreparations went to Paris for a conference and never went home.[37] He left his family behind in Russia and wound up in Britain. One of the scientists who debriefed Pasechnik for the British was Jack Melling. "Pasechnik chose Britain," says Melling, "because he thought the U.S. still had an active biological warfare program and he didn't want anything more to do with making weapons. He didn't think the same of Britain."[38] According to Melling, what Pasechnik told Britain's MI–6 raised even more alarm about the U.S. and British chemical anthrax vaccines. Pasechnik said that Moscow had created antibiotic-resistant super-strains of anthrax, plague and tularemia. Although Pasechnik's British handlers couldn't verify this, it sounded plausible enough to them—in part because making germs antibiotic-resistant was relatively easy to do, and in part because the Soviets had published several papers in the 1980s disclosing that they had developed a veterinary vaccine that immunized against all three of these microbes.[39] Intelligence analysts had been asking themselves why Soviet livestock would need to be vaccinated against plague, tularemia and anthrax—the three agents regarded by bioweapons specialists as the most likely ones to be used in a biological warfare attack. They could not come up with a good answer.

Back in Maryland, Fort Detrick now had at least four viable prototypes of a single-shot vaccine that they thought was safe. All were made from the protective antigen protein or pieces of it.[40] Three were recombinant vaccines; Fort Detrick had cloned the protective antigen gene into *Bacillus subtilis*, baculovirus and vaccinia. All of these prototypes were formulated with squalene or squalane. The ones showing the most promise were the protective antigen vaccines combined with these oils. According to Ivins and his Fort Detrick colleagues, just one dose of these new vaccines gave protection equivalent to three doses of the licensed U.S. vaccine . . . *and the new vaccines were ready for clinical trials.*[41] All Fort Detrick needed now was the right time and place to test them.[42]

Chapter Four

The Opportunity

If any nation was caught more flat-footed by the Iraqi invasion of Kuwait than Kuwait, it was the United States. Saddam Hussein was a son of a bitch, but Washington had worked hard to make him *our* son of a bitch. When extremist Shiite clerics orchestrated the exile of the Shah from Iran in 1979, Saddam and his secular Baath Party overnight became America's bulwark against Islamic fundamentalism. That meant perks for Saddam. These included a big line of credit, an easing of trade restrictions, massive shipments of rice and wheat—and other materiel that was decidedly less benign.

America sold Saddam anthrax. Between May 1986 and September 1989, Iraq went on a shopping spree for germ warfare agents here, importing seven anthrax strains from a U.S. repository of infectious agents called the American Type Culture Collection—including Vollum, the former U.S. and British weapons strain. This was the strain that Iraq, in turn, would also weaponize.[1] From the same non-profit company that provided the anthrax, Iraq also received several strains of *Clostridium botulinum* (the source of botulinum toxin), *Brucella abortis* and *Brucella melitensis* (the causative agents for brucellosis) and West Nile Virus.[2] Iraq acquired elsewhere the precursor chemicals to make nerve agents and mustard gas. Between 1983 and 1988, it used chemical weapons "approximately 195 times" to incapacitate or kill an estimated 50,000 Iranians, many of them civilians.[3] Though a signatory to the 1925 Geneva Protocol banning chemical weapons, Iraq was now brazen in their use.

By August 1990, Saddam not only had mustard gas, he had "dusty mustard"—a powdered form of the agent bound to silica nanoparticles so fine they could conceivably seep through a soldier's protective uniform and masks.[4]

The Invasion

At 1 A.M. on August 2, 1990, four divisions of Saddam Hussein's Republican Guard cranked their engines and crossed the border from Safwan, Iraq, into Kuwait.[5] Some five hours later they rumbled into the capital, Kuwait City, from the west.[6] From the east came the air assault—a battalion of Iraqi Special Forces on board a swarm of Soviet-made Mi–8 helicopters, escorted by heavily armed gunships, flying low over Kuwait Bay out of the rising sun.[7] The muezzins were just finishing the azan, their plaintive call to Morning Prayer, as the formation of some fifty helicopters started their descent. It was a textbook "vertical envelopment"—a pincer attack in three dimensions designed to entrap an opponent from either direction, and from above. The outcome was almost foreordained. The invaders swept into the city virtually unopposed. Fighting at the emir's palace was intense but ended quickly; Sheikh Al-Sabah had already taken flight in his limousine. A coordinated land-air attack with more than 100,000 troops took the capital in less than a day. In forty-eight hours, the entire country was occupied; three Republican Guard divisions had taken up positions in the Al-Wafra oilfield on the northern border of Saudi Arabia. Nothing stood between Saddam's tanks and the world's largest oil producer except open desert.

Six days after the invasion began, Rear Admiral Joseph P. Smyth, the Medical Readiness Officer for the Joint Chiefs of Staff, received the "first mention of BW in monitored [Iraqi] message traffic."[8] A secret communiqué sent to the Joint Chiefs on August 8th asserted that Iraq had a "mature offensive BW program."[9] The very next day, the 82nd Airborne Division arrived in Saudi Arabia; the day after that, the 24th Infantry Division, Mechanized—the only heavy armored division specifically trained for desert warfare—left the United States by Fast Sealift Ship for the Persian Gulf.[10] The troops would be at their most vulnerable when they first disembarked from transport planes and ships. It wasn't Iraqi armor or infantry that had the generals worried; it was Iraqi biological and chemical weapons. Of the two threats, U.S. military planners were more concerned about America's lack of readiness for a biological attack. The armed forces had detectors that could alert troops to the presence of a chemical agent. The only detector America had for anthrax walked on two legs and carried an M–16. There was no way to know if Saddam had used anthrax until soldiers actually succumbed to it.

Two weeks into Operation Desert Shield, the Navy and Marine Corps sent an urgent request to the Army Surgeon General for 150,000 doses of anthrax vaccine and botulinum toxoid; Britain's Air Marshall Kenneth Hayr contacted the Joint Chiefs wanting to know how the United States planned to defend U.S. forces from biological attacks and how it would treat bioweapons casualties.[11]

The Army had meager stockpiles of an anthrax vaccine that it didn't think would work. Its biggest worry was "time-to-immunity"—an estimated six months after the first shot with the U.S. chemical vaccine, eight months with the British version, provided all the boosters were given at the proper intervals. Even if there had been enough vaccine to start immunizing right away, troops would be at risk from biological attack as soon as they arrived "in country." They couldn't be immunized in time to ensure any protection.

The U.S. faced an enemy with weapons for which it had no adequate defense—weapons the enemy had acquired partly through America's indifference and partly through its direct help. Not everyone in the military, however, saw this as a potential disaster. For some, it was an opportunity.

An Ugly Military Tradition

One month after Saddam invaded Kuwait, the head of the Armed Forces Epidemiological Board (AFEB), Navy Captain William M. Parsons, Ph.D., put the Army's predicament in a different light. "Operation Desert Shield presents *unique research opportunities*," he wrote to the commander of the United States Army Medical Research and Development Command. The Army's medical R&D command controlled USAMRIID (where Bruce Ivins worked) and the Walter Reed Army Institute of Research (where Carl Alving worked). It was the mission of the R&D command to come up with better ways to protect troops from medical threats; this could mean a better gas mask or a better chemical weapons detector . . . or a better vaccine. Desert Shield offered a chance for the Army to put its latest inventory to use, and Parsons wanted US-AMRDC to inform the Epidemiological Board about the steps "being taken by the medical research community to capitalize on these opportunities."[12]

Coming from AFEB, the words "research" and "opportunities" conveyed a chilling nuance. On the face of it, the board was an innocuous entity; its members were civilian doctors and scientists who advised the Assistant Secretary of Defense for Health Affairs and the Surgeons General of the Army, Navy and Air Force on matters of public health. Whether by design or by default, the board was also a means by which faculty members from top universities across the nation were enmeshed in a system that endangered the very troops it was supposed to help protect. Faculty members appointed to the board received funding for their institutions from the Department of Defense to run experiments. Most of these experiments were performed on animals; some were performed on human volunteers. Others were done on humans without their consent.

Since its inception in January 1941, the board has organized its field research around "commissions" that looked at specific medical problems threatening the health of U.S. troops. There was, for instance, a Commission on Meningococcal Meningitis, a Commission on Parasitic Disease and a Commission on Pneumonia. One experiment, conducted by AFEB's Commission on Streptococcal Diseases, looked at how strep infections spread at Frances E. Warren Air Force Base (AFB) in Cheyenne, Wyoming. Under AFEB contracts with New York University, Case Western Reserve, Vanderbilt and the University of Illinois, civilian doctors beginning in March 1954 conducted an experiment in twelve barracks.[13] There were forty-three airmen in each barrack. The idea was to determine "the effect of crowding on disease rates" and the "route of transmission."[14] To do this, each barrack was assigned one carrier of Type A streptococcus; the doctors knew exactly who they were. Each of these carriers was given a specially selected bunk; by design, they would expose the rest of their barrack mates to strep. By the standards of this era, when other U.S. military personnel were exposed to atomic fallout with no more protection than a pair of Ray-Ban sunglasses, the AFEB strep experiments seem relatively benign. Except that a strep infection can do serious damage. Left untreated it can progress to rheumatic fever, which can permanently damage the heart valves. AFEB doctors deliberately withheld antibiotics from airmen suffering from "acute rheumatic fever" to get data.[15]

In another strep study at Warren AFB, the sick were randomly divided into two groups: "Treatment" and "No treatment."[16] While all the patients received cortisone (a steroid used to treat rheumatic fever), doctors wanted to know if an ongoing strep infection determined whether a patient suffered valve damage. By design, some of the infected airmen were denied antibiotics to determine the extent of the harm this caused, if any. Only airmen in the "Treatment" group received gantrisin, penicillin or tetracycline.[17] Denying viable treatment for a disease was what made the infamous Tuskegee syphilis study so offensive. In rural Alabama, doctors with the U.S. Public Health Service withheld penicillin from poor black men with syphilis in order to observe the disease's progress. There were 399 men in the study; as many as 100 of them died from syphilis-related complications.[18]

One might take reassurance in thinking that such studies were excesses of bygone times, when AFEB and the U.S. public health establishment were less enlightened in their thinking about informed consent. But that would be incorrect. Using the men and women of the United States Armed Forces as unwitting test subjects is a practice that continues to this day.

The Unfinished Experiment

One series of experiments is still unfinished, in the sense that decades of testing on military personnel have never yielded a licensed product. The product is a vaccine for the common cold. Outbreaks of respiratory illness are among the biggest disruptions to unit readiness. Up to eighty percent of all new recruits develop adenovirus infections; twenty percent are hospitalized as a result.[19] To limit these outbreaks, the military medical command, usually upon the direct recommendation of the Armed Forces Epidemiological Board, has been testing unlicensed influenza and adenovirus (common cold) vaccines on troops for more than forty-five years. The experiments were run intermittently at bases around the United States from 1952 to 1998—and were only halted in the '90s by the manufacturer's inability (or unwillingness) to continue making the vaccine.[20]

In the winter of 1955, the military began injecting its first "inactivated" adenovirus vaccines into recruits at Lowry Air Force Base, outside of Denver.[21] Gradually the experimentation expanded to other bases. Ten years later, the Armed Forces Epidemiological Board recommended the expansion of adenovirus vaccine trials to other bases and other services—including Camp Lejeune (Marine Corps), Great Lakes Naval Air Station (Navy), Fort Ord (Army), Fort Dix (Army), and Keesler Air Force Base (Air Force), while continuing to use ADV vaccine at Lowry AFB.[22] By June 1970, the board wanted the military to run experiments on troops to test a new "subunit" adenovirus vaccine—the same design the Army used to make its licensed anthrax vaccine.[23]

Although a flu vaccine, or one for the common cold, sounds benign, there was in fact cause for concern. For over thirty years, at the recommendation of the AFEB's Commission on Influenza and under contract to the U.S. Army Research and Development Command, doctors from medical schools around the country injected experimental influenza and adenovirus vaccines into U.S. military personnel that sometimes included oil additives.[24] Even the viruses themselves, the main component of these vaccines, posed a greater risk than anyone anticipated. The military discovered that certain lots of experimental adenovirus vaccines were contaminated with SV–40, a monkey virus that causes mesothelioma—a slow-developing cancer affecting cells on the external surfaces of many organs.[25] Scientists then learned that certain types of adenoviruses themselves caused cancer in baby hamsters.[26] There was more. When they injected adenovirus Type 4 into monkeys, the monkeys developed lesions in their central nervous systems.[27] U.S. military personnel were not told about this. They weren't even told they were being immunized with experimental adenovirus vaccines in the first place. To this day, if any service member developed chronic illness as a result of these vaccinations, they would not begin to know why.

Business as Usual

All this has been done without secrecy . . . as was the U.S. Public Health Service's Tuskegee Study. When the Associated Press broke the story of the Tuskegee syphilis experiment in 1972, many newspaper editors assumed the work had been done clandestinely. To the contrary: doctors had published reports on the study in leading medical journals and discussed it openly at conferences.[28] Based on the number of scientific papers published about it, one

Public Health Service official, Dr. John Millar, estimated that more than a hundred thousand physicians knew about the experiment.[29] Government funding had endowed it with a patina of respectability, as did publication in peer-reviewed medical journals; far from aberrant, it was embraced matter-of-factly by the U.S. public health establishment. If any doctors felt the slightest pangs of conscience over it, they had made no effort to register their dismay with letters of protest to journal editors. Or, if protests were sent, the editors chose not to publish them.

The same was true of the infamous hepatitis experiments at Willowbrook State School on New York's Staten Island. Between 1956 and 1972, New York University Professor Dr. Saul Krugman injected hepatitis into severely retarded children at Willowbrook in order to study the progression of the disease.[30] It was no secret that Krugman was doing this. A distinguished pediatrician and member of the Armed Forces Epidemiological Board, he performed the Willowbrook experiments under the aegis of his university.[31] Krugman's bona fides were impeccable—president of the American Pediatric Society, consultant to the Bureau of Biologics, member of an advisory panel for the WHO, fellow of the American Academy of Arts and Sciences, member of the Institute of Medicine and National Academy of Sciences, and AFEB Commission Deputy Director.[32] Although the parents of the children in the Willowbrook experiments signed consent forms, there were some complaints of passive coercion. The school was overcrowded. According to a Department of Energy report on human experimentation in America, some critics charged that parents could only get their kids into Willowbrook by signing them up for the hepatitis study. Before Krugman began the experiments he consulted many colleagues; he also sought and received the express approval of the Armed Forces Epidemiological Board, which funded the study. When the British medical journal the *Lancet* published a letter to the editor attacking Krugman's work as "unjustifiable," the editors of America's two most respected medical journals—the *New England Journal of Medicine* and the *Journal of the American Medical Association*—defended it.[33]

This was no isolated incident. When Henry K. Beecher, a professor of anesthesia at Harvard Medical School, published his now legendary article on unethical clinical research, he cited twenty-two examples from the year 1964 alone. None of them were secret—all were published in "an excellent journal," he said, by doctors and scientists from "leading medical schools, university hospitals, private hospitals, governmental military departments (the Army, the Navy, and the Air Force), government institutes (the National Institutes of Health), Veterans Administration hospitals and industry."[34] Beecher's very first example was a study of streptococcal respiratory infections by military researchers who withheld penicillin from 109 servicemen. Two from this group developed acute rheumatic fever and one developed acute nephritis.[35] Like all the other studies Beecher cited, this was published in the open literature. So it may come as no surprise to some that the ongoing military practice of immunizing U.S. troops with experimental vaccines is a matter of public record—published in scientific journals available in many libraries, and in some cases, documented on Department of Defense websites.[36]

This was the backdrop to the proposals made by Army and Navy doctors for Desert Shield. The public health bureaucracy viewed the first principle of the Nuremberg Code developed in the wake of World War II—"the voluntary consent of the human subject is absolutely essential"—as something that didn't apply to soldiers. By tradition and practice, and later by explicit agreement with the FDA, the military had gotten an exemption from the principle of informed consent.

—

The military's use of experimental medicines is as old as the nation itself. The first U.S. military leader to order the use of an experimental medical procedure was none other than General George Washington. When smallpox struck the Northern Department of the Continental Army in 1775, it had 10,000 troops under the command of General Horatio Gates; more than half of Gates's men, 5,500 of them, would become casualties of smallpox. Enlistments stopped; men began deserting.[37] To halt the epidemic and the desertions, the Northern Army resorted to "variolation." Doctors cut incisions into a healthy person's arm and then deposited in the wound pus from an active smallpox sore. This gave the patient a case of smallpox, but the infection was milder; fewer people died from the disease when it was induced.[38] The following year, Gates's army, now free of smallpox, defeated the British at the Battle of Saratoga. Seeing this result, Washington persuaded the Continental Congress to approve variolation for all new recruits.

It would be another twenty years before Britain's Edward Jenner developed the world's first smallpox vaccine. A controversial medical procedure (calling it "experimental" is anachronistic as there were no licenses in those days) saved the lives of American troops and may have even turned the course of the war in the colonists' favor.[39] Although military historians are too circumspect to put it this bluntly, the implication is there in their writings: were it not for variolation, Americans today might be drinking tea and singing "God Save the Queen."

In military medicine, the mission, not the patient, comes first. As Edmund G. Howe of the Uniformed Services University puts it: "The military physician . . . accepts the obligation to place military interests over his own interests and those he might otherwise have as a civilian doctor when he becomes a military officer; he is, in this sense, primarily a soldier with special technical expertise. Thus, when during combat, the soldier comes to the military physician with an injury, both the soldiers and the physician have agreed to prioritize the needs of the military."[40] This is what turned Dr. Harold Appel into a conscientious objector. During his conscientious-objector hearing in 1969, Appel quoted Navy documents that led him to believe that "the purpose of the Medical Corps was to enable the fighting force to attain its mission, not to heal the sick."[41] In a letter published in the New England Journal of Medicine, Appel urged any doctor considering a military career to think about this. "Patient-centered ethics," he wrote, "is fundamentally antagonistic to the military's goals. The military physician is a soldier first and a doctor second."[42]

In war, greater moral weight is given to the effort to save many lives at the expense of some. No commander will refuse an order to take a hill because some of his soldiers will die in battle. The same is expected of a military doctor. While they might balk (as they did in Vietnam)[43] at placing the badly wounded in the back of the queue, there has been less reluctance to risk a soldier's health or even his life with experimental immunizations. George Washington resorted to an unproven medical procedure to help him prosecute a war. The Army used an experimental vaccine to defend against a possible biological warfare attack in World War II. To protect troops, the Army has been doing that ever since, regularly using experimental flu and adenovirus vaccines to maintain operational readiness and to prevent an outbreak of killer flu like the one in 1918 that left more than twenty million people dead. At the time, the index patient in that pandemic was an Army cook named Albert Gitchell. Although he fell ill, it was his job to help feed some 56,000 new recruits at a hastily built cantonment called Camp Funston, on the Fort Riley military reservation in Haskell County, Kansas.[44] If Camp Funston is in fact where it all started, then the catastrophic Spanish Flu pandemic of 1918 should have been called the "Army Flu" pandemic. Everyone has a stake in how the military prevents infectious disease.

The danger is when the wartime mentality takes hold of researchers conducting experiments on military personnel. Because "soldiers give their lives during combat if necessary," Howe warned that "researchers may also inappropriately generalize [the soldiers'] 'expendability' during combat to the research setting."[45] That is precisely what happened in the CIA's experiments with LSD, performed on military personnel. In defending these experiments, one officer explained the rationale this way: "You have to look at the experiments like a combat operation. You start taking casualties in combat, and you don't stop. You press on. You take the objective. That is the way it was in these experiments. They were very important to national security, and we pressed on. It's unfortunate that somebody died. But we had to know what these drugs could do to people and how we could use them."[46] Note the subtle shift in thinking contained in those last six words: If it's ethical to experiment on soldiers without their consent in order to save their fellow soldiers' (and civilians') lives, it's also ethical to do so for weapons development.

Common to all experiments performed on human subjects without their informed consent is the attitude that some people—*other* people—are expendable. In a strict sense the subjects of such experiments are *all* expendable because any one of them may receive an unproven treatment or none at all. By the precepts of the Nuremberg Code, what separates a legitimate human experiment from an illegitimate one is a patient's choice, not a doctor's; a patient must choose to participate.

When we look back at the experiments performed on concentration camp prisoners at Buchenwald and Dachau, we are looking into a cracked mirror, but a mirror nonetheless. This was, in fact, the Nazi doctors' chief defense—that in some cases they only did what Americans were doing. Brigadier General Gerhard Rose, who oversaw infectious disease experiments at Buchenwald and Natzweiler concentration camps, became "exasperated" at the repeated insistence by American prosecution witness Dr. Andrew Ivy that "human experimental subjects must be volunteers."[47] Rose and his fellow defendants protested that American physicians did involuntary research on patients, citing several examples. The malaria experiments at Dachau, for instance, bore more than a passing resemblance to the malaria experiments run by Dr. Alf Alving of the University of Chicago (whose son Carl Alving would grow up to become the Army's chief expert on vaccine adjuvants and one of the nation's biggest advocates for the use of squalene).[48] Alf Alving ran experiments to test the antimalarial drug, primaquine, on more than 400 inmates of the Joliet-Stateville branch of the Illinois State Penitentiary thirty-five miles southwest of Chicago.[49] The U.S. and Nazi experiments were both performed on prisoners in an attempt to find preventive medicines for malaria to protect soldiers, and both were done at the same time (the Dachau malaria experiments ran until April 1945; the Stateville experiments ran between 1944 and 1946).[50] There remain unanswered questions about whether every Stateville prisoner understood he would be infected with malaria, but despite Nazi protests to the contrary, the similarity ends there. The prisoners at Stateville volunteered; the concentration camp prisoners at Buchenwald and Natzweiler did not. Researchers with the U.S. military and public health service considered themselves to a degree exempt from the Nuremberg Code, arguing that it really only applied to war criminals; and they were not war criminals.[51]

That, however, did not prevent the Americans from trafficking with them. The U.S. Army granted General Ishii Shiro and his fellow Unit 731 officers immunity from war crimes prosecution in exchange for data from their biological warfare experiments—a devil's bargain made upon the recommendation of scientists from Camp Detrick.[52] Between 1945 and 1955, the United States also brought Nazi scientists into the country under "Operation Paperclip." Operation Paperclip put 765 skilled German and Austrian nationals to work, in part to prevent them from helping re-remilitarize Germany.[53] In some cases, where you had worked before didn't matter. In 1951, under "Project 63," the U.S. Army Chemical Corps hired Kurt Blome, the *Reichsgesundheitsfuehrer* (Reich Health Leader) who had personally conducted plague vaccine experiments on concentration camp inmates on the orders of SS Chief Heinrich Himmler.[54]

A Long Way from Valley Forge

By engaging evil, Americans to some extent had been touched by it. Health law scholar George Annas sees World War II as a kind of moral Rubicon for American science and medicine. Before the war, human experimentation was treated as deviant activity by U.S. courts—"itself evidence of malpractice." After the war, writes Annas, "Human experimentation became a mainstream, legitimate, and valued activity."[55] War moved from the "realm of quackery to the realm of science."[56]

The exigencies of the Cold War justified all manner of previously unacceptable conduct by doctors and scientists. U.S. soldiers lined up at atomic test sites were given a pair of Ray-Bans, nothing more, to protect them from a nuclear flash. Pregnant women got injected with plutonium; mentally handicapped children were fed radioactive porridge.[57] "The connection between those horrendous acts [by the Nazis] and our every day investigation was not made for reasons of self interest, to be perfectly frank," says William Silverman, a pediatrician who did research at Columbia University from the 1940s through the 1960s. "As I see it now, I'm saddened that we didn't see the connection, but that's what was done. We wrapped ourselves in the flag. . . ."[58]

Excusing such conduct in the interests of national security has been a slippery slope. Always it was the least among us who were targeted: the mentally ill, prisoners, alcoholics, retarded children, ethnic minorities, the poor. As Eileen Welsome pointed out in her book *The Plutonium Files,* doctors who carried out these experiments confessed that "poor patients often were selected because they were easily intimidated, didn't ask questions, and belonged to a different social class."[59]

But following the revelations of Willowbrook and Tuskegee in the early '70s, the public outcry against such experimentation so embarrassed the federal government that in 1974 it adopted regulations to protect the subjects of any medical experiment, especially those that were federally funded.[60] From then on, no institution conducting human experiments could receive federal funding without an Institutional Review Board (IRB) to oversee the work.[61] The Bureau of Prisons, long a source of human subjects who happily volunteered their bodies for cash, curtailed this activity.[62] Researchers now had to look elsewhere for a readily available pool of human subjects. There was just one population left. The military.

The Only Game in Town

If you look at a composite picture of people who volunteer to serve in the U.S. armed forces, it looks an awful lot like Eileen Welsome's profile of the kind of people used as guinea pigs. They are poor (the scions of America's upper crust have better options than an Army private's base pay of $12,776.40 a year);[63] they can be easily intimidated (a private is always easily intimidated by a sergeant, especially in boot camp); they don't ask questions.

Soldiers, sailors, airmen and marines provide a "stable, long-term permanent study group," to borrow Albert Sabin's phrase—more so than civilian volunteers who may quit a study at any time, pack their bags and move, never to be heard from again. Military personnel can't do that. They are on a short leash. They also can't refuse any medical treatment that has been ordered by their superiors. New recruits must accept all immunizations, no questions asked, or face court martial.[64] For these and a variety of other reasons, military personnel make an ideal population for medical testing. Since Tuskegee and Willowbrook they have been the only game in town.

So when America started to mobilize troops for war in the Persian Gulf, Captain Parsons of the Armed Forces Epidemiological Board may well have assumed that the tradition of doing medical studies on military personnel would simply continue. It had been a given since World War II. When Parsons wrote to the Army's Medical Research and Development Command in September 1990 to point out the "unique research opportunities" that had just fallen into their laps, he was just asking to be kept in the loop.

Moreover, in the case of vaccine development there was a need for government intervention. Because of low profit margins and high risk of product liability lawsuits, big pharmaceutical companies couldn't get out of the vaccine business fast enough.[65] The public health establishment had to do something before vaccine manufacturing in the United States disappeared altogether. By forming strategic partnerships in the 1980s with big pharmaceutical companies and then running clinical trials with experimental vaccines on U.S. troops, the military was serving a clear public interest. Large-scale vaccine trials on military personnel could entice pharmaceutical companies to keep making vaccines by reducing their exposure to litigation and thereby improve their bottom lines.

Which brings us to the other reason why American troops make such inviting test subjects: they can't sue the government for injuries due to negligence.

This is a controversial doctrine resulting from a Supreme Court ruling more than fifty years ago. After Lieutenant Rudolph Feres died in a barracks fire at Pine Camp, New York, in 1947, his widow sued the government for negligence, alleging that the Army knew the barracks was unsafe. Three years later, the U.S. Supreme Court ruled that Feres's widow had no right to sue the government under the Federal Tort Claims Act for injuries sustained while on active duty due to "negligence of others in the armed forces."[66] The ruling applies to everything that might happen to military personnel, from accidental deaths during combat to slipping on a wet floor in the Pentagon. It specifically includes injuries resulting from medical treatment. Thus, if a service member gets hurt by medical malpractice, or by the use of an investigational drug or vaccine, no one is accountable. The Department of Defense indemnifies companies manufacturing its vaccines, and DOD cannot be sued for damages due to negligence. Military doctors don't carry medical malpractice insurance, because they don't have to.

Since the 1970s, the military has maintained an Institutional Review Board, like every other body engaged in human experimentation. In theory, the military is held to standards similar to those governing civilian institutions. But if you think these boards truly protect people from becoming guinea pigs without their knowledge or consent, think again. The Department of Health and Human Services (HHS) wrote exceptions to the rules: IRBs can "approve a consent procedure which does not include, or which alters, some or all of the elements of informed consent"—the requirement of informed consent can be "waived" if the "research could not practically be carried out without the waiver or alteration."[67]

If the existing IRB regulations are disturbingly vague about the circumstances under which such waivers might be granted for experiments on civilians, they are more specific when it comes to the military. The military gets a special loophole courtesy of the FDA. In 1974, the same year the government passed legislation to allegedly impose strict guidelines on human experiments, the FDA also drafted a special agreement that enabled the Department of Defense to conduct its experiments secretly. When necessary for "national security," a Memorandum of Understanding between the FDA and the Department of Defense permits the military to administer investigational drugs to its personnel without informed consent, and without having to disclose this decision to the public, by classifying the trial.[68] Whether a clinical trial is classified or not is solely at the Pentagon's discretion. This is a loophole bigger than a barn door; it is, in practice, wider than an eight-lane Interstate.

Hepatitis A and Lennette's Law

By the time the FDA updated this Memorandum of Understanding in 1987, the military was already using this system to develop a hepatitis A vaccine. Working under an "Investigational New Drug exemption," the Walter Reed Army Institute of Research (WRAIR) developed a "crude prototype" hepatitis A vaccine jointly with the Salk Institute in Swiftwater, Pennsylvania.[69] Having already tested this prototype in troops at Fort Lewis in Washington, the Army published a "Request for Proposals."[70] This invited pharmaceutical companies to submit proposals for developing WRAIR's prototype vaccine in collaboration with the Department of Defense. The companies would become the Army's industrial partners. Smith Kline Beecham and the Swiss Serum Institute signed "no-dollar agreements" to work on the experimental vaccine at no cost to the Army. What they got in exchange was access to the Army's research: "We provided them with extensive information on the production of hepatitis A vaccine and continued our own in-house development efforts," states an Army report assembled just prior to the Persian Gulf War.[71]

The system was a kind of club whose biggest perk was access to human subjects; not just a dozen or so volunteers, but tens of thousands of human subjects for clinical trials on a scale that even the largest pharmaceutical companies could never contemplate. Jonas Salk's trial of the influenza vaccine at Fort Dix, New Jersey, involved over 44,000 soldiers who were stationed there between 1951 and 1953; the Army and civilian teams from various medical schools followed these subjects for decades afterward. No company could afford to run a trial this size; no single university could either. Better still, these almost unlimited numbers of human subjects were available without the risk of product liability lawsuits. In the case of the military's hepatitis A vaccine, the Army started modestly, testing Smith Kline Beecham's product first on 125 volunteers from the 101st Airborne Division at Fort Campbell, Kentucky; then it ran more trials on troops at Fort Lewis outside of Tacoma, Washington, and at Fort Detrick. The Army then conducted a "field efficacy study" with the Smith Kline Beecham vaccine in 40,000 children in Thailand.[72] Merck Sharp

Dohme had a prototype hepatitis A vaccine too, and the Army obligingly planned to test it in soldiers with the 25th Infantry Division stationed at Schofield Barracks in Hawaii.

This system was in full swing when Saddam invaded Kuwait. The hundreds of thousands of American men and women being called up to serve in Desert Shield were a vast new pool of human subjects in which the Army could test its experimental vaccines. A longtime consultant with the Armed Forces Epidemiological Board, Edwin Lennette, used to say that it was "impossible to evaluate a vaccine in the absence of the disease, which the vaccine was supposed to prevent."[73] In AFEB circles this became known as "Lennette's Law." The Saudis had hepatitis A; the Army had a vaccine. How better to test whether these new vaccines worked? Using them would give the Army a "two-for"—the Army could get its data *and* protect its soldiers. An opportunity like this might never come around again.

In 1990, there was one potential disease in the Persian Gulf that worried military planners a lot more than hepatitis A; it was a disease that worried them more than all the others combined: anthrax.

Chapter Five

The Battlefield Laboratory

In October 1990, war with Iraq was just months away. The Pentagon was drawing up plans to send nearly 700,000 troops to fight in the Persian Gulf—over a hundred thousand more than it had fighting in Vietnam at that war's height.[1] Anthrax was the one biological weapon in Saddam Hussein's arsenal that Pentagon planners feared above all others; and they had no way to protect troops against it. At the time, there was not enough vaccine to go around, and no device in the Army's inventory to quickly detect an anthrax attack if the Iraqis mounted one. According to a secret medical log kept by the officer in charge of medical readiness for the Joint Chiefs of Staff, the Army only had 60,670 doses of the licensed anthrax available on October 18, 1990.[2] That was enough to give just over 10,000 soldiers the six-shot series of vaccine thought necessary by the FDA to provide protection. That amounted to just 1.5 percent of the total coalition fighting force. In other words, fewer than two soldiers out of every 100 could get immunized against this weapon. The situation looked so grim that the Pentagon even approached the Russians about buying stocks of their vaccine (the Russians wouldn't sell any).[3]

The prospect of quickly getting big batches of anthrax vaccine from the somewhat decrepit production plant at the Michigan Department of Public Health in Lansing was poor even in the best of times. It was an aging facility

accustomed to producing limited quantities at a leisurely pace. Since getting
the Army contract to make anthrax vaccine in 1971, Michigan had produced
350,000 doses—but had taken nearly two decades to do it.[4] Even with twenty
years to perfect the process, making a good batch of the vaccine was still
tricky; some lots invariably failed their potency tests.[5] The Pentagon's medical
planners were in a race to organize a way to defend American troops from anthrax. It was going to be a hard sprint. It seemed inevitable that even more
vaccine lots would fail their potency tests, and the staff working for Secretary
of Defense Richard B. Cheney knew it.[6] His office was keeping close tabs on
this situation. A biological attack with anthrax could send a lot of Americans
home in body bags. So Cheney's staff reviewed the Michigan plant's track
record for producing anthrax vaccine and found it was not encouraging. Prior
to 1990, two of the nineteen lots produced by Michigan had failed.[7] "Under
the stress of accelerated production, a higher percentage of failures is likely,"
said a report issued by his office.[8] This prediction was proving true. "To date
in 1990, 3 of 32 lots have failed."[9]

That was not good enough. On October 3, 1990, Cheney ordered Assistant
Secretary of Defense for Health Affairs Dr. Enrique Mendez to "take the necessary actions, on a priority basis, to acquire *a second source* to produce biological vaccines to protect against anthrax and botulinum toxin" [italics mine].[10]
Two days later, Mendez had the Army charter a "Tri-Service Vaccine Task
Force"—a team of doctors and scientists from the Army, Navy and Air Force—
to get the job done. This team would answer directly to the Surgeon General
of the Army, General Frank Ledford, and the Deputy Assistant Secretary of
Defense for Medical Readiness, Dr. Peter Collis. Its mission was to investigate how quickly private industry could start manufacturing biological warfare
vaccines for the military, to find companies willing to do this, and to recommend ways to "surge" BW vaccine production on short notice.[11] To make sure
the military didn't get caught with an anthrax vaccine shortage again, the task
force was also supposed to come up with "long-term options."[12]

They convened their first meeting on October 10, 1990, in the commander's conference room of the United States Army Medical Research and Development Command at Fort Detrick. Nine people attended, including two
who would play key roles in the procurement of anthrax vaccine in the coming
months—Dr. Walter Brandt of the United States Army Medical Material Development Activity (USAMMDA) and Dr. Anna Johnson-Winegar of Fort

Detrick—both of whom had worked with Joe Jemski in the 1980s to make the Army's new and improved anthrax vaccine. The task force members chose a new name: Project Badger.

Over the next three months, Project Badger's Anna Johnson-Winegar would contact 172 companies and government institutions to see if they could take on the job of making a giant batch of anthrax vaccine in a big hurry.[13] She did not have much luck. Not many companies could handle the job even if they wanted it, and not many wanted it. Johnson-Winegar identified nineteen firms in the United States with the facilities and the know-how to produce vaccine; and four organizations overseas—including the Swiss Serum and Vaccine Institute in Switzerland and Porton International in England.[14] In the end only three of the 172 prospects agreed to help—Lederle-Praxis Biologicals and the National Cancer Institute in the United States, and Porton International.[15]

There were a lot of disincentives to making anthrax vaccine, not the least of which were FDA regulations.[16] To make vaccines from spore-forming and virulent organisms like B. anthracis, the FDA required "a totally separate and dedicated area, at least biocontainment level 2 (BL–2) and in some cases BL–3."[17] Workers would have to be vaccinated; extra insurance taken out for them.[18] A building with special containment might have to be constructed. Because of the possibility of live anthrax spores going astray, the building could never be used for anything else. The companies also cited objections unrelated to production—including "adverse publicity" and "potential targeting by terrorists." But most importantly, from a business point of view, there was no telling when the Army would need a big batch of anthrax vaccine again. And if the Army was not going to keep buying it, who would? Assisting in the "surge production" of anthrax vaccine would require a big capital investment with no guaranteed return in the long run. Making anthrax vaccine was a high-risk, low-return proposition, and it did not take a rocket scientist to figure that out. Just about every company politely but firmly declined.

There was at least one other option. Another way to prevent vaccine shortfalls was to reduce the amount of vaccine you needed to make. To immunize a force of 697,000 troops with the full six-shot series would require more than four million doses. If you could reduce the number of shots required to achieve immunity, you could cut the amount of vaccine you needed to make.

At the time, there was only one conceivable way to cut the dosage: with an adjuvant. With an adjuvant you could theoretically get more immunity with less vaccine. It was one way to stretch a limited supply—by cutting the amount you needed. Cheney's office knew this. The Army was already trying to "reduce the number of inoculations" with one of those oily vaccine additives—specifically material "incorporated into microvesicles" (Col. Carl Alving's "Walter Reed liposomes"), which would "act as adjuvant."[19] Cheney's office had issued two thick reports that October: one for recommendations on how to solve the vaccine problem for the war that was about to commence, and the second report on what do about this same problem after the war, so it would not happen again. The second report, titled "Long Term Expansion of Production Capability for Medical Defense Against Biological Warfare Agents (S)," discussed the possibility of a new vaccine design—one made by "recombinant technology."[20] A recombinant anthrax vaccine could be made in BL–2 conditions, which were barely more secure than a high school chemistry lab. This is because the vaccine would be created by inserting a little bit of anthrax DNA into the genetic code of a completely different organism, a harmless one. In other words, it did not require working with live anthrax spores to make an anthrax vaccine. This could exponentially increase the number of companies that might be willing to make emergency stocks of anthrax vaccine in support of any future war effort.

All of these initiatives by Project Badger and Dick Cheney's office were logical and, on the face of it, responsible enough—except that somewhere along the line, some members of Project Badger veered from their narrowly defined mission, going beyond the effort to procure more anthrax vaccine and botulinum toxoid to protect troops: they started to plan experiments.

Old Habits Die Hard

A spin-off group from the Project Badger group started to draw up plans to test experimental vaccines on military personnel "in theater"—same staff, different hats. For this purpose, they called themselves the Desert Shield Medical Issues Working Group. In a memorandum written on December 7, 1990, the group justified these proposed experiments by the fact that since the Vietnam War, "USAMRDC . . . has switched its emphasis from diseases of mobilization (i.e., vaccines to prevent meningococcal diseases) to diseases of deployment (i.e., vaccines to prevent wound sepsis)."[21] One reason the Army was now less concerned about "diseases of mobilization" was that its experimental adenovirus and influenza vaccines had allegedly succeeded in preventing a big outbreak of respiratory disease among new recruits. Now, after the experience of sending half a million troops to Vietnam, USAMRDC was preoccupied with diseases that affected troops on deployment. If anyone failed to see the opportunity the Gulf War presented, Project Badger's chairman, Col. Edmund C. Tramont, brought it into sharp focus: "a major impediment to the determination of product efficacy," he wrote, "has been the lack of a true operational deployment scenario."[22] What Tramont said next summed it all up. "Thus we have the research requirement of determining true efficacy during times of actual deployment."[23]

The Persian Gulf was about to become one big laboratory.

While there were numerous loopholes by which the Army could run such experiments, they could still only be done under certain conditions. The cardinal rule of the Nuremberg Code—that the *voluntary consent* of human subject is *absolutely essential*" [italics mine]—had been watered down by the World Medical Association's "Declaration of Helsinki," which states that a doctor "must be free to use a new diagnostic and therapeutic measure, if in his or her judgment it offers hope of saving life, reestablishing health or alleviating suffering."[24] That a new treatment be "therapeutic" was the key. Using an experimental medicine or vaccine could be justified to *treat* someone who needed it. Experiments that had no clinical benefit to their subjects—those intended strictly to get data for the economic benefit to an individual researcher or corporation—were still prohibited: "In research on man, the interest of science and society should never take precedence over considerations related to the well-being of the subject."[25] That is fairly restrictive, but under existing military policies at the time of Desert Shield, there was even less wiggle room than this. A formerly top-secret memo for the Secretaries of the Army, Navy and Air Force entitled "Use of Human Volunteers in Experimental Research"—written at the same time as the Helsinki Declaration—reiterated the cardinal principle of the Nuremberg Code, that it was "absolutely essential" that human subjects be "volunteers."[26] The human subject, this memo said, must have "legal capacity to give consent; should be so situated as to be able to exercise free power of choice, without the intervention of any element

of force, fraud, deceit, duress, over-reaching, or other ulterior form of con-
straint or coercion."[27] Given the corporate alliances that the U.S. military
medical command and FDA officials had been forging in the 1980s, assessing
"product efficacy" during a wartime deployment could be corrupted by potential profiteering, at great risk to soldiers' health.

Even with incorruptible motives, giving experimental medicines and vaccines
to troops, even for their own good, would constitute a de facto experiment.
There was no way to anticipate how these products would affect the health of
troops. But the Badger spinoff group went forward anyway; and based on the
declassified minutes from its meetings, there was almost no time spent on discussing the morality of these plans. With more than a hint of grandiosity, the
group started referring to its plans as the "Manhattan Project." Five medicines
were slated for special "evaluation": Oral cholera vaccine, Centoxin (a human
monoclonal antibody that would help prevent death from septic shock induced
by certain kinds of bacteria), hepatitis A vaccine, typhoid vaccine (Ty21A) and
Shigella vaccine (to prevent diarrhea).[28] Though it was not specifically slated for
evaluation in the "Manhattan Project," the Army also made plans to ship its
stocks of an experimental anti-viral drug, Ribaviran, to the Gulf.

Another Fort Detrick committee proposed a study that skated right on the
edge of what was legal; some would say it skated over that edge, breaching the
standards to which military as well as civilian doctors are held accountable. It
was the proposed research for leishmaniasis—which is caused by a parasite
transmitted by the bite of sand flies—that went too far. The Army Medical
Research and Development Command had three experimental drugs available
for cutaneous leishmaniasis: Pentostam, Ketoconazole and Itraconozole. Two
of them, Pentostam and Ketoconazole, were under Investigational New Drug
status; these were the two the Army wanted to try out.[29] Few would argue
with this. There were three types of leishmaniasis endemic to the region (*L.
major, L. tropica* and *L. donovani*) and no licensed medicines for any of
them.[30] Although the disease wasn't fatal, it was a little more than just incon-
venient. People infected with leishmaniasis developed a "non-healing skin ulcer" that sometimes led to a bacterial "superinfection."[31] The disease was bad
enough to induce the Iranians to inoculate some 300,000 troops against the
disease each year.[32]

The Army wanted to do more than just treat leishmaniasis with Pentostam
and Ketoconazole; it wanted to run a clinical trial with one of them, Ketocona-

zole, in "a study situation."[33] In order to do that, the Army planned to have one group of infected soldiers get a "vitamin placebo" only.[34] In other words, one groups of soldiers, randomly selected from all those infected, would be left untreated. These untreated service members, all of them infected with a nasty disease, would be the control group. Defense Department investigators would evaluate the drug's effectiveness by comparing how well infected soldiers treated with it fared next to those who got nothing but a vitamin.[35]

The most reliable medicine of the three, Pentostam—the one the Army knew best—was in short supply (the Army could only get enough from the British manufacturer, Wellcome Trust, to treat sixty patients). Army investigators were instructed to hold Pentostam in reserve only for those soldiers who failed treatment with Ketoconazole.[36] Available data for Ketoconazole showed that it cured up to 70 percent of patients infected with *L. major*, which was the predominant form of the disease in Saudi Arabia and Iraq.[37] By rights, the Army should have instructed its "investigators" to give every infected soldier Ketoconazole. Instead, the Army's Leishmaniasis Steering Committee decided to pursue the "unique research opportunity" presented by Southwest Asia's sand flies. Patients would be "randomized"—some would get Ketoconazole; some would just get a vitamin placebo. As experiments go, this was a classic way to conduct a clinical trial. But even by the more relaxed standards of the Helsinki Declaration, it was out-of-bounds. Army investigators planned to deliberately withhold the best available medicine from infected U.S. troops in combat. It would be a mini-Tuskegee in wartime.

There is no available evidence that FDA officials knew about the experiments being organized by Project Badger or its spin-off, the Desert Shield Medical Issues Working Group, when they agreed to amend the informed consent rules for Desert Shield. The Pentagon had made a persuasive case for the *therapeutic* use of investigational drugs without informed consent. It would be strictly to save lives. In a letter to the FDA on October 30, 1990, the Assistant Secretary of Defense for Health Affairs argued that taking an experimental drug or vaccine could not be left to the discretion of an individual soldier when a refusal could jeopardize that soldier's life and the lives of his comrades:

If a soldier's life will be endangered by nerve gas, for example, it is not acceptable from a military standpoint to defer to whatever might be the sol-

*dier's personal preference concerning a preventative or therapeutic treat-
ment that might save his life, avoid endangerment of the other personnel
in his unit and accomplish the combat mission. Based on unalterable requirements of the military field commander, it is not an option to excuse a
non-consenting soldier from the military mission, nor would it be defensi-
ble militarily—or ethically—to send the soldier unprotected into danger.*[38]

FDA Commissioner David Kessler concurred, but he agreed to waive the
informed consent requirement only on a drug-by-drug basis. The Defense Department didn't have carte blanche to do anything it wanted. Kessler still insisted on some restrictions. Codifying his decision in a new general
regulation, Rule 23(d), Kessler granted waivers for the use of two INDs
only—pentavalent botulinum toxoid (to protect against botulinum toxin) and
pyridostigmine bromide pills (which were supposed to offer some measure of
protection from the nerve agent soman).[39] The FDA granted this waiver for
one year.[40]

When the *Washington Post* broke the story about the FDA decision, the day
after it was made, most greeted the news as a necessity of wartime.[41] The
New York Times published an editorial endorsing the decision, saying that "the
military is acting more like Florence Nightingale than Joseph Mengele."[42]

To Vaccinate, or Not to Vaccinate

Not everyone in the military chain of command thought it was a good idea to
vaccinate troops against anthrax. Among those who opposed the idea: the
CINC (Commander-in-Chief, in theater), General H. Norman Schwarzkopf.
General Schwarzkopf had been pressing Washington since early December to
make a decision about when to start vaccinating troops against anthrax.
Weeks before the FDA's decision, Schwarzkopf started raising "questions
about the medical recommendations."[43] He sent an "Eyes Only" message to
General Colin Powell, Chairman of the Joint Chiefs of Staff, saying he
needed to know more than just when to start immunizing; since there wasn't
enough vaccine to go around, he needed to know who got the shots.[44] According to a December 6th entry in a special "Medical Biological Defense" log
maintained by the Army, Schwarzkopf thought it all had more "political over-

tones than operational."[45] According to government sources familiar with Schwarzkopf's objections—who have requested anonymity as a condition of talking about it—Schwarzkopf's chief complaint was that giving vaccine to some troops could hurt the morale of those who didn't get it. They would be left asking why they were the expendable ones.

The lack of vaccine was just one of many good reasons why the Defense Department put off the decision to vaccinate. Another big concern was how the public would receive the news. Would it cause undue panic? How would the coalition allies react? Starting to immunize U.S. and British soldiers against anthrax would signal to troops from the rest of the coalition that they were at risk too. Would they bolt if they thought Iraq was going to use anthrax and they had no protection? The State Department circulated a report titled "Managing Fallout from British BW Inoculations."[46] So the Joint Chiefs understood Schwarzkopf perfectly when he messaged that the decision had "political overtones."

Meanwhile, the Armed Forces Medical Intelligence Center (AFMIC) kept issuing ominous reports of Baghdad's alleged bioweapon activity; its "dual-use" equipment purchases (equipment that could be used for both peaceful and military purposes) were especially worrisome. The Iraqis had "acquired 40 high performance aerosol generators" the previous spring, and "high capacity spray dryers."[47] AFMIC reported more evidence that the Iraqis had "anthrax, botulinum (serotype still unknown), SEB (staphylococcus enterotoxin B) and C. Perfringens."[48] There was no evidence that Iraq had plague, but it was "possible because of Soviet programs." The intelligence analysts at AFMIC anticipated the possible use of biological agents "for wide area attack and against ships."[49] A handful of Iraqi Republican Guards, Saddam's elite forces, had defected to Saudi Arabia that month; serum samples were taken from them for analysis at USAMRIID,[50] which would test for the presence of antibodies to "anthrax, plague, Tularemia, Q-fever, Botulinum toxins (all strains), Ricin, VEE, CCHF, Sand Fly Fever, Clostridium perfringens and Smallpox."[51] If the defectors tested positive for antibodies against agents like anthrax or plague, the Army could reasonably conclude that they had been vaccinated to protect them from Iraq's intended use of these agents in battle. But the report USAMRIID gave the Defense Intelligence Agency in late December was ambiguous: "Positive samples conform to plausible expectations resulting from natural exposure to endemic disease agents or non-specific cross reactions."[52] It didn't look like they'd been vaccinated against anthrax; still, the Army couldn't ignore the possibility that Saddam might use it even if it meant killing his own troops.

A Matter of Timing

By December, though, it was too late to immunize troops with the licensed vaccine and expect them to have a meaningful level of protection. Going by what was believed at the time, that the vaccine provided optimal protection around six months after the first shot, it was already too late to start vaccinating all the way back when Saddam invaded Kuwait in August 1990. To be protected in time for "H-hour" on January 15th (the UN-imposed deadline for Iraq to pull out of Kuwait), the troops needed to get their first shot *the previous July* and their fourth shot no later than December. The British, with their slightly different formulation, faced the same problem, only worse. The British estimated their version of the single protein vaccine achieved optimal immunity after eight months.[53] To send its troops into battle with "full immunity," the Ministry of Defence would have had to have immunized its troops beginning in *May 1990*—a full eight months before the start of "Operation Granby," the British code name for Desert Storm.

When you read the logs kept by officers assigned to the Joint Chiefs and the Army Surgeon General's office, the timing issue comes up again and again. It was raised at the very highest levels of the military chain of command.[54] Colin Powell even went to the President about it.[55] But by mid-December, no U.S. or British soldier had received even one dose of anthrax vaccine, let alone the required six shots.

The One-Shot Wonder

For all the energy that Project Badger had poured into "surging" vaccine production that fall, the Pentagon was now way behind the eight ball. Anthrax was the chief biological warfare threat in the Persian Gulf—the one that could send thousands of men and women of the United States Armed Forces home to their families draped in American flags. As an NBC News correspon-

dent assigned to Department of Defense Quick Reaction Pool #5, I once visited one of the Air Force's new Air Transportable Hospitals near the eastern
port city of Dharhan. Basically, it was an "inflatable ER"—stuffed with state-
of-the-art surgical equipment, an operating theater and intensive care unit.
The Air Force medical personnel manning it were working inside what
amounted to an air-conditioned hot air balloon; you could comfortably bounce
off the walls. Outside, along the tarmac, were rows of gleaming aluminum
containers stacked six feet high. From a distance they looked like some pristine new munitions, but no one would leave such things unattended out in
the sun. When I got closer, I saw what they really were. They were coffins.
Stacks and stacks of shiny new coffins. My cameraman started shooting video.
The public affairs officers at JIB (Joint Information Bureau) didn't want anyone seeing pictures of these coffins when they were empty. No one wanted to
see those coffins filled . . . pictures or no pictures. Pentagon planners were
faced with the real prospect of seeing such pictures on American TV screens
and on the front pages of newspapers and magazines, and anthrax was one of
the major nightmares . . . unless the Project Badger team figured out a way to
get more anthrax vaccine out of the Michigan Department of Public Health or
some other source.

By December, however, Project Badger had managed to acquire enough
vaccine to immunize only about 100,000 troops, maybe a little more, with an
abbreviated three-shot dosage—which meant that only one out of seven U.S.
troops in the Persian Gulf could get any protection at all. And it was too late to
start vaccinating anyway.

Timing wasn't the only issue with the licensed U.S. and British anthrax
vaccines. There were in fact lots more:

- The licensed vaccines couldn't protect against every strain—especially
  the Ames strain, which the Iraqis had been trying very hard to get their
  hands on.[56]
- A large dose of anthrax bacteria could overwhelm the vaccine; every
  U.S. analysis circulated during Desert Shield said so.[57]
- Until recently, there had been an estimated 3,000 Soviet military advi-
  sors in Baghdad; British intelligence had informed the United States
  that the Soviets had antibiotic-resistant anthrax and might have assisted
  Iraqi scientists in making it.[58]

Troops were arriving in-country every day, disembarking from ships and transport planes; they were even coming by commercial airliner. Two weeks before hostilities were due to commence, the Army's biodefense strategy still had its pants around its ankles.

As bad as things looked, there was a "research opportunity" here; maybe even the clear prospect of saving lives. The scientists at Fort Detrick and Porton Down had other options and this was the time to try them out.

Some protection would be better than none. The British Ministry of Defence decided to use an adjuvant. This would speed the immune response to its anthrax vaccine and give troops some measure of protection in the short time left before the war. Britain's CBD com (Chemical Biological Defence Command) recommended boosting the U.K. anthrax vaccine by injecting it along with a vaccine for whooping cough. Its core ingredient, the *Bordetella pertussis* organism, was a known adjuvant. The Ministry of Defence elected to give pertussis vaccine simultaneously with anthrax vaccine to British "squaddies."[59] This was the same "microbial supplementation" technique that Porton Down's Peter Turnbull had been working on—the one on which he presented a paper the year before at the International Workshop on Anthrax at Winchester.

By December 1990, the month before the first Persian Gulf War, Project Badger's scientists had run out of time. They did not have enough vaccine to go around, and what little they had was of debatable value. It was too late to start vaccinating with the licensed six-shot vaccine to do any good. For Project Badger, the International Workshop on Anthrax was a godsend. Project Badger's Anna Johnson-Winegar went to England to confer with Porton Down scientists in the frantic run-up to the war.[60] It was Johnson-Winegar's job to find other sources of BW vaccines for the war effort. Now she wanted copies of the workshop proceedings. The workshop's coordinator, Peter Turnbull, sent four copies to Johnson-Winegar and eight more to Fort Detrick's Colonel Arthur Friedlander.[61] If you read Turnbull's workshop paper, he reports that his method "markedly enhanced" the protectiveness of the U.K. vaccine.[62] The British vaccine did not perform well in trials with the "vaccine-resistant" Ames and New Hampshire strains.[63] But with Turnbull's pertussis adjuvant, as many as 88 percent of the guinea pigs survived.[64] The protection with Turnbull's adjuvant declined over time, though. When challenged six months after vaccination, two-thirds of the guinea pigs survived;

at fourteen months, only half survived.[65] It was an improvement, but far from guaranteed protection.

There was something much better. Only one paper presented at the workshop reported near perfect results—100 percent protection from the Ames strain with just one or two shots.[66] As an old Marine Corps expression goes, this particular paper "sparkled like a diamond in a goat's ass." USAMRIID's Bruce Ivins had reported at this very same workshop that his "one-shot wonder"—protective antigen or mere fragments of it combined with oil additives—protected every animal challenged with Ames with a single injection.[67] Ivins explained to anthrax experts from around the world that all he needed to do was mix the protective antigen protein with either "Triple Mix" or "DeTox"—both of them squalene-based emulsions.[68] The resulting vaccine generated as much protection to the Ames strain of anthrax as did three shots of the licensed U.S. vaccine.[69] More immunity in less time with one shot— just what the Army needed. This was the ticket. Ivins's vaccine was undeniably superior, and as far as anyone knew at the time, it was safe.

This was, as Project Badger's Colonel Tramont had taken pains to point out, the kind of opportunity that only a deployment could present. To try the new anthrax vaccines in this predicament was more than a "research requirement"; theoretically, they were better vaccines. They could save lives, maybe tens of thousands of lives. Regulations or no regulations, who could reasonably deny U.S. troops the best possible protection from anthrax?

In one of the last meetings of the Badger spin-off group before Desert Shield became Desert Storm, committee members convened in the Army Surgeon General's Office to discuss the "Manhattan Project" again. This is what Col. Michael J. Kussman of the Medical Command wrote in his minutes from the meeting:

> Establishment of a "Manhattan Project" was discussed to evaluate vaccines
> in Saudi Arabia was discussed [sic]. Committee members felt that the time
> for trials in theater was not right at present. There is too much else going on
> right now. If Operation Desert Shield becomes a prolonged operation, then
> trials may be possible.[70]

The committee recommended against using typhoid TY21A vaccine in the Gulf; they would give hepatitis A vaccine strictly as a pre-deployment immunization for new recruits, but not to troops in Saudi Arabia.[71] Oral cholera was a question mark.[72] Centoxin was a go.[73] So was Ribaviran.[74] Both would be shipped to Saudi Arabia along with botulinum toxoid and pyridostigmine bromide pills.[75]

There is no mention of Bruce Ivins's PA vaccine with "Triple Mix" or "DeTox" in the Working Group minutes or in other declassified Desert Shield/Desert Storm materials in my possession. The only available reference to evaluating it and other "new candidate vaccines" was in Dr. Anna Johnson-Winegar's letter to Peter Turnbull dated November 26, 1990. Of all the potential biological warfare threats posed by Saddam, anthrax was the most likely, and arguably the most lethal, of all the bioweapons allegedly in the Iraqi arsenal. Given the insurmountable shortcomings of the old vaccine at the time, who could balk at using the new one?

On January 5, 1991, the U.S. military finally started immunizing its troops against anthrax.[76] The vaccine was administered to 150,000 U.S. military personnel in the United States and Saudi Arabia. They would get no more than two shots apiece. Many would only get one. The British started immunizing that same week.[77]

The anthrax vaccine was the only immunization given during the Gulf War that was classified "Secret."

Chapter Six

The "New and Improved" Vaccine

In Desert Storm, the United States Armed Forces proved that they were superior in numbers, firepower, organization and technology—not just to the Iraqi Army, but arguably to any army on the planet. Saddam had promised to surprise the coalition with "the mother of all battles," but the only surprise was how one-sided it was. This imbalance was reflected in the official casualty rates. In 1990–1991, the United States deployed 697,000 troops to the Persian Gulf. A total of 293 Americans died in this war: 148 in combat, another 145 from accidents or illness. That's a death rate of 0.042 percent. Of the 50,000 British troops who fought in the war, twenty-four died . . . nine by U.S. friendly fire. That's a death rate of 0.048 percent.

Not everyone who returned injured was noted in the official casualty count.

———

"It burned like hell." That's all Gregory Dubay remembers about getting injected with anthrax vaccine, which happened twice—the first time on January 13, 1991, and the second time two weeks later on the 27th. For Dubay, giving the vaccination to others was a lot more memorable. In Saudi Arabia, as commander of the Army Reserve's 129th Medical Company based out of Mobile, Alabama, Dubay oversaw the immunization of more than 14,000 troops against anthrax in one 72-hour marathon completed just a few days shy of the U.N.'s January 15th deadline for Iraq to pull out of Kuwait. The Army gave the 129th a special commendation for this achievement. But what really sticks out in Dubay's mind are the extra precautions he and his "shot teams" took in giving troops the injection—precautions that, even today, strike him as peculiar. "Each soldier had to read a classified sheet of instructions, stating that he, or she, was receiving a secret shot, and that this was for reasons of national security. You don't want to tell the enemy that you're getting protection against one of his weapons," says Dubay.[1]

"And why was that?" I ask.

"Well, because the enemy might then switch to another weapon for which we had no vaccine. Our battalion commander also told us there wasn't enough anthrax vaccine to go around. Only combat support troops were getting the shot; we were supposed to keep quiet about it so the front line guys didn't get upset about not getting the vaccine. It was a morale issue."[2]

"Was the botulinum toxoid shot as big a secret?"

"No . . . well, it didn't seem to be at the time. I don't recall anyone having to keep that particular shot a secret. But I'm not sure. My guys didn't give out botox."

"Let me get this straight. The botulinum toxoid shot was experimental, and it was no secret that U.S. troops were getting it; it was even reported in the U.S. press. The anthrax shot was licensed, but getting it was supposed to be a big secret?"

"That's correct. Photography was not permitted, the event was classified *secret*. In fact we had MP guards all around the locations, to insure the operations security was maintained.[3] A little strange isn't it? I was even under orders *not* to record the inoculation in the soldier's medical records." Dubay, on the other hand, insisted that his own shots be recorded in *his* records. There are annotations for both of them logged in his World Health Organization "International Certificates of Vaccination." Every soldier is issued one of these cards. "If a soldier really put up a stink about not having a record of the anthrax shot, battalion instructed us to write 'Vaccine A' or 'Vac A' on that little yellow WHO immunization card. 'Vac A' was supposed to be for the first anthrax shot; 'Vac B' was for the second one. On my card I made sure that next to 'Vac A' and 'B,' it said anthrax."[4]

"You couldn't decline that shot?"

"No, you couldn't," says Dubay. "You were just marched through. You signed a roster, so at least someone knew you got the shot, and that was it. Then our commander told us to destroy everything connected with it—the empty vials, the boxes, and the package inserts. We burned them all in 55-gallon steel drums back behind the tents."[5]

Dubay got sick in Saudi Arabia. "First with diarrhea, fatigue, weight loss, muscle aches, weakness and not sleeping good," he says.[6] Then came "confusion, disorientation and memory loss and difficulty in concentrating to a task."[7] His memory and concentration have improved, but he is still fatigued, he still has achy muscles, and it is still a struggle to get to sleep sometimes. Since we last talked, five years earlier, Dubay has gotten divorced and married again. He is fifty-four years old and has a cleft in his chin like Clark Gable's—a resemblance that I imagine is still accentuated by his dark hair and his mustache. One the phone, Dubay is alert and in good spirits. It is June 2004; I have called him after all this time to ask him something I never asked him before.

"Did anyone ever say anything to you in Saudi Arabia," I begin, "about a 'recombinant DNA' anthrax vaccine or 'squalene' or a 'new and improved' anthrax vaccine?"

"I never heard anyone talk about a recombinant DNA anthrax vaccine. I never heard anyone say anything about squalene either." He pauses for a moment. "But a 'new and improved' anthrax vaccine? That's what battalion told us we were giving out. There was supposed to be something wrong with the old vaccine. I don't remember now what it was. Something was wrong with it, so we were giving troops a new one . . . the best the Army had available."[8]

"Are you sure about that?"

"I'm *absolutely* sure. I remember that clearly. Battalion said it was a new vaccine and that it was better than the old one . . . the best the Army had available at the time."

I wait a couple of days before calling Dubay again. "Greg, are you *sure* you heard your senior officers tell you that you were injecting troops with a 'new and improved' anthrax vaccine?"

"I'm positive. I remember that very clearly. It was new and it was supposed to be the best the Army had available."[9]

"No doubts?"

"No doubt about it. That's what they said."

———

"I passed out," recalls Lieutenant James Patrick Rudicell. "After my second shot I was walking across the examining room in our clinic at Khobar Towers and I passed out cold . . . busted my head on a marble baseboard and started bleeding pretty bad." Rudicell was a member of the Army Reserve 129th Medical Company—the unit Greg Dubay commanded. He recalls the 129th arriving in the Saudi capital, Riyadh, on January 4th, then heading east to Dharhan in eastern Saudi Arabia. In Dharhan, the 129th set up shop in "Khobar Towers." Khobar Towers was a monument to a truly harebrained experiment in social engineering through urban planning—an eight-story concrete tower block for Bedouins. For millennia the nomadic Bedu have lived in tents in close proximity to their beloved "Ata Allah" ("God's Gift"), the camel, a gruesomely flatulent 1,500-pound beast that can guzzle twenty-one gallons of water in less than ten minutes, and spit. Not surprisingly, the Bedu, and their camels, declined to move in. This left members of the 129th with their choice of pristine three-bedroom apartments complete with stainless steel kitchen countertops and marble baseboards. At one point, the 129th moved to a place called "TV Center"—a one-story dormitory off a highway outside of Dharhan built for the kingdom's foreign workers, a kind of Saudi housing project for infidels. Most members of the unit called the place "Tones and Bones," because it was temporary quarters for a signal unit (Tones) and medical battalion (Bones). From "Tones and Bones," the 129th sent shot teams to "Cement City," which was really a canvas tent city the Army put up at the site of a dusty cement factory and the nearby ports of Dammam and Al Jubayl.

The night before a scheduled vaccination, members of the 129th would fill hypodermic needles with vaccine drawn from ten-dose vials called aliquots, then put the caps back on the needles to keep them germ-free. The next day, a five-to-seven-member shot team, armed with hundreds of these syringes, would head to one of the Army's makeshift clinics.[10] There troops would be lined up outside of tents large enough to accommodate eight people standing up in addition to the shot team. At the rear of each tent were a couple of cots (for those really indisposed after receiving the vaccine) and some chairs to sit on. After reading a special briefing statement about the vaccine, troops would sign the "Alpha roster" before entering the tent. Next to each signature, a member of the shot team would log either "A–1" for the initial shot or "A–2" for the booster; for many veterans of this war this would be the only record that they received the vaccination. Time and again, members of these shot teams rejected requests to log the anthrax vaccination into a service member's WHO immunization card. Some of the older soldiers and officers—the ones who'd served in Vietnam—couldn't re-call any other time when an immunization was classified a secret.[11] In over twenty years, these service members had never read a "briefing statement" before getting a shot; never before did anyone refuse to document a shot in his or her personnel records.

In addition to the secrecy, Rudicell remembers something else that was strange. "We only gave out two shots. That was the 'series.' I know that li-censed vaccine calls for 6-shots, but as I recall, we never planned to give any-one more than two."[12]

What he doesn't recall is banging his head on the baseboard. "One of the nurses had to tell me what happened; I was unconscious. I just keeled over, busted my head, and then I started shakin'. I have no memory of this. The nurse told me everything. She said my knees started shakin' and bangin' to-gether. There was blood on the carpet and I was unconscious, shakin'—she said I was having a *petit mal* seizure." When Rudicell came to, he was on a lit-ter in the back of a HUMVEE ambulance on his way to the 85th Evacuation Hospital at Dharhan International Airport—one of those air transportable hospitals that looked like a cross between a circus tent and a hot air balloon. "They sewed me up . . . I got about 6 stitches, as I recall."

While in Saudi Arabia, Rudicell started experiencing joint pain. He felt tired all the time and suffered from intermittent low-grade fevers. He went up to Kuwait four times with the Defense Reconstruction Assistance Organiza-tion (DRAO).[13] Sometime in between his June and July trips to Kuwait, he began to lose his hair. "My hair came out in circular clumps."

When he finally left active duty in August 1991, Rudicell was 25 years old but felt like 55. He ached all over. His fatigue wouldn't go away. Back home in Marion, Alabama, Rudicell broke out in rashes. He was getting scared. He had always been strong and able to take a lot of physical punishment. In high school, Rudicell was a jock—an outfielder on the baseball team and a defensive back on the football team. After graduating from college he started coaching both sports at the Marion Military Institute upstate in Marion, Alabama; he was 6 feet tall and a trim 175 pounds. After he returned from Saudi Arabia and Kuwait, his weight dropped to 127 pounds, and instead of looking trim he began to look emaciated.

In November 1992, a scant year and a half after he left the Persian Gulf, doctors at the University of Alabama Medical School in Birmingham diagnosed Rudicell with systemic lupus erythematosus (SLE).

He had never heard of it before.

SLE occurs when the immune system's natural tolerance for the body's own cells, cell constituents and proteins breaks down. It is a debilitating and incurable disease. If the immune system's attack cannot be arrested and controlled, SLE can be fatal. It mainly destroys the skin, joints, body cavity linings and kidneys, but it can affect just about every other organ in the body. As the *Merck Manual* puts it, "SLE may begin abruptly with fever, simulating acute infection, or may develop insidiously over months or years with episodes of fever and malaise."[14] SLE patients may also suffer from neurological disorders: "headaches, personality changes, epilepsy, psychoses, and organic brain syndrome."[15] One hallmark of this disease is the "butterfly rash"—a deep ochre eruption that appears above the cheekbones and continues over the bridge of the nose. These rashes, and those on other parts of the body, are often photosensitive—meaning they get worse in sunlight. Sometimes they spread so profusely that they merge into one another, forming a giant red patch over which the skin gets scaly. SLE patients develop rheumatoid arthritis, an autoimmune inflammation of the joints. The skin inside a patient's mouth can ulcerate, too, though this is rare.

One of the most dangerous consequences of SLE is the occurrence of antibodies against phospholipids in the bloodstream; phospholipids prevent blood clots in the absence of physical injury. When the patient starts forming antibodies to a phospholipid like cardiolipin, he can be in deep trouble. Any patient making anticardiolipin antibodies will have a tendency to thrombosis—to form clots.[16] Abnormal clotting can lead to strokes (clots that lodge in the brain) or pulmonary emboli (clots that lodge in the lungs), either of which can be fatal. In women, anticardiolipin antibodies are associated with a tendency to spontaneous abortion.[17] Doctors can control SLE most of the time, but they can't cure it. It is a lifetime sentence. Rudicell now faced the prospect of struggling with a physically and mentally impairing disease for the rest of his days.

One other thing was odd about Rudicell's diagnosis. SLE is both gender and race specific; it mainly affects women. About 1 out of every 700 women will develop SLE. It is also more common, and more severe, among American black women.[18] About 1 in every 245 American black women will develop this disease, making them three times more prone to it than women in general.[19] Women are exponentially more susceptible to SLE than men. Ninety percent of all lupus patients are women.[20] Most male lupus sufferers are in their fifties or sixties.

Rudicell was a twenty-seven-year-old white male. He belonged to the demographic least likely to develop the disease.

———

When Navy Lieutenant Mary Jones sifts through the letters she wrote home from Saudi Arabia (there is a giant pile of them) and her medical records from the Gulf War, one thing stands out: Mary is one of the few veterans to have a record of her anthrax shots. They are logged as "Anthrax Vaccine," not as "Vac A1" or "Vac A2," "Vaccine Apple" or "A-Vax." She received two shots:

Fleet Hospital 5
1 MEF
FPO San Francisco, CA 96608–5409
OPERATION DESERT STORM
11 Jan 91 Anthrax Vaccine 1st dose 0.5 ml sq
29 Jan 91 Anthrax Vaccine 2nd dose 0.5 ml sq
T.R. Zajdowicz
CDR, MC, USN

Although the mailing address is the Fleet Post Office in San Francisco, Fleet Hospital 5 was in Jubayl; Mary and others in her unit had the shots

entered into her records back in the States after the war was over. She remembers them well. "It didn't hurt going in, but it burned like heck afterwards. It left a golf ball size swelling where they injected it." Like others
who received these shots, Mary also remembers the secrecy involved in getting it—something she'd never experienced in getting any other immunization. The other odd thing about this record is the entry "sq" after the dosage.
"SQ" is often used as an abbreviation for "subcutaneous" in place of the
more common "SC." These abbreviations refer to the way a shot had been
administered, in Mary's case, subcutaneously, under the skin. But subcutaneous is the FDA-approved way to administer the licensed anthrax vaccine;
in other words, it is the *only* way to administer it; it is how it has been done
for decades. Because of this, it is unheard of to bother noting the route of
administration in anyone's records. It is not done with anthrax vaccine, or
with any other vaccine for that matter. It is an entirely superfluous annotation unless someone is performing an experiment and it is necessary to compare how different routes of administration, e.g., subcutaneous (SC) vs.
intramuscular (IM), might affect the safety or effectiveness of the shot.
That is the *only* circumstance when scientists note the route of administration. If you examine Mary Jones's immunization records, the route of administration is not specified for any other shot that she received during her
entire military career. Nor is it specified in anyone else's records that I have
seen. Of all the shot records that I have examined over the years, I have
never seen another with this "sq" annotation. The unanswered question
about its presence in Mary Jones's Gulf War records would only become an
issue many years later—for reasons that would leave Mary, and many others
in her predicament, feeling astonished and betrayed.

A maddening rash broke out on Mary's hands after she came back from
the Gulf. "It was on top of my hands and they were constantly red, raw,
cracked and bleeding with blotchy areas. I would almost get like paper cuts
on my fingers and hands that would open up and bleed." Sometimes it
hurt, especially where her skin had split open, and then, when she aggra-
vated it, it "would itch like a son of a gun." At first she thought it "was from
being a nurse and washing my hands all the time." Other possibilities
crossed her mind, too. "I thought maybe it was because I still had two children in diapers; maybe I was allergic to something in New Hampshire, or
was it a new soap."

THE "NEW AND IMPROVED" VACCINE 97

Nothing Mary tried made it better. "I tried putting cotton gloves on at night. My mom told me to call the VA . . . that she heard on the news that other Gulf War vets were getting these strange persistent rashes."

Mary started going to the VA hospital to treat what looked like eczema, but no sooner had she gotten that under control than her muscles started to twitch uncontrollably, and in an unusual place. "It was first on top of my upper left thigh." People under a lot of stress can develop a nervous twitch, but as far as Mary recalled that sort of thing occurred around the eyes, not big, bulky muscles like the thigh. "I would feel it on and off for a couple of days and then it would go away; sometimes it would last for months at a time." Mary says if you put your hand on her leg, you can feel it twitch or quiver for two to three seconds at a time. "It was driving me bananas so I told my husband to put his hand on my leg and try to feel it."

She almost felt relieved when her eye started to twitch, too. "The only other place that twitched a couple of times is my left hand, below my thumb, palm side. You could actually see the muscle moving involuntarily." The VA told Mary that other veterans were complaining of the same thing.

Other problems started cropping up in New Hampshire—sleep disturbances and short-term memory loss; she also had problems concentrating. She started getting tired all the time and her muscles hurt. Her joints felt fine, but her muscles hurt without her having exercised or injured them. The pain has been mostly confined to her left hip area (not the joint) and she has been getting steroid shots to alleviate it.

Mary still doesn't know what it was about the Gulf that seemed to trigger all these ailments. "I had absolutely no health problems before going to Saudi. I felt great."

All the talk about vaccines has Mary thinking—not about her own military service but about her mother's.

"When she was a student nurse at the Massachusetts General Nursing School in Boston she was given BCG shots. These were anti-TB shots." BCG stands for "Bacillus Calmette-Guerin," which is a species of bacteria that can cause tuberculosis. Mary's mother, also a Navy nurse, got injected with BCG vaccine sometime in the late 1940s or early 1950s. At some recent nursing school class reunions, her mother's classmates said that "there was a higher incidence of cancer in the people who received the BCG shots." Mary's mother has advanced lung cancer. She is on painkillers now; the cancer has so bloated her lungs that "it cracked her ribs." When the diagnosis was made, around Christmas 2003, Mary recalls being asked if her mother ever received the BCG vaccine. "My mom told me it was a controlled study."

"Do you know anything about the BCG vaccine?" I ask.

"Only that it's supposed to be a vaccine for TB," says Mary.

"Well, depending on the country, that could be right or that could be wrong."

"What do you mean?"

"BCG vaccine is licensed in other countries to protect people from tuberculosis, but it is not licensed for that purpose in the United States," I tell her. "Here it is only licensed as a special therapy to protect against the recurrence of bladder cancer."

"Oh," she says.

"Mary . . . there's one other thing."

"Yes."

"You know when your mother got the BCG vaccine?"

"Yes."

"It wasn't licensed yet," I tell her.

"What do you mean?" asks Mary.

"I mean it was experimental. BCG vaccine wasn't licensed in the United States until 1990.[21] That's about forty years *after* your mother got injected with it. Did your mother know that?"

"No . . . I don't think she did," says Mary.

"Well, if your mother didn't know that it was experimental at the time, then she may have given her consent to receive the shot, but it wasn't *informed* consent," I say.[22] "Did anyone in Saudi Arabia say anything about getting an 'experimental' anthrax vaccine or a 'new and improved' anthrax vaccine?"[23]

Mary gets very quiet on the other end of the phone.

———

Army Sergeant Scott Siefken suffered from ailments that mystified his doctors for almost a year. He served with the National Guard's 1133rd Transportation Company out of Mason City, Iowa. After he returned home his body temperature began to rise and fall without explanation; one moment he felt very cold, the next moment he was warm. Nothing else seemed out of the ordinary until the spring of 1993, when the rashes appeared. At first they were tiny red bumps on his torso that looked like a heat rash; Scott's mother thought it could be an allergic reaction to a detergent. But heat rashes eventually go away; so do allergic reactions to a new laundry soap, provided you change the soap. Every time Scott's rash disappeared, it would come back again, only worse. By fall, he had two lesions in his mouth, one on the side of his tongue, the other on the inside of his cheek. They were holes about the size of a pea, and they hurt like the blazes.

"Mom, take a look at this, willya?"

Scott opened his mouth as wide as he could to let his mother, Ardythe (pronounced AHR-dith), take a look at the sores with a flashlight. "I don't know, Scott," she said. "I think you've got to get that looked at right away." She couldn't bring herself to say what she really thought . . . that her son might have some sort of mouth cancer.

Scott's doctor thought he might have a disease called lichen planus—an inflammation of the mucus membranes in the mouth that can be caused by drugs like bismuth or even exposure to color photograph developers.[24] But lichen planus lesions are whitish around their edges with irregular shapes. The ulcers in Scott's mouth looked like someone had burned holes into his cheek and tongue with a lit cigarette. They were raw and painful.

Because of the sores in his mouth, eating anything that required chewing became excruciating. Scott's wife, Lydia, started pureeing his food, which he would sip through a straw. By the winter of '93, even that hurt too much. By then he had lost forty pounds.

His doctors put him on a steroid called Prednisone, which is often used to control autoimmune disease. The drug made Scott's body swell until it seemed like it would burst. "My God, Ardie," said Scott's father, "if we met him on the street we probably wouldn't have known him."[25] While Scott's appearance and his weight would seesaw, its overall direction was unmistakable: it was getting worse.

Scott was thirty-three, 6 feet 2 inches, and a very fit 190 pounds when he went to the Persian Gulf. Like Pat Rudicell, he had been a high school football player. Now he could barely walk.

It was the sores on his feet that made it difficult. The rash on his torso had spread to his toes. By then, it had become something else altogether. The raised red bumps had turned to blisters the size of half-dollars. At the slightest contact, they would break, leaving open, weeping sores that caused him great pain. One of his younger sisters said "it was if his blood were boiling to the surface of his skin."

The skin is one of our most vital organs. It helps regulate body temperature and is the body's chief barrier to infection. The ruptures in Scott's skin became gaping portals to invading pathogens. Scott started running a fever.

The VA hospital in Des Moines wanted to transfer him to a burn unit in Texas. That was when he received the diagnosis of SLE. When he first heard it, Scott was elated. He thought if the doctors knew what he had, they could help him.

No sooner had VA doctors given Scott a diagnosis than they transferred him to the University Hospital in Iowa City. The doctors there didn't think Scott had lupus. "If it was lupus we could control it; we can't control this," Ardie recalls one of them saying. The doctors then resorted to a radical procedure called debridement, a treatment for severely burned patients that entails the removal of dead skin from a burned area. Doctors removed Scott's skin, which was not dead but diseased. From his scalp to his toes, Scott Siefken was, in effect, skinned alive. Some 99 percent of his skin was peeled and abraded away. For temporary protection, doctors performed a "xenograft"— they covered Scott in pig skin. Xenografts are a stopgap to prevent infection until a burn area is sufficiently healed to receive an "autograft"—the grafting of healthy skin from an unaffected part of the victim's body. Except that Scott didn't have any healthy skin left.

With the epidermis and the uppermost portion of his dermis removed, Scott was a mass of raw flesh and exposed nerve endings. His room had to be kept at a constant 98° because the loss of skin left him perpetually cold. When the xenograft started to slough off, he was given "burn baths"—water jets that would peel away dead pig skin that clung stubbornly to his body. Scott's body would grow a tiny patch of new skin, only to lose it a day or so later. Nurses fed him through a tube, gave him antibiotics to ward off infection, and dosed him up with morphine to dull the pain. Ardie recalls Scott's courage during those times. His family would read to him; when they mispronounced a word, he would gently correct them. Throughout his ordeal, Scott never lost his sense of humor, but even that became a burden to him. When he smiled, his lips would bleed. His parents, his wife, his sisters and his friends couldn't kiss him or hug him; they could not lay a finger on him for fear of causing him pain or giving him a fatal infection. The sight of him without skin was so hideous that the family dared not let Scott's children see him. His suffering was almost indescribable, yet when he expressed worry it was always for his family, not himself.

"I'll never quit trying to find out what made you sick," Ardie told Scott.

"Go for it, Mom," he said.

At 3 A.M., on October 5, 1994, seven weeks after his surgery and just over two years after returning home from Desert Storm, Scott Siefken died. He was thirty-seven years old.

The medical examiner attributed Scott's death to "lymphoma," "kidney failure" and "blood poisoning." That is what his autopsy records say. The University of Iowa Burn Unit doctor who treated Scott told the Siefkens that "he had never seen anything like it before, and he had no idea what he was dealing with." For Ardie, these memories remain like Scott's affliction; they don't heal. To this day, she feels the military is withholding answers from her; she feels betrayed by a government to whom the Siefkens have given a great deal. Scott's father, Rollie, served in the Army. Of the six kids he and Ardie had together, four of them served a total of sixteen years in the Navy, including Scott, who later joined the Iowa National Guard to stay closer to home. "We're angry. We're frustrated. We're so scared this may happen to another family. We're trying to get answers before it's too late for you," Ardie wrote in a letter published by the *American Legion Magazine* back in August 1996.

"I still don't have answers," she says today.

"Did Scott get vaccinated against anthrax during the war?" I ask.

"I don't know," says Ardie. Ten years after Scott's death, the Siefkens still haven't been able to get his immunization records.

———

"Colonel Smith," said Dr. Michelle Petri, "you have systemic lupus erythematosus. It's embarrassing to look over your medical records and see the failure to diagnose it when the answer was right there at all times."

Dr. Petri's remarks, if faithfully recalled by Col. Herb Smith, were not meant for anyone else's ears but Smith's. Even so, Smith, a retired colonel in the Army Reserve Special Forces, cannot resist recounting it. "When I was hurtin' I would lay in bed with tears rollin' down my face. And when you're hurtin' like that, you want to die. *I* wanted to die. My joints were burning. Now, most of the time, they just ache. Occasionally, they're just like they're on fire . . . like a hot needle's been stuck in 'em. I get headaches so bad it hurts to comb my hair." What makes him madder still is that in 1997, he already knew he had lupus; he had known for almost two years. A Memphis-based rheumatologist named Dr. Kevin Asa ran the lab tests and diagnosed it back in 1995. He reviewed Smith's medical records and believed there were clinical indications as early as July 1991 that suggested Smith might have an autoimmune disease.

"Col. Smith was examined and found to have multiple arthralgias (joint pain) in June 1991," wrote Dr. Asa in a letter to Walter Reed Army Medical Center (WRAMC) in Washington, D.C.[26] Asa was as astonished, as Dr. Petri would later be, that anyone in the Army had missed the clinical indicators that Smith had a problem with his immune system. "In July," Asa continued, Smith "had swelling of the left leg, ankle, and foot which resolved. Abnormal liver functions tests were also shown. Later in July, he was found to have a monoclonal gammopathy. Additionally, there was swelling and tenderness of the DIP joints, elbows, ankles, wrists and MTP joints bilaterally. . . . In October 1991, chronic headaches, fatigue, low-grade fever, and carpal tunnel syndrome were noted. In December 1991, Col. Smith had developed dizziness, vertigo and an unsteady gait. In 1993, wrote Asa, "the Army documented vestibular dysfunction."[27]

All of these observations consistent with autoimmunity were made by Army doctors at WRAMC.[28] Walter Reed also ran the initial lab tests indicating autoimmune disease. Yet Army doctors there, including Major Michael J. Roy who was treating Smith, disagreed. In consultation with other Army doctors, Roy diagnosed Smith with a psychiatric problem called "somatization disorder." Smith's ailments, in other words, were imaginary.[29] As Kevin Asa pointed out to Maj. Roy, this diagnosis could not account for Smith's positive lab results for genuine physical ailments. The mind can create pain, numbness or even, in extreme cases, paralysis—but one thing it cannot do is alter the results of lab tests. "After reviewing the DSM-III [the American Psychiatric Association's *Diagnostic and Statistical Manual of Mental Disorders*]," said Asa, "I cannot see how [Smith] would fit the criteria of having somatoform disorder in that this diagnosis is appropriate only in those cases where there is no evidence of organic disease."[30] Kevin concluded that laboratory evidence contradicted Roy's diagnosis. "Col. Smith has had positive clinical and laboratory findings for the past 4 and a half years indicative of autoimmune disease," Asa wrote.[31] "Most of the tests were done at WRAMC. He is currently on a treatment protocol of strong immune suppression in order to stop the destruction of his tissues by his own immune system . . . by diagnostic criteria appropriately applied, he does not have a somatoform disorder."[32]

Smith doesn't remember who was sitting across the dinner table from him the night he first noticed he had a problem. He just remembers what the guy said:

"Herb . . . your hand . . . it's shaking."

Smith stared at his right hand, the one holding the fork. It looked like it was shivering, as if Smith had just been trudging around in subzero weather without a jacket—except he was in Saudi Arabia, where the average daytime temperature in January often climbed above 70°. There was an irony to someone like Smith getting sick. He was in the Persian Gulf to prevent illness. His job was to organize medical care for the Kuwaitis after the war was over. A veterinarian by training, Smith was a Green Beret colonel who in 1987 had joined the 352nd Civil Affairs Command as a Public Health Officer. In December 1989, he went to Panama in Operation Just Cause and was there until June 1990. Less than two months later, the Army put him on alert for Desert Shield. He was glad to go: he was bucking for promotion to general, and the fastest route to promotion in the Army is through a combat zone. As the leader of the U.S. Army's public health team for Kuwait, Smith was the designated counterpart to the Kuwaiti Minister of Health. Together, they would draw up an Emergency Medical Care Plan for non-combatants that would commence once the country was back under the Kuwaiti flag. After the Iraqis were ousted, Smith's unit, the Kuwait Task Force, was also supposed to help get the country's health-care system functioning again.

Smith kept staring at his right hand. Even with the air conditioning at full blast, he wasn't cold. His brain said "stop trembling," but the hand wouldn't stop. It was almost as if it were attached to someone else's body.

After that, watching his hands tremble became almost a daily event at mealtimes. Sometimes it was his right hand, sometimes his left; it was never both at once. By May 1991, hand tremors were the least of his problems. "My joints were hurting," says Smith, "and my lymph nodes were swollen, and I was feverish and I had a rash. I felt real fatigued. It hurt to walk, especially up and down stairs. Every day it just seemed to get worse."

Smith kept hoping whatever it was making him feel lousy all the time would just go away. He didn't want to admit he had a serious problem. He had always been a little arrogant, even vain, about his fitness. He had been an NCAA Division I wrestler at Auburn and had a black belt in karate. In 1966, he graduated No. 1 in his class from Jump School (Airborne) at Fort Benning, partly because he was in such good shape; he could do a thousand push-ups a day while barely breaking a sweat. He was no one's candidate for a psychosomatic illness. It wasn't just his physical prowess; it was his gung-ho attitude. A hyper-competitive, if not combative, man, Smith sought out grueling physical challenges that he could not have mastered without a commensurate level of mental toughness. When the Army made him a Special Forces instructor in 1968, refusing to send him to Vietnam because he graduated too high in his class, Smith quit the Army in frustration. It's not that he was so eager to kill, or risk being killed. It was his ferocious desire to advance himself. Warriors prove their mettle in war, and war offered Smith the chance to achieve yet another career milestone. Vietnam was an arena in which to excel.

Even after joining the Army Reserve, Smith never lost a competitive edge that, for some people, bordered on the obnoxious. It wasn't enough for him to be good; he had to be better than everyone else. As a "semi-civilian," Smith continued to work out like he was still on active duty in the Special Forces. He had a "six-pack of abs" before anyone thought to call them that. In the 1980s, he ran Army PT programs, putting troopers half his age through their paces.

"Everybody had a good time," Smith says with a faintly wicked gleam in his eye. "I got the name 'Dr. Death.'"

As fanatical about his fitness as he was, Smith didn't get sick much either. So it was hard for him to accept that, whatever this illness was, he couldn't shake it. He had never known what it was like to get winded climbing stairs. Dr. Death didn't get fatigued or have trouble carrying his ruck. Dr. Death was the only one left standing when everyone else was red-faced on the deck with their chests heaving. Most of all, Dr. Death wanted that goddamn promotion and he wasn't going to get it if he had to bail on this deployment too soon.

"'You know,' they said, 'there's an opportunity to excel here,'" Smith remembers. "'You can stay another year if you like.' And I really wanted to stay another year. But I felt that something was wrong. I wasn't doing well in the desert."

He wasn't doing well back home in Maryland either; that is, when he could find his home. At the time, Herb Smith lived in Ijamsville (pronounced EYE-yumsville), Maryland—close to Frederick and Fort Detrick, where Smith used to work. He lived with his wife, Pamela, in a kind of upscale no-man's-land of architectural conformity that typifies many new subdivisions—a spacious ranch home in a community with two-acre lots, but offering a strangely empty vista. Smith's house sat atop a hill that looked as though it had been scraped free of every tree within a five-mile radius. On either side of him were golf courses with broad green fairways that had further denuded the landscape. Even with good directions and a road atlas, it wasn't easy for me to find Smith's home. The trouble was Smith had been having difficulty finding it too.

It shouldn't have been that tough. Herb Smith was a Green Beret colonel. He knew how to orienteer. Smith was the kind of guy who would think GPS was for wimps; with a quadrant map and compass he was once able to bushwhack through an unmarked swamp full of alligators. Now he had a hard time finding his own house.

It was the seizures that waylaid him. Smith started having them not long after returning to the United States. These seizures did not involve falling and shaking uncontrollably on the floor, as happened to Pat Rudicell at Khobar Towers. Smith's were "complex partial seizures." He could walk around his home without it being obvious to anyone that he was having an attack. Doctors call this phenomenon "automatization," which is action without thinking—a patient experiencing such a seizure can act robotically without any awareness of what he is doing. "One day I was in a car driving toward Baltimore on I–70," says Smith, "and the next thing I know, I'm just outside of Washington, D.C., on I–95, and I've got no clue how I got there." The one thing Smith couldn't do when he had a complex partial seizure was remember what he was doing when it struck. His mind was like a tape with gaps in the recording. Whole hours of his life got erased with no hope of retrieval.

One night Smith had an episode that lasted for an hour, maybe an hour and a half. It was long enough for him to get good and lost.

Smith had called his wife, who was waiting for him to get home. When she answered the phone, Dr. Death—the tough-as-nails Green Beret who delighted in humbling twenty-year-olds with almost superhuman shows of stamina—started to quietly weep. "Pam, I don't know where I am."

Things could have been worse; he could've forgotten his phone number too. "I had to call my wife on the phone to find my way home. That's when I knew I really had a problem. And even then I resisted seeking medical care until the pain got so bad I couldn't walk around, and was so dizzy and so nauseous I kept passing out."

As early as 1991, Army physicians were documenting symptoms associated with autoimmune disease, by the following year there was clinical evidence of it. In a series of ten laboratory tests for autoimmune dysfunctions, Smith tested positive in every one. Smith's immune system was producing antibodies to his microsomes—the energy-producing organelles in the cell—and to his own muscles. One lab result in particular, a below-normal C3 complement level, was a possible indicator of lupus.[33] "Complement" is a collective term, referring to thirty different types of proteins that play a part in an intricately choreographed series of immune responses.[34] When complement is activated, it serves at least three main functions. First, it amplifies the antibody response, telling antibody-producing cells to make more antibodies. Second, complement is a kind of marker in a process called "opsonization." When complement coats the surface of an invading germ, it is like ringing a dinner bell. It signals to macrophages—the Pac-men of the immune system—to start consuming those germs marked for destruction. A low level of complement indicates overactivation of the immune system. Finally, complement is part of a cascade of interactive responses called the "membrane-attack complex," or MAC.[35] MAC is a set of biochemical reactions that perforate the germ's outer membrane, killing it.

When this complement system is activated against your own constituents it gets overtaxed; there is literally too much to attack. The body starts to use up complement faster than it can make it; hence the deficit of these proteins—especially in an autoimmune disease like systemic lupus erythematosus, in which the immune system attacks multiple constituents of the body all at once.

In order to diagnose somatization disorder—a neurotic manifestation of real symptoms like headaches, nausea and vomiting (in the absence of demonstrably physical manifestations of disease like antibody production)—Dr. Kevin Asa complained that the Army physicians treating Col. Smith offered no rational explanation for dismissing the implications of his lab work in favor of a psychiatric disorder that seemed inappropriate to Asa. Somatization disorder is almost unheard of in men. The latest edition of the *Diagnostic and Statistical Manual of Mental Disorders,* known as DSM-IV-TR, states that somatization disorder "occurs only rarely in men in the United States," and overall in "less than 0.2% in men" everywhere.[36] It mainly affects women (1 to 2 percent of the female population), starting in adolescence or early adulthood.[37] In both men and women, the symptoms, according to the manual, are "often present by adolescence."[38] In fact, the complaints *"must begin before age 30* and occur over a period of several years" [italics mine].[39]

Herb Smith didn't fit this profile. He was a man and his complaints began after the age of fifty-one. There was one other major objection. The American Psychiatric Association says "unexplained symptoms in Somatization Disorder are *not intentionally feigned or produced* [italics mine]."[40] Yet that is precisely what Roy insinuated that Smith had done—intentionally faking his illness.

"He accused me of bleeding myself to fake my anemia," says Smith. "He also accused me of knowing—I also have a degree in chemistry as well as a Doctor of Veterinary Medicine . . . chemistry, zoology and a DVM degree—anyway, he said [Smith is] a pretty smart guy, so he also knows how to screw up lab results, so he can lower his complement levels."

Roy denies "accusing" Smith of anything. He says he only "suggested" that Smith might have faked his anemia. Roy also points out that the diagnoses for cases like Smith's were discussed among "multiple subspecialists." So, according to Roy, he was not the only doctor at Walter Reed who reached these conclusions about Smith. But the doctors in Walter Reed's Gulf War clinic could not have it both ways. They could not diagnose somatization disorder in which unexplained symptoms "are *not* intentionally feigned or produced," and then suggest that Smith was committing what amounted to a devious kind of malingering—contriving to artificially induce his anemia to lower his complement levels. Asa says Roy offered no evidence to support his speculations about Smith. If Smith had been bleeding himself, there should have been signs of it—like a wound. Roy did not specify such a sign. How much blood did Smith allegedly drain from his body? Roy did not say. According to the Asas, donating a unit of blood at a hospital would not accomplish what Roy was suggesting; in fact, no amount of blood loss would. A complement level does not change with the amount of blood in the body, says Asa; it is a *ratio* of these proteins per unit of blood. The ratio at the time it is measured will remain constant whether it is in a cubic centimeter of blood or a liter.

Smith could have lost a lot of blood and it still would not have lowered his complement levels.

Kevin Asa had heard enough. He saw Smith's lab results; he was certain of Smith's diagnosis—systemic lupus erythematosus. Having already challenged the conclusion that Smith had a psychosomatic illness, Kevin Asa was then taken aback by Roy's audacity at even suggesting Smith had been bleeding himself. He wrote another letter to the Army:[41]

> *Thank you in advance for helping this severely impaired veteran to obtain benefits for a condition which clearly had its origins during the period while he was on active duty in the Persian Gulf. It seems incredible to me that anyone could suggest that a man whose major life interests include martial arts, physical fitness and health, and skydiving would make himself an invalid for the minimal monetary benefits he received as a pension. He could easily make far more income in his work and would far prefer to work than to suffer from his pronounced physical and intellectual impairments with which he is now afflicted.*
>
> *Sincerely,*
> *D. Kevin Asa, M.D.*
> *Board Certified–Rheumatology*
> *Board Certified–Internal Medicine*

Still, Dr. Roy refused to accept Asa's diagnosis. An associate of Roy's from Walter Reed Army Medical Center, Lt. Joe N. Flowers, even wrote a letter requesting that Asa cease treating Herb Smith.

By then, Smith's patience had run out too. He wrote a letter to the commanding general of Walter Reed Army Medical Center, General Ronald Blanck, "and I told him," says Smith, "that I had an officer, a major, accuse a superior officer—a colonel, me—of conduct unbecoming of an officer, and perjury." Blanck assigned Smith another doctor.

"Then once I got the other doctor," says Smith, "he comes in and he says, 'Well, you know, Dr. Roy says you got all these psychological problems.' And I said: 'What about the VA findings?' [The VA concluded Smith had an autoimmune problem, too.] 'The VA . . . they're wrong. They don't know what they're doing.' I said, 'Well if you don't believe the VA, whom will you believe?' They said, 'Well, we'll believe either NIH, or Johns Hopkins.'"

Exasperated by Roy's intransigence on the diagnosis, Kevin Asa advised Smith to get a second opinion from a rheumatologist in the Baltimore area. If Smith could get in to see her, Dr. Michelle Petri, a Professor of Medicine in the Rheumatology Department of Johns Hopkins School of Medicine, was one of the world's leading authorities on lupus. "And so she reviewed my medical records," says Smith, "and she called me up and said, 'Dr. Asa was correct, that's the correct diagnosis,' but she said she was going to have to confirm it because she's had problems with Walter Reed before." So Petri ordered up some blood work and a brain SPECT (Single Photon Emission Computerized Tomography) scan for Smith; this enabled Petri to observe the blood flow to various regions in Smith's brain, which determined how well those areas would function. The results were unambiguous: Smith had lupus. In case any of the doctors at Walter Reed Medical Center didn't get the message, Johns Hopkins backdated its diagnosis. The subsequent lab report referred to Smith as a patient with a "history of SLE *since 1992* [italics mine] with CNS involvement."[42] It was 1997. Upon review of the contents of Smith's medical chart, Johns Hopkins determined that Smith had had systemic lupus erythematosus as early as 1992.

As the Johns Hopkins lab report clearly suggested, Smith's lab results had pointed towards autoimmune disease years before. Smith had lupus, and somebody should have spotted it a lot earlier. According to Smith, the fact that his symptoms began shortly after his second anthrax immunization was a potential tip-off to a vaccine connection; even one of Smith's friends in the 352nd Civil Affairs Battalion suspected it, and said so in Kuwait just before Smith boarded a plane to return to the States.

"He says: 'I think you're sick as a result of the vaccine you got,'" recalls Smith.

"And I said: 'What vaccine?'

"'The so-called anthrax shot that we got,'" says the other fellow, an M.D. who doesn't wish to be identified.

As long as Smith's illness remained unidentified, it could not be traced to his vaccinations, or to anything else.

—

In 2004, after much effort, I finally got a chance to speak to Dr. Roy. Roy says he knew nothing about the use of a new and improved anthrax vaccine during the Gulf War. He vehemently denies ignoring any of Smith's lab results. "We did not ignore any data, but used all available data to make the most accurate diagnoses we could," says Roy. He did admit suggesting to Pam Asa, an immunologist married to Kevin, that "as a veterinarian [Smith] had the expertise to bleed himself" to fake his anemia, and stands by his original conclusion that Smith's problems were psychological.

"I hope COL Smith is doing better these days," Roy said in an email, "but he had become a professional patient. Both he and the military were best served by severing their relationship, so that he could move on with his life." It has been nearly eight years since Smith has been in Roy's care. Roy still insists that he and his fellow doctors at Walter Reed made no error in diagnosing Smith with "somatization disorder." "If he wanted to call his condition lupus, fine, and he was compensated accordingly," says Roy. "Perhaps some of the toxic therapies even induced lupus, for all I know. But when I saw him he did not have lupus. I would have to say that one of the more disillusioning aspects of my work with Gulf War veterans was how a few veterans with personality disorders could occupy inordinate time with Congressional inquiries and so forth."

Pam Asa says the diagnosis given to Smith at the Walter Reed Army Medical Center is a potential concern for other sick Gulf War veterans. Roy was not just any doctor at Walter Reed Army Medical Center. He was not just Smith's doctor either. Dr. Michael Roy was the Clinical Director of the Gulf War Health Center (GWHC) at Walter Reed. This was the clinic that screened a lot of the veterans who returned sick from the Persian Gulf War. "The great majority of the Gulf War veterans I saw, who truly needed help," says Roy, "were very satisfied with the treatment we provided, and acknowledged their gratitude." Still, if you review Smith's medical chart, his illness had been variously diagnosed as somatization disorder, chronic fatigue syndrome[43] and multiple chemical toxicity syndrome[44]—anything but lupus. The unanswered question is whether or not Smith was an isolated case.

———

Many other veterans have been suffering from ailments with known links to autoimmunity or have since been diagnosed by civilian physicians with an actual autoimmune disease. In Herb Smith's case, military doctors at the Army's original clinic for the treatment of Gulf War ailments had diagnosed him with a somatoform disorder even when there was laboratory evidence that his illness was real and not a figment of a neurotic mind. In September 1997, the Veterans Administration reached the same conclusion, awarding Col. Smith 100 percent disability for "systemic lupus erythematosus with central nervous system involvement." A previous VA evaluation attributed Smith's problems to "chronic fatigue syndrome." Doctors at Walter Reed—and as Dr. Roy points out, at the Mayo Clinic as well—had diagnosed Smith with a psychiatric disorder.[45] Any predilection for such psychiatric diagnoses at Walter Reed or elsewhere—if indeed any existed—would have distorted the epidemiological picture for any discussion on Gulf War Syndrome. As long as Gulf War illnesses remained a vague cluster of ill-defined symptoms like headaches or chronic fatigue, they could be attributed to just about anything; and they were. The Army started funding research into everything from flea collars to microwaves as possible sources of an allegedly faux malady. Had anyone diagnosed these problems as autoimmune, it would have narrowed the field of potential causative agents; flea collars and microwaves do not cause autoimmunity.

Pam Asa was convinced that there was a common link to these autoimmune ailments and that at least some Army doctors knew what it was. As yet, there was no evidence that any of these sick veterans had been injected with the new anthrax vaccine containing an unlicensed oil adjuvant; the autoimmune diseases were a clue, but not proof. Major Greg Dubay had been briefed that his Army Reserve medical company would be giving troops a "new and improved anthrax" vaccine, but he says no one ever said anything to him about squalene. Pam Asa was determined to find out what was making these veterans sick. What seemed to be an abnormally high incidence of autoimmunity in male Gulf War veterans raised a lot of questions she could not answer. It seemed to Pam Asa that in Herb Smith's case at least, Army doctors did not want to know the answers. She wanted to know why.

Chapter Seven

The Unraveling

Pamela B. Asa, an immunologist with a Ph.D. in molecular biology—Kevin's wife—had no idea what she had gotten herself into. For nearly fifteen years, Army doctors and scientists had been trying to come up with a better anthrax vaccine, and in their view they had just about succeeded. By the time Pam Asa entered the picture, the Army's work on a recombinant anthrax vaccine was like a big freight train about to arrive at its destination, and she had just stepped in front of it.

As soon as the war was over, the Army took steps to ensure that it would never again be caught unprepared to face an enemy with anthrax. The next time, the Army would be ready. All of its troops would be vaccinated, and it would have more than one source of vaccine. In April 1991, less than two months after the Iraqi surrender, the Army issued a task order to the Salk Institute in Swiftwater, Pennsylvania, to push this process along.[1] Salk would help get the recombinant DNA anthrax vaccine with squalene out of its R&D phase and into full-scale production. By the end of the war, Fort Detrick's Col. Arthur Friedlander had identified which of the Army's new and improved anthrax vaccines to scaleup.[2] This meant taking it from the lab bench to the next level—refining the techniques for small-scale production runs of the Army's candidate second generation anthrax vaccine. With Friedlander as the Army's designated point of contact, Salk would also initiate "work to identify adjuvants suitable for humans to be used with the PA [protective antigen] protein."[3]

In a parallel effort, the Army commenced plans to make recombinant PA at the National Cancer Institute, the only government institution that had agreed to join Anna Johnson-Winegar's prewar effort to "surge" anthrax vaccine production. At the time, the National Cancer Institute's laboratories at Fort Detrick were managed by a subcontractor called Program Resources, Inc. (PRI). By August 1991, the Army had started processing the paperwork on a $15.4 million contract to make PRI and the National Cancer Institute (NCI) its second source of anthrax vaccine.[4]

The very next month, Brigadier General Ronald R. Blanck held a secret briefing for the Joint Chiefs.[5] It took place in "the tank"—the secure briefing room at the Pentagon. Blanck informed the chiefs about the Army's plans to make anthrax vaccine at NCI, but for reasons left unexplained in his notes, he made no mention of Salk. When we read this material many years later, with the benefit of knowing what would happen next, two things stand out. The vaccine made by NCI would require a separate contract with the licensed producer, the Michigan Department of Public Health, "for potency test, bottling, labelling, and storage."[6] In other words, vaccine made at NCI's Fort Detrick laboratories would be bottled and labeled at Michigan. According to FDA regulations, only anthrax vaccine made by the sole licensed facility by means expressly approved by the FDA could be injected into humans. Vaccine made anywhere else, by any other means, would be a de facto investigational new drug, requiring express permission from the FDA for use.

The other item that stands out from Blanck's briefing is his timetable for the completion of this work: Blanck told the chiefs that the "recombinant anthrax vaccine" would be ready in "less than five years."[7] Given the date of this briefing—September 13, 1991—that would make the target date for the availability of the new vaccine no later than the fall of 1996. Remember that date.

Anna Johnson-Winegar had the job of finding other sources of anthrax vaccine before the war; it was only logical that she continued doing so afterwards. She had a new job by then—Biological Sciences Administrator of the Military Disease Hazards Research Program. This meant she would help oversee the creation of a new and improved anthrax vaccine that she herself had tried to make at Fort Detrick more than ten years before. To make this new vaccine, there was something Johnson-Winegar had to make sure everyone understood: the vaccine's chief ingredient, protective antigen, was "only one component of a final second generation vaccine."[8] There was a second and equally vital constituent; without it, the new vaccine wouldn't work any better than the old one. In fact, without it, the new vaccine would be virtually identical to the old one—just protective antigen made with up-to-date technology; that was all. "The PA alone cannot be used as a vaccine candidate," she wrote in a memo dated February 28, 1992, "but rather requires an adjuvant."[9]

The squalene-based adjuvants the Army had mixed into its earlier prototypes (Triple Mix, DeTox and Walter Reed Liposomes) had proven too toxic.[10] Salk's adjuvant studies would help remedy that. One candidate already looked especially promising. It was called MF59—another adjuvant made from squalene, the oil that DOD and NIH scientists still considered safe. For Blanck and Johnson-Winegar, everything seemed to be on track, except for one thing: troops returning from the war were getting sick.

By 1994, America's newspapers and airwaves were filled with reports about ailing veterans of Desert Storm. The ubiquitous Michael Fumento—a journalist specializing in science and health issues, media iconoclast, and self-proclaimed debunker of modern myths—counted "no less than 11 television programs" that had aired reports on the ill-defined "Gulf War Syndrome" affecting veterans of this war.[11] Some facetiously called this affliction "Saddam's Revenge"; Fumento, with some justification at the time, suggested it was "chemophobia in a fascinating new guise."[12] It seemed impossible to diagnose. The symptoms were consistent enough—aching joints and muscles, rashes, fatigue, weight loss, weight gain, alopecia or hair loss, sore gums, diarrhea, nausea, swelling, short-term memory loss and headaches. But considered individually, they could be attributed to just about anything. A headache or fatigue might be due to anything from a bad day at the office to the onset of flu. Achy joints or memory loss could result from aging or even a hangover. Either these veterans were being incapacitated by some crypto-pathogen, or they were succumbing to some sort of stress-induced hysteria. Public opinion was divided. The media played up its mysterious origins. Primary care physicians seemed perplexed.

With everyone primed to think these illnesses were either bunk or something so new that it defied diagnosis, it apparently failed to occur to military doctors at the time that the symptoms, when considered collectively, also suggested an improperly functioning immune system. Primary care physicians, the doctors who treat patients for generalized complaints like fatigue, might be forgiven for missing this. That thousands of veterans could have developed autoimmune diseases as a result of service in the Gulf, even today sounds implausible, maybe even ridiculous, unless you know about the Gulf War "Manhattan Project" and the history of Army doctors testing oil adjuvants on military personnel. Autoimmunity is a rarity among men—especially young men, its principal victims. Some doctors recognized the symptoms as hallmarks of autoimmunity; but attempted to link the phenomena to things like bug repellent and pyridostigmine bromide pills that have not been previously associated with autoimmune disease.[13] According to the *Merck Manual*, pyridostimine is, ironically, a treatment for autoimmune disease (myasthenia gravis), not a known cause of it.[14]

Having convinced themselves that Gulf War illness was some cyptopathology, public health officials and media mavens alike tried to define it by reversing the traditional order of what physicians normally do in making a diagnosis. Since the mid-19th century, pinpointing a causative agent began first by identifying the disease. How else could one rationally discuss a cause? The cause of what? As illogical as it may seem, doctors did the opposite with Gulf War Syndrome. Unable to identify a common illness among these sick veterans, they seized upon something they could establish, toxic agents to which soldiers might have been exposed in Southwest Asia—e.g., the bite of a sand fly, mosquito repellent, micro-doses of nerve agent, or stress—none of which had known links to autoimmune disease. The cart was conspicuously before the horse, and not surprisingly, the cart didn't go anywhere.

In 1994, two groups of Senate investigators got tantalizingly close. Concern about the use of unlicensed drugs and vaccines in the Persian Gulf only intensified after the war—fueled initially by a lawsuit and then by subsequent media reports. On the eve of Desert Storm, the FDA issued rule 23(d) to permit the use of experimental drugs without informed consent because consent was "not feasible in a specific military operation involving combat or the immediate threat of combat."[15] After the FDA granted informed consent waivers for the use of two IND drugs in the Gulf, pyridostigmine bromide and pentavalent botulinum toxoid. "John Doe," a U.S. soldier deployed to Saudi Arabia, and his wife tried to halt it by filing a lawsuit against then HHS Secretary Louis Sullivan and Secretary of Defense Richard B. Cheney.[16] John and Mary Doe lost their case and their appeal, but their efforts raised sufficient concern about the issue to help inspire an investigation by the Senate Committee on Veterans' Affairs. The resulting report, *Is Military Research Hazardous to Veterans' Health? Lessons Spanning Half a Century*, contains an item that, at the time, appeared to be a dead end.

Blanck, by 1994 a major general and commander of the Walter Reed Army Medical Center, told the committee staff that "Anthrax vaccine should continue to be considered as a potential cause for undiagnosed illnesses in Persian Gulf military personnel because many of the support troops received anthrax vaccine, and because DOD believes that the incidence of undiagnosed illnesses in support troops may be higher than that in combat troops."[17] Epidemiologists could have substantiated this by cross-referencing medical complaints from Gulf War veterans against their immunizations records—except that, as the Veterans' Affairs Committee soon found out, the Army had given express orders against logging the anthrax vaccinations into anyone's records. "Unfortunately," reported committee investigators, "medical records and shot records of individuals who served in the Persian Gulf frequently do not report the vaccines they received."[18]

A second investigation, conducted by the Senate Committee on Banking, Housing, and Urban Affairs, contained another lead that seemed to go nowhere. In a report titled *U.S. Chemical and Biological Warfare-Related Dual Use Exports to Iraq and Their Possible Impact on the Health Consequences of the Persian Gulf War*, the Committee stated that it had "received reports of recurring rumors that experimental recombinant DNA (rDNA) biological defense vaccines were used by the military during the Persian Gulf War."[19] At the time, the committee could not find any proof of this. The evidence would come from somewhere no one ever thought to look.

Getting a Grip on the Problem

Pam Asa sat still in her office, concentrating. She was pulling it all together. Or, perhaps more accurately, she was pulling it all apart. Herb Smith was a loose thread . . . the sort that, when you tugged it, would start to unravel everything. Like Herb, all these sick veterans had an autoimmune problem. For Pam Asa it was obvious. She had read the Gulf War Syndrome stories in the newspapers and couldn't believe that other people couldn't see it too: all these soldiers were complaining of rashes, joint and muscle pain and fatigue—hallmarks of autoimmune disease. She first spotted Herb Smith on a *60 Minutes* segment about the syndrome's possible links to nerve agent exposure. But when the camera cut away to Smith's hands, something caught Pam Asa's eye. His knuckle bones were swollen. "His MCP joints are rheumatoid," she said aloud to herself in front of the TV. Because of her suspicions, she started corresponding with veterans on the Internet, through a website chat room called "Military City" on AOL. All of the postings complained of the same thing. Rashes. Muscle and joint pain. Fatigue. Memory loss. Headaches. It was textbook autoimmunity. For any doctor familiar with autoimmunity, it couldn't be plainer . . . provided they considered the symptoms as a cluster. "It's like a constellation," she explained to some of her friends. "You don't look at the one star; you look at the group of stars to perceive the pattern."

For many veterans, the pattern was diagnosable. One of Pam Asa's Internet correspondents in Pennsylvania, Sgt. Peter Parks, had lupus. Herb Smith had lupus. Pat Rudicell had moved to Memphis and by pure coincidence had walked into Kevin Asa's practice seeking treatment for lupus. Pam helped manage Kevin's practice at the time, and got to know his patients. Rudicell had been in Kevin's care for a while before it occurred to Pam that she should ask Pat a question about something that wasn't in his chart. "Pat, were you in the Gulf War?" she asked. "Yes, ma'am," he replied. "Why do you ask?" Another veteran, Randy Wheeler, of Birmingham, Alabama, started seeing Kevin, too. Unlike all the others who were Army veterans, Wheeler was an ex-Marine—3rd Battalion, 11th Marines, Task Force Ripper, Echo Battery 212. When Sgt. Wheeler's lab work came back, there was no getting around it. He had lupus.

Pam Asa didn't like the implications of all this. "It can't be," she thought, "but it *has* to be." This mental tug-of-war was giving her a headache. She didn't want to go where the logical side of her brain kept taking her. Finally she stopped resisting the awful logic in Herb Smith's hands. As if solving a math problem, she walked through each step in her mind. Herb had lupus. So did these other men. This was weird. Lupus rarely affected men, especially younger men. Something must have induced it. Only troops from four countries complained of these health problems: the United States, Britain, Canada and Australia. Even more puzzling, veterans who never deployed to the Persian Gulf had developed the same problems—rashes, joint and muscle pain, memory loss. Whatever the causative agent was, it had not been confined to the Gulf. Pam Asa knew of only a few things that had been proven to induce autoimmunity in controlled laboratory experiments; even fewer things had been proven to induce autoimmune disease in several animal species—including humans.

"Oh, no," she said to herself, unable to evade the conclusion any longer. "They injected these guys with an adjuvant."

She started to cry.

———

Systemic lupus erythematosus is nothing a humane person would wish on their enemies. The worst cases, like Scott Siefken's, are so aggressive that nothing can slow the disease progress. For sufferers whose lupus is less severe, its ill effects can be fought to a relative standstill with immunosuppressant drugs (drugs that inhibit the immune response) like prednisone (a steroid) or Cytoxan (a cancer-fighting drug). Although the mildest cases invariably worsen over time, they can be managed.

There was something about Sergeant Jeff Rawls's illness that defied every effort to manage it. In September 1992, Jeff fell down and broke his leg. It was a bad break. Because he was in a cast for six whole months, Jeff's doctors in Utica, New York, told him that when it came off, he would have problems with his balance. When the doctors removed Jeff's cast in 1993, his balance was indeed imperfect, but it never got better. That year Jeff developed a noticeable ataxia—he couldn't walk straight. He also started slurring his words. Between his wobbly gait and his slurred speech, some of the patients Jeff assisted as a nursing student at the Mohawk Valley Community College accused him of being drunk. But Jeff didn't drink. He didn't do drugs either. His family grew alarmed. There was something bizarre about seeing a perfectly sober twenty-six-year-old man incapable of walking a straight line, but Jeff couldn't do it. He decided to seek help from the VA. Jeff was an ex-Marine

Reservist—the commander of an M–60 tank during Desert Storm—so he was eligible for care from the VA hospital in nearby Syracuse. But VA doctors told Jeff that he was "faking it." As Jeff recollects their comments, his father, Don, a Vietnam veteran who was present when VA doctors said this to his son, looks equal parts astonished and angry at the way these doctors treated his boy. But there is no hint of it in his voice. "They kept tellin' this kid that it's all in his head," says Don Rawls calmly. The VA doctors did not realize at the time that Jeff's problem was, indeed, in his head. His brain was shrinking.

By 1995, his cerebellum, the part of the brain that controls motor skills, had shrunk to less than a third of its original size. "All the testing they did," his mother Carol recalls with lingering frustration, "everything was normal. All the blood tests, everything." When it finally became clear from Jeff's MRIs that he had an unmistakably physical problem, his VA doctors concluded his problem was probably genetic, only according to the Rawlses, the VA refused to run the lab tests to verify it. "They wouldn't do it," says Carol Rawls, "they said it was too expensive." The VA wouldn't say how much it would cost, leaving the Rawlses thinking that it might cost thousands of dollars. They kept asking the VA to run the tests and the VA kept balking. This went on for months. As the Rawlses found out later, the DNA testing didn't cost thousands of dollars. It cost $350, which they could afford. But after all that dickering, the tests were a dead end. They were negative. Jeff Rawls did not have any genetic predisposition to a cerebellar degenerative disorder. That's when Jeff's VA doctors suggested that his problem might be due to chemical weapons exposure.

Jeff wasn't buying it.

"If it was a chemical weapon, more people would've had the same reaction," he protests. "You wouldn't see it like seven years later still in your system. It doesn't stay in your body that long."

This is consistent with everything I learned about nerve agents from the Army. During the Gulf War, I reported from Saudi Arabia and Iraq for NBC News. Like many other reporters who covered it, I received chemical warfare defense training from the Army, and those of us who stayed at the Dharhan International Hotel in eastern Saudi Arabia got extra training from an Englishman the hotel had hired to help protect its guests from such an attack—a middle-aged fellow who said he was ex-SAS (British Special Air Services). Nerve agents, he said with authority, act quickly. Even the slightest exposure could kill us. This is what the Army taught too: nerve agents take effect within a few seconds. A big dose will cause convulsions, paralysis, respiratory failure and death. It won't shrink your brain. Nor is there any evidence that they can cause problems that only become manifest several years after an alleged exposure. Jeff's ataxia appeared for the first time two years after the war.

"How did you know that?" I ask Jeff . . . about nerve agents not staying in the body very long.

"Just my chemical weapons training," he said.

"Did you get that training as a Marine?"

"Right," he says. Jeff speaks slowly and with great exertion. His speech sounds as if it had been recorded on tape, then played back at half speed. Speaking is a struggle, but telling this story is important to him. "Everything that I have been taught before—like from private on up to sergeant—is that if you are exposed to chemicals it'd be reacting instantly. It would not stay in your system for so long."

Whatever made Jeff sick, it did not wait for the VA to figure out what it was. Jeff's cerebellum kept getting smaller. His movements had become spastic and he could not walk in a straight line.[20] On a perfectly flat pavement, Jeff staggered back and forth as if on the deck of a ship in rough seas. He no longer had full control over what his arms would do. It was as though they were taking orders from someone else's brain. Writing was out of the question. He could barely hold a pen, and when he put the tip of one down on a page, all he could manage was a scrawl. Even a remotely legible scribble was beyond his abilities. The cerebellar atrophy had so impaired the muscles in his face and jaw that his speech was practically incomprehensible. As accustomed as his parents were to hearing him speak, they were now struggling to understand each word he said. Don was Jeff's chief interpreter at the VA hospital. "And even I had a hard time understanding him to relay the information to the doctors," says Don, "because they couldn't understand him anymore."

Another year went by, and Jeff's doctors still could not figure out what was wrong. His primary care physician, Dr. Joseph Booth, had grown particularly fond of him. Jeff had a particularly endearing quality; despite his catastrophic illness, he never complained. The initial suggestions that Jeff's problems were due to drinking appalled Booth. "You may occasionally see cerebellar degeneration with alcohol abuse," says Booth. But "Jeff does not drink. Jeff is as clean-cut as they come, a Marine reservist, nursing student, all-around nice guy. If there's anybody who's got a bad thing to say about Jeff Rawls . . . I know of nothing adverse in his records at all."

No one remembers exactly how they learned about Pam Asa, but they recall it had something to do with Herb Smith. Herb had become something of a poster child for Gulf War Syndrome. When he wasn't in the newspapers or on TV, he was messaging fellow veterans on the Internet about his illness. Word had spread via the web that Herb finally got a diagnosis when he went to Tennessee to see Kevin and Pam Asa.

When the Rawls family asked Dr. Booth to call Pam, he did not hesitate. He didn't admit this to the Rawlses, but calling Pam was almost an act of desperation. Jeff wasn't responding to any treatment—none of Jeff's doctors could figure out what they were supposed to treat. A consulting neurologist at the VA hospital in Albany, Dr. Arnulf Koeppen, thought Jeff might have something called "sporadic olivopontocerebellar atrophy" or "multiple system atrophy," but he couldn't be sure. "The only way to make a definitive diagnosis is through autopsy," he said.[21]

Booth didn't want to alarm the Rawlses, but something had to be done for Jeff, and soon, or the question of what was making him sick would be irrelevant. Booth picked up the receiver and dialed Memphis.

"No one is doing anything to help this boy," Asa recalls Booth saying. "If something isn't done for him, he's going to be dead in six months."

Pam Asa hung up and began doing some research on cerebellar atrophy. She found a paper published in France showing a possible link between this type of brain damage and autoimmunity.[22] It was a long shot, but she knew from Booth that Jeff was a Gulf War veteran. She called Dr. Booth back. After the two of them discussed the matter at length, Dr. Booth recommended that Jeff begin therapy with prednisone. Jeff and his family agreed. Now all they could do was wait and see.

A month went by, then another and another. The wait was excruciating, but now Booth could be certain of his results. The shrinkage had stopped.

Jeff would live.

"To be honest with yah as a parent," says Don Rawls, "this kid woulda been dead if it hadn't been for those treatments. The shakes that this poor kid was havin' . . . and the breathin' trouble that he was havin'. . . ." There is a slight hitch in his voice. He pauses. Thinking about how close his son came to dying is almost too much for him, but he regains his composure. "Between Dr. Booth and Pam Asa," he says, "they're the reason this kid is still alive."

"What do you think?" I ask Jeff. "Do you think you might've died from this?"

"I know I would've," says Jeff.

After his DNA tests came back negative, he became convinced that his Gulf War immunizations were to blame for his condition, only he couldn't find out what those immunizations were. His records were missing.

"American Legion can't find 'em," Jeff says. "VFW can't find 'em . . . League can't find 'em. Disabled American Veterans can't find 'em."

This makes Don Rawls even more suspicious about the shots. The military keeps records on everything, Don insists. "Our family history shows that my great, great grandfather fought for an Alabama regiment and was a prisoner of war in the state of Ohio. I can get my records from Vietnam. I can call Jefferson Barracks—the Air Force, that's where they keep 'em, and get those records."

Carol Rawls doesn't buy it either. She cannot believe there is not some record, somewhere, of her son's immunizations. "They don't exist," is what they told him. "Somebody's got 'em," Carol insists.

"Not on file is what they tell yah," says Don. "It's not on file."

Jeff says he grew even more skeptical when he asked the VA doctors if anyone else in his unit had ever been to the hospital. He says they replied that he was the only one.

"And I found out later I wasn't."

"Sixty-eight out of seventy-two individuals in his unit," says Don. (Later I called the highest-ranking non-commissioned officer in Jeff's unit, Master Gunnery Sergeant Bill Gleason, who said this was true.)

"They all got somethin'," Carol chimes in. "And they told him [Jeff] he was the only one."

Not to mention saying "that it's all in his head," Don says shaking his own head in disgust. Don looks at his son, sitting across from him at the dining room table. "The VA," he says to Jeff, "more or less, sent yah home to die and be forgotten."

———

That prednisone halted the shrinkage in Jeff's brain did not prove that he had an autoimmune problem. It also did not prove that Jeff had been injected with an unlicensed oil adjuvant. The prednisone had kept Jeff alive—that much Booth and Asa knew—but beyond that they could say very little. Pam did, however, take Jeff's case as further evidence, albeit anecdotal, that the problems afflicting sick Gulf War veterans were autoimmune—whether their diseases turned out to be lupus or not.

So far, when it came to diagnosing these veterans, Pam Asa had made the right call every time. Herb Smith had drifted through the VA system for years—saw doctors at the Mayo Clinic, University of Texas Southwestern Medical Center and the Walter Reed Army Medical Center—without anyone treating him for autoimmunity until Pam Asa spotted his swollen knuckles on *60 Minutes*. But however observant she had been as a clinician, it was immaterial when it came to proving her thesis about adjuvants. Until she had evidence to support her views, all she had was a hunch.

Before she could link these diseases to injection with an adjuvant, she first needed to know which one it was.

Patient X

Pam Asa was in the process of trying to figure that out when she met someone who could help her. I will call this person "Patient X." Patient X had gone to the Senate Veterans' Affairs Committee to report having symptoms that matched Gulf War Syndrome. Only Patient X hadn't been in the military, had never been to Saudi Arabia or Iraq, and had never inhaled so much as a single lungful of oil fire smoke. Patient X had never worn a flea collar (as some soldiers allegedly wore)[23] or a desert battle dress uniform impregnated with the arthropod repellent Permethrin. Patient X had never fired a depleted uranium shell from a tank, or had been near a vehicle hit with one. Patient X had never taken a pyridostigmine bromide pill, or got injected with either anthrax vaccine or botulinum toxoid. In other words, Patient X had not been exposed to a single agent cited as a possible cause for Gulf War Syndrome. Patient X had been injected with an experimental oil adjuvant.

Like most people, no one on the staff of the Senate Veterans' Affairs Committee had ever heard the word *adjuvant*. Senate staffers are busy people with lots of things competing for their attention. If you don't have an appointment and you're not a constituent, chances are you won't get much attention from a Senate committee staffer, assuming you actually get past the guards on Capitol Hill. Patient X might have been stranded on the wrong side of a Capitol Hill metal detector were it not for the fact that Patient X had a certain credential that piqued the committee's interest in this adjuvant thing. Patient X was a doctor.

Patient X had enrolled in a trial conducted by the National Institutes of Allergy and Infectious Diseases (NIAID) for an experimental herpes vaccine. The study was designated "93–1–0141, Chiron V5P13 Vaccine Trial."[24] Its principal investigator was Dr. Stephen E. Straus, who would be evaluating the vaccine as a therapy for people already infected with genital herpes.[25] Other than having genital herpes, "participants had to be 'healthy' in order to be eligible" for enrollment.[26] It was "placebo-controlled" study.[27] This meant that some of the participants would get injected with a non-therapeutic substance, a placebo—usually something harmless like salt water or a vitamin—while others received the actual vaccine. Those who received the placebo would constitute the "control group." The experiment had been organized to see if this new vaccine could actually cure genital herpes or diminish its effects. If the vaccine provided any benefit whatsoever, it would theoretically show up in the patients inoculated with it. To assess the degree of benefit, assuming that there was any, Straus would compare the condition of infected patients injected with vaccine against that of infected patients injected with a placebo. Getting a shot of saline or vitamin B12 was supposed to be tantamount to getting a shot of nothing at all.

NIAID's new herpes vaccine was a "sub-unit" preparation. Like the Army's anthrax vaccine, it did not contain a whole germ, or even parts of one. It was created from two herpes virus proteins that had been reproduced inside another microbe by recombinant DNA technology. Because of the weakness of such preparations, it was necessary to add an adjuvant. What set this study apart from ones done in the past was the placebo. It wasn't saline. It also wasn't a vitamin. The placebo used by Straus and his team was the adjuvant.

Two weeks after receiving one shot of adjuvant, Patient X developed "fibromyalgia" (a prolonged aching of joints and muscles), "suffered for extended periods from fasciculations" (the same muscle twitching experienced by Lt. Mary Jones after her anthrax shots), "rashes," "fatigue," "tingling in limbs" and "probable auto-immune peripheral neuropathy" (autoimmune damage to the peripheral nerves).[28] This type of damage could account for the tingling in Patient

X's limbs, the muscle twitching and fatigue. It can occur with lupus, multiple sclerosis, rheumatoid arthritis, polyarteritis nodosa, sural nerve vasculitis, Guillain-Barré syndrome, Sjögren's syndrome and amyotrophic lateral sclerosis (ALS)—all of which are autoimmune diseases with neurological dysfunction.

The Senate Veterans' Affairs Committee referred Patient X to Pam Asa. The two of them met at the Marriott Hotel in Crystal City, Virginia, not far from the Pentagon. Patient X said the symptoms first appeared about three weeks after the shot. The adverse reactions were so severe, Patient X had to take time off work; the muscle and joint pain, and the rashes still hadn't gone away. Patient X told the Senate Committee, and then Pam Asa, that the symptoms induced by this oil adjuvant were so similar to Gulf War Syndrome that it was conceivable these veterans had been injected with one too.

"I got injected with a placebo, which was the adjuvant," Pam recalls Patient X saying.

"An adjuvant is not a placebo," Pam said. She remembers Patient X looking surprised to hear that the practice of using an adjuvant as a placebo was a departure from standard protocols in the past. A placebo was supposed to be inert. It was not supposed to be an active pharmaceutical ingredient with possible side effects, which was the basis of Patient X's complaint. The people conducting the study had warned their subjects that there could be problems arising from the immunizations; the question is whether that warning had been sufficient. Patient X's attorney argued that the NIH failed to disclose that the adjuvant "is itself an experimental drug whose side effects are not yet fully known, and for which there had not yet been done adequate human testing to know at what levels different toxicities are to be expected."

"So what was this adjuvant?" Pam asked.

"MF59," said Patient X.

"And what is that?"

Patient X had researched this, and was ready for the question.

"MF59 is squalene and water."

NIH's Eyes on the Prize

At the time this meeting took place, little had been published on the toxicity of squalene since Frances Beck's research at UCLA in the 1970s.[29] No laboratory—government, academic or commercial—had followed up with experiments meant to relate Beck's findings to the oil's effects in humans. Nearly fourteen years had passed since researchers at the National Cancer Institute first extolled the merits of squalene in a paper that made scant mention of Beck's discovery that it could induce the animal version of multiple sclerosis.[30] Narrowly focused on squalene's effectiveness at boosting the immune response to weak vaccines, NIH investigators promoted the oil's use in a variety of immunizations. Were it only a matter of developing a vaccine for genital herpes, there might have been less incentive to find a new adjuvant, and perhaps less of the carelessness that comes with haste. And there *was* haste. NIH's eyes were on a different prize—AIDS. By 1990, AIDS had become a leading cause of death in America. More than 100,000 Americans had died from this disease in the previous decade. A third of those deaths came in 1990 alone. So with some justification, NIH wanted this new adjuvant, and fast.

Maybe too fast. Scientists had identified human immunodeficiency virus (HIV), the virus causing AIDS, back in 1984, yet by 1990 only one HIV vaccine study had paid any attention at all to adjuvants, and this study did not concern itself with adjuvant safety.[31] So intent were NIH investigators on developing an effective vaccine against HIV that the question of squalene's safety does not appear to have come up. The NIH wasn't looking at this issue and wasn't going out of its way to fund anyone who did.[32]

Patient X's herpes vaccine trial was an example of NIH's larger strategy for combating incurable diseases like HIV. Chronic viral infections had proven unresponsive to antiviral medicines. So in the late 1980s, Jonas Salk—the same Jonas Salk who ran the Army's experiment with oil adjuvants given to troops at Fort Dix—and the Army's leading HIV vaccine researcher, Lt. Col. Robert Redfield, started promoting the idea of "therapeutic" vaccines. This idea wasn't just novel, it was revolutionary. Since Edward Jenner developed the world's first vaccine in the eighteenth century, there had never been such a thing. Vaccines were conceived as a means to prevent infections, not to cure them once they had occurred. Salk and Redfield proposed to somehow enhance and amplify the immune response to an infectious agent, specifically HIV, with a vaccine in an attempt to mitigate its effects.[33] This was what Straus's herpes vaccine trial ultimately was all about—postinfection immunotherapy that could lead to an effective treatment for AIDS.[34] "The ability to influence the frequency of genital herpes outbreaks with this vaccine inspires optimism that similar successes may be possible for other chronic viral diseases such as AIDS," Straus wrote.[35]

Such was the mentality that had taken hold of the U.S. public health establishment by the late 1980s. It's not that it was reckless or lunatic, though you can find people who will say it was both. I prefer to see it as pushing the envelope. Conventional approaches to combating HIV and AIDS were not working. Infections were multiplying exponentially each year. While some of the ideas that were proposed seem ridiculous in retrospect, AIDS was a problem that desperately needed new thinking. The phenomenon of inherently cautious scientists shrugging off conventions to take chances on a new idea was only to be commended.

—

Still, even if the proper groundwork had not been laid for testing the stuff in humans, by the time of Stephen Straus's herpes vaccine trial with MF59, experiments in animals clearly indicated that oil additives, and squalene in particular, were a lot less safe than they were reputed to be. In 1992, scientists at the Massachusetts Institute of Technology compared Freund's Complete Adjuvant—which had proven too toxic for human use as far back as the 1930s—to Ribi adjuvant, the commercial name for the Triple Mix concoction that the Army had been mixing into its breakthrough single-shot anthrax vaccine. Ribi was a modified Freund's. By design it was nearly identical—bacterial fragments emulsified in oil, only different fragments in different oil. Unfortunately, the MIT group got more or less the same damage too. Ribi did produce a better antibody response than Freund's, which was a good thing, but Ribi also caused similar destruction to tissue.[36] Mice injected with Ribi developed granulomas, just as they did when injected with Freund's. Granulomas are lesions—abnormal changes in tissue—that are caused when a foreign antigen is so irritating to the body that the immune system literally tries to wall it off.[37] Immune cells surround the irritant—which can be a particle of something like silica or a germ—and fuse together into larger masses called "giant cells." These giant cells then form a kind of cytoplasmic gasket that seals off a pathogen from the surrounding tissue. Granulomas are a bad thing. If too many of them form, necrosis or tissue death can occur. Mice injected with Ribi not only developed granulomas, scar tissue formed in their viscera. The scar tissues acted like an adhesive (they are called "adhesions") that made the abdominal organs of MIT's mice stick to one another, or to the walls of their abdominal cavities. This was a bad thing too.

But having reported this type of damage associated with a squalene emulsion, MIT's investigators concluded their report by saying "we are encouraged by the preliminary success of the Ribi system."[38] Success . . . but at the price of inducing granulomas and scar tissue? You get a better antibody response with Ribi adjuvant, but your organs will stick together and your tissues could die? These conclusions were strangely out of sync with the data.

A year later, scientists working for the Dutch government published similar findings to MIT's in a study conducted out of entirely different concerns— cruelty to animals. Freund's Complete Adjuvant caused too much pain and distress in animals injected with it. In the hope of finding a more humane oil adjuvant, the Dutch scientists compared the effects of what was commercially available at the time, including two squalene emulsions—Ribi and Hunter TiterMax.[39] They discovered that the two squalene emulsions caused "severe effects" and "considerable lesions" in rabbits—but without the benefit of the improved antibody responses observed at MIT.[40] The rabbits got pain but no gain. In this particular study, Ribi proved the most harmful, producing "the largest number and most severe lesions when compared with the other adjuvants."[41] The Dutch group concluded that only a formulation called Specol, which did not contain squalene, might be an acceptable alternative to Freund's.[42]

Most of the research showing problems with squalene emulsions was published overseas. In 1994, two scientists published some of the most damaging findings yet. Injecting rats with pure squalene, with nothing else in it, caused severe arthritis.[43] This was an astonishing result given the conventional wisdom of the times. Squalene was supposed to be safe because it was "metabolizable." When it did cause disease in previous experiments, it had always been mixed with something else. Now scientists had proven for the first time anywhere that squalene alone could initiate an autoimmune disease. Not surprisingly, the two scientists who proved this were foreign—Japanese, and working in Australia at the time. In the United States, there was too much riding on squalene to criticize it.

Given NIH's considerable investment in squalene, these results from the Pacific Rim were positively subversive. Yet, no one at NIH attacked this work. No one said, "We reject this result because it threatens billions of dollars' worth of HIV vaccine research." Instead they did something worse: they ignored it. The Japanese scientists, Shin and Junko Yoshino, had discovered something of great relevance to vaccine research at the National Institutes of Health. But you would never know it. If you review the U.S. research published in the '90s on prototype HIV vaccines and then the papers published specifically on adjuvants, you'll have a hard time finding a single citation to the Yoshinos' paper. You won't find references to the Dutch research either, or even that at UCLA or MIT. It's as if this work didn't exist.

And people suffered for it. In one of the earliest publicly acknowledged human experiments with a vaccine containing squalene, scientists at Baylor College of Medicine injected five volunteers with an influenza vaccine combined with an earlier formulation of MF59 called MF59–100 (which also contained squalene).[44] The five volunteers given flu vaccine without MF59–100 had little to complain about. Two of them developed "mild tenderness at the injection site."[45] One felt nauseated for "a brief period immediately after injection."[46] That was all. The five volunteers injected with vaccine containing MF59–100, on the other hand, had a different experience. After just one shot, all of them suffered "moderate to severe local and systemic reactions."[47] Within twelve hours after inoculation, they were suddenly beset by "chills, myalgia (muscle ache), headaches, malaise or fatigue, and nausea."[48] Two of the five volunteers given the vaccine plus adjuvant "reported dizziness"—one of them "vomited."[49] Three out of the five developed a "fever of over 100°F (37.7°C)."[50]

The adverse reactions in the Baylor study should have influenced what NIH did next if for no other reason than geography; Baylor was in America, and the work was published in a U.S. medical journal, not a veterinary journal like the Dutch and MIT studies. In addition to the class divide between medical and veterinary researchers, there is in American scientific circles an unspoken suspicion about data published overseas. There are notable exceptions to this attitude, of course. The British journal *Nature* is acknowledged by many to be the world's best; its American counterpart *Science* is a close second. Both of these publications are intellectually omnivorous. By reputation, they publish the most significant new findings in a range of scientific disciplines. Then there is a presumed hierarchy among specialist journals—those devoted to orthopedics or cardiology or endocrinology. The degree of respect accorded to these publications is related to their longevity. Some of the oldest medical journals, like the *Journal of the American Medical Association* (JAMA) or the *New England Journal of Medicine* (NEJM), are held in high esteem—in part because of their vintage (both date back to the nineteenth century), and aggressive self-promotion. (Their British equivalents, the *Lancet* and the *British Medical Journal,* also command worldwide respect.) This hierarchical milieu is supported by academic snobbery. If a team of American scientists publishes abroad in any but the top British publications, I have heard U.S. scientists ask dismissively, "Couldn't they get it published here?" Scientists jokingly refer to this is as "NIH syndrome"— Not Invented Here.

By the early 1990s, however, NIH's "see-no-evil" stance on squalene could no longer be understood in nationalistic terms. Scientists at UCLA Medical Center, MIT and Baylor College of Medicine—highly respected academic institutions in the United States— were detecting problems with squalene emulsions. Baylor observed these problems in humans, in a study partially funded by NIH.[51] What's more, three of the six authors listed on the Baylor paper worked for Chiron Biocine, the manufacturer of MF59–100 and MF59.[52]

There is no evidence that Dr. Straus—the Chief of Laboratory Investigations at NIAID and the principal investigator for the NIH herpes vaccine trial in which Patient X participated—knew about the accumulating data on squalene's toxicity in animals, or the problems with Chiron's squalene emulsion at Baylor. He makes no reference to Beck's work in his reports of the study, nor of any other work concerning adjuvant toxicity. Published papers saying squalene emulsions like TiterMax are a "safe, effective and chemically defined alternative" to Freund's Complete Adjuvant were reassuring.[53] Yet Straus *did* know there were safety questions about an MF59 variant from another trial, because Chiron wrote to him about it.

In a letter dated 6 July 1993, Dr. Straus informed his superiors at the NIH that a suit had been brought against Chiron by a former participant in a vaccine trial that Chiron had "conducted elsewhere in 1991."[54] The plaintiff claimed to have developed "persisting pain in the muscle and joints beginning several minutes after a vaccine that trial [sic]," wrote Straus. "The suit," he went on, "claims induction of fibromylagia by the vaccine."

The plaintiff in that lawsuit had been injected with a prototype herpes vaccine containing MF59–100—the same stuff that caused similar adverse reactions in the study at Baylor. It is unclear whether Chiron was aware of this study, or of the autoimmune diseases that Beck at UCLA had induced with squalene, or the work by the Dutch or by the Japanese scientists in Australia that generated similar results. At the time, Chiron made no reference to any of these studies in its publications on MF59–100 or MF59. But NIH had copies of these studies in its database where I found them myself. However NIH investigators continued to put squalene emulsions into their prototype vaccines for cancer and HIV.

Patient X did not know about this research at the time; nor did any other participant in the Straus study. The NIH consent form simply told them that "3 out of 63 subjects enrolled in another study had developed some painful sensations in their arms or legs or muscle aches that in one patient resembled fibromyalgia." The only indication that MF59 itself might be a problem was limited to a single sentence: "These subjects [i.e. the three who dropped out of the other study] had received a vaccine with herpes proteins plus MF59 or MF59 alone."[55] Patient X's attorney protested to the NIH that "By no definition is a one sentence statement that the placebo vaccine has side effects adequate to provide [Patient X] or other participants with sufficient information to make an informed consent."[56] Patient X's attorney had no idea how inadequate this one sentence truly was. Neither, apparently, did the court that ruled on the case; it threw out Patient X's lawsuit. As for NIH, its clinical investigators did not need lawsuits to raise doubts about the dangers of injected squalene. They need only have spent time in their own library. All of the papers showing squalene's toxicity in animals and its possible links to adverse reactions in humans were all archived just down the street in Bethesda, at the National Library of Medicine.

The lines between negligence and carelessness, and carelessness and laziness, are blurry ones. In the NIH documents concerning this specific vaccine study there is no evidence of deliberate negligence to advance a scientific or commercial agenda. Two things, however, deserve further scrutiny. First, Patient X left the study because of illness, yet Straus reported in his paper about the study that "No subject refused revaccination or withdrew from the study because of side-effects."[57] The second question concerns the side effects that

Straus observed in patients who remained. "Reactions to vaccination were extremely common," he writes. How common? Out of 98 participants, 93 experienced adverse reactions, including "44 out of 49 placebo recipients." So *ninety percent* of the patients immunized with the squalene emulsion, MF59, suffered side effects. The adverse reactions recorded by Straus included fevers (101° F or 38.3°C), chills, myalgia (muscle pain), arthralgias (joint pain) and nausea.

The reactions were "typically mild," Straus reports, but however mild the reactions to the placebo immunizations allegedly were, there should have been none at all. Placebos were originally conceived as "dummy treatments" that were supposed to have no pharmacological effect. They were given strictly for psychological reasons. The mind exerts a powerful influence on the body; those given a drug or vaccine might *think* they felt better merely because they knew they were getting treatment. To compensate for that possibility, control patients, those given a placebo, received in essence no treatment at all. The placebo injections might have contained salt water or a vitamin, but nothing that could actually improve their condition. In the late '80s and early '90s, when scientists came up with the idea of immunotherapeutic vaccines, they started immunizing patients with experimental adjuvants as a placebo because they rationalized that adjuvants worked "non-specifically." When injecting someone with a herpes vaccine, its intended target is the herpes virus. Adjuvants were supposed to promote more robust responses from the immune system, but not act directly on the infectious agent. The researchers needed a group injected with the adjuvant alone; otherwise, they couldn't know whether the effects they observed came from the adjuvant or from the active ingredient.

The problem with using experimental adjuvants as a placebo was this: as Straus himself noted in his study, the squalene adjuvant he used, MF59, had side effects. Adjuvants were not inert substances. They had a clear pharmacological effect. Giving one group a vaccine containing adjuvant, and the control group the adjuvant only, meant every patient got a dose of something with proven risks. The side effects "did not differ significantly between the groups," wrote Straus in his paper.[58] Of course they didn't. Both groups got injected with the oil adjuvant. If there were any side effects specifically associated with MF59, then injecting it into the control patients would make the extent and severity of those side effects less obvious. Using the newest generation of oil adjuvants as placebos would be an effective way to mask the problems.

The equivalent of "read the fine print" for a scientific paper is "read the data." The interpretation of the data can be skewed by an author to support a larger agenda. Or an author can make mistakes.

Based on the absence of any rigorous discussion on squalene's safety in the open scientific literature at the time, or in unsealed court documents, there remained unanswered, indeed unasked, questions about whether or not the NIH or its sister agency, the FDA, had handled this matter responsibly. There is also a question of whether the Army had acted any more responsibly, because by 1995, Fort Detrick had abandoned use of Tri-Mix and DeTox—the squalene emulsions it had been using prior to the Gulf War. Now the Army was evaluating MF59 for inclusion in its second-generation anthrax vaccine.[59]

———

Pam Asa first wrote the Pentagon about her theory that Gulf War veterans were sick with autoimmune diseases due to injections with a squalene adjuvant—specifically MF59—in 1995. In return, the Pentagon did not send her a congratulatory bouquet.

She had mounting evidence that sick Gulf War veterans were suffering from neurological damage caused by autoimmunity. Because the majority of these victims appeared to be men, she suspected that their autoimmune diseases resulted from something other than random exposure to some cryptotoxin in the environment. Some of the mysterious ailments tentatively linked to service in the Gulf were allegedly being transmitted to family members, but in these cases the illnesses did not appear to be autoimmune.

By the mid-1990s, it would have been clear to anyone reading the latest scientific papers on cutting-edge vaccines that squalene emulsions were the preferred adjuvants for two of the most powerful medical research bureaucracies in America—the Department of Health and Human Services and the Department of Defense. For a lone immunologist in Tennessee, whose main job was raising four kids, Pam Asa had taken on formidable opponents. She had a theory based on clinical observations that she had made in a limited number of cases, but no hard evidence. Her idea that military personnel were suffering from adjuvant-induced autoimmunity presumed conduct by military doctors that may have breached regulations for clinical trials with devastating consequences on the health of U.S. troops. Pam Asa was not about to get the support of military doctors or NIH investigators in proving that their adjuvant-of-choice had made people incurably ill. Without government funding, she would have no way to acquire the data necessary to prove her point. Pam Asa faced a lopsided fight in which she had virtually no ammunition. If there was any time for her back off, this was it.

Chapter Eight

The Antibodies

Pam Asa will tell you that her refusal to back down from something she believes in is a trait she acquired from her father, Lou Burdette. Before Lou was a NASA engineer, he was a Marine. He fought at Guadalcanal—America's first offensive of the Pacific War—where he learned to be fearless about what he needed to do and was fortunate enough to survive that lesson. Lou Burdette was 6 feet 4 inches tall and weighed about 200 pounds; he didn't scare easily. But once the ramp of his Higgins boat dropped down on that empty beach at Guadalcanal and Lou walked into the treeline of a malarial jungle so dense with cassia, liana vines and twisted creepers that in places he could not see an enemy five feet in front of him, he was scared. Everyone was. He was scared the first night the Japanese infantry charged through the waist-high kunai grass near the perimeter of Henderson Field, shrieking *"Banzai! Totsugeki!* [Charge!] *Banzai!"* He was more scared the night a Marine officer shouted: "Nobody moves! Just die in your holes!" And he didn't stop being scared when the fighting was over, when his enemies lay dead before him, their blood still glistening on his Kabar knife. Some of the Marine raiders, stunned by these fanatical assaults, staggered away from their positions, but they were ordered back. Had they refused to return, on any of those nights when the Japanese charged from the jungle waving samurai swords and firing Nambu light machine guns from their hips, it would have left gaps in the line. The whole company could have been overrun.

On those terrifying nights, near cathedrals of soaring banyans, ipils and eucalyptus, Lou Burdette came to believe that some things in life were more important than his own survival. He stayed put, like all those other gyrenes less fortunate than him—the ones who fell defending their positions. A lot more would have died in those attacks had they made a different choice. But they chose to fight, in some places until only one man was left standing. Had Henderson Field fallen to the Japanese, the entire island could have been lost. Had Guadalcanal been lost, the Japanese would have regained mastery of the sea lanes between Australia and the United States. Had the Japanese been able to land their Zeroes and Bettys at Henderson, an airstrip they had started building before losing it to the Marines, it would have given them control of not one but two airfields, one on Rabaul and one on Guadalcanal, and Japanese planes would have threatened Allied shipping for nearly a thousand miles in every direction. The choice made by each of those Marines to stand and fight helped alter the course of the Pacific war.

Decades later, when Lou was responsible for quality control at NASA's Redstone Arsenal, he caught a big U.S. corporation cutting corners on the manufacturing of a Saturn rocket part to save money—something that could endanger the lives of American astronauts. He didn't flinch when an executive with that corporation got ugly. "Either you make that part the way it's supposed to be made," said Lou, recounting the story for his daughter, "or I'm gonna call a federal marshal." Then, he told Pam, to prevent the corporation from tampering with the disputed parts or removing them to conceal what it had done, "I threatened to clear the building and padlock the doors." Pam still remembers how angry her dad was, and how proud she was of him. For Lou there was only one way of doing something and that was the right way. When he told his daughter about this showdown, he repeated something that he'd told her over and over as she grew up: *never compromise on safety*—an admonition to a child that might sound strange coming from anyone else but a quality control officer at NASA. It was the one part of his job that Lou took home with him. Safety was always on his mind—it didn't matter if it was a Titan II rocket, making a campfire with the local Boy Scout troop or changing a tire.

So Pam Asa didn't find long odds daunting. She was not the sort of person to go looking for a fight, but she wouldn't run from a fight either. For Pam, this fight was necessary. She had personal reasons for being concerned about the safety of vaccines being given to the military. Two of those reasons were her cousins—both Marines who had served in Vietnam, one of whom had a son who received an appointment to the Air Force Academy.[1] She felt protective of her nephew. She couldn't bear the thought of military doctors injecting him with something that could give him lupus or MS. And then there were her own sons, Chris, Michael and Bryan. If there was ever a draft, she didn't want the same thing happening to them that happened to Carol Rawls's boy.

When it dawned on Pam that military doctors might have immunized Gulf War troops with an oil adjuvant, she wrote letters about her theory to officials at the Pentagon. It never occurred to her that because her thesis presumed ethically dubious conduct by military doctors it might not receive the fair hearing that she expected. Even when she read articles on the case of Lt. Col Robert Redfield, one of the Army's leading vaccine researchers who used oil additives in his prototype HIV vaccine, she remained upbeat, even Pollyannaish. Had she read the articles more closely, a little cynicism might have been in order. Redfield stood accused by his own colleagues of altering his statistics to make it appear that his prototype HIV vaccine worked better than it really did. When two senior Air Force doctors reviewed a paper that Redfield published in the *New England Journal of Medicine,* they were scathing.[2] They said Redfield had been "sloppy or, possibly, deceptive." His statistical methods were at best "unorthodox." At worst his methods "abuse the data" to come up with desired conclusions. The Army refused to allow an independent review of Redfield's account. Instead it ran its own investigation, which concluded the evidence "does not support the allegations of scientific misconduct." Few people were convinced by the Army's self-investigation (run by a former chairman of Project Badger), not even other Army scientists.[3] "The Army had the fox in the hen house for this one," a colleague of Redfield's told a reporter from *Science* magazine. "I'd like to see another formal investigation done by the Navy, Air Force, and Army together."[4] That didn't happen.

While Pam Asa was personally convinced that the Army's investigation of Redfield was a whitewash, she still believed that the service could be impartial when it came to evaluating *her* allegations. This was not her father's belief in doing what was right no matter the cost. This was something else. Pam Asa had convinced herself that had the military's doctors, indeed, given troops an oil adjuvant, they would be grateful to know how dangerous it really was because it would give them a chance to fix the problem. However unlikely this was, given the Army's handling of the Redfield case, Asa clung to this view with an almost religious conviction. They would recognize their error and re-pent of their mistake. Once they were blind; now they would see.

But it was a toss-up who was blinder. Tangling with the Pentagon is a full-contact sport that doesn't favor women. Much as the Pentagon might protest to the contrary, gender still mattered. Asa's chief Pentagon contact at the time, Air Force Col. Ed Koenigsburg, even told her matter-of-factly that because she was a woman, the generals would take her less seriously. She suffered from just about every conceivable disadvantage in any fight with the military's doctors and scientists. In a world of "insiders"—where to be truly "inside" one needed to be tenured at a major university, preferably an Ivy League one—Pam could not have been more of an outsider. Not only was she a woman, she was a Southerner. She wasn't a faculty member, tenured or otherwise, at any university. She saw patients in her husband's clinical practice in Memphis, Tennessee—far from the ivy-festooned quadrangles of the northeast, and in Elvis country no less. Believing that she, a southern woman whose sole aca-demic credentials were her Ph.D. and a handful of published papers, could unravel one of the biggest medical mysteries of our time was like believing David could defeat Goliath without a sling.

On the other hand, being an outsider gave Pam Asa the freedom to pursue her theory in the first place. Working outside of academia meant she worked outside a system where the boundaries of intellectual freedom were drawn by what the NIH and U.S. Public Health Service—or even the Department of Defense—were willing to fund. Pam Asa did not need a grant from NIH or USPHS or DOD, which was a good thing, because the prospects of her get-ting one to prove this particular hypothesis were nil.

By 1997, hundreds of millions of dollars had been spent testing the efficacy of vaccines formulated with squalene adjuvants. NIH's investment in squa-lene, however presumptive, could not be reversed without cadres of govern-ment scientists, by reputation some of America's best and brightest, losing face and funding. The National Cancer Institute had been conducting re-search with squalene-boosted vaccines for nearly two decades. The Depart-ment of Defense began incorporating squalene adjuvants into prototype anthrax vaccines in 1987; the National Institutes of Allergy and Infectious Diseases began animal research with squalene adjuvants a year later.[5] NIAID-sponsored clinical trials in humans with squalene began at the same time as Operation Desert Storm, in January 1991.[6] Over the next six years, NIAID would fund twenty-three clinical trials to test vaccines with squalene adjuvants; nineteen of those trials were for prototype HIV vaccines.[7] The Department of Defense had run five of its own trials to test squalene-boosted immunizations for malaria and HIV.[8] Squalene adjuvants were a key ingredient in a whole new generation of vaccines intended for mass immunization around the globe, including two vaccines for diseases considered a threat to both U.S. military readiness and national security—HIV and anthrax. If squalene was as dangerous as Pam Asa maintained, NIH and the Pentagon had a lot to lose.

Unknown to Asa at the time, the Department of Defense, the FDA and the NIH were about to form a "Working Group" to accelerate the development of the Army's second-generation anthrax vaccine. The scientists at Fort Detrick had chosen which of its recombinant DNA systems it would use to make the new vaccine. All they needed now was an adjuvant; two of the five leading candidates, including MF59, contained squalene.[9]

Asa was a threat to the single most important franchise in U.S. biodefense planning. The Pentagon and its partners would have to take steps to protect it.

The Flavor of the Month

When Pam Asa finally got a response from the Deputy Assistant Secretary of Defense for Health Affairs, it was a lengthy attack that attempted to demolish her theory without a single reference to the existing data showing squalene's toxicity. A more cynical observer might have thought this inevitable, but Asa was stunned. She read the report with incredulity. An independent contractor had reviewed her allegations for the Department of Defense and concluded that it was "generally unsupported."[10] Before Pam Asa even had a chance to read the report and respond to it, the Pentagon had posted it on the Internet. Alum, it said, was the only adjuvant given to U.S. military personnel in the Gulf.[11] According to the report, calling the alleged problem a "Human adjuvant disease (HAD)," as Pam had done, was old-fashioned and therefore misleading; HAD, said the author of this report, was a term "generally not used by most informed physicians today." And while admitting that "There is a similarity between HAD and Gulf War syndrome," the report insisted that HAD took years to develop, "not months."

This report was hardly as independent as the Pentagon alleged. Its author was Dr. Walter E. Brandt, one of the two members of Project Badger responsible for procuring a second source of anthrax vaccine for the Persian Gulf War, and a scientist who helped oversee the postwar scale-up of the Army's recombinant DNA anthrax vaccine combined with squalene emulsions.[12] Brandt sent his critique of Asa's theory to the Commander of the U.S. Army Medical Research and Materiel Command, the Fort Detrick bureaucracy in charge of developing this new vaccine. Brandt had also sent his review to Dr. Anna Johnson-Winegar—the same Anna Johnson-Winegar who sat at a Fort Detrick lab bench back in 1980, working on the Army's first attempts to make an improved anthrax vaccine after the incident in Sverdlovsk; the same Anna Johnson-Winegar who led Project Badger's effort to find a second source of anthrax vaccine prior to the Gulf War, and who along with Brandt after the war, had directed further development of the new vaccine. Johnson-Winegar, who was steadily climbing the military's medical defense bureaucracy, was paying close attention to this crazy new theory from a Memphis housewife and part-time clinician named Pam Asa.

The connection between Brandt and Johnson-Winegar is enough to cast doubt on the impartiality of Brandt's critique, but there was more. When Brandt wrote his attack on Asa's theory, he worked for Science Applications International Corporation (SAIC). SAIC operated the National Cancer Institute facilities at Fort Detrick, where the Army first started producing large batches of the new anthrax vaccine; SAIC managed payrolls and vacation schedules and other administrative tasks. It also helped coordinate NIH efforts to develop vaccines for both cancer and AIDS. If there was a single common denominator to these vaccines, it was squalene. SAIC, like NIH and NCI, had a franchise to protect. According to SAIC's website, the company possessed the "the largest single research contract awarded by the Department of Health and Human Services." All of this made Brandt's and Johnson-Winegar's connection to any attack on Asa especially suspicious because of what the National Cancer Institute was doing at the time. NCI was making the first batch of recombinant protective antigen for the Army's second-generation anthrax vaccine.

NCI was supposed to be one of Anna Johnson-Winegar's alternate sources of anthrax vaccine for the Gulf War. But the Army's plans to make anthrax vaccine at NCI for Desert Storm had foundered; NCI couldn't get its new fermenters running in time.[13] Next time NCI would be ready. As the sole government institution that had agreed to join the prewar effort to "surge" the production of the old vaccine, it had a head start on making the new one. It wouldn't have the same start-up problems it experienced before because it would be making a different vaccine in a different facility. This time NCI would rely on another of its Fort Detrick labs, with an older and smaller fermenter that could nevertheless produce sizable batches of protective antigen . . . provided it was made by the new recombinant DNA method.

The National Cancer Institute had several laboratories at Fort Detrick, including the two that were given the task of making protective antigen for the new vaccine. According to U.S. Army sources who have requested anonymity to protect their careers, the work began in Building 325, South Wing, then moved to Building 472, a two-story structure of Korean War vintage not far from the old Eight Ball. Many of the buildings at Detrick are spread out from each other. Building 472 is tucked in one of the more cramped areas where brick chimneys and above-ground steam pipes abound. It could be anywhere in America's rust belt—not the sort of place where you'd expect to see cutting-edge science being done. For the Army, this arrangement couldn't have been more convenient.

The lab is still there. Next to the entrance is a small sign that says:

BUILDING 472
RECOVERY PLANT
GMP PRODUCTION FACILITY
AUTHORIZED PERSONNEL ONLY

By Fort Detrick standards, this facility is unique; it is a "GMP"—Good Manufacturing Practice lab. "Meaning that [materials produced there] would be suitable for use in humans," says one of the Army sources directly involved with making this material, "that it meets the documentation and quality standards of the FDA."

"If you are making vaccine components strictly for research work in animals," I ask, "is it common practice to manufacture these components under GMP conditions?"

"No," says this source. "Material for doing pure experiments is not produced under GMP."

By the time Pam Asa had reached the troubling conclusion that Gulf War troops had been injected with an unlicensed oil adjuvant, Army scientists had produced enough of the recombinant protective antigen in the NCI lab for a large-scale clinical trial. According to confidential military sources, by the summer of 1996 the lab in Building 472 had produced enough recombinant anthrax protein for at least 10,000 doses of new vaccine.[14] This was the year that General Ronald Blanck had told the Joint Chiefs the Army's new recombinant anthrax vaccine would be available for general use. Blanck was now Army Surgeon General, and Fort Detrick had switched from "Triple Mix," the original squalene emulsion in its new and improved anthrax vaccine, to another adjuvant, MF59. MF59, as Patient X had informed Pam Asa, and as anyone could read for themselves in published scientific papers, consisted of water, a detergent and squalene.

It is a wonder that the attack on Asa was not even more severe. It had been almost a year since she sent Col. Koenigsburg a summary of her theory that specifically identified MF59 as a potential problem. She called it "Report on Gulf War Syndrome"—a title so bland it gave no clue as to its inflammatory contents; in it she cited no fewer than nine recently published scientific papers on prototype vaccines with MF59 in which the authors had simply assumed it was safe.[15] What concerned Asa, but not apparently anyone else, was that these trials directly involved scientists from the Chiron Corporation, the company that made MF59. It was in Chiron's financial interest to conclude that its product was safe, even when, as Pam Asa saw it, there was evidence to the contrary. "It has been very disturbing to find it used in humans with adverse side effects (influenza and herpes) without seeing more preclinical studies and toxicological studies being done," she wrote in her report to the Defense Department.[16] "We have tried to obtain this information from the company along with the teratological data. The company would not send this nor could it be obtained from the NIH."[17]

It was also in the Army's interests. Fort Detrick had just completed production of a big batch of recombinant protection antigen for possible clinical trials in humans; it was now formulating its prototype anthrax vaccine with squalene adjuvants, including the increasingly ubiquitous MF59. As a solver of mysteries, Pam could not have had more auspicious timing; from Fort Detrick's point of view, her timing could not have been worse.

But the scientists at Fort Detrick were not the only ones inconvenienced by Asa's squalene theory, and for reasons other than the Army's new anthrax vaccine, now co-sponsored by the NIH. Many of the prototype HIV vaccines then in development at the NIH contained MF59. Scientists working on these vaccines had discovered that their chief ingredient—a glycoprotein produced by the virus called "gp120"—did not stick to alum particles very well.[18] They tried adsorbing gp120 onto alum, just as the Army did with the protective antigen protein in its licensed anthrax vaccine. But after doing this, the gp120/alum particles "desorbed"—they fell apart. Without an adjuvant, gp120 barely elicited an immune response. So scientists working on HIV vaccines resorted to MF59. MF59 was not just flavor of the month; it had become the only flavor. There were few viable alternatives. By questioning the safety of squalene, Asa imperiled more than 80 percent of the existing NIH-sponsored clinical trials for vaccines to prevent HIV—America's number one public health priority.

For myriad reasons other than squalene's alleged links to Gulf War Syndrome, scientists working for the Army and NIH had a lot riding on Pam Asa's being proven wrong. This was the drama occurring behind the scenes; even Asa was unaware of how extensive and Byzantine it truly was. She was acutely aware, however, of another unfolding drama. Played out in front of network television cameras, it drew attention away from any possible link between the military's experimental vaccines and sick Gulf War veterans.

The Nerve Agent Theory

It did not begin as a diversion. The idea that chemical weapons might have caused Gulf War Syndrome came from the veterans themselves. On June 30, 1993, several of them appeared before the Senate Armed Services Committee to report on unexplained incidents during the Gulf War that they believed to be unacknowledged chemical warfare attacks.[19] One month later, more evidence emerged that seemed to corroborate suspicions that Gulf War troops had been somehow exposed to chemical weapons. Czechoslovakia's Minister of Defense reported that a Czech chemical decontamination unit had detected the nerve agent sarin in northern Saudi Arabia during the war.[20] These detections did not result from an actual attack, the Czechs concluded, but from unanticipated fallout from the bombing of Iraqi chemical weapons plants.[21] An investigation into the possible causes of Gulf War Syndrome conducted by the Senate Committee on Banking, Housing and Urban Affairs supported "the conclusion that U.S. forces were exposed to chemical agents."[22] When the Senate Banking Committee released its report in 1995, the Defense Department estimated there were hundreds of sick veterans; the Veterans' Administration guessed thousands.[23] Belief in the chemical weapons scenario spread among the sick. Even Herb Smith became a convert. It was Smith's appearance in that *60 Minutes* broadcast on alleged chemical weapons exposures in the Gulf that brought him to Pam Asa's attention. "We were getting hammered with a lot of information that we were actually affected by chemicals," says Smith. "I was getting sick enough where I couldn't argue with anyone. I was really very, very passive."

By 1997, it was clear that some of the most common complaints among Desert Storm veterans were neurological.[24] That was the year the CIA and the Department of Defense jointly released a computer model of an alleged plume of sarin and cyclosarin nerve agents released by the demolition of an Iraqi ammunition dump at Khamisiyah.[25] The Pentagon had previously denied that the Iraqis had stored chemical munitions close enough to coalition troops to affect them had those munitions been blown up. The Khamisiyah revelation seemed to be a rare government admission that it had made a mistake. The Army's 37th Engineer Battalion had blown up 122mm rockets containing sarin and cyclosarin. According to the CIA, on March 10, 1991, and for the next three days, a lethal plume emanated from Khamisiyah.[26] Because of shifting winds, the CIA reported, this plume blew in several directions—one day blowing downrange more than 180 miles south into Saudi Arabia, another day over the Euphrates River Valley. Sarin is highly volatile, which means it quickly evaporates. But the evaporation rate slows if the agent seeps into the ground and saturates wood debris, which occurred at Khamisiyah, according to the CIA. Evaporating agent from the soil and wood "refreshed the plume," said the CIA, sending up "new tendrils" of sarin into the atmosphere.

As political theater goes, the Khamisiyah revelation had a lot going for it—elements of mystery, the hint of a cover-up, sympathetic victims, and a villain, Saddam Hussein, that everyone in America loved to hate. Nerve gas/neurological damage; the implied message was that it was all really Saddam's fault.

Had he not ordered chemical munitions into the Kuwait Theater of Operations, we wouldn't have blown them up. The whole scenario sounded reasonable, and the media bought it largely without question. According to the
CIA/DOD simulations, this plume might have blanketed as many as 100,000
troops. Perhaps a little too conveniently, this was almost precisely the number
of Desert Storm veterans complaining of chronic ill health.[27]

There were many flaws in this scenario as an explanation for Gulf War
Syndrome, and they should have been obvious to Congressmen and reporters
alike, starting with one of the more remarkable symptoms associated with
the Khamisiyah demolition—glowing vomit. A Humvee driver who witnessed
the operation, Pfc Brian Martin, told a congressional panel that "during PT
(physical training) I would vomit Chemlite-looking fluids every time I ran, an
ambulance would pick me up, putting IVs in both arms, rushing me to Wom-
ack Community Hospital. This happened *every* morning after my return from
the war" (the emphasis is Martin's, as noted in the official transcript).[28]
Chemlites are chemical lights that glow when the separate tubes containing
those chemicals are snapped, allowing their contents to mingle; the Army
mostly uses a Chemlite that was fluorescent green. By Martin's own description then, his breakfast, which he regurgitated daily, was green and glowed in
the dark.

Sarin has been around since 1938.[29] In the nearly seventy years that it has
been in use, no one has ever observed a victim producing fluorescent green
vomit. But the hue of one man's partially digested breakfast was just one of
many reasons to dispute the theory that nerve agent exposures made Gulf War
veterans sick. It is important to recount them here because the nerve gas/neu-
rological damage connection has become so entrenched in the thinking of
many veterans, partly because the theory was advanced so aggressively by media organizations like the *New York Times* and CBS *60 Minutes*. The media
stampede to cover this story missed important details, such as in the Defense
Department's conclusion that the Khamisiyah plume it had so elaborately illustrated probably did *not* affect any coalition troops.

There is a strange duality to the DOD/CIA investigation into the alleged
sarin release from Khamisiyah. While seeming to substantiate it with meteor-
ological charts, data on the rate of evaporation and computer-simulated
plumes, these agencies then went on to conclude that nerve agents probably
did *not* cause chronic, long-term disease in veterans. In a July 1997 press

release from the Department of Defense, entitled "Troops Not Exposed to Dangerous Levels of Chemical Agent," both DOD and the CIA "confirmed that *no* U.S. units were close enough to the demolitions to experience any noticeable health effects at the time of the event" [italics mine]. With this elaborate retelling of the Khamisiyah story (a CIA analyst first heard Pfc Martin tell it on the radio), both agencies went to considerable lengths to legitimize the theory that low doses of nerve agent *could* have caused the neurological damage observed in Gulf War veterans. Then, based on the limited scientific data available, these same agencies reported that nerve agent injuries were improbable. "Little is known about delayed effects from a brief, low-level exposure to nerve agents such as might have occurred in this case," said the press release; "however, current medical evidence indicates that long term health problems are unlikely."

The doublespeak in this press release verged on Orwellian. DOD and CIA seemed to be going to extraordinary lengths to please everyone—on one hand, the senators and veterans who were convinced that troops were exposed to nerve agents, and on the other, the scientists on the Presidential Advisory Committee on Gulf War Illnesses who had just issued their own report saying: "Current scientific evidence suggests that subclinical exposure to OP (organophosphate) CW (chemical warfare) nerve agents does not result in long-term neurophysiological and neuropsychological health effects."[30]

There are many ways to cause neurological damage, including blunt trauma and autoimmunity, but the means by which nerve agents do this damage is so distinctive that it constitutes a kind of fingerprint—a fingerprint that is conspicuously absent from the medical charts of sick Gulf War veterans. Linking nerve gas to neurological damage was deceptively straightforward, and the simplicity of this connection helped make it stick in people's minds. The media didn't help. Because of the almost forced superficiality of my profession, the case against nerve agent poisoning, in particular the mild poisoning from an allegedly low dose, got ignored—if for no other reason than its complexity. In light of reporting by influential news organizations that conveyed the impression that the entirely theoretical Khamisiyah plume (there are no data to confirm that it ever existed) made a far more conclusive case for nerve agent poisoning than it really did, it is important to reexamine why this is not only unlikely, it is preposterous. There are many reasons for this, but five of them, I think, are insurmountable.

First, the alleged plume of nerve agent, if it ever existed, was selective about whom it poisoned. There were thirty-four nations in the Gulf War coalition.[31] Only four of those nations—the United States, Britain, Canada and Australia—have reported troops suffering from illnesses matching a widely accepted case-definition of Gulf War Syndrome.[32] A non-sentient plume of chemicals would have been less discriminating. Why did Syrian troops escape its ravages? Egyptian troops were unaffected, as were Belgian sailors.[33] This makes no sense. The armored units from Saudi Arabia, Egypt, Syria and Kuwait were sandwiched between U.S. and British forces—the U.S. First and Second Marine Divisions on the Arab right flank, and four U.S. Army divisions and the British 1st Armored Division on the Arab left.[34] If the syndrome's causative agent were truly some crypto-toxin in the environment, how then did Saudi, Egyptian, Syrian and Kuwaiti troops all escape Gulf War Syndrome? The French 6th Light Armored Division fought alongside the U.S. 82nd Airborne at the extreme western end of the coalition line.[35] The French did not report a single case of Gulf War Syndrome.

There was no "Passover" in Desert Storm—no lamb's blood mark to tell God's killer angels to pass over the occupants of one tent or one tank, over another's. If U.S. and British troops—with their charcoal-lined chemical suits and, as it turns out, hypersensitive chemical detectors—were truly harmed by occult exposures to sarin, how did the people who lived in the region year-round, people who did not have such protection, escape harm? Yet they did.[36]

Another cohort from which Gulf War Syndrome was conspicuously absent is the media. There were 1,400 reporters in Saudi Arabia covering Desert Storm, four times the number that reported on the Vietnam War at its height. Many of the Desert Storm reporters were in the same locations as troops who would later become sick. Yet there is not one reported case of Gulf War Syndrome among the press. Out in the field, I remember how many times the chemical alarms went off, how many times we reporters donned our charcoal-lined suits and sweaty rubber gas masks along with everyone else. My former colleague Arthur Kent became known as the "SCUD Stud" after a broadcast he made during halftime in an NFL play-off game, in which a SCUD exploded just over the horizon. It was early in the war, and it was still unknown if the Iraqis, in an act of desperation, would launch chemicals. Arthur, normally the picture of cool in his Italian leather jacket, looked uncertain about whether to continue broadcasting or retreat from the platform—it was not only his own safety he had to be concerned about; his decision affected the producers and TV crews that were out there with him. Another former colleague from my NBC Radio days, Charles Jaco, then with CNN, smelled something that he thought was gas (sarin is odorless, by the way, cyclosarin is said to have a faint fruity aroma, and tabun supposedly smells like camphor). While the cameras were live, Jaco went for his mask. Kent and Jaco are tough reporters who have been in more dangerous spots than Saudi Arabia. If nerve agents did not affect them, stress certainly did. Yet neither of them developed Gulf War Syndrome, nor did any other reporter.

A second problem with the Khamisiyah story concerns the known symptoms of nerve agent poisoning. These symptoms have not been observed in a single Gulf War veteran—not one.[37] In 1998, the U.S. Air Force published its widely referenced "case definition" of Gulf War Syndrome.[38] Based on the answers to questionnaires given to Air Force personnel, doctors identified a collection of symptoms associated with the syndrome. There were a total of thirty-five symptoms divided into three categories—"fatigue, mood-cognition, and musculoskeletal." According to this approach, an Air Force veteran qualified as having the syndrome if he or she had one or more chronic symptoms from two of the three categories.[39] Among the most common complaints were headache, fatigue, joint pain, memory loss, concentration problems, joint stiffness, difficulty sleeping, rashes or sores, numbness or tingling, muscle pain and depression.[40]

Missing from the Air Force list are the telltale signs of even mild sarin poisoning. According to the Centers for Disease Control, these signs include miosis (constriction in the pupils of the eye to pinpoints), eye pain, dimness of vision, runny nose, tightness in the chest and difficulty breathing.[41] Moderate symptoms include drooling, excessive sweating, blurred vision, severe nasal congestion, increased tightness in the chest, more breathing difficulty, nausea, vomiting, diarrhea and cramps.[42] A severe exposure to sarin results in "involuntary defecation and urination, very copious secretions, twitching, jerking, staggering and convulsions, cessation of breathing, loss of consciousness, coma and death."[43]

Military doctors did not treat a single Gulf War veteran for miosis or dimness of vision; none drooled or had noses running like faucets. No soldier mysteriously lost control of his bowels, stopped breathing and blacked out.

There are no records of any service member going into a coma and dying after one of the Army's M8A1 chemical alarms went off; and those alarms went off thousands of times during the war. Sarin does not give you a rash or sores. It does not induce joint and muscle pain. An exposure to the vapor from a few drops of sarin does not result in difficulty sleeping; it results in difficulty *living*. Without the swift administration of the antidote, atropine, a victim of sarin poisoning can die—but he will not get autoimmune disease. According to the Defense Intelligence Agency (DIA): "U.S. medical personnel stationed in the Gulf were especially watchful for symptoms associated with CBW agents. During the entire Persian Gulf crisis not one person, military or civilian, was treated, hospitalized or died as a result of CBW exposure."[44] The failure to spot this discrepancy in symptoms was, by 1997, inexcusable. The Japanese doomsday cult Aum Shin Rikyo had released sarin into the Tokyo subway system in 1995 and was suspected of another sarin attack in the city of Matsumoto in the Japan Alps the year before. These two attacks resulted in nearly 6,000 casualties, varying in severity from transient headaches (which resolved themselves with minimal treatment) to death.[45] These two incidents were proven exposures to sarin, not theoretical ones like Khamisiyah. The dosages ranged from mild to fatal. Years later, none of the victims suffer from anything resembling Gulf War Syndrome, or from autoimmunity, as a result of these attacks.[46] Detailed descriptions of the sarin injuries from Matsumoto and Tokyo were published in several peer-reviewed scientific journals shortly after the attacks, well before the media focus on Khamisiyah reached its zenith.

A third reason for doubting the Khamisiyah explanation for Gulf War Syndrome is the absence of this syndrome among Iraqi military personnel and civilians. Most of the chemical weapons facilities were in central Iraq, many of them near Baghdad. Yet Iraqi physicians did not treat injuries consistent with nerve agent exposure, or any mysterious illnesses resembling Gulf War Syndrome. The Iraqis would have recognized such injuries; they had considerable experience using chemical weapons against Iran and against their own Kurdish minority. Had Iraqi civilians been injured or killed by nerve agent fallout from coalition bombing, would Saddam Hussein, a cynical despot who never let pass any opportunity to enlist international sympathy through propaganda (e.g., the accidental bombing of a factory making baby milk powder)— would such a man fail to exploit injuries or deaths among Iraqi civilians from chemical weapons, even if they were his own? It would have been a propaganda bonanza. And if the Iraqis who lived in close proximity to bombed chemical weapons facilities (not just one facility but several) did not develop Gulf War Syndrome as a result, why would U.S. military personnel deployed hundreds of miles away be affected? "When one considers that cases of Gulf War Syndrome have been reported by soldiers stationed all over the Saudi Arabian peninsula and that the vast majority of CBW targets were much farther north than Nasiriyah, it quickly becomes apparent," writes the DIA, "that the lack of evidence of massive Iraqi military and civilian deaths associated with releases from bombed Iraqi CBW targets, argues very strongly against the theory that coalition soldiers were exposed to airborne CBW agents released from bombed Iraqi CBW targets literally hundreds of miles away."[47]

The fourth reason is the absence of any confirmed chemical weapons detections. State-of-the-art laboratories in the United States and Britain tested soil, water and air samples suspected of containing these agents. According to the DIA, "These samples were taken before, during and after the war from suspected 'hot' areas in Saudi Arabia, Kuwait and Iraq."[48] All of the samples "were negative." During the entire war there was only one nerve agent detection, made by a Czech chemical warfare decontamination unit on January 19, 1991, that was judged credible, though not confirmed.

The fifth reason, according to the DIA, is that long-term, low-level exposure to nerve agent "defies the laws of physics."

> The law of diffusion states that any substance, particularly a gas or liquid, naturally moves from an area of greater concentration to lesser concentration. If in one area or time the concentration is low—as in the Czech detection— at some other area or time the concentration must be high. Therefore, other detections would be expected near by, possibly resulting in casualties; this did not happen. Further, the only possible explanation for long-term low-level exposure below detection range is the deliberate, continuous release of very small amounts of agent throughout the area where exposure was to have occurred—in this case, much of the Saudi Arabian peninsula. The facts simply do not support this theory.[49]

All the reasons put forward by the DIA are consistent with what the Marine Corps taught Sergeant Jeff Rawls and what the Army taught me. As part of our training to cover Desert Storm, Army instructors educated me and other reporters about the effects of sarin and VX. Nerve agents do not destroy nerve cells. They affect the *communication* between nerve cells. To protect muscles and organs from overstimulation, the body produces an enzyme called acetylcholinesterase (AChE), which acts like a chemical "off switch." When a nerve agent like sarin inhibits the production of AChE, a contracting muscle will keep on contracting; muscle paralysis sets in, you can't breathe and you die of suffocation. As the DIA reported, no one died like this during Desert Storm; no one was treated for even a *mild* case of sarin poisoning.

To cause damage, sarin must either be inhaled or pass through the skin. The amount needed to bring on severe distress is astonishingly small. But ensuring even the slightest exposure to sarin in the vast reaches of the Arabian Desert—where high temperatures would accelerate evaporation and hot dry winds would dissipate the vapor—would require enormous quantities of agent. According to the DIA, for sarin to have registered at the low levels detected by the Czechs near the Saudi town of Hafar Al Batin on January 19, 1991, the bombing of the nearest Iraqi CBW target (at An Nasiriyah) would have had to release eighty tons of sarin—eighty tons, as in 160,000 pounds. The destruction of an estimated 500 rockets filled with sarin and cyclosarin at Khamisiyah did not generate anything remotely close to an eighty-ton release, assuming it released anything at all. The inevitable dissipation of a vapor in any open space, let alone the desert, is why Aum Shin Rikyo planned their Tokyo attack in a subway. The indoor release in the Tokyo subway resulted in an almost tenfold increase—5,000 injuries and eleven deaths.

In retrospect, the DOD/CIA reports on Khamisiyah appear to be an earnest attempt to appease senators who were misinformed about the effects of sarin—senators who, in turn, were trying to appease the sick veterans in their constituencies who wanted answers. In the rush to judgment, military and intelligence bureaucrats tried to provide answers that refuted the nerve agent theory without insulting anyone. Those answers were, in fact, fairly accurate. The bureaucrats reached the only scientifically supportable conclusion: that Gulf War Syndrome could not be attributed to nerve agents. But an uninformed press corps that did not bother to educate itself on the effects of nerve agent poisoning—or even, apparently, to read the report very carefully—used the report to draw the opposite conclusion.

Eventually, the military's own epidemiologists published data that discredited the nerve agent theory, and an angry Senate criticized both the Army and the CIA for releasing highly speculative, spurious information. I wondered why the CIA and the Army would have tried to sell a theory that in time would surely come to be revealed as bogus and subject them to deserved ridicule.

The Stress Test

The military doctors, however, were not cowed by the Senate. They returned with a vengeance to their original position—that Gulf War Syndrome was nothing more than an unrelated constellation of symptoms, not a disease with a known causative agent and understood mechanism. And the most likely cause of these disparate symptoms was war-related stress. Blue-ribbon panels organized by the Institute of Medicine, the Defense Science Advisory Board and a Presidential Action Committee all concluded that there was no unique disease, or disease process, common to sick veterans. Stress could be an underlying factor in a wide array of diseases that otherwise share no similarities. Elements in the media embraced this conclusion with almost as much enthusiasm as the nerve agent theory.

The stress theory fails the commonsense test too. If Gulf War Syndrome resulted from stress, then why did it affect more support troops than those who actually saw combat? As General Ronald Blanck told Senate investigators back in 1994, the Department of Defense had already observed at that early date a prevalence of Gulf War Syndrome among support troops, leading Blanck to suspect anthrax vaccine because it was mainly given to troops in the rear echelon.[50] Who experienced more stress? Troops in the rear or assault troops in combat?

As I discussed in Chapter 6, the U.S. military's casualty rates in Desert Storm were the lowest in its history. There was no Omaha Beach in Desert Storm; no Arnhem or Bastogne or Tarawa, no Chosin Reservoir or Khe Sahn. This was unlike any war that U.S. or British soldiers had fought before—less mud, less blood and big-screen TV's. When I joined the 24th Infantry Division, Mechanized as an embedded reporter (before anyone thought to call it that), I walked into a tent to find a Mitsubishi projection TV, a big-screened monster, with a well-stocked video library. One night our public affairs officers drove us out into the desert to see something truly surreal—a bank of perhaps twenty payphones in the middle of nowhere hooked up to a satellite dish, courtesy of AT&T. Soldiers could actually phone home from the front lines; all they needed was a credit card. On a clear night under the stars, the Arabian Desert was beautiful—more like a painting than a war zone. If there was crippling stress out there, you almost had to go looking for it.

By 1997 I knew that veterans who had never shipped out—that is, veterans who had never left the United States—were also suffering from illnesses identical to Gulf War Syndrome, and that civilian doctors, treating soldiers who had shipped out to the Persian Gulf as well as those who never left these shores, were not finding these symptoms vague or indicative of stress. With relative ease and remarkable alacrity, some veterans who took the trouble to see civilian rheumatologists discovered that they were suffering from some sort of autoimmune disease, which was odd, because autoimmunity is a pathology that mainly afflicts women and most of the sick veterans were men. Still other physicians and scientists, all of them civilians, began suggesting another connection, one that I began to follow closely as well—a connection between Gulf War Syndrome and the vaccines given the troops, both those who had shipped out to the Gulf and those who had not. That is when a former CIA officer suggested that I contact Dr. Pamela Asa.

The Antibody Hunt

By the time I met Asa in 1998, she had acquired clinical evidence to support her theory that Gulf War Syndrome was, in fact, a constellation of autoimmune diseases induced by injections with squalene. She had done this by doing something that had never been done before. She found a way to detect antibodies to an adjuvant.

This was nothing short of subversive. Most of the time, finding a new antibody is fairly humdrum stuff. But finding one related to squalene, a substance deemed vital to the future of a whole new generation of vaccines—and a substance that at that point had already been injected into hundreds of thousands of people—was unnerving. If, as Pam Asa maintained, these antibodies were a trail of bread crumbs leading to something that might cause incurable disease, then billions of dollars were at stake, not to mention the health of those who already had had squalene put in their veins. If antibodies to squalene truly existed, they were a Pandora's box that the NIH and the Army dared not open.

Antibodies are one of the marvels of the living world. The human body is capable of producing almost an infinite number of different antibodies—each of them utterly unique. Antibody-producing cells actually reshuffle their DNA to form a custom fit to a molecule. Immunologists like to compare this phenomenon to a lock and key. On the surface of molecules are three-dimensional structures called epitopes—these are the keys. The antibodies produced by a B-cell form a custom-fitting lock around that key, as if the cell were creating a mold to fit the key's specific shape. An antibody that fits one of these keys will usually work only for that key. The difference of a single atom can determine why an antibody will bind to one molecule and not another. Antibodies react to the molecules for which they were specifically made, and (generally) to no others. They are like a fingerprint.

Antibodies can be raised to just about anything. The Nobel Prize–winning immunochemist Karl Landsteiner first demonstrated this back in the 1930s by creating in his laboratory molecules that did not exist in nature, and then raising antibodies to them.[51] Because you can raise an antibody to just about anything, it was a breathtaking assumption on the part of adjuvant-makers to assume that the immune system would not react to squalene simply because the human body makes it. Although, under normal circumstances, the body will not react to its own molecules—a phenomenon that immunologists called "tolerance"—tolerance can be broken. This is the essence of autoimmunity. Antibodies against self, or autoantibodies, are associated with debilitating and sometimes fatal autoimmune diseases.

When Pam Asa first suggested that Gulf War Syndrome might be due to anti-squalene antibodies, many scientists balked. They said it couldn't happen: the immune system could not form antibodies to a lipid or fat like squalene because these molecules were too small. On the face of it, this was foolish because, for decades, anti-phospholipid antibodies had been a key test for lupus. The scientists who didn't know this were probably going by something presumed to be true decades ago—that only relatively large molecules like proteins could induce the production of an antibody.

There is at least one other reason why many smart, impressively credentialed scientists presumed that the immune system would not produce antibodies to squalene. For the better part of the twentieth century, scientists have believed that adjuvants stimulate a non-specific immune response. In other words, they supposedly activated a robust immune response to everything but themselves. Scientists conceived this idea before they knew where antibodies came from or how they worked, and then clung to that idea as scientific gospel. When vaccine designers at the NIH and Fort Detrick started using squalene, they were counting on this concept to be true. As molecules go, squalene was relatively light; it was small and it was an adjuvant—qualities that theoretically added up to no immune response or a non-specific response. But if the human immune system made antibodies specific to squalene—if squalene activated the immune system's whole cellular repertoire—then it would be undeniably dangerous. It might even be the single most dangerous oil to come out of a hypodermic needle. Triggering an immune response to squalene would be promoting an attack on "self," as immunologists somewhat awkwardly put it, and a particularly vital part of "self" at that—not just a molecule found in a knee or an elbow, but one found all throughout the nervous system and the brain. The brain and nerve damage in animals following injection with squalene is not theoretical. It has been proven.[52]

In every community, there exists pressure to conform to certain norms of behavior and thinking. We have different names for this—"political correctness" on a college campus, "groupthink" in a business meeting, the "conventional wisdom" in politics or the "orthodoxy" of the church. In detecting antibodies to squalene, Asa was not only defying the conventional wisdom of her field, she was becoming something of a heretic. If the antibodies were truly evidence that injecting squalene caused incurable autoimmune diseases in humans, it threatened to shut down every NIH-sponsored clinical trial involving vaccines formulated with it. Asa's discovery challenged a long-standing scientific orthodoxy on adjuvants at a time when a powerful new adjuvant was considered essential to the development of the next generation of ultra-pure, genetically engineered vaccines.

For some individuals, the stakes couldn't be higher. Just as Karl Landsteiner's discovery of blood types in 1901 would later be used to help police solve murders, Pam Asa's anti-squalene antibodies were a forensic as well as diagnostic tool. Opposition to the existence of these antibodies was not just a matter of saving face or protecting a grant. For any scientist or physician who might have administered squalene-boosted vaccines to military personnel without their informed consent, these antibodies were evidence of a possible wrongdoing.

Asa found the antibodies with the help of Dr. Robert Garry, Professor of Microbiology and Immunology at Tulane University Medical School. Bob Garry is one of the world's leading virologists, who specializes in retroviruses like HIV. He runs a busy lab at Tulane Medical School, supervising more than half a dozen Ph.D. candidates in microbiology. In the absence of documentation showing that Gulf War veterans had been injected with squalene, Pam Asa needed some way to prove, or disprove, that it had been done. Finding an antibody would do this. But in 1997, an assay system that could detect antibodies to squalene did not exist. She called Bob Garry because one of his doctoral students, Scott Tenenbaum, had just published a paper in the *Lancet* reporting that he had discovered antibodies to a very different kind of molecule that shared an important chemical property with lipids—it was hydrophobic, meaning it had little or no affinity for water.[53] A friend of Pam's, a fellow immunologist in Memphis who also happened to be a colonel in the U.S. Army Reserves, suggested that she call Bob Garry and ask if he could adapt his antipolymer assay to detect antibodies to a lipid. When Pam finally got him on the phone and asked him if he thought it could be done, Bob said "sure."

Maybe he spoke a little too quickly. Like Asa, Bob Garry did not quite know what he was getting himself into. He knew he would be looking for an antibody to a lipid, but he didn't know which one. Asa would send him serum samples that she had collected from sick veterans as well as some from people who were healthy; these people would act as one of several control groups in the study. If anti-squalene antibodies were specifically linked to illness in Gulf War veterans, then, in theory, healthy people should not have them. The lipid she would also send to Bob Garry—several different samples of it in unmarked bottles.

Antibody hunting is a fairly routine task for immunologists looking for a possible viral or bacterial cause of a disease whose origins were as yet unknown, and there are few better at it than Bob Garry. He had helped create the assay that Pam Asa now wanted him to adapt to detect squalene antibodies. The Western Blot assay to confirm HIV infection in a patient, a standard laboratory test run millions of times a year around the world, was developed in the 1980s by Bob's brother-in-law, who worked for a biotech firm in Rockville, Maryland. Bob advised the company on how to grow the virus. Bob Garry also helped confirm the identity of the first American to die of AIDS—a fifteen-year-old black male who died in St. Louis, Missouri in 1969.[54] Using the same assay that he would use to find antibodies to squalene, in 1997 Bob Garry assayed the boy's serum and autopsy specimens, which had been frozen by St. Louis City Hospital when he died. The assay confirmed the boy had been infected with HIV–1.[55]

Laughing comes easily to Bob Garry. He likes a good joke and though he takes his work as seriously as you would expect any professor at a major medical school to do, he is more inclined to listen than he is to talk. When he does talk, it is generally about something that he or one of his students is working on. He does not like to talk about himself. If there is a gene for narcissism, he does not have it. But his laid-back manner is deceptive. No one with a half-inch-thick bibliography, including over a hundred scientific papers published in some of the world's most highly regarded scientific journals—among them *Nature, Science,* the *Journal of the American Medical Association* and the *Lancet*—lacks ambition or intensity. Bob Garry does not talk much about himself because he is busy doing more important things.

By temperament, he is not inclined to seek controversy, nor flee it when it finds him. It has found him only once before. When his student, Scott Tenenbaum, discovered antipolymer antibodies, Tenenbaum organized an experiment to see if silicone breast implant patients had them. This was a minefield and the mines were nuclear. The dispute over whether ruptured silicone breast implants caused rheumatological disease was arguably the single most polarizing issue in science and medicine in the 1990s. The insistence by some breast implant patients that silicone induced lupus, rheumatoid arthritis, skin rashes, memory loss, chronic fatigue, headaches, body aches and hair loss provoked the most expensive mass litigation in history. In 1994, the nation's largest implant makers, Dow Corning, Baxter and Bristol-Meyer, offered a $4.2 billion "global" settlement to more than 440,000 women who had filed claims against them; the deal later collapsed. The crush of litigation would ultimately sink one of America's largest chemical companies, Dow Corning, into Chapter 11 bankruptcy.

Silicone was a known immunostimulant. In the 1970s, Dow Corning investigated the possibility of commercializing silicone as a vaccine adjuvant, and though the company abandoned the idea, silicone has in fact been used for this purpose, notably by Col. Carl Alving at the Walter Reed Army Institute of Research, who in the mid-nineties used silicone to induce antibodies to cholesterol.[56] The question was whether, in addition to being an adjuvant, silicone also caused disease—an assertion vehemently disputed by silicone manufacturers, the makers of silicone prosthetic devices and the plastic surgeons who implant them. In 1997, Tenenbaum reported that he and Bob Garry had detected antipolymer antibodies in silicone breast implant patients, and that the prevalence of these antibodies in patients appeared to be proportional to the severity of their illness. This was purportedly the first objective laboratory marker for the body's reaction to silicone polymers, in addition to being evidence that a silicone-related disease process was under way in sick people. The article appeared in the midst of Dow Corning's attempt to reach a settlement to limit any further liability from more than a quarter million litigants still seeking damages against the company for its silicone-based products (Dow Corning would settle separately for $3.2 billion in July 1998). When Tenenbaum and Garry published their data in the *Lancet,* several scientists wrote letters to the journal savaging their paper. They accused the Tulane scientists of having too few participants in their study for it to be meaningful, and for not recruiting specific types of control patients that would rule out the possibility that the antibodies resulted from something other than silicone exposure. In the most inflammatory accusation, one scientist alleged financial conflict of interest because Tulane would receive royalties from the assay, having licensed it to a private biotech firm, Autoimmune Technologies.[57]

Along with Tenenbaum's paper and the responses to it, the *Lancet* published something I have never seen a scientific journal put in print before. Each of Tulane's attackers had to append personal information to their letters, divulging their connections to the implant makers, or lack thereof. Of the six correspondents publishing criticisms of the Tenenbaum/Garry paper, four had either conducted research for the implant manufacturers (which found no links between the implants and autoimmunity) or testified on their behalf as paid consultants or expert witnesses.[58] The fees for such work can be considerable.

Welcome to the world of high-stakes science. Bob Garry, who had never testified either for or against implant litigants, got himself embroiled in a controversy that was really a sideline to his work with retroviruses. It was an unpleasant foretaste of what lay ahead.

When Garry ran his assay adapted for squalene antibodies he didn't know what to expect. On the initial run, there were just five patients. He knew four of them were Gulf War veterans. The fifth was a patient that had been injected with an adjuvant; Bob Garry knew that too, but he didn't know which adjuvant. He set to work in the morning; it would be a long day. The Western Blot assay uses little paper strips soaked in various chemicals to detect the presence of antibodies in human sera that is also applied to the strips. If antibodies are present, the strips will turn varying shades of blue/black—the higher the concentration of antibodies in a patient's sera, the darker the strip. It took Bob Garry's colleague, Dr. Yan Cao, a whole day to run the assay. It is tedious work. One reagent must be applied to the strips, which must then be dried before applying the next one, and then the process is repeated all over again until every chemical has been applied, not to mention the patient's serum. Garry and Cao did not know the names of any of the patients. Each strip had a number; that was all. Garry and Cao also didn't know which lipid they had used in the assay. It was a clear liquid in various unmarked bottles.

When the test was done, all of the strips were dark. Bob Garry scored the intensity of shading on the scale of zero to +4. A zero score meant no antibodies; +4 meant a very high concentration (or "titer") of antibodies. All the patients in this run were either +1 or +2.

Bob Garry called Pam Asa on the phone the next morning.

"Pam, all of your patients were positive," he said.

"Are you kidding?" Pam's voice went up an octave . . . "Omigod!"

"Oh, and by the way, I had all these other blood samples from Gulf War patients frozen away," he said. "The VA sent 'em to me back in '93. Some of them were sick Gulf War vets and some were controls. They never told me which were which. When your people tested positive, I remembered these other samples and I went and got 'em out and tested them too. About two-thirds of them tested *hotter* than your patients."

Military doctors had sent 300 serum samples to Bob Garry to check for antibodies to retroviruses.[59] He didn't know anything about these patients either, except that some were sick Gulf War veterans and others were healthy controls. The samples were randomly jumbled together with code numbers on the test tubes. There were no names; Bob Garry did not have the code. Why the military asked him to check for retrovirus antibodies in these veterans was unclear to him; the military didn't say. But Garry knew the serum samples had come from the rheumatology clinic at a VA hospital in Little Rock, Arkansas, and a hospital ward for Gulf War Syndrome patients at the Henry M. Jackson

Foundation in Washington, D.C. For Pam Asa, these connections had troubling implications. The serum sent from the Little Rock VA's Rheumatology
Clinic indicated that someone, at that particular VA hospital back in 1995,
was already seeing veterans coming back from the war with some sort of autoimmune disorder. Looking for the cause of an autoimmune problem would
have been the logical reason to send their sera to Bob Garry to test. Bob was
already renowned as one of the world's leading authorities on the links between retroviruses and autoimmune disease.

"So what's adjuvant?" he asked.

"Squalene," said Asa.

"Omigod." Garry went silent for minute. As an HIV specialist, he knew that
virtually every prototype HIV vaccine contained squalene. He knew the assay
results would not be well received in Washington. Even worse was the question for which he had no good answer: Why were Gulf War veterans testing
positive for an experimental vaccine additive?

Over the next month, Garry and Cao ran Tulane Medical School's new
anti-squalene antibody assay on a total of 234 serum samples. Eighty-six of
these samples were from Gulf War veterans. In this group, the breakdown was
stark. Of the sick Gulf War veterans who deployed to the region, 95 percent
tested positive for the antibodies.[60] That group included three British Gulf
War veterans. The number of healthy Gulf War veterans with the antibodies
was *zero*.[61] The next group was arguably the most damning of all. This group
consisted of six Gulf War veterans suffering from autoimmune diseases who
never went to the Persian Gulf. These veterans, whose complaints were identical to the sick veterans who deployed, were *not* exposed to depleted uranium, low doses of nerve agent, Kuwaiti oil fire smoke, sand or the stress of
combat. All six, 100 percent, were positive for anti-squalene antibodies.[62]

Among the sick deployed veterans who tested positive for the antibodies
were Col. Herb Smith, Lt. James Patrick Rudicell, Lt. Mary Jones and Sgt. Jeff
Rawls. The two patients from the NIH clinical trial for an experimental herpes
vaccine combined with MF59—Patient X, who received a single injection of
MF59 only, and a second patient, Patient Y, who was immunized with the actual vaccine—were both positive. Patient X was +1. Patient Y, who received
three injections of the experimental herpes vaccine with MF59, was +3. Both
the NIH patients told Pam Asa that they had rashes, memory loss, dizziness,
joint and muscle pain, chronic fatigue, severe headaches and hair loss.

To see if their antibodies could be linked to anything else, Asa and Garry tested randomly selected members of the public, patients suffering from systemic lupus erythematosus of unknown origins, patients complaining of chronic fatigue and women with silicone breast implants. None of the patients suffering from idiopathic autoimmune disease (autoimmunity from unknown origins) were positive. No member of the general public tested positive. None of the healthy Gulf War veterans were positive. Three out of the thirty breast implant patients were marginally positive for the antibodies, but the shadings on their strips were little more than faint shadows. The call was a toss-up between scoring them a 0 or a +1. So no one could accuse him of being biased in his scoring, Bob Garry called them +1. The absence of the antibodies in the control patients meant that healthy people in general, civilian or military, did not have anti-squalene antibodies. Because the lupus patients whose illness could not be linked to adjuvant exposure were all negative, the anti-squalene antibodies were not a marker for lupus in general, or for chronic fatigue. The sick veterans who never went to war had just one thing in common with the sick veterans who did: vaccinations.

Pam Asa and Bob Garry knew these results meant trouble. Their data not only suggested that anti-squalene antibodies were a "marker" for Gulf War Syndrome; they were a clear indication of what the syndrome might actually be. More to the point, they were an indication that Gulf War "Syndrome" might not be a syndrome at all. It might actually be an array of fully diagnosable autoimmune diseases like lupus, multiple sclerosis, rheumatoid arthritis and autoimmune thyroid disease—all of which had occurred in animals after they were injected with adjuvants formulated with squalene.[63] What Herb Smith and Pat Rudicell had was no mystery. They had lupus. So did Randy Wheeler, a former sergeant in the 3rd Battalion, 11th Marines. According to VA doctors in New Hampshire, both Marine Corps Captain Wes Davis, who flew a Cobra attack helicopter in the Gulf War, and Air Force Sgt. Jeff Swan were suspected of having lupus. Wheeler, Davis and Swan all tested positive for anti-squalene antibodies. Swan, a non-commissioned Air Force intelligence officer, never set foot in Saudi Arabia, Kuwait or Iraq. He spent the entire Gulf War in Egypt. Army Reserve Captain Martin Hall of Soldotna, Alaska, had a bad reaction to a shot he received at Fort Richardson in Anchorage when he was preparing to deploy in February 1991. He got a headache so bad that he couldn't see. He then developed joint and muscle pain, and a rash that appeared on his left hand then crept all the way up his left shoulder; it is still advancing. That was soon accompanied by numbness in his hands and arms, chest pain, fatigue and short-term memory loss. His headaches come and go, but they are a constant feature of his life now. He doesn't know which vaccine he got; the Army didn't tell him. He says the Army took his shot records away for reasons that he does not recall ever hearing. The Army, he says, never returned his records. Hall is +3 for the antibodies. All of these sick Gulf War veterans had antibodies to a vaccine additive that scientists at Fort Detrick and the NIH had grown to rely on. This additive was experimental. It was not licensed for human use by either the FDA or its British equivalent, the Medicines and Health Products Regulatory Agency.

The presence of anti-squalene antibodies in sick Gulf War veterans did not prove these men and women had been injected with it, but it was a strong indication that they had. Without some sort of trigger to break the body's natural tolerance for this molecule, there would be no antibodies. Swallowing squalene would not induce them; rubbing squalene on your skin would not do it either. Getting immunized with squalene made the most sense; it was the *only* thing that made sense. All things being equal, Pam Asa thought the simplest explanation was also the most likely one—"the law of economy" or Occam's Razor, championed by the fourteenth-century English philosopher and theologian William of Occam: *"Pluralitas non est ponenda sine necessitate,"* "plurality should not be posited without necessity." In other words, don't introduce needless complications into your theories. Occam's Razor made vaccination with squalene seem like the most likely answer to Bob Garry, too. But a deduction, however logical, was still no substitute for data. Asa and Bob Garry remained cautious about what they said publicly, but they harbored suspicions that they couldn't quite shake.

Too many troubling deductions were making too much sense. Some of the serum samples given to Bob Garry back in 1995 came from Victoria Polonis at the Henry M. Jackson Foundation. The Henry M. Jackson Foundation for the Advancement of Military Medicine was where Col. Robert Redfield and Victoria Polonis had been developing the Army's prototype HIV vaccine. This vaccine contained squalene. A sick Gulf War veteran had sent Pam Asa a copy of a Project Badger document about Fort Detrick's plans to run a "Manhattan Project" to test experimental vaccines in Saudi Arabia during Desert Shield. Pam Asa recalled that before the Gulf War, politicians in Washington kept referring to the need for a "Manhattan Project" to develop an HIV vaccine. Pam Asa had ruled out anthrax vaccine. Everyone knew that the troops got anthrax vaccine during the war, which was licensed and contained the FDA-approved additive, alum, not squalene. And too few troops got injected with botulinum toxoid, only 8,000 by the Army's record books, to account for the number of sick veterans. A lot of Pam Asa's patients did not have their shot records. Like Captain Hall, their records had been taken and not returned, or if they did have their records, the shots they received for the war were not recorded. That left a few patients with an odd annotation in their yellow, passport-sized immunization cards from the WHO. The entries said: "Vaccine A." What was Vaccine A? What reasons would the military have for keeping the identity of this shot a secret? If she suspected it before she had the data proving her patients had antibodies to squalene, she was even more suspicious of it now. An HIV vaccine, she thought, was the Army's top R&D priority. When Asa informed her patients of their test results, they asked her which vaccine she thought the squalene had been in.

"I don't know," she said. "But one real possibility is HIV."

Chapter Nine

"*Vanity Scare*" and the Taming of the Crews

I first talked to Pam Asa in the spring of 1998. By then I had read several articles based on her suspicion that a prototype HIV vaccine had been tested on U.S. troops during the Gulf War. The first one, by a journalist named Paul Rodriguez, had appeared in the *Washington Times* under the title "Anti-HIV Mix Found in Gulf Veterans."[1] Rodriguez, a former *Washington Times* reporter and by then Managing Editor of its sister publication, a magazine called *Insight on the News,* started publishing a series of articles in the magazine emphasizing squalene's connections to HIV vaccines. A friend of Asa's from Tennessee knew Rodriguez and tipped him off to her work. Rodriguez called his first article in the magazine on squalene "Sickness and Secrecy."[2] This, too, emphasized the link between squalene adjuvants and HIV. "It is from the experimental HIV clinical trials run by private firms—and in conjunction with high-level government research projects including those by the U.S. military—that the presence of squalene in the bodies of the sick gulf-war veterans takes on the potentially fiendish qualities of a nightmare," he wrote.[3] Rodriguez pursued the HIV vaccine angle doggedly, calling his next article "Gulf War Mystery and HIV."[4] In the course of his investigation, Rodriguez reported that both the Department of Defense and NIH had conducted extensive testing with squalene-based adjuvants combined with vaccines for influenza, herpes, malaria, and one that Rodriguez put particular emphasis on—HIV. In all of his writings on squalene, he made no mention of anthrax vaccine. I had a big problem with this, and after we talked a few times, I asked Pam Asa about it.

"You know, Paul makes no mention of anthrax vaccine in any of his articles," I said.

"So," said Pam, a bit defensively. "I ruled out anthrax vaccine."

"Ruled it out? Why was that?"

"A doctor at Fort Benning sent me the package inserts for all the vaccines given to troops sent to the Gulf," she said. "The one for anthrax vaccine showed it contained alum, not squalene. Besides, someone with the Senate Veterans' Affairs Committee showed me a document saying the Army only had about 12,000 doses of anthrax vaccine when the Iraqis invaded Kuwait. Twelve thousand doses can't account for all those people who got sick. It *had* to be something else."

"Like what?" I asked.

"I told Paul that some of these patients got shot up with something called 'Vaccine A.' The Army's big priority, just like everyone else's up there in Washington, was an HIV vaccine and the Army's HIV vaccine contains squalene."

"Pam, if all these other new vaccines were formulated with squalene—influenza, herpes and malaria, just to name a few—what evidence do you have that these troops were injected with an HIV vaccine? It could have been any of the others," I said. "Antibodies to squalene do *not* prove it was an HIV vaccine."

"Well, what about Vaccine A?" Her voice was rising now. "Anthrax vaccine was a licensed vaccine. Why call it Vaccine A? And what about all those serum samples that Vicky Polonis sent to Bob Garry? What's an HIV vaccine specialist doing sending samples to Bob asking him to test for retroviruses?"

"That's circumstantial," I objected. "It's not evidence, not if all you've got are antibodies to squalene; you don't have anything to substantiate your theory. You can't go beyond the limits of your data."

"Look," I said. "I have no evidence that you and Paul Rodriguez are wrong about HIV. I just don't have any evidence that you're right. What I do know is this: the Army might have been sinking tons of money into an HIV vaccine, just as you say, but an HIV vaccine wasn't going to save anybody's life in Desert Storm. Maybe you're right, and the Army's scientists were so cynical that they'd test any old vaccine they wanted on troops just because they could. But if there was any new vaccine the Army was arguably *justified* in using, it was anthrax. They were scared of anthrax. They thought anthrax, not HIV, could send a lot of Americans home in body bags. And besides," I said, "apart from the fact that anthrax begins with an 'a,' there's an irrefutable reason why Vaccine A is anthrax vaccine, and not HIV."

She hesitates a moment. "And what's that?"

"Because the Army says so. I've got the Army's declassified documents from the war. They all say Vaccine A—and all its variants, Vac A and Vaccine Apple—it's anthrax vaccine."

The Dear Abby of Anthrax Vaccine

Pam Asa still didn't believe me.

Back in 1998, I was writing an article on Tulane's antibody findings for *Vanity Fair* magazine, and I had lost a lot of time investigating Asa's HIV theory before coming across the Rosetta Stone for Vaccine A—a cache of documents at the National Archives that stated Vaccine A, and all its permutations (Vac A, A-Vax, Vaccine Apple, etc.), was anthrax vaccine; some of these documents were available on the Department of Defense's own website.[5] They were consistent with the entry that Major Greg Dubay personally made in his WHO shot card, which says: "Vacc anthrax A and Vacc Anthrax B."[6] Herb Smith got one of his anthrax shots logged as "Vac A"; so did several other veterans who tested positive for anti-squalene antibodies.[7]

Lieutenant Colonel John Czerwinski had "Vaccine A" entered into his WHO immunization card, too, and something he recalls hearing the week before Desert Storm began has always bothered him.[8] Czerwinski was commander of the Army Reserve's 324th Personnel Administration Battalion from Livingston, Alabama, now headquartered about a twenty-minute drive southeast of the Saudi capital, Riyadh, near Al Kharj. Something he remembered seemed consistent with Dubay's recollection of immunizing troops with a "new and improved anthrax vaccine." Czerwinski, who like Smith was positive for anti-squalene antibodies and suffered from autoimmune thyroid problems, recalled his commander, Brigadier General Thomas Sikora, saying that units in the area were getting a "substitute shot, but would not be getting the real vaccine." Czerwinski took this to mean that the other units would be getting a placebo. He recalls Sikora saying that John's unit, the 324th, would get the real shot because they were so "critical to the maintenance of unit strength in theater." Czerwinski remembers the exact date of this conversation, January 8, 1991, and even the time of day, 1800 hours, at the commander's daily staff meeting. Was the placebo an adjuvant, as it was in the case of Patient X? And why would the Army bother to immunize troops with a placebo in the middle of a war if it wasn't for an experiment, and an important one at that? I have not been able to track down Sikora to corroborate Czerwinski's recollections.

The information from Lt. Col. Czerwinski was one of those interesting factoids that pointed toward a destination, but did not actually get you there. I decided to use whatever time I had left to run down a lead that seemed more promising. In 1997, the Department of Defense made anthrax vaccination mandatory for all military personnel and by the following year a growing number of service members were complaining that they were getting sick after their shots. The list of complaints sounded all too familiar: fatigue, headaches, joint pain, dizziness, tinnitus (loud ringing in the ears), memory loss and rashes.[9]

One person in direct contact with hundreds of the so-afflicted was Lori Greenleaf of Morrison, Colorado, a suburb of Denver. Lori's son, Erik Julius, a sailor who did launch and recovery on the flight deck of the USS *Independence*, called home from the ship to ask his mother for help. The *Independence* was on cruise in the Persian Gulf when Erik's commanding officer announced that everyone on board would have to take anthrax shots; the immunizations would commence in twenty-four hours. Sailors were alarmed. Some of them had heard that the vaccine might be linked to Gulf War Syndrome and this rumor spread quickly around the ship. When Erik got his mother on the phone, he asked her to find out anything she could about the shot. Lori started searching the Internet for information, and what she read frightened her; a lot of military personnel were complaining of severe reactions to the shots. Some of them alleged that it had made them chronically ill. Lori couldn't call the ship and tell her son what she had found, and Erik couldn't call back until after he reluctantly took his first shot. He listened to what his mother said and decided to refuse the second shot; his tour of duty would be up in three months and he was going to leave the Navy; he didn't see why he had to take the shot. When Erik refused, his mother says, Erik's commanding officers reduced him in rank and threatened him with brig time if he didn't take his shots. That's when his shipmates, fifteen to twenty of them, started to email Erik's mother for information too. Without intending to, Lori became the Dear Abby of anthrax vaccine. Soon sailors from another ship on patrol in the Persian Gulf, the USS *Stennis,* stared emailing her too. Then email started arriving from the *Kitty Hawk* and the *Abraham Lincoln.* Lori was buried in email. When she heard about the reprisals the Navy took against her son for refusing the shot (he eventually caved and took all three), Lori called her senator to complain and then went to the media. When the TV show *Extra* broadcast a segment on her and put her email address on the screen at the end of it, men and women from all the other services started to email her too. Before the year was out, Lori had some 7,000 service members getting information from her. Even I had heard of Lori Greenleaf. When I wanted to find sick military personnel who'd be willing to have Tulane test their serum for the antibodies, Lori was the natural person to ask for help. One of the first soldiers she put me in touch with was Technical Sergeant Earl Stauffer, a loadmaster for C-5 Galaxies at Dover Air Force Base in Delaware.

When Earl got his first shot, on January 1, 1999, a painful nodule developed at the injection site that lasted for about ten days.[10] After his second shot more than three weeks later, both his hands started to tremble after two or three days; the involuntary hand tremors lasted for two days.[11] This time, the nodule that developed on his right arm lasted for weeks. His ears started ringing after his third shot on February 5th; not the kind of ringing that some people typically hear when they've been in a noisy place and then abruptly go somewhere quiet. This was an alarm-clock loud, incessant ring that was driving him to distraction. A month after this third shot, he developed a raised red rash on his face after being out in the sun. That's when his "gray-outs" started. Earl called them gray-outs because he didn't actually black out. He would feel himself losing his balance, as if he were on the verge of teetering over. His speech would slow; he would lose his train of thought. Time itself seemed to slow down. Sometimes he felt so weak he couldn't walk. His family says at these times, Earl looked like he was eighty years old; his jaw would hang slack, making him look "as though he was drugged." His wife, Barbara, saw him fall several times "like a staggering drunk." These episodes would occur once or twice a week and last for about eight hours. Fluorescent lights seemed to affect him; after he went into a store lit with fluorescent bulbs, his wife, who was with Earl at the time, said he couldn't find the car afterwards. He forgot why they made the trip and didn't even know where he was. "Every day, I wonder if he's going to die," says Barbara, "it's like overnight he got Alzheimer's disease." Earl's family doctor suspected autoimmunity; he was, according to this doctor, developing "either lupus or MS."[12]

Earl had been healthy all his life. In high school he was a varsity swimmer, he played lacrosse and ran cross-country. As an adult, he took up kick-boxing. He is a compact man with a mustache, who at his age (forty-five at the time of his vaccinations) still looks athletic. He is fair-skinned with reddish blond hair, which might make him especially sensitive to the sun, but he has never before broken out in chronic rashes. When he is well, he speaks quickly, in short staccato bursts. His speech is peppered with military-speak: "Roger that" and "Watch your six." You can tell he was an energetic man with a positive outlook; you could hear it in his voice, even in the way he spoke. Earl was so robustly healthy and upbeat that many pilots at Dover took notice when he became ill. If the shot could take him down, they thought, it could flatten anybody.

According to his medical records from the Walter Reed Army Medical Center, Earl had "short term memory loss, intermittent loss of balance, joint pain in his hands, knees and feet, recurring right-side headaches 5–6 days every week, with the pain shooting down the right side of his face behind his right ear." The memory loss was getting expensive; he was paying the same bills twice.

I got Earl's email address from Lori. He said he'd be glad to have Tulane test him for the antibodies; Lori's son Erik, now back home from the Navy, sent his blood in too. In March 1999, both Earl Stauffer and Erik Julius tested positive for anti-squalene antibodies. Earl had received three injections from anthrax vaccine lot number FAV030; Erik received three shots from lot number FAV020.

I published this information in the May 1999 issue of *Vanity Fair,* though I did not identify Earl by name. He outed himself. When the magazine hit the newsstands, he went on the Internet and identified himself as the anonymous airman in the article who had tested positive for the antibodies. The United States had started bombing Kosovo just four days after the article's publication; it got ignored by the media, but not by military personnel. Dover Air Base was in an uproar. The base commander, Col. Felix Grieder, suspended the anthrax immunizations at his base until he and his staff could learn more about the vaccine. A lot of his people were getting sick. He saw this with his own eyes and he wanted time to find out why. He would pay for that decision.

The Taming of Dover AFB

On May 11, 1999, Air Force Surgeon General Charles H. Roadman II convened one of the oddest briefings in the annals of the United States Air Force. A standing-room-only crowd of about 130 pilots, engineers and loadmasters squeezed into a conference room at Dover Air Force Base in Delaware to hear Roadman speak. They sat in the aisles, leaned against the walls, peered through an open doorway from the corridor. Not even President Bill Clinton, on his last visit to the base, had attracted so large and rapt an audience. But what made this meeting really noteworthy was Roadman's subject matter.

"Let me say this as succinctly as I can," he said. "There is not, there never has been, squalene as an adjuvant in the anthrax immunization, period . . . if you have anti-squalene in your body, we do know one thing, and one thing we do know, it didn't come from the anthrax immunization. And that's a fact."[13]

Squalene? Adjuvant? What manner of Air Force briefing was this? A mostly young, mostly male crowd, the kind you'd expect to see gathering for *Monday Night Football,* had come to hear a gynecologist, General Roadman, hold forth on molecular pathology and immunology. To someone unfamiliar with recent events at Dover, this might have seemed risible. This crowd was hardly the most scientifically literate bunch. If the "fighter pukes" were the aviation equivalent of Formula I drivers, Dover's C-5 Galaxy crews were long-haul truckers, and proud of it. The enlisted men called their massive cargo planes "Fred"—homage to Hanna-Barbera's working-class hero, Fred Flintstone; the smaller C-17 Globemaster III, flown out of bases like Altus AFB in Oklahoma and McChord AFB in Washington State, was "Barney." Under different circumstances, a word like *adjuvant* might have elicited, at best, a shrug of the shoulders at a place like Dover, or blank stares. Even at an immunology convention, *adjuvant* is not a word you hear sprinkled in casual conversation. But the beer-chugging working stiffs of the Air Mobility Command weren't shrugging or head-scratching; they were transfixed. In fact, several members of Roadman's audience could actually define the word *adjuvant.* They had heard Earl talk about adjuvants, they had read about them in the *Vanity Fair* article, which was virtual contraband on the base (airmen stuffed it between the pages of other magazines to conceal it from officers) and they had talked about adjuvants directly with Pam Asa.

Intent on quashing all talk of squalene, Lieutenant General Roadman, the highest-ranking medical officer in the Air Force, put the full weight of his three stars behind the message. This is a "red herring," said Roadman. "You've got to take my word as an officer, my word as a physician at face value . . . if you have anti-squalene antibodies in your body . . . it didn't come from the anthrax immunization." General Roadman knew he wouldn't be preaching to the choir at Dover, so he brought his own choir—an entourage of eleven military scientists and physicians, specialists in epidemiology, microbiology and even such exotica as membrane biochemistry, who all sat in the first couple of rows.

When Roadman assured everyone that the licensed vaccine offered complete protection against every strain, an Army microbiologist, Colonel Arthur Friedlander, backed him up. Colonel Carl Alving, a membrane biochemist and by reputation the Army's chief adjuvant expert, said he wouldn't be surprised if "enormous numbers of people" had "naturally" occurring antibodies to squalene that were "unrelated to injection." All this talk of squalene wasn't science, "it was journalism," Roadman said, as if "journalism" were something unclean. After all, the general complained, the antibody data that I had reported in *Vanity Fair* had not yet been published in a peer-reviewed scientific journal, which was true and an entirely justifiable criticism. Then Roadman administered a *coup de grace*. With a note of triumph in his voice, he told the audience that a "civilian" lab, Stanford Research International (SRI) in Menlo Park, California, had tested lots 020 and FAV030 for squalene. "I have on laboratory letterhead, 020 and 030 are negative."

Six weeks after General Roadman gave everyone at Dover his word "as an officer and a physician" that there was no squalene in anthrax vaccine, and especially not in the two vaccine lots that I had cited in *Vanity Fair,* the FDA would prove him and SRI wrong.[14] The FDA would find squalene in both lots, and in three others already known to Pam Asa because patients injected with those lots had developed the antibodies. The question is, what did Roadman know that day, and just as important, what *should* he have known as the Air Force Surgeon General? The following was declassified information available in open sources.

1. In 1998—the year the Anthrax Vaccine Immunization Program commenced—the FDA, the National Institutes of Health and USAMRIID formed the "NIH Working Group" to *fast-track* the Army's new recombinant protective antigen anthrax vaccine (rPA) into clinical trials;[15]
2. At the time, rPA formulations contained two different squalene emulsions, MF59 and MPL, as well as Col. Carl Alving's cholesterol-based liposomes;[16]
3. Colonel Alving was the Army's chief adjuvant expert and recommended the incorporation of squalene emulsions into rPA. Colonel Friedlander helped develop the new anthrax vaccine from its inception;
4. The United States had a Memorandum of Understanding (MOU) with the governments of Canada and the United Kingdom to develop the rPA second-generation anthrax vaccine. The Army referred to this agreement as the "CANUKUS MOU";[17]
5. The British formulated its version of the rPA vaccine with the Tri-Mix— the same squalene emulsion used by USAMRIID before the Gulf War;[18]
6. The next-generation anthrax vaccine was considered vital to the national security interests of the United States for the following reasons:
   a) rPA, theoretically, "would provide greater protection";[19]
   b) rPA "would require fewer doses to produce immunity";
   c) rPA, theoretically, would have "fewer adverse effects than current vaccine";
   d) Genetic engineering would eliminate the necessity of working with live spore-forming anthrax;
   e) The need for fewer doses of vaccine to confer protection = "greater flexibility and fewer time constraints in fielding a protected force";
   f) rPA, in theory, cost less to produce, and increased the number of companies that might be willing to make the vaccine (eliminating the Army's reliance on one unreliable producer, BioPort);
7. Scientists in Australia (1994) and Sweden (1999) had proved that injection with squalene caused rheumatoid arthritis in animals;[20]
8. Scientists in the United States (1976) and Poland (1997, 1999) had proved squalene injections caused neurological damage in animals;[21]
9. Scientists in the Netherlands (1994, 1998) had proven that squalene adjuvants incorporated into rPA vaccine candidates were toxic;[22]

10. Scientists in the United States (1993) had already recommended against injecting certain squalene-based formulations into humans.[23]

Contrary to General Roadman's strenuous protests, various batches of the new anthrax vaccine *had* contained squalene since 1987. Maybe he didn't know this. But what he and his entourage omitted from their presentation that day, for whatever reasons, misled Dover's personnel into thinking the detection of anti-squalene antibodies in Earl Stauffer was a trivial finding. Their audience might have judged otherwise had they known the prologue to this unfolding drama at Dover—information that Colonels Friedlander and Alving undeniably had but didn't share with their audience. By May 1999, nearly half a dozen laboratories affiliated either with major medical schools or with government laboratories in the United States and Europe had proven that injected squalene caused autoimmune disease. If Roadman and his colleagues did not know this, it was their responsibility to know it.

But the Department of Defense scientists had already established a see-no-evil pattern for managing the hullabaloo at Dover by the way it suppressed attention to Pam Asa's theory when she first brought it to their attention. DOD officials delegated their inquiry on adjuvant disease to the command that had developed the new anthrax vaccine with squalene, the United States Army Medical Research and Development Command (USMARDC), which then delegated the allegedly independent analysis of the Asa theory to the company that ran the lab making the first batches of the new vaccine, Science Applications International Corporation (SAIC). SAIC, in turn, assigned the task of writing a report on the Asa theory to a former Project Badger scientist who was responsible for the post–Gulf War development of the new vaccine. From start to finish, the Department of Defense review of the Asa theory was run by insiders with pronounced conflicts of interest. If the game wasn't rigged, it certainly gave the appearance of being so.

When it became necessary to test the vaccine for the presence of squalene, the testing was handled by the very institution that was promoting the use of squalene emulsions in the second-generation anthrax vaccine, the Walter Reed Army Institute of Research (WRAIR), which, in turn, hired a longtime military contractor, SRI International, to get the job done.[24] A company like SRI, which did business with the Pentagon, would know that its failure to provide the answers that WRAIR wanted might jeopardize any future contracts with the Department of Defense. What's more, SRI was one of the companies that Dr. Anna Johnson-Winegar had contacted to make anthrax vaccine for the Gulf War.[25]

A conflict of interest is not proof of wrongdoing, but it raises questions about SRI's failure to detect squalene in six lots of anthrax vaccine when it was, in fact, there. SRI's original reports to William Ellis, Chief of the Department of Chemical Information at WRAIR, stated on May 7, 1999, that its test had a lower detection limit, below which SRI would not be able to "see" any squalene if it were there.[26] Then, just over a month later, to SRI's embarrassment, the FDA's Center for Biologics Evaluation and Research (CBER) found squalene in five lots of anthrax vaccine in which SRI had reported none; all the concentrations found by the FDA were far below SRI's stated detection limit.[27] For anyone to find squalene in anthrax vaccine using SRI's method, the sample would have to contain almost twice the highest concentration of squalene detected by the FDA.

So there was now a logical explanation for why SRI failed to find squalene in all seventeen vaccine lots it tested—SRI's test was not sensitive enough. Believe it or not, in the vast arcana of published science, someone had actually determined the best way to detect the presence of squalene in an emulsion, *and SRI wasn't using it.* SRI employed a technique called high performance liquid chromatography, or HPLC. Way back in 1982, nearly twenty years earlier, scientists had proven that the best way to detect squalene was gas chromatography or GC.[28] GC was more sensitive and more accurate that HPLC. SRI didn't find squalene in anthrax vaccine using liquid chromatography, and nobody else would either. Was that the intent? SRI gives no explanation for using a test that would invariably fail to find squalene in the amounts detected by the FDA in anthrax vaccine. The SRI scientist who performed the tests, Dr. Ronald Spanggord, repeatedly refused to explain his choice of liquid chromatography to me, finally saying that he thought it would be a waste of time because I would not understand his answer. That was a peremptory, but reasonable enough dismissal. After all, I did find his responses to my other questions confusing.

The question is whether confusion was, in fact, the intent in all of these efforts by Army doctors and scientists. Strictly speaking, SRI stated—accurately—that it did not find squalene in seventeen anthrax vaccine lots in concentrations above its stated test limitations. At no time did SRI declare the vaccine unequivocally free of squalene. That, however, was how it was inter-preted by General Roadman at Dover, and also by representatives of the Army's Anthrax Vaccine Immunization Program. They overstated their case. After the FDA found squalene in five of the same lots tested by SRI, the Army ran more tests and found squalene in a sixth lot.

Almost without exception, doctors and scientists working on the second-generation anthrax vaccine for both USAMRIID and HHS gave reporters and members of Congress false information about squalene. Insisting that there was no squalene in the anthrax vaccine was just one misstatement among many. In 1997, when the Senate's Special Investigation Unit on Gulf War Ill-nesses inquired about "a recent theory" that "vaccines administered during the War contained squalene," the FDA resorted to equivocation.[29] FDA offi-cials informed Senate investigators that "extremely minute quantities of squa-lene could be found in vaccines manufactured using eggs, since eggs are rich in squalene and cholesterol."[30] The FDA officials provided no proof of this; no data in the existing scientific literature supported their assertion that growing a microbe in an egg contaminated a vaccine with squalene. Even if this en-tirely speculative proposition proved to be true for some vaccines, it could not have been true for anthrax vaccine. Eggs are sometimes used to grow viruses for vaccines, but *Bacillus anthracis* is a bacterium. The culture medium for growing *B. anthracis* is a broth made from amino acids, salts and some sugars, but no eggs. The FDA had licensed the formula for this medium, along with the vaccine, in 1970. So when FDA officials told the Senate that the use of eggs could "affect vaccines in general, and not just vaccines administered to Gulf War veterans," they were being disingenuous. As Pam Asa protested at the time, influenza virus is cultured in eggs for vaccines, which would make flu vaccine the most likely to be contaminated with extraneous egg antigens and squalene. But patients immunized with flu vaccine did not test positive for anti-squalene antibodies.

Second, the FDA also told Senate investigators there was "no peer re-viewed literature that comments on the health effects of such exposure to squalene."[31] This too was demonstrably false. By 1997, when the FDA made this statement, at least half a dozen scientific papers on squalene's proven ability to induce autoimmunity in several species of animals had been pub-lished in peer-reviewed journals that could be found on the shelves of the Na-tional Library of Medicine, if not at the FDA itself.

The FDA made no mention of the fact that squalene was an integral part of the Army's new anthrax vaccine, or of its discussions with the NIH and US-AMRIID at the time about "fast-tracking" the new vaccine through FDA's newly streamlined licensing pipeline. Failing to mention these facts successfully prevented any discussion of them. To date, they have never appeared in any Congressional report or in the media.

FDA officials and military doctors also propagated misleading information about the licensed anthrax vaccine. General Roadman and Colonel Friedlander told Dover's air crews that the licensed anthrax vaccine protected against every strain. This was inconsistent with the Army's argument for a new anthrax vaccine, which was partly based on the fact that some strains of *Bacillus anthracis,* such as the Ames strain, killed animals immunized with the old vaccine. The effectiveness of the licensed vaccine varied according to a number of factors. The vaccine dosage was one variable; the animal species was another. The number of spores to which an animal was exposed and the means by which it was infected—injecting them directly into its muscles or having the animal inhale them from an aerosol—also mattered. So military scientists had all sorts of data with which to support any conclusion they wished. To argue the need for a new vaccine, Army scientists complained that the old vaccine failed to protect guinea pigs against every strain.[32] This was true. To date, scientists at Fort Detrick have found at least thirty-three wild strains of *B. anthracis* that will kill one or more animal species immunized with the licensed vaccine. But that discussion was chiefly meant for internal consumption. For the public, military doctors and government officials said just the opposite. To reassure troops that the old vaccine did, in fact, protect against every strain, Army scientists and government officials could point to experiments with vaccinated monkeys that survived aerosol challenge from the same lethal Ames strain spores that wiped out vaccinated guinea pigs.[33] This they did whenever in close proximity to a podium, microphone or switched-on TV camera. There was data for every occasion. Exactly which data was recited by military doctors and scientists seemed to depend entirely on their audience.

Even the GAO skirted these issues. In its March 1999 report titled *Gulf War Illnesses: Questions About the Presence of Squalene Antibodies in Veterans Can Be Resolved,* the GAO made scant mention of the new vaccine.[34] The actual discussion of it is limited to one paragraph in a twenty-five-page report:

The anthrax vaccine experiments began in 1987, and some of the results have
been presented at conferences and published in several medical journals.
(See App. IV for a list of some of DOD's animal research on adjuvant formulations with squalene). DOD's animal studies are of interest for two reasons.
First, because animal studies are generally performed before human trials,
they represent the first step of vaccine research and present a more complete
picture of the state of research on adjuvant formulations with squalene before
the Gulf War. Second, since vaccines against biological warfare cannot be
tested for efficacy in humans, animal research is considered essential by researchers.[35]

Again, what is said is often less important than what is left unsaid, and the
GAO left a lot unsaid. By the time the GAO published its report, the NIH
Working Group to fast-track the new vaccine was already busy.[36] The Army
had scaled back its research on an HIV vaccine; the second-generation anthrax vaccine was its top priority. In 1998, Fort Detrick's scientists had three
versions of the new vaccine that protected monkeys from the deadly Ames
strain with only one shot. A decade had passed since Bruce Ivins first reported
that he had made a single-shot vaccine that worked in guinea pigs; now Ivins
had monkey data showing the same result.[37] The new vaccine was ready for
clinical trials. At least two versions of it contained squalene. The Department
of Defense now had a willing partner in the Department of Health and Human Services to carry out those trials. (This was particularly problematic since
HHS was supposed to ensure that such clinical trials were done safely, not
grease the wheels for them; HHS was also the sole government agency that
could approve waivers of informed consent for clinical trials.) Britain had also
commenced its own research with a recombinant anthrax vaccine combined
with squalene. The United States had made plans with Britain and Canada to
formally adopt the new vaccine. The GAO mentions none of this in its report.
    There are other puzzling omissions. While the GAO discussed Project Bad-
ger's failed attempt to organize production of the old anthrax vaccine at the
National Cancer Institute in time for the Persian Gulf War, the report failed
to mention that NCI had, in fact, produced material for the new vaccine *after*
the war. The GAO report also ignored plans by Project Badger scientists to
run clinical trials for experimental vaccines during Desert Shield, and did not
mention the Defense Department's long track record of testing experimental

drugs and vaccines on military personnel. Perhaps the most glaring GAO omission of all concerned the growing body of peer-reviewed scientific literature showing how squalene induced autoimmunity. This data was relevant to the discussion. Not only was it available in many university and public libraries, Pam Asa had personally photocopied copies of some of the papers and sent them to GAO investigators.

None of these complexities were hinted at in General Roadman's talk at Dover, delivered two months after the GAO report came out. If these gaps in his narrative were, indeed, sins of commission, as opposed to sins of omission by a gynecologist out of his depth in immunology, then he was only doing what everyone else seemed to be doing, including the GAO. Roadman's lawyerly equivocation reached its zenith in his repeated insistence that there has never been squalene in the anthrax immunization, "period." Strictly speaking, this was true . . . if you were speaking *strictly* about the licensed vaccine. It was the new anthrax vaccine, the so-called second-generation vaccine, that contained squalene, and service members weren't told about it. Without that information, no one could put two and two together. Military personnel immunized with vaccine lots confirmed by the FDA to contain squalene were not only developing the antibodies, they were developing diseases that matched those induced in animals injected with the oil. The diseases were autoimmune.

Error Begets Error

When Earl Stauffer began experiencing what he called "meltdowns" or "grayouts," he sought treatment at the Army's Walter Reed Army Medical Center. A neurologist there diagnosed Earl with "conversion reaction," which is in another way of saying somatization disorder (the same diagnosis given to Herb Smith and seen by physicians at Walter Reed). At first, Earl was shocked at being told his problems were all psychological. Then he got angry. But being told his problems were psychosomatic was probably the least insulting thing that military doctors might have said about his illness. Other people reporting sick at Dover were being tagged as "malingerers, liars and hypochondriacs."[38]

There was, however, clinical evidence to the contrary. These people were not experiencing run-of-the-mill post-injection soreness in their arms. Dover's vaccine casualties were developing autoimmune problems. After her second anthrax vaccination from lot FAV030, the same ones given to Earl Stauffer, Captain Michele Piel, a C-5 pilot, began suffering from dizziness so severe she could not drive; she could not read the writing on a piece of paper. Her vision was blurry, "which is very critical to me," she told members of the Congressional Committee on Government Reform; "it affects my career as a pilot."[39] Another C-5 pilot, Captain John Richter, developed joint pain following his second shot from lot FAV030.[40] His right shoulder started to ache; a few days later it was his left. A week later the pain was in the "center of my spine, to the point where I had some difficulty getting out of bed in the morning." The pain seemed to migrate—first to his ankles and feet, and then to his hands and then his hips. "I am a 36-year-old man with no previous history of arthritic symptoms," he told the committee, "and I was perfectly healthy before my first anthrax shot."[41] Later, both Captain Piel and Captain Richter were diagnosed with rheumatoid arthritis; both of them also tested positive for anti-squalene antibodies.

There were other problems consistent with injection with an oil adjuvant—like cysts. After his anthrax vaccinations, Air Force Captain Bill Law developed cysts all over his body. Stauffer developed cysts too; one of them had to be removed from his spine. Like Stauffer, Bill Law learned the meaning of "gray-out." He experienced one in the cockpit of his C-5 Galaxy after his fourth shot. On July 8, 1999, Law had been at the controls for about four hours when he had an "episode."[42] It was midday; Law's Galaxy was on autopilot over the Atlantic near the coast of Newfoundland. He checked his instruments. Air speed: 550 knots. Altitude: about 33,000 feet. The sky was an unblemished expanse of blue as far as the eye could see, except for a few streaks of wispy cirrus cloud to the right of the aircraft. Law remembers thinking how much he loved flying, even these routine milk runs across the Atlantic from Prestwick, Scotland. That's when it hit him. It felt as though someone had pulled a plug at the bottom of his brain and let the blood drain out of it. His eyeballs started to roll. His shoulders sagged. He called out to his flight engineer for help. "I'm not going to make it," Law said, as he slumped behind the yoke. Law was flying solo; his copilot had gone to the bathroom. The flight engineer got on the intercom and hailed the copilot forward, then helped Law out of the cockpit. By reputation, Law was a solid pilot or a "good stick" as they say in pilotspeak. He was also a calm man who avoided exaggeration. Yet without a hint of melodrama Law says that episode might've ended in tragedy had he been flying "single seat." One hundred fifty tons of aircraft, with eleven crew members and a score of passengers, might've gone down because of an anthrax shot.

Law had received his fourth anthrax shot on May 8, 1999. On May 12th he reported to the flight surgeon with a large cyst on his right buttock. By the time of his "gray-out," the cysts were spreading all over his body. Cysts are a proven adverse reaction to oil adjuvants in animals—something I suspect Law still does not know. He then developed endocarditis, an autoimmune inflammation in his right aortic heart valve. By the autumn of 1999 he was "DNIF," or "duh-niffed," as they say in the Air Force. DNIF stands for "Duties Not Including Flying."

Dover, a base responsible for one-quarter of America's total strategic airlift capabilities, had a record number of pilots and air crew whose status was "DNIF" since taking their anthrax shots. Lt. Colonel Jay Lacklen, chief pilot of the 326th Air Mobility Reserve Squadron, told me in 1999 that he couldn't remember a time in his thirty-year career when there were so many people sick. "I've lost more than half my squadron," he says. "In terms of percentages, we didn't lose this many people at Omaha Beach. Saddam Hussein and the Bosnians didn't knock out a fraction of the pilots we're losing to this damn vaccine!" Lacklen is a vaccine casualty too. When he got his first shot, his joints began to swell, especially in his hands. After his third shot, Lacklen says it felt like steel rods were shoved through his knuckle joints. He finds it difficult to grip anything with his left hand. X-rays show deterioration in the knuckles of both hands. Despite the sudden onset of arthritis in his hands, Lacklen decided to take his fourth shot. "I've got mouths to feed," he says. Taking care of his family is the only reason Lacklen took another dose of a vaccine that he believes is toxic. Lacklen has a history of rheumatoid arthritis in his family, but he did not have this disease before receiving his anthrax shots. Being a pilot with newly acquired arthritis wasn't the only thing Lacklen had in common with Michele Piel and John Richter. He also tested positive for anti-squalene antibodies.

Many of these reactions were documented by Capt. Richard Rovet, a nurse at Dover at the time. Rovet grew up a devout Roman Catholic. He makes frequent references to God and prayer in ordinary conversation. At times he seems better suited to being a chaplain than a nurse. Some people might interpret this as softness, but Rovet has a tough guy side to him, picked up on the streets of Bay Ridge—a working-class Brooklyn neighborhood where he grew up playing stickball and learning how to use his fists. Rovet is fidgety. He chain-smokes. He paces back and forth. Rovet is wound pretty tight.

Yet dozens of people turned to him for guidance. He was Dover's Lori Greenleaf—the man that base personnel went to for straight answers about the anthrax vaccine. He carefully recorded the illnesses that seemed to get worse with every shot—illnesses that the Air Force almost too predictably dismissed as psychosomatic. Rovet ordered laboratory tests done, and these tests verified the existence of physical, not psychological disease. According to records he kept during 1999, more than 100 people got sick after taking their anthrax shots.

They were developing verifiable autoimmune problems that could be definitively linked to the vaccine. When physicians at Walter Reed diagnosed Captain Michele Piel for an autoimmune thyroid condition, the medical center's chief immunologist, Col. Renata Engler, decided to analyze a sample of Piel's pre-vaccination serum kept in frozen storage at the Center for Health Promotion and Preventative Medicine (CHPPM) outside of Washington. Piel had passed her intensive flight physical in October 1998 with "flying colors." She was not ill, and there was no evidence of any occult illness in her blood work. The day after her flight physical, on October 21st, she received her first anthrax vaccination from lot number FAV030. Weeks later she became ill, but it was manageable. After her second vaccination she became severely ill and had to stop flying. The symptoms consistent with autoimmunity, and the lab work verifying this condition (anti-nuclear antibodies and rheumatoid factor), only manifested *after* her anthrax shots. A "conversion reaction" might give you headaches, but not antinuclear antibodies or RF. Here was straightforward evidence of causality—before her anthrax shots, Captain Piel did not have an autoimmune disease; after two shots she did.

None of this might have come to light were it not for Richard Rovet's doggedness. It was Rovet who kept collecting data, compiling a record he called "The Matrix" (no relation to the movie). In the statement Captain Piel gave to Congress, she said: "There would be no data collection at Dover Air Force Base if it wasn't for the fact that Lieutenant Rovet pursued the issue . . . and all of his efforts were met with resistance and discouragement. This resistance and discouragement came from the top." According to various personnel at Dover, the officer in charge of health care for the base, Thomas Fadel-Luna, at the time a major, suppressed the information. When she got sick, Luna called Captain Piel, an Air Force Academy graduate and accomplished pilot, a "malingerer, a liar and a whiner," says Rovet. By December of 1999, Rovet, who was still a lieutenant at the time, had documented sixteen confirmed cases of autoimmunity among Dover personnel; he had rarely seen autoimmune disease in patients over his then nine-year career in the Air Force and here was an undeniable cluster of them, but no one listened. That is when the Air Force had him transferred to another base. The Air Force had had enough of Richard Rovet and his matrix. For trying to prevent further harm to the men and women under his command, the Dover Air Base commander, Col. Felix Grieder, a highly regarded senior officer on track to make general, got sidelined. Today he is retired from the Air Force but with no regrets over his decision.

I have a copy of Rovet's matrix. Among the listed adverse reactions are "vertigo, black-outs, gray-outs, muscle and joint pain, chronic tinnitus or ringing in their ears, dizziness, fatigue, cramping, nodules, memory loss and headaches"—all following the shot, all of them consistent with autoimmunity. Even the base public health officer, a flight surgeon, suffered acute anaphylaxis after one shot. According to sources at the base who requested anonymity, she collapsed and had to be resuscitated with oxygen. Still the FDA, by this time an active participant in efforts to accelerate the licensure of the new anthrax vaccine, declined to intervene.

A verified autoimmune problem had also appeared elsewhere just months after the force-wide anthrax immunization program began. The Navy recorded an autoimmune reaction following anthrax vaccination in a sailor the same year the problems cropped up at Dover. On May 17, 1998, a twenty-four-year old sailor aboard the USS *John F. McCain* became noticeably weaker after his third anthrax shot.[43] Within forty-eight hours, he could not even climb stairs. The Navy evacuated him to Bahrain International Hospital in Manama, where he was diagnosed with an autoimmune disease called Guillain-Barré syndrome. Guillain-Barré syndrome is described in the Navy document that recounts the incident as "an acute, sporadic, relatively rare disease wherein the body's own immune system is stimulated by an outside agent to attack the nervous system, specifically the mylen [sic] sheeths [sic] of the nerves." The Navy investigator reached the following conclusion: "In this case, in the absence of any known preexisting infection or condition, the anthrax vaccine cannot be ruled out as a possible cause of this sailor's disease."

If the FDA needed more evidence that anthrax vaccination caused autoimmune disease, it could have found it a lot closer to home than Manama, Bahrain. This evidence linked autoimmunity specifically to injection with anthrax lots proven to contain squalene by the FDA. On June 25, 1999, for reasons it did not explain to health-care personnel at Dover, the Air Force transferred the remaining stocks of one lot of anthrax vaccine containing squalene, FAV030—the one that caused problems for Sgt. Stauffer, Captain Piel, Captain Richter and Lt. Col. Lacklen, among others—to Battle Creek, Michigan, home of the 110 Fighter Wing of the Michigan Air National Guard. When the Air Force started vaccinating members of this wing with FAV030, they became sick, too. They complained of symptoms identical to the ones afflicting personnel at Dover as well as Gulf War veterans. After receiving three shots from vaccine lot FAV030, Air Force Staff Sergeant Randi Allaire developed chronic fatigue, abdominal cramping, migraines, joint and muscle pains and memory loss.[44] She couldn't remember computer passwords that she used every day at work.[45] Two out of four Michigan Air National Guardsmen tested by Tulane had the antibodies. This was an epidemiological trail lit as brightly as an Air Force runway after dark, but no one in the Air Force, Walter Reed Army Medical Center, or the FDA seemed inclined to follow it.

Military personnel were getting sick after their anthrax shots. Those who didn't get sick saw others who did. None of them knew why some people got gravely ill after their vaccinations while others stayed healthy. If service members couldn't get a straight answer from their generals or from the FDA, they weren't getting them from the media either. The media largely ignored the *Vanity Fair* article even if the Pentagon and the FDA did not. It was in response to *Vanity Fair* that the FDA tested the anthrax vaccine for squalene, specifically lots FAV020 and FAV030.[46] And while it found squalene in both lots, as well as three others, FDA officials withheld this information from the public for another year and a half. The director of the Anthrax Vaccine Immunization Progam, Major Guy Strawder, simply came out swinging. I was "reckless, irresponsible and wrong," he told a Navy public affairs specialist.

There were two other attacks, and I discuss them here only because it is conceivable that both were sufficiently influential to have discouraged anyone in the media or in Congress from taking a closer look at the link between an-thrax vaccine and squalene. The first was an article by Laurie Garrett of *News-day*, who wrote a piece entitled "Healthy Shot of Distrust" that is, in retrospect, remarkable for how extravagantly wrong it was about squalene and autoimmunity.[47] It ran nearly 3,000 words, an exceptionally long piece by newspaper standards, which in itself lent a certain gravitas to its content. What's more Garrett had won a Pulitzer Prize for her reporting on an Ebola outbreak in Zaire. So when a reporter of Garrett's stature quoted military sources "who argued that the anthrax vaccines used at the time of the Gulf War were manufactured long before squalene was even considered for use as an adjuvant in any vaccine," no one thought to question it. Garrett's sources were incorrect. According to declassified military documents, the Army had fewer than 20,000 doses stockpiled when Saddam Hussein invaded Kuwait, so most of the vaccine used in the Gulf War was made after August 1990. If Bob Garry had succeeded in identifying an antibody to squalene, wrote Gar-rett, "this would constitute the first time in the history of immunology that anti-fat antibodies have been found." This statement left Garry and Asa, both immunologists, slack-jawed. Antibodies to fats or lipids had been known to ex-ist for decades. Antiphospholipid antibodies are a hallmark of systemic lupus erythematosus; to diagnose lupus, doctors routinely test for this lipid autoanti-body. In the '80s, the Army's adjuvant expert, Col. Carl Alving, published sev-eral papers on his success at inducing autoantibodies to cholesterol, which is not only a lipid but a molecular cousin of squalene.

That made two egregious errors on squalene's alleged links to anthrax im-munization and Gulf War Syndrome in Garrett's piece; there were at least two more. She reported that alum, the only licensed vaccine adjuvant in America, caused rheumatoid arthritis in animals. If this were true, one might wonder why the FDA ever licensed it for use in vaccines. Alum has been around since the 1930s, when it was first used to boost the immune response to tetanus and diphtheria toxoids. In nearly seventy-five years of use, alum has never been shown to cause rheumatoid arthritis or any other autoimmune disease in animals or humans. If you search the database of the National Library of Medicine you will not find a single paper supporting Garrett's assertion about alum. In fact, one study has recently shown the opposite might be true—that animals could actually be protected from autoimmunity by immunizing them with a protein affixed to particles of alum.[48]

Finally, Garrett was also incorrect about the backgrounds of Bob Garry and Pam Asa. Because the anti-squalene antibodies found by Tulane "constituted the only evidence that might indicate the Pentagon is lying," Garrett argued that it was necessary to examine Garry and Asa's personal backgrounds. Both, she said, "were previously in the public eye, in the silicone breast implant controversy." Garry, she reported, had testified in lawsuits against Dow Corning, alleging that silicone leaking from implants caused antibodies that induced autoimmune diseases. Although his doctoral student had written that controversial paper published in the *Lancet,* Bob Garry had never testified in any lawsuit regarding silicone breast implants; neither had Pam Asa.

Which brings me to the background of the source who told Garrett there was no squalene in the anthrax vaccine used during the Gulf War. Garrett's source for this information was General Phillip K. Russell, former commander of the United States Army Medical Research and Development Command at Fort Detrick at the time of the Gulf War. General Russell oversaw the early development of the second-generation anthrax vaccine with squalene. During the '90s, when he joined the faculty of the Johns Hopkins School of Public Health, Russell became an outspoken proponent of the new vaccine as it was being shepherded through the FDA's licensing labyrinth. Judging by Garrett's failure to mention these facts in her article, one may wonder whether General Russell ever informed her of them. If he did not disclose the existence of the Army's prototype anthrax vaccines, which had been formulated with squalene since 1987, or disclose his relationship to their very creation, then General Russell's oversight raises questions about his motives or his memory.

Error begets error, and STATS, the Internet-based Statistical Assessment Service of the Center for Media and Public Affairs one-upped *Newsday* in its wielding of the hatchet. According to the STATS home page, "STATS monitors the media to expose the abuse of science and statistics before people are misled and public policy distorted." STATS Managing Editor Trevor Butterworth compared me unfavorably to Garrett. She: "award-winning science reporter." Me: "susceptible journalist." Butterworth called his piece "Vanity Scare."[49] As with Garrett's *Newsday* piece, the errors in "Vanity Scare" could have been averted with a routine search on PubMed, the National Library of Medicine's database for scientific papers and abstracts. Failing to do so was an especially egregious lapse for Butterworth whose bread and butter was not only web-based journalism (he should have known how to use PubMed then), but also throwing brickbats at inaccurate journalists or as he most charitably insinuated about me: "a journalist susceptible to such inaccuracies." Butterworth, an Englishman who has recently taken aim at the allegedly error-prone ways of British journalism, not only repeated Garrett's mistakes but liberally quoted them, which no doubt delighted the Department of Defense. The department promptly photocopied "Vanity Scare" and circulated it to members of Congress.

Of the many flaws that Butterworth sought to expose was my assertion that Patient X in the NIH herpes vaccine trial had been injected with the MF59 adjuvant as a placebo. "This paragraph makes no sense," Butterworth decried. "A placebo is chosen precisely because it has no physiological effect—in other words, it is a blank." I could not agree more. "Scientists do this," he went on, "in order to have a control group of patients against which to measure the experimental effect. They wouldn't risk interfering with the integrity of the control by using a potentially potent substance, obscuring the effects of the real medicine under investigation." Butterworth actually laid out the case as well as anyone could for why the NIH's use of oil adjuvants as a placebo was scientifically and ethically dubious. The practice was so outrageous that Butterworth could not conceive how anyone but a moron such as me, not to mention the two *Vanity Fair* researchers who spent a full month reverse-engineering every sentence I wrote, could have allowed such a howler to get into print. Assumption is a child of arrogance.

After reading "Vanity Scare," I decided to call Butterworth, if for no other reason than to find out how a media watchdog organization that purportedly sought to "hold U.S. journalists to the highest standards" could publish such calumny without checking its facts.

"Why didn't you call me or Dr. Garry or Dr. Asa?" I asked. "We could have given you the documents and scientific references that support the allegations."

"Because whenever I write a piece such as this, I restrict myself to the text," he said.

"I majored in English literature, Trevor. You did not restrict yourself to the text. You quoted *Newsday* and scientists who were not in my article. Those quotes were *extra*-textual. If I get something wrong," I continued, "then by all means bash me. But you got your facts wrong, and that doesn't help anybody. For instance, Bob Garry's assay wasn't developed to test for antibodies to silicone; it was originally developed to detect antibodies for HIV, which it does so well that it is used millions of times a year around the world."

Butterworth, who was more polite on the phone than he was in print, was listening. "As for the NIH, it is, in fact, using oil adjuvants as a placebo, and you don't have to take my word on that. You know the herpes vaccine trial that you say *couldn't* have used an adjuvant as a placebo? Well, it did. And the NIH scientists who ran that trial published a paper on that particular experiment five years ago. They clearly state that they used MF59, which is squalene in water, as a placebo. You can read it for yourself."[50]

"Oh," he said somewhat sheepishly.

"But never mind me, Trevor. What about the people who may have been harmed by this stuff? Did you know that the Department of Defense has been working on a recombinant anthrax vaccine for more than a decade, and that starting around 1987 the prototypes were mostly formulated with squalene? And if you quoted Laurie Garrett, which went beyond my text, you could have also gone beyond my text to quote some of the scientific papers on squalene's ability to induce autoimmunity. Had you bothered to check, you would have discovered quite a few of them."

Butterworth paused before he spoke again. "What would you like me to do then?" he asked. "I could take it [the article] off the website."

"Don't bother," I said. "The damage is already done. DOD is passing 'Vanity Scare' around the halls of Congress. It's on the Defense Department website. You can take it off your website, but you're not going to get it off the Pentagon's."

I was glad I got that off my chest, but one criticism leveled by General Roadman, Carl Alving, Laurie Garrett and Trevor Butterworth was legitimate, and I could not do anything about it. At the time of the *Vanity Fair* article's publication, the Tulane data had not yet been published in a peer-reviewed scientific journal. Articles about scientific data usually appear after it is published, not before. Pam Asa had informed me that I was in a "horse-race with JAMA" (the *Journal of the American Medical Association*) to get the information published. But JAMA never published it. After the *Vanity Fair* article was already in production, JAMA's editor, Dr. George Lundberg, got ousted.[51] Tulane's squalene antibody paper got shelved. To be taken seriously, Asa and Garry's data needed to be published in a peer-reviewed journal. This would not have validated every single assertion they made, but it would have signaled to other scientists that their data was sufficiently credible to warrant further scrutiny, if not acceptance.

At Dover, General Roadman referred to this controversy over squalene in anthrax vaccine as a "battle of the Internet." I was caught up in an information war, and until Tulane got its paper published, I was firing blanks. The *Vanity Fair* article did provoke the FDA into testing the vaccine, and the discovery by the FDA, and later the Army, that squalene was indeed present in six lots of anthrax vaccine would become a critical piece of forensic evidence—perhaps the most important piece of evidence after the antibodies themselves. But in the absence of either set of data—the Tulane paper would not be published for another eight months and the FDA data would not be released to the public for a year and a half—the squalene issue got buried in an accumulating sludge of disinformation.

Not knowing what to think, an increasing number of sick military personnel rejected the idea that squalene could have gotten them sick.

Chapter Ten

A Dose of Reality

By the time Pam Asa and Bob Garry published their first paper on squalene antibodies, in February 2000, there was a growing consensus that the anthrax vaccine was somehow linked to chronic illnesses in Gulf War veterans. But you would never know it from the media. If reporters missed the forest for the trees, it was because they had been told, incessantly and with great authority by public health officials and the military, that there *were* no trees. Gulf War Syndrome didn't exist. An Ivy League professor of English even published a book called *Hystories,* lumping Gulf War Syndrome with alien abduction, satanic ritual abuse and recovered memories as examples of "hysterical epidemics." GWS, she argued, was a kind of mass hysteria abetted by a gullible if not cynically irresponsible press.[1]

The U.S. media, having cycled breathlessly through each new theory as if it were the definitive answer to the problems afflicting Gulf War veterans, had exhausted itself. As each new theory fizzled, editors grew yet more weary of the story. It was too insubstantial; the facts were too elusive. The conventional wisdom that emerged on Gulf War Syndrome had gone from mystery to history (as well as "hystory"). It was old news.

In a sense it was. The federal government had spent $133.5 million on 145 different research projects on GWS; by the spring of 2000, forty had been completed, another 105 were under way, and nothing had been turned up.[2] As the VA noted in a fact sheet published at that time, even the term "Gulf War

Syndrome" was of "limited value."[3] The so-called syndrome, said the VA, did not "identify a characteristic organ abnormality nor reflect consensus on any set of inclusionary or exclusionary symptoms, laboratory tests or medical signs."[4] The problem with all this criticism was that Asa and Garry's data in fact satisfied all these criteria. It identified a *characteristic abnormality*: autoimmunity and its attendant *symptoms*, which were a close match for the complaints made by sick veterans. The Asa/Garry assay was a *laboratory test* that showed evidence of an abnormal immunological process under way in both sick Gulf War veterans and active-duty military personnel. The antibodies detected by this test were a marker for the alleged causative agent: the oil adjuvant squalene, as well as an alleged marker for the source of that agent, an anthrax vaccine.

By 2000, more and more epidemiologists and even government researchers had reported links between the syndrome and biological warfare vaccines, specifically anthrax vaccine. Their papers, however, although published in peer-reviewed journals, barely received any attention from the wider media. This was odd because the anthrax vaccine was in the news for related reasons. Military personnel, fearing its alleged ability to induce Gulf War Syndrome–like illnesses, were refusing to take the shot. The mandatory anthrax vaccination program, which ran from 1998 to 2000, had provoked the single most corrosive policy dispute to divide the ranks of the military since the Vietnam War. It caused more disruption than the decision to put women in combat or the "don't ask, don't tell" policy on homosexuality. In an organization that demanded unflinching submission to authority, where people had been drilled to obey orders even when there was a slim chance of surviving what they had been told to do, there was outright insubordination over the contents of a hypodermic needle. Hundreds have chosen to end their military careers in order to avoid the shot. Some left the service; some chose court-martial. Some Air Force reserve squadrons were decimated by resignations.

Dover Air Force Base hemorrhaged pilots. Lt. Col. Lacklen, who had been flying for nearly thirty years, starting with C-7s and B-52s in Vietnam, had never seen anything like it. "The big bleed was 'drill weekend,'" says Lacklen. "The wing commander said that weekend everyone would have to take the shot. Almost half didn't show up. My wing, the 512th, lost 55 out of 120 pilots just in that one weekend. They were pilots. They saw what happened to Michele Piel, her vertigo; pilots can't afford to get vertigo. What happened to

Richter and Stauffer, that made a difference too; these were solid guys, respected around the base. What's it cost these days to train a pilot? A million? Do the math!" I did the math. That weekend the U.S. Air Force lost about $55 million in pilots at just one base.

The media, its eyes glazed over by seemingly endless and inconsequential scientific mumbo jumbo about GWS, missed the accumulating evidence of a vaccine-related illness in military personnel. It is not that the outlines of this story were too inchoate; they were simply too big.

In 1999, five months before the appearance of my *Vanity Fair* article or the Asa/Garry paper, epidemiologists from the University of London published a Pentagon-funded study of British Gulf War veterans showing that "vaccination against plague and anthrax before deployment to the Gulf correlated highly with illness."[5] That conclusion was made by none other than Dr. Stephen E. Straus of the NIH, the principal investigator in Patient X's herpes vaccine trial, who wrote a kind of précis to the British paper. Both the paper and Straus's commentary were published in the same issue of the British medical journal the *Lancet*. The authors of the actual study, British epidemiologists who worked in the Gulf War Illness Research Unit at Guy's, King's and St. Thomas' College Medical School at the University of London, had asked more than 12,000 British servicemen to fill out a general health questionnaire. In another of those Orwellian moments that continued to crop up during this saga, a Presidential Advisory Committee in the United States had just reaffirmed that there was no such thing as Gulf War Syndrome, but the CDC had a definition of one.[6] Using the CDC criteria to define the allegedly indefinable disease, the University of London investigators learned that "servicemen who received vaccinations against biological warfare agents were more likely to report long-term symptoms. Those who received routine vaccinations were generally not at increased risk."[7]

The British epidemiologists would go on to investigate whether U.K. veterans were suffering from some sort of overload from the cocktail of vaccines they received during the Gulf War. But multiple vaccinations were a feature of every deployment, and no corresponding syndrome had appeared as a result. The same was true for the thousands of tourists traveling each year to equatorial countries; they receive multiple vaccinations without getting sick. Likewise, the *Lancet* study did not support a link between Gulf War illness and multiple vaccinations. It was more specific than that: "A striking relation between retrospective recollection of side-effects of vaccines at the time and later illness seemed to explain the association between individual vaccines and illness, but not multiple vaccines and illness."[8] Which vaccines? According to this study, only two: anthrax and plague.

More and more epidemiologists were finding links between "nonroutine immunizations (anthrax and plague)" and veterans suffering from the CDC definition of Gulf War illness. The Canadians were the first to make this connection, in 1998, followed by the University of London study.[9] In 2000, British epidemiologists reported more evidence of a link between GWS and vaccines, speculating that it might be a result of a toxic combination of multiple vaccinations and stress.[10]

But not every clue was coming from investigators outside the United States. An epidemiologist with the Kansas Commission on Veterans Affairs, Lea Steele, published data that was consistent with the British and Canadian findings, noting evidence of "excess morbidity" among Kansas veterans. That is epidemiology-speak for more illness. Steele provided another tantalizing bit of information: more evidence of Gulf War illness in veterans who never went to the Persian Gulf. And non-deployed veterans who received vaccines during the war were far more likely to get sick than those who did not (12 percent versus 4 percent).[11] Gulf War illness was least prevalent among deployed veterans who left the Middle East before the war (9 percent) and most prevalent among those who left in June or July of 1991 (41 percent).[12] Not only were non-deployed Gulf War–era veterans sick; those who received vaccinations were three times more likely to get sick than those who did not.

The Canadians and the British vaccinated against anthrax and plague.[13] The United States vaccinated against anthrax and botulinum toxin. So far, concerning the Australians, I have been able to confirm only that they vaccinated against anthrax. Only one biological warfare vaccine was administered by all four nations reporting veterans suffering from the CDC case-definition of Gulf War illness: anthrax vaccine.

One more clue came from overseas—one that went unreported here in the United States. In the late 1990s, British Defence Minister Nicholas Soames informed Britain's Parliamentary Defence Select Committee that Britain had administered a whooping cough (pertussis) vaccine to British Gulf War troops as an adjuvant to accelerate the immune response to the anthrax vaccine. There was no known link between pertussis vaccine and autoimmunity, but in admitting the use of an adjuvant for anthrax vaccine, Britain let something out of the bag that U.S. military doctors and scientists were not telling troops. The licensed U.S. and U.K. anthrax vaccines were weak; they required too much time to induce any reliable level of immunity. To get a quicker response, both vaccines required a more powerful adjuvant. Since the late 1980s, U.S. and British military scientists had experimented with several candidates; most of them contained squalene.

Laboratory tests proved that people have become sick after taking the vaccine. Yet published research, and decades of prior experience with the vaccine, also showed that it was safe. These two facts seemed irreconcilable, and yet both were true. If this epidemiological riddle seems as vexing as a Buddhist koan, it was because the solution lay in a third set of facts, known to few people outside the inner circle of the military's medical command. The vaccine had changed.

If It Looks Like a Duck

In September 2000, the FDA finally provided what was perhaps the most definitive evidence of a clandestine experiment with squalene—ironically, while trying to persuade Congress that squalene's presence in anthrax vaccine was a wholly natural phenomenon. Having found squalene in five lots of vaccine after the publication of "The Pentagon's Toxic Secret" in *Vanity Fair,* the FDA withheld this evidence from the public.[14] It had given the results in the winter of 2000 to Norma Smith, an assistant to former Representative Jack Metcalf—Metcalf being the congressman who asked the GAO to investigate the squalene issue in the first place. Smith told me she held onto this information for another six months without telling anyone, because she didn't know what the FDA findings meant.[15] She said the FDA told her that the amounts of squalene its scientists had detected in the vaccine were minuscule and nothing to worry about. After she and Representative Metcalf released a final report on their investigation in late September, the deputy director of the FDA's Center for Biologics Evaluation and Research (CBER), Dr. Mark Ellengold, informed the House Government Reform Committee that the "trace" amounts of squalene detected in the five lots of anthrax vaccine were in the parts-per-billion range and therefore harmless.[16]

Ellengold also told the committee that squalene was probably found in all vaccines. CBER, he said, had found squalene in similar amounts in a sample of the diphtheria vaccine manufactured by Wyeth as well as Connaught's tetanus vaccine. Ellengold made no mention to Congress of the Army's recombinant protective antigen (rPA) vaccine with squalene or of FDA's direct involvement in fast-tracking its licensure. Pharmaceutical companies routinely test experimental drugs in the parts-per-billion or nanogram range for effectiveness, but Ellengold didn't explain this to the congressmen.

There was something else about the findings that Ellengold didn't point out. CBER found the following concentrations of squalene in the five lots of anthrax vaccine:[17]

FAV020	11 ppb
FAV030	10 ppb
FAV038	27 ppb
FAV043	40 ppb
FAV047	83 ppb

What escaped everyone's notice, perhaps even Dr. Ellengold's, was a discernible relationship in this sequence of numbers. After the first two lots, which contained virtually identical amounts of squalene, each successive lot contained roughly twice as much as the previous one.

I reported these figures to Dr. Frank Engley, a former chairman of the Department of Microbiology at the University of Missouri and a longtime consultant to the Armed Forces Epidemiological Board, with which he was affiliated at the time of the Gulf War.

"The arithmetic is showing us what?" I asked.

"Doubling," he said.

"And what are the chances of this doubling phenomenon occurring randomly in nature?"

"Impossible," said Engley. "That's really impossible. Things don't occur that way. Someone back there in production in the labs was making twofold dilutions . . . twofold increasing amounts."

"I'm not sure I understand you," I said.

"That's how you do things," he said. "Your first tube is what you call a 1:2, and the next tube is 1:4, and the next tube is 1:8, and 1:16, 1:32, 64, 128, 256, 512, 1024. See how fast I can do that?"

Frances Beck, the scientist who first demonstrated squalene's ability to cause autoimmune disease, back in the 1970s, agreed with Engley—it was a twofold serial dilution. "That would be the first thing I would think about," she said. "When you do a dose-response, you can do a 1:5 or a 1:10 . . . this is about a 1:2. It's not quite. 10, 20, 40, 80 would be a 1:2. This is a little off, but it may be that it was based on a curve rather than a straight line."

"What about the FDA's egg explanation for the presence of squalene?" I ask Dr. Beck. "Just assume for the sake of this argument that anthrax is grown in eggs—which it isn't, I know—but if it was, could eggs or any other contaminant account for these concentrations of squalene?"

"So you're going to tell me that some eggs have 11 parts, some have 27, some have 40, and some have 83? . . . *I don't think so.*"

"Well, what do you make of this, then?"

"They did a Phase I clinical trial without informed consent," she said, without missing a beat. "The government thinks we're dumb."

It looked that obvious to me, too, but as much as I trusted Dr. Beck and Dr. Engley, two scientists with whom I had consulted for years, I wanted to put the same questions to other scientists with whom I had never spoken before. I "cold-called," as we sometimes say in journalism, a nationally recognized specialist in clinical pharmacology, Dr. Lewis B. Sheiner, an M.D. and Ph.D. on the faculty of the University of California at San Francisco, which, in a recent *U.S. News & World Report* survey, had the No. 2-ranked school of pharmacology in the nation. I did not mention the words "squalene" or "anthrax vaccine" in our discussion because they were such hot-button topics, and would be for Professor Sheiner. In addition to being a Professor of Laboratory Medicine, Medicine, and Pharmacy at UCSF, Sheiner is active in the AIDS Clinical Trials Group (ACTG) of the U.S. National Institute of Allergy and Infectious Diseases (NIAID), and a member of the Antiviral Advisory Committee of the U.S. Food and Drug Administration. Because of his affiliations with both NIH and FDA, I was concerned that if he knew the subject was squalene—an adjuvant used in most prototype HIV and oncology vaccines in addition to the Army's recombinant vaccine for anthrax—it would politicize our discussion, skewing his comments in one direction or another. I wanted his objective evaluation on two issues only: whether or not the FDA concentrations had any discernible relation to each other, and whether or not nanogram doses of a drug could affect anyone.

I told him what Drs. Engley and Beck said without mentioning their names. Sheiner concurred that the concentrations represented a dilution series.

"Well, yeah, I mean 80 to 42 to about 20 to about 10, so it looks like they're dilutions to twofold, sure, true enough," said Dr. Sheiner.

"They're not an exact doubling," I pointed out. "They're a little off. Do you have a problem with that?"

"They meant it to be 10, 20, 40, 80, but of course, little errors occur and so they got 27, 83 and 11 instead of exactly 10, 20, 40, 80, you know . . . that's fine, sure," says Sheiner. "Typically, you can't measure things with better than 5 to 10 percent error, so 83 is essentially the same as 80, as far as you know. It's conceivable that when they made the dilution a little extra drop of stuff got in there. I mean, nanograms are very hard to deal with; it's an extremely small amount. If somebody told me 'I made up a twofold serial dilution,' and I sent it off to the lab to assay what was actually in these dilutions and I got these numbers, I'd say you were doing pretty good."

That was three for three. All three scientists, none of whom knew each other, or Pam Asa or Bob Garry, looked at these numbers and saw the same thing.

I called Dr. Beck again to see if she wanted to tone down her remarks. She had been rather vehement about the FDA's reported concentrations being evidence of a clinical trial.

"They did a dose-response," she reiterated. "I mean, that's what it is. There's no other way that somebody would run a study and use varying doses unless they were running a dose-response trial, because you do all of this before you give it to humans. This is what a Phase I trial does. You give it at one dose, and you look at it, you evaluate the data, and then you go to the next dose, give it to another bunch of people and you evaluate the data, and then you do it again."

"Bottom line: knowing what you know about squalene, given your own experiments, would you ever inject it into a human being?"

"No," said Beck.

I put the same question to Dr. Johnny Lorentzen at the Karolinska Institute, who has also done groundbreaking research showing squalene's ability to induce autoimmunity in animals.

"Would you risk injecting it?" I asked.

"I would be cautious," he replied. "I would not do it to myself."

I started going through Chiron's published papers on MF59 again; there were some figures I wanted to look at again from a dose-ranging study that Chiron did with an influenza vaccine mixed with MF59. I found them in a book called *Vaccine Design, The Subunit and Adjuvant Approach*.[18] I wrote them down on a piece of paper, then lined them up side by side with the FDA's squalene concentrations in anthrax vaccine. "Pam Asa's not going to believe this," I said to myself.

In the early '90s, Chiron Corporation, in Emeryville, California, the manufacturer of MF59, the vaccine adjuvant that Col. Carl Alving said he would recommend for use in the anthrax vaccine—and the same adjuvant that Dr. Stephen Straus used in the NIH herpes vaccine trial with Patient X—rediscovered what Frances Beck and her colleague Michael Whitehouse found all those years ago: squalene was an immunostimulant. When scientists at Baylor College of Medicine recommended against using an influenza vaccine formulated with Chiron's earlier squalene emulsion that contained a protein fraction called muramyl tripeptide (MTP-PE), Chiron removed the MTP-PE. It was superfluous.[19] Chiron concluded that squalene was the "primary adjuvant."[20] In light of this, the company did the logical thing: it organized a dose-ranging study for MF59.

Now take a look at FDA's squalene concentrations in BioPort anthrax vaccine on the left, next to the concentrations on the right from Chiron's 1995 dose-ranging study for MF59—which, by the way, Chiron has been developing in cooperation with the U.S. Army and NIH.[21]

FAV020	11ppb	Chiron	.11 mg
FAV030	10 ppb		
FAV038	27 ppb	Chiron	.22 mg
FAV043	40 ppb	Chiron	.43 mg
FAV047	83 ppb	Chiron	.86 mg

The FDA's ratios were a close match for Chiron's. Remember, the FDA found parts per billion or nanogram concentrations of squalene in anthrax vaccine. The Chiron dose-ranging study uses milligrams—an amount which is a million times greater. So I am comparing *ratios* not quantities. Now consider the Chiron dilution series on the right: there is a precise doubling between each dilution—double 11 and you get 22; double 22 and you get 44 (well, 43 is pretty close); double 43 and you get 86. Now look at the FDA nanogram concentrations for squalene in anthrax vaccine on the left. The first two vaccine lots contain, for all intents and purposes, identical amounts. In nanograms, which are one billionth of a gram each, a difference of one nanogram is negligible. Now let's look at the first lot. FAV020 contains 11 nanograms; double that and you get 22—5 nanograms less than the concentration of squalene in FAV038. That bothered me at first, but when I asked Sheiner about this comparison, he described this as a negligible difference and one that could be accounted for by a sampling error. "You've got a number of places where you can make a mistake here," he said. "You can't measure volumes perfectly, and so when they were measuring to make the dilution, you know, they make a little error in the measurement of the volume that you're diluting, and then the gas chromatography has an error. In other words that 27 could be 20 and I wouldn't be surprised. The next time you assayed it, it might not come out to be 27, it might come out to be 22, and a time after that it might come out to be 30, and so on and so forth. So it's in a ballpark of 27."

For the sake of this argument, let's use this 5 nanograms margin of error; subtract 5 nanograms from FAV038's 27 and you get 22. Double 22 and you get 44 (that's off by just 1 from the comparable Chiron ratio of 43); and double 44 and you get 88 (again, well within our 5 nanogram tolerance). To give you an idea of how small these amounts are, scientists at Cornell University have compared a nanogram or part per billion to "a pinch of salt in ten tons of potato chips" or "one drop of impurity in 500 barrels of water."[22] That's not much. At these low nanogram concentrations, someone has done a masterful job of mixing a twofold serial dilution. With these 5 lots of anthrax vaccine, someone could bracket which nano-dose of squalene, mixed with this anthrax protective antigen, would provide optimal performance with the least amount of toxicity. "That's why you do dose-responses," says Beck. "What range will give you the response, or the desired response that you'd look for? And what range would give you an undesirable response, because you don't want to exceed that range."

After the FDA announced that it found squalene in five lots of vaccine, the Army retested the vaccine using a more sensitive method and found concentrations ranging between 1 and 9 ppb squalene in three different vials from a sixth lot, FAV008. Lot FAV008 was administered at Dover Air Force Base to personnel who subsequently developed anti-squalene antibodies and autoimmune disease, specifically polymyositis; and it was first distributed on January 22, 1991—during Desert Storm.[23]

According to a confidential inventory I received from a source at BioPort, the corporation, in its previous incarnation as the state-owned Michigan Biologic Products Institute in Lansing, Michigan, made 72,880 doses of FAV008. The lot verified to contain squalene, FAV008, was not only distributed to U.S. military installations but also to foreign countries, including the Federal Republic of Germany, Israel, Canada and Taiwan. Based on the number of different times that the Michigan producer packaged this lot of vaccine, something seemed odd about FAV008. Something was. Based on the Army's testing, we know it contained squalene. Based on the dates listed in this inventory, we know it was first distributed during Desert Storm. Anthrax vaccine Lot # FAV008 is evidence, then, that Desert Storm troops may have been injected with at least one anthrax vaccine lot verified to contain squalene, which is consistent with Tulane University's detection of anti-squalene antibodies in Desert Storm veterans and the autoimmune diseases afflicting them.

As for the trace amounts of squalene that Dr. Ellengold considered harmless, parts-per-billion doses do indeed sound inconsequential when you're thinking in terms of household measures like teaspoons and ounces. But in immunology, parts per billion are a substantial dose. When an immunologist refers to antibodies reacting to a germ, it is a simplified way of describing what really occurs. Antibodies respond to molecules, and even then, not a whole molecule. Antibodies bind to specific sites on a molecule—the epitopes or antigenic determinants that I discussed in Chapter 8. Any one molecule might have several different epitopes to which unique antibodies can form. So when someone like Dr. Ellengold says 10 parts per billion is a trace amount, it is in a casuistical sense true. Relative to the number of teaspoons of coffee to make a quick cup of morning java, 10 parts per billion is a trace amount. But in immunology and pharmacology, 10 parts per billion can be a big dose. A mere 10 ppb concentration of squalene in 0.5 ml of liquid translates into approximately 184 trillion molecules of squalene.[24] So the number of potential immune responses to a 10 ppb concentration of squalene in 0.5 ml of liquid may exceed 184 trillion by a considerable amount.

"Could that be active? Sure," says Sheiner. "I mean, it depends on the kind of drug. For example, a drug that imitates a hormone. Hormones are often active in that range, in nanograms per mil. Digoxin is a famous drug that's been around for several hundred years, that's active in nanograms per mil concentrations. Opiates can be in that range and be quite effective. So it really depends on the body's amplification system. The body does have certain systems where it's extremely sensitive, and amplifies the signal a great deal. And so a very small amount of a stimulus can cause a very large effect."[25] In fact, at the time Dr. Ellengold addressed the House Committee on Government Reform, many biotech companies and universities were developing medicines for which the proposed dosage was in nanograms.[26] A Swedish company, Isconova, has been researching a "mucosal" or inhaled tuberculosis vaccine in which the chief pharmaceutical ingredient, the vaccine antigen, is present in mere "nanogram doses."[27]

That dosing was being done in these minuscule amounts was not something only a top-rank research pharmacologist like Dr. Sheiner would know. By the time Dr. Ellengold spoke to Congress, nanogram doses were not only routinely used in drug testing, they were also being tried with vaccines, which were Ellengold's specific area of responsibility with the FDA.

At the time Ellengold provided his advice to Congressman Metcalf's committee, his boss was Dr. Kathryn Zoon, and it's worth asking what influence Zoon could have had on his comments. As the director of the Center for Biologics Evaluation and Research, where Ellengold worked, Zoon was not only a proponent of the Army/HHS agenda to fast-track the licensure of the new anthrax vaccine, she publicly advocated testing the new vaccine in humans in 1999, when U.S. military personnel were being immunized with anthrax vaccine lots containing a twofold dilution series of squalene. She proposed such testing in a special issue of the journal *Emerging and Infectious Diseases,* which is published by the Centers for Disease Control.[28] "Comparisons of immune responses in human cohorts receiving new [i.e., experimental] or licensed vaccines should be performed," she wrote. Judging from the mass spectrometry data from CBER's own laboratories, that research was already under way.

That particular issue of *Emerging and Infectious Diseases* was devoted to the hottest topic in public health at the time: bioterrorism. The paper immediately preceding Zoon's was written by General Phillip K. Russell, who was commander of the United States Army Medical Research and Development Command at Fort Detrick in the late 1980s when Bruce Ivins and colleagues developed their single-shot anthrax vaccine with squalene. General Russell took this opportunity to plug the new vaccine, too:

A vaccine based on purified protective factor made by recombinant technology has been protective in animals. Use of a modern adjuvant with purified protective factor should make it possible to have a very effective two-dose vaccine. A recent report by the Institute of Medicine Committee on Research and Development to Improve Civilian Medical Response to Chemical and Biological Terrorism makes a strong case for a major research and development effort leading to an improved second-generation vaccine.[29]

What makes Dr. Zoon's and Dr. Russell's (General Russell is an M.D.) comments in the CDC's journal so significant is what they represent. Zoon was at CBER; General Russell, former commander of USAMRDC, was now a professor at the Johns Hopkins School of Public Health; the journal was the CDC's; the initial batches of the second-generation vaccine were made in a National Cancer Institute laboratory; NIH had organized a working group with the FDA and the Defense Department to rush the new vaccine through the licensing pipeline; the Institute of Medicine and the Armed Forces Epidemiological Board also promoted the adoption of the new vaccine.[30] The Armed Forces Epidemiological Board, which had promoted the use of experimental vaccines on troops for decades and invited research proposals from military scientists for experiments to run on troops during Desert Shield, became particularly outspoken in its support for the mandatory anthrax immunizations and for the new vaccine. In the same year that AFEB dismissed the first Asa/Garry paper on the antibodies, it also published fulsome support for the mandatory anthrax immunizations and the new anthrax vaccine. "The AFEB considers anthrax vaccine to be a safe, preventive agent against anthrax and wishes to congratulate the anthrax vaccine immunization program agency for the attention it has paid to this important program."[31] "The Board," wrote its president, Dr. Marc LaForce, "also encourages continued clinical research into newer anthrax vaccines and studies using the current vaccine." That was in spring 1999. That summer, LaForce wrote, "The AFEB is concerned about delays in the development of the 'next generation' anthrax vaccine."[32] Sandwiched in between these recommendations was AFEB's attack on the Asa/Garry paper that reported antibodies to squalene—the toxigenic oil in several versions of the new vaccine—were a marker for Gulf War Syndrome. "The paper contains numerous shortcomings, several of them serious, that combine to invalidate the authors' conclusions," wrote the board.[33] But the "shortcomings" were the same ones that Asa and Garry had already answered and shown to be invalid.

These Byzantine connections are more than a game of six degrees of separation. They help explain what has been happening to U.S. military personnel since Desert Storm. The flip side of synergy is herd thinking. What looks like a sterling example of interdepartmental cooperation can erode the normal processes of critical thinking that are supposed to govern science, including the science of vaccine development. The Department of Health and Human Services—which presides over the FDA, CBER, NIH, the CDC and the U.S. Public Health Service—is supposed to regulate human experiments, not just fund them. The particular danger posed by HHS's open advocacy of an Army vaccine, especially one that is deemed vital to national security, is the existence of a system that allows experimentation on military personnel without informed consent under conditions just such as these. This is why CBER's detection of a serial dilution of squalene, the very adjuvant that Fort Detrick and WRAIR had been using for more than a decade in its new anthrax vaccine—and FDA's failure to act on this finding—raises questions about the wisdom of big-government synergy in regulating drugs and vaccines. Who is watching over the guardians? The troubling answer appears to be that they're all looking to each other for validation.

Unexpected Allies

Scientists with the Army and HHS were not the only ones ignoring the accumulating evidence for squalene's toxicity. So were General Blanck's "Internet paranoiacs"—the vaccine refuseniks fomenting opposition to the mandatory anthrax immunization program. There was nothing paranoid about them, as the evidence showed even then, but the reasons that they repeatedly cited for their concerns were medically and epidemiologically unsound.

One problem cited by the refuseniks and just about everyone else who listened sympathetically to them—members of Congress as well as producers with network magazine shows like *60 Minutes*—were the alleged health violations by BioPort, the maker of the licensed anthrax vaccine. In 1998, as the NIH Working Group began orchestrating the adoption of the second-generation vaccine, the FDA, a member of this group, began censuring BioPort for breaching Good Manufacturing Practice standards with the old vaccine.[34] Vaccine lots had expired. Some had failed potency tests. Others failed sterility tests. BioPort had not monitored how long some vaccine was exposed to room temperature. There was rust on steam generators, there were germs on tabletops.

All this sounds perfectly dreadful. Except on closer examination, BioPort's GMP violations could not explain why people were developing rheumatoid arthritis and lupus following immunization with its anthrax vaccine. The first reason was the most obvious one. Most of the vaccine lots cited in the FDA complaints were not administered at bases where troops were getting sick. So the lots did not correlate with illness. As a proposed source of a Gulf War Syndrome-like disease, most of the problematic lots identified by the FDA failed this basic epidemiological test.

This particular fact makes all the other charges moot, but they are worth addressing as they were cited over and over again by anxious military personnel—and the lawyers and reporters who listened to them—as cause for alarm. Failing the potency test, for instance. A lot that failed a potency test wouldn't protect anyone; it wouldn't be potent enough. But that didn't mean it would get anyone sick. Failing a sterility test sounds like it could be more of a problem until you look at the list of organisms: "*Penicillium, Bacillus subtilis, Staphylococcus capitis, Rhodococcus, Bacillus cereus, Corynebacterium, Cladosporium, and Propionibacterium acnes.*" The FDA inspector found most of these organisms on "critical surfaces," which means they were not actually in the vaccine. Strike one. When FDA detected a contaminant like *Bacillus cereus* in its initial sterility test, the supposedly contaminated vaccine lot then passed the subsequent retest. Strike two. Finally, none of the organisms found by FDA had any known association with autoimmune disease. *Propionibacterium acnes* causes *acne vulgaris* or zits . . . not lupus. Strike Three. Finally, expired vaccine is not rotten vaccine. Vaccine does not putrefy like butter or a carton of eggs.

The other theory promoted by some of the refuseniks concerns mycoplasma—one of the most ubiquitous microorganisms on the planet. Two biochemists and an emergency room physician from Maine, Garth and Nancy Nicolson and Meryl Nass, proposed the theory that Gulf War illness was somehow associated with anthrax vaccine contaminated with mycoplasma bacteria. From the outset, this theory had a problem: there is no history of mycoplasma causing anything resembling Gulf War Syndrome. *Mycoplasma pneumonia,* for instance, is the most common pathogen linked to respiratory infections among children and young adults. It has never been proven to cause long-term chronic illness of any sort.[35]

Only three types of mycoplasma are known to cause disease in humans: *M. pneumoniae,* which causes atypical pneumonia; *M. hominis,* which causes sore throats; *Ureaplasma uerealyticum,* which causes urinary tract infections. The strain that was supposed to be a problem in anthrax vaccine, *M. fermentans* strain incognitus, has been weakly associated with rheumatoid arthritis, but never proven to cause it, or any other autoimmune disease. "Association does *not* mean causation," says Pam Asa. "For instance, everybody who gets cancer breathes air; therefore breathing causes cancer? No. You have to meet certain criteria to identify an organism as the etiologic agent of disease. They're called Koch's Postulates and they've been around for more than a hundred years. No one's ever fulfilled Koch's Postulates with mycoplasma and rheumatoid arthritis."

Mycoplasma failed another elementary test for validity. It was not in the vaccine. The sterility tests done by FDA did not list mycoplasma among the possible contaminants. Further confirmation that anthrax vaccine was mycoplasma-free came from USAMRIID and the National Cancer Institute, which tested four different lots of anthrax vaccine and did not find it.[36] If the vaccine were really contaminated with mycoplasma, it would have failed FDA's sterility tests.

Finally, the environment in the vaccine itself is inhospitable for mycoplasma or any other microorganism. The vaccine contains formaldehyde, a stabilizer, and benzethonium chloride, a preservative. The preservative kills germs. It apparently did in anthrax vaccine. USAMRIID added mycoplasma to a fifth lot of anthrax and "they did not survive for even 1 day."[37]

All this controversy suited the proponents of the second-generation anthrax vaccine just fine. They used the clamor against the old vaccine to promote the new one. To calm the jangled nerves of military personnel anxious about the safety of mandatory anthrax immunizations, government officials assured them that a new and improved vaccine was on the way—one that was more pure than the old and allegedly adulterated vaccine. "We're working on it night and day," NIH scientist John Robbins told the *Wall Street Journal.*[38] The new vaccine was not only "purer," said Robbins; it contained, in the reporters' words, "an added ingredient intended to more quickly and more thoroughly mobilize the body's immune system against a possible future anthrax infection." What was this hush-hush ingredient? Could it have been squalene? Tellingly, Robbins declined to name the ingredient, saying only that "The people who should know about it do know, but we're not saying much."[39]

While the Department of Defense, NIH and FDA remained secretive about the fact that several formulations of the new vaccine were made with squalene,

Army scientists continued to attack the Tulane antibody data as junk science. Bob Garry, with whom the Defense Department had consulted in the past because of his internationally recognized expertise in retroviruses and autoimmunity, was portrayed as some sort of renegade. Pam Asa, an "unaffiliated scientist" (she was, in fact, affiliated with Tulane as a Visiting Professor), was dismissed by some inside the Beltway as a "Coal Miner's Daughter." And the former director of the Army's anthrax vaccination program, Major Guy Stander, said I was a writer of "fiction" who was "reckless, irresponsible and wrong." The research done in laboratories proving squalene's toxicity might as well have been done on a different planet because it was never referenced.

Dr. Anthony Allison, who helped create Syntex Adjuvant Formula (SAF-1)—an oil-based adjuvant used by USAMRIID in the very early prototypes of the second-generation anthrax vaccine—said squalene, and its molecular cousin squalane, both "have a good record in toxicology studies."[40] To support this assertion, Allison cited a 1982 study published in the *Journal of the American College of Toxicology*.[41] This report is not easy to find. After visiting several medical libraries, I tracked it down at the New York Academy of Medicine—an oasis of calm and scholarship just across the street from Central Park on New York's Upper East Side. When a library assistant brought the journal to me (researchers are not allowed into the stacks at the Academy), I was more than a little startled by what I read. The paper, a report of a test of squalene and squalane done by a panel of the American College of Toxicology (ACT), did indeed conclude that these oils were safe, but not quite in the way that Allison led people to believe. In the report's conclusion, the author wrote "it was the panel's expert opinion that both squalene and squalane were safe . . . as *cosmetic* ingredients" [italics mine].[42] The report that Allison cited as proof that these oils were safe to inject had, in fact, nothing to do with immunization. It was written, as its author clearly stated, as a "Cosmetic Ingredient Review." Squalene and squalane are safe to rub on your skin as a moisturizer or as an emollient in makeup. To interpret this report as an endorsement of squalene's safety for *immunization* would require extreme inattention to detail.

Even the Institute of Medicine (IOM), which on its website touts itself as an "independent scientific adviser" to the nation, providing all of America with "advice that is unbiased, based on evidence, and grounded in science," cited the American College of Toxicology report in its 2002 book, *The Anthrax Vaccine: Is It Safe? Does It Work?*, as evidence for squalene's safety.[43] What I find especially troubling about this citation by Anthony Allison and the IOM is that the ACT paper is not entered into the National Library of Medicine database called PubMed. PubMed is the mother of all databases for medicine— the logical starting point for anyone wanting a snapshot of what has been published on any given medical topic from the 1950s forward. The ACT's final report on squalene is not listed on PubMed because it is not medical; it is a paper about the safety of cosmetic ingredients. To support the assertion that squalene was safe to inject, then, somebody had to go to the trouble of tracking down a cosmetics paper published more than two decades ago, which had nothing to do with vaccination. To be as "independent" and "unbiased" as it claims to be, the IOM should not have cited this paper as evidence for squalene's safety in a vaccine. The Institute also should have disclosed in its book that it had been an unabashed advocate of the second-generation anthrax vaccine for several years prior to the book's publication, but it did not do so.

The book also makes no mention of the FDA's finding of squalene in five lots of anthrax vaccine; nor does it refer to any of the published scientific papers on squalene's proven ability to induce autoimmune diseases in animals. There are more than two dozen such papers, all of them published in peer-reviewed science journals available in medical libraries around the world. Many of those papers were written by scientists at the world-renowned Karolinska Institute in Stockholm. With the right search terms and a few quick keystrokes, you can find all of them on PubMed. The IOM's silence on squalene toxicity is evidence that where squalene is concerned, it is less "independent," "unbiased" and "grounded in science" than it wants the public to believe.

Other scientists promoting squalene adjuvants did the same thing: omit from their papers any reference to the data on squalene's toxicity. Researchers in Italy, where a squalene-boosted influenza vaccine called FLUAD has been licensed since 1997, have published five papers on this vaccine without a single mention of autoimmunity. A sixth paper on FLUAD was published as a collaboration between U.S. and Italian scientists.[44] FLUAD contains MF59, which is made by Chiron; paper after paper coauthored by Chiron-employed scientists in Italy have reported MF59 safe. If autoimmunity was not observed in patients immunized with FLUAD it may be that this vaccine was as safe as Chiron's Italian studies insisted. Or it may be that a flaw in the study design prevents researchers from seeing the vaccine's real risks. The patients injected with FLUAD were old. They were residents of nursing homes; their average age was 71.5.[45] Testing FLUAD in a patient population that old made sense because the influenza virus poses the greatest danger to the elderly. But limiting the trials to patients who were sixty-five or older would also tend to obscure autoimmune problems. Lupus mainly affects younger women. Testing the vaccine in elderly patients increased the likelihood of Italian primary care physicians missing autoimmune reactions to the vaccine—if in fact they did occur. The toxicity of oil adjuvants is a discussion that has been confined almost exclusively to specialist papers in experimental immunology. Most doctors have a hard enough time keeping up-to-date with new data in their respective fields; they are unlikely to go out of their way to research the effects of injected oils. They would have little reason to. Until recently, no oil adjuvant has been licensed for human use. If autoimmune symptoms did occur in geriatric Italians, doctors might not have attributed these symptoms to an oil adjuvant because there would not have been an obvious connection in the elderly between joint pain and anything else besides old age. If seventy-two-year-old Giuseppe started complaining of aching joints or feeling tired, chances are his doctor would see it simply as a sign of old age and advise him to take it easy. As it is, autoimmunity is notorious for taking years to diagnose because the early symptoms (e.g., headaches, joint and muscle pain and fatigue) are so vague; primary care physicians often fail to recognize it. It would be even less obvious in the elderly. A large Phase IV trial did not even bother to analyze the "common post-immunization reactions" in study participants, recording only those adverse events severe enough to require a doctor's visit "within 7 days of immunization."[46]

In another study done jointly by the University of Siena and Chiron, clinical investigators noted the local and systemic reactions for seven days after vaccination and no more. Although they continued to observe patients for as long as 180 days, the investigators only recorded an adverse reaction as "serious" if a patient was hospitalized or died.[47] Think about that for a moment. In this particular vaccine trial, only two things qualified as a "serious adverse event"—admission to a hospital or death; anything else wasn't recorded.[48] Autoimmune diseases rarely require hospitalization and develop over a period of years, not weeks. Once again, the design of the study, whether meant to do so or not, would ensure that autoimmune diseases, if in fact they occurred (they might not have), would likely go unreported.

With all the adverse reaction data from animals injected with squalene so accessible on the Internet, what was the Chiron scientists' reason for not discussing the published data showing squalene's proven ability to induce autoimmune disease, specifically with neurological damage, and designing studies? One possibility was the profit motive. Chiron reported that its vaccine sales increased from $357 million in 2002 to $678 million in 2003.[49] That's a 190 percent increase in revenues. A lot of it came from selling flu vaccine. According to its annual report, Chiron is now the world's second-largest manufacturer of flu vaccines. It sells at least five different brands, each with a different formulation, and it considers the overseas market for flu vaccine an "important driver" of revenue growth in the "near to mid-term." If marketing is a kind of warfare, as some business mavens like to argue, by establishing the alleged safety of its MF59 squalene emulsion with a single-shot flu vaccine given to the elderly, Chiron is creating a kind of beachhead that could potentially break through regulatory obstacles to oil emulsion adjuvants that have existed for decades because of their toxicity. Once MF59 is approved in a flu vaccine, what is to prevent its licensure in prototype vaccines for HIV, hepatitis B, cytomegalovirus and human papillomavirus—all of which Chiron has developed? With its regulatory breakthrough in Europe, Chiron is looking at a revenue bonanza on its horizon with its growing list of oil adjuvant vaccines currently in the licensing pipeline.

In light of the considerable body of recently published data on squalene and autoimmunity from scientists in Sweden, the Netherlands, Poland, Australia and the United States, any objective evaluation of FLUAD—or any other vaccine containing squalene emulsions marketed for human use—should involve monitoring vaccinated patients for autoimmunity over an extended period.[50] The question is whether scientists working for pharmaceutical companies are intentionally designing studies so as to miss adverse reactions that inconvenience their marketing strategy. Chiron's conclusions about squalene's safety are at odds with recent data from studies in both animals and humans. To predict how a new drug or vaccine could affect a human being, scientists test those products in animals first. That is standard operating procedure. There is even an established progression up the evolutionary ladder in these tests—from mice to rats to guinea pigs to rabbits to monkeys; then human beings.

Since the 1980s, the FDA has streamlined this process for selected medical products approved for "fast-tracking." If Chiron or Ribi ImmunoChem Research, Inc. (Corixa Corporation acquired Ribi for approximately $56.3

million in cash and stock June 10, 1999) have conducted toxicology studies in animals with squalene, they have not published their results. Although squalene's advocates—which include the U.S. Army's Carl Alving—argue that the Karolinska's data from animal experiments do not necessarily predict what will happen in a human being injected with squalene, which is true, a perfunctory dismissal of the data calls into question time-honored methods for drug and vaccine safety testing. What's more, the Karolinska is not the only laboratory that has linked squalene injection with the induction of autoimmune disease in animals; ten laboratories in five countries, including the United States, have shown similar results: these laboratories have all reported that injecting squalene-based adjuvants or squalene alone will induce autoimmunity in mice, rats and rabbits.[51] "The autoimmune diseases in animals injected with squalene have been completely consistent with what I've seen occur in humans who've tested positive for antibodies to squalene since the first Gulf War," says Pam Asa. "It's remarkable to see how well the animal models correlate with disease in humans."

These animal models, and the experience of many sick veterans injected with squalene, are consistent with what you'll find on the new package insert (starting on January 31, 2002) for BioPort's anthrax vaccine, which lists systemic lupus erythematosus among its adverse reactions. They are also consistent with the symptoms listed among the adverse reactions for FLUAD. I had a certified translation of the FLUAD package insert translated from Italian into English. Among the listed adverse reactions are rashes, malaise, fever, myalgia (muscle pain) and arthralgia (joint pain), weakness and sweating. Among the allegedly "rare" reactions are vasculitis (an autoimmune inflammation of blood vessels) accompanied by "transitory renal involvement," and "neurologic disturbances" such as encephalomyelitis, neuritis [which has been documented in Air Force personnel immunized with anthrax vaccine], and Guillain-Barré syndrome [which has been known to occur with flu vaccines that do not contain squalene, but as previously noted, also has been documented in a sailor immunized with anthrax vaccine]. "Rashes, malaise, fatigue, muscle pain, joint pain, weakness and rare occurrences of neurological problems" make for a list that reads like the Air Force case-definition for Gulf War Syndrome.

These symptoms are also associated with autoimmune diseases. Chiron reports that "the undesirable side effects disappear with treatment after 1 to 2 days," but it does not specify what that treatment is, nor does it provide any data to support this assertion. The general symptoms listed on Chiron's package insert for FLUAD cannot be definitively characterized as autoimmune (though vasculitis and Guillain-Barré are undeniably so).

UCLA proved that squalene with neurological tissue (ground-up guinea pig spinal cord) injected into rats could induce the animal version of multiple sclerosis. The Karolinska Institute, along with the Royal Adelaide Hospital and University of Queensland in Australia, proved injection with squalene alone could cause the animal version of rheumatoid arthritis. A study at the Department of Neuropathology at the Polish Academy of Sciences showed how squalene caused severe damage to the nerves and brains of rats. And it was the University of Florida Medical School that demonstrated for the first time that squalene induced the autoantibodies that are diagnostic of lupus. These autoantibodies were induced with one shot of squalene in mice that were specifically bred to be resistant to autoimmune disease. The Florida researchers write cautiously about leaping to conclusions about their data's relevance to vaccines containing squalene: "Whether this is relevant in human vaccination is a difficult issue," they write, "due to the complex effects of vaccines and the fact that immunotoxicological effects vary depending on species, route, dose and duration of administration."[52]

As inclined as they are to understatement and caution, the scientists at the University of Florida could not ignore the inescapable implications of their data. "The present data argue that caution should be exercised in the use of oil adjuvants in human and veterinary vaccines."[53]

A Game of Whack-a-Mole

Trying to deal with the misinformation on squalene has been like playing the carnival game Whack-a-Mole—where you bop the mechanical mole on the head with your mallet and three more pop up somewhere else. A few more of the "moles" in this dispute over squalene are worth bopping on the head, if for no other reason than that they are found on the website for the U.S. Secretary of Defense (they went up before Donald Rumsfeld assumed the post). The file is called THE FACTS ON SQUALENE and it is riddled with inaccuracies, which, when understood in the context of the information in this book, appear intentional.[54] The "facts" are presented in question-and-answer form.

To give you a sense of what the Defense Department has been telling U.S. military personnel about squalene, consider this question posed by the SECDEF's Assistant Secretary for Health Affairs, and his answer:

5. Is it possible that extremely low doses of squalene might trigger the immune system?[55]

Here is the answer:

There is no scientific evidence to support the concept that squalene triggers the immune system.[56]

If there really is no scientific evidence to support the concept that squalene triggers the immune system, then U.S. taxpayers will want to know why the NIH and the U.S. Department of Defense have spent billions of taxpayer dollars on developing recombinant DNA vaccines boosted with squalene. Why would they waste money on a product that doesn't do what it is supposed to do? Of course, the answer to that question is that DOD and NIH do not believe that they have been wasting taxpayers' money. They know full well that squalene is an immunostimulant.

When DOD decides to misinform its troops, there are no half measures. Two more questions and answers are less obvious howlers; I want to address them here because they help illustrate the extent to which troops have been misled and how difficult it would be for them to evaluate the information that they have been given by their most senior leaders in the military medical command. Here is DOD's Question # 6 on squalene:

6. If you wanted to use squalene as an adjuvant, what form would it take?

Here is part of the answer, which will give you its gist:

If you wanted to use squalene as an adjuvant (to boost antibody responses) you would have to multiply the amount of squalene found by the FDA *one million times* [italics mine].

Here is what DOD omitted from its answer:

Chiron Corporation, the manufacturer of the squalene-in-water adjuvant MF59, reports immunological activity in animals with a 200 nanomolar concentration of MF59.[57] According to Pam and Kevin Asa, a 200 nanomolar concentration is about equivalent to 82 parts per billion, which is almost identical to the 83 parts per billion concentration that the FDA found in anthrax vaccine Lot # FAV047. In that lot, the FDA found 83 parts per billion squalene. In reviewing this matter for Representative Jack Metcalf before he left office in 2002, Dr. Dorothy Lewis, an immunologist and a member of the Advisory Council to the NIH's National Institute of Allergy and Infectious Diseases, had this to say:

"More research needs to be done to answer these questions, but it is possible that very small amounts of a biologically active product could induce an immune response, either to the molecule itself or it could boost immune responses to other agents in the mixture."[58]

Dr. Lewis, an immunologist who had no hand in either discovering anti-squalene antibodies or in developing the Army's second-generation anthrax vaccine with squalene, could not ignore the potential significance of the concentrations of squalene FDA found in anthrax vaccine. Why? Because Dr. Lewis knew, as all immunologists knew, that the possibility of an immune response to a minuscule amount of antigen was consistent with decades of research in mainstream immunology. As Pam Asa, Bob Garry and their colleague Russell Wilson would state in a paper published in 2002, "The immune system is exquisitely sensitive to small quantities of antigen . . . before the molecular nature of antibodies was fully appreciated, it was accepted that as little as a single molecule of antigen could stimulate antibody production (Cannon, 1942)."[59] Asa, Garry and Wilson were putting into context their discovery that U.S. military personnel had developed antibodies to squalene *and* gotten sick, following immunization with vaccine lots containing trace concentrations of squalene: 10 parts per billion in Lot # 030 (according to the FDA) and 1–9 parts per billion in Lot # 008 (according to the U.S. Army).

Let's look at one more question and answer.

12. Where did the squalene in anthrax vaccine come from?

Here is DOD's answer:

The most likely source of the trace squalene is from the bacteria used to produce the vaccine. Squalene is not added to anthrax vaccine or any US-licensed vaccine.

First, let me give the Pentagon its due. DOD is telling the truth here, though a bit too cleverly. Squalene is not added to anthrax vaccine—provided you are talking about the *licensed* vaccine. Squalene *has* been added to various formulations of the second-generation anthrax vaccine since its creation around 1987. DOD is also telling the truth when it says squalene is not added to any licensed U.S. vaccine. It is, however, added to many genetically engineered vaccines in the military and NIH development pipeline.

Setting aside these subtle prevarications, let me now address the outright baloney. *Bacillus anthracis* does not make squalene. It is a microorganism too far down the food chain to have any need to biosynthesize a relatively complex lipid like squalene. Asserting this without supporting data, however, would amount to speculation. There is no need for speculation. The absence of squalene in *B. anthracis* was proven a long time ago. Two types of laboratory analyses performed on *B. anthracis* show that the germ only makes monounsaturated lipids (lipids with only one double bond between carbon atoms—all the other carbons are connected by single bonds), with a maximum of seventeen carbon atoms.[60] Squalene contains thirty carbon atoms connected by six double bonds. It is a much bigger molecule than any lipid *B. anthracis* makes.

The Department of Defense was not alone in suggesting the organism was the source of squalene in the vaccine. To support this idea, the FDA's Dr. Mark Ellengold informed Congress that his laboratory also found comparable squalene concentrations in samples of tetanus toxoid made by Wyeth and a Connaught diphtheria toxoid.

There are two objections I have to this. The first goes back to the number of carbon atoms in squalene. Scientists have done a thorough job of analyzing bacteria for their lipid and fatty acid content. All bacteria make lipids or fatty acids composed of 10–20 carbon atoms.[61] Remember, squalene is a 30-carbon chain—so that rules out *Clostridium tetani* and *Corynebacterium diphtheriae* as makers of squalene, just as it rules out *B. anthracis*.

The second issue concerns which companies produce licensed tetanus and diphtheria toxoids. Aventis Pasteur, GlaxoSmithKline, North American Vaccine, Inc., SmithKlineBeecham Biologicals and the Massachusetts Public Health Biologic Lab make FDA-licensed tetanus and diphtheria toxoids distributed for use in the United States. Note the companies missing from this list: Wyeth and Connaught. According to the FDA's list of licensed vaccines, Wyeth does *not* make an FDA-licensed tetanus toxoid and Connaught does *not* make an FDA-licensed diphtheria toxoid. It appears that CBER's laboratory found squalene in lots of what may be experimental tetanus and diphtheria toxoids. Ellengold omitted this detail from his presentation to Congress. Did the FDA—a member of the NIH Working Group fast-tracking the new anthrax vaccine—test samples of unlicensed toxoids that had been experimentally boosted with squalene? Why aren't Wyeth tetanus toxoid and Connaught diphtheria toxoid on the FDA's list for "Vaccines Licensed for Immunization and Distributed in the US?" This list can be found on the website for the FDA's Center for Biologics Evaluation and Research where Ellengold works. When Dr. Ellengold omitted these details from his presentation to Congress, he was, in one of those moments of almost cosmic irony, testifying to the House Committee for Government Reform.

If patients in the Italian or NIH clinical trials with MF59 were never informed of all the data on squalene's proven ability to induce autoimmunity in animals, did those patients really give their informed consent to participate in those trials? Wasn't it uninformed consent? Can anyone truly volunteer for an experiment without being fully informed of the risks? The line between volunteer and guinea pig is not merely a fine one; here it has become indistinguishable. As for U.S. military personnel, the issue of ethical experimentation is even more critical because they have been victims of unethical conduct so many times in the past.

In 1998, the NIH Working Group pressed ahead to license a new anthrax vaccine and it needed a new adjuvant. Otherwise the new vaccine would be virtually identical to the old one—the active pharmaceutical ingredient in both vaccines still being the same insufficiently protective anthrax protein, the wistfully named "protective antigen." Protective antigen, whether made by conventional or cutting-edge means, would still fail to protect guinea pigs from the deadliest strains. And it would still take months to induce any level of protection at all. It would be purer, but in immunology purity translates into weakness, so the only ingredient in the new vaccine capable of accelerating the immune response to the same old protein would be a new adjuvant. The NIH Working Group had a range of new adjuvants it wanted to test, and several of them contained squalene. But no published data existed on how little squalene you could use and still achieve an effect. Remarkably, five lots of anthrax vaccine then showed up with squalene concentrations that add up to a twofold dilution series capable of generating the needed dose-response curve to squalene—the Working Group's preferred vaccine adjuvant.

Equally remarkable was how these allegedly random squalene concentrations in anthrax vaccine matched up with the serial dilutions employed by Chiron to test its proprietary squalene-based adjuvant, MF59, in an experimental flu vaccine. We have seen cosmic irony in these events; why not cosmic coincidence—a pharmaceutical lottery in which Mother Nature by pure chance came up with the winning numbers. Accomplished scientists, with decades of experience in their respective fields, don't buy it. But whether or not the squalene in anthrax vaccine is there by accident or design, it is there. And while DOD and FDA continue to insist that there is no evidence that squalene is dangerous to humans, they have likewise offered no evidence that it is safe.

Data now exists that squalene is clearly unsafe for human use . . . and that data was acquired at the expense of what may be tens of thousands or more U.S. military personnel.

Chapter Eleven

The Real
Biological Weapon

While the director of the Army's mandatory Anthrax Vaccine Immunization Program, John Grabenstein, told reporters that the anthrax vaccine was perfectly safe, the vaccine's manufacturer, BioPort, on January 31, 2002, quietly published information contradicting him. Obligated to disclose all adverse reactions to its product to avoid charges of "Failure to Inform," BioPort published its new package insert with some astonishing information. The percentage of people suffering adverse reactions to anthrax immunization had skyrocketed to 5–35 percent.[1] According to a file on the AVIP website called "Myths and Facts About Anthrax Vaccine," these new figures were "about the same as other vaccines."[2] The problem is that the rate of serious adverse reactions to anthrax vaccine was much lower before 1990.

Before the vaccine's licensure in 1970, BioPort reported data from one study involving 7,000 textile workers who received 15,907 doses of anthrax vaccine over a five-year reporting period.[3] During that time only four systemic reactions—reactions like fever and chills that affect whole systems in the body—were reported. That was a minuscule systemic reaction rate of 0.06 percent. The lower end of the new rate, 5 percent, was still 83 times higher than the one reported in this "open-label safety study," which was used to make the case for licensing the vaccine in the first place. If you calculate the difference using the higher end of the range, 35 percent, the new systemic reaction rate is 583 times higher.

After the Department of Health and Human Services licensed the vaccine, the systemic reaction rate climbed to 0.2 percent, which is still—relative to other vaccines—fairly low. BioPort does not report this figure in its new product insert; it is found on the old insert dated October 1987.[4] Again, for comparison's sake, five percent is 25 times higher than the systemic reaction rate reported on the package insert issued by BioPort's previous incarnation—the Michigan Department of Public Health. The 0.2 percent rate stood for fifteen years until January 2002. The high end of the new range reported by BioPort, thirty-five percent, is a whopping 175 times higher than the 1987 systemic reaction rate. These are astronomical jumps. Interestingly, the Army started documenting reactions again in 1990, which coincided with the creation of the new anthrax vaccine with squalene.

"Change in the Composition"

The GAO found even more discrepancies that led it to ask whether someone had altered the licensed vaccine. To start with, the GAO's own survey of Air National Guard and Reserve personnel showed the adverse reactions to anthrax vaccine may be much higher than reported by either BioPort or the Department of Defense. The GAO limited its survey to those who received their shots between September 1998 and September 2000. That's when the Department of Defense made anthrax immunization mandatory for all military personnel, and incidentally, when the dose-ranging concentrations appeared in at least five lots of vaccine. Eighty-four percent of those surveyed reported experiencing adverse reactions or side effects from the vaccine.[5] That means more than eight out of every ten men and women in the Air National Guard and Reserves experienced some sort of untoward reaction from the vaccine. And not just one or two reactions. The average respondent in the GAO survey reported having "about seventeen reactions or events thought to be attributable to the vaccine."[6]

The GAO also estimated the rate of systemic reactions to be "more than a hundred times expected in the product insert in effect at the time of our survey."[7] The actual difference may be much higher than either of these figures.

This is because the GAO also reported that most of the personnel experiencing problems did not know where to report those problems—the FDA's Vaccine Adverse Event Reporting System or VAERS.[8] That kept the numbers artificially low. So did the way the Department of Defense started counting the vaccine reactions. At the outset of the mandatory vaccination program, the Defense Department counted only those reactions that led "to either hospitalization or the loss of 48 hours or more of duty time."[9] Those criteria eliminated a lot of adverse reactions that might have been otherwise counted. DOD only lifted this restriction after many complaints. Whatever the true reaction rate was, it was bound to be much higher than the ones reported by either the FDA or Department of Defense officials—who relied on the relatively modest number of filed VAERS reports to argue the vaccine was safe.

The difference in reactions between September 1998 and September 2000 was so much higher than the one reported by the Department of Defense and BioPort that even the hyper-cautious GAO concluded that something might have been done to change the contents of the vaccine:

> The rates disclosed in the survey and the DOD studies are each significantly higher than those stated in the vaccine product insert until recently. *Such marked variances from the product insert data suggest the possibility of change in the composition of the vaccine originally approved in 1970* [italics mine].[10]

The GAO identified at least two changes to the manufacturing process that raised concerns. A previous GAO report suggested that an increase in the amount of protective antigen protein in the vaccine—the vaccine's main ingredient since the 1950s—might be to blame.[11] The GAO attributed the increase to the manufacturer's new fermenters (an installation unapproved by FDA) and the manufacturer's switching the type of filters used to strain out bits of leftover anthrax cells from the vaccine.[12] According to the GAO, an unpublished Department of Defense study showed "a hundred-fold increase" in the amount of protective antigen protein in vaccine lots produced after the filter change took place in 1990.

In other words, there was now a lot more of the same protein in each dose of vaccine. But as a potential source of disease, this did not make much sense. For fifty years, the whole idea behind using this protein was to safely prevent anthrax, and in fifty years no evidence had emerged to show that it caused disease. The whole point of the filter changes was to get more protective antigen protein into each dose. Historically, whatever protective antigen's shortcomings were, toxicity was not one of them. Its perennial problem was weakness. Ironically, it was weakness that not only made the protective antigen protein safe, but made a booster like an oil additive necessary in the first place.

As of January 31, 2002, the date on the new product insert, BioPort now disclosed that recipients of anthrax vaccine had reported allergic reactions and autoimmune disease as a consequence of anthrax vaccination. The new product insert lists the following "serious adverse events" as "infrequently reported" by recipients of BioThrax: "pemphigus vulgaris, endocarditis, angiodema and other hypersensitivity reactions, idiopathic thrombocytopenia purpura, collagen vascular disease, systemic lupus erythematosus, multiple sclerosis, polyarteritis nodosa, inflammatory arthritis, transverse myelitis and glomerulonephritis."[13] All are dysfunctions of the immune system or diseases that are specifically autoimmune.

As extensive as this list was, it could have been longer. BioPort missed at least two other autoimmune reactions to its vaccine—both of which affect the eyes. Air Force doctors reported two cases of optic neuritis in patients thirty-nine and twenty-three years of age, respectively.[14] Optic neuritis is an inflammation of the optic nerve. It can come from a viral infection or from an autoimmune attack on nerve sheaths, which is what occurs with multiple sclerosis.[15] At least one of these optic neuritis cases was autoimmune. While both patients recovered, the second one had to have his immune system regularly suppressed in order to save his eyesight.[16] An Army recruit named Robert Shively was not so lucky. "He went blind," says Pam Asa. "A week or so after his fourth anthrax shot, Shively developed anterior uveitis, another kind of autoimmune inflammation that affects the eyes." Shively tested positive for the antibodies before the FDA announced its test results. "It turns out he got four shots of vaccine from lots that contained squalene (FAV038 and FAV043); that's what his wife told me," says Pam Asa. Shively was twenty-three years old when he became blind. "If he ever has kids," says Asa, "he won't be able to see them. That's what these injections took away from him." Optic neuritis and anterior uveitis are not listed on the package insert as diseases associated with anthrax vaccination.

Although the Air Force and Army scientists reporting this problem concluded that this one case of autoimmune optic neuritis resulted from anthrax immunization, they could not explain why. Exactly how they tried to establish a link between anthrax vaccination and optic neuritis is important. They tried to establish a dose-response relationship with the contents of the vaccine by looking for something in the Army's licensed anthrax vaccine that resembled something in the patients' retinal or optic nerves. Specifically, they looked for epitopes—those three-dimensional structures on the surface of molecules to which antibodies form. The question was whether there was an epitope on the surface of any molecule in the licensed anthrax vaccine that was identical, or at least very similar to, epitopes found in the optic nerves of humans. If there was such an epitope, antibodies responding to it in the vaccine would "cross-react" with those in the human eye. Protective antibodies would thus become destructive antibodies, attacking structures in the eye and resulting in a disease that could cause blindness.

The military doctors did not find such an epitope.[17] What's remarkable about this explanation is what these doctors didn't do: they didn't entertain the possibility that these cases of nerve damage were caused by the ingredient known to cause nerve damage—namely squalene. In addition to a long list of autoimmune diseases now associated with anthrax vaccination by the manufacturer itself, BioPort now reports that six deaths occurred among people given the vaccine.[18]

In contrast to all the above, Col. Grabenstein's list of "Myths and Facts About Anthrax Vaccine" says, "There is no evidence that life-threatening or permanently disabling immediate-onset adverse events occur at higher rates in individuals who have received AVA [Anthrax Vaccine Adsorbed] than in the general population." Grabenstein does not disclose the basis of this assertion and nowhere on his list of Myths and Facts is there any mention of the data from BioPort's new package insert.

None of this occurred before 1990, when the Army had its new anthrax vaccine with squalene ready for testing—no military personnel or civilians immunized against anthrax developed a documented case of autoimmune disease. No one died. The first appearance of a chronic syndrome characterized by symptoms associated with autoimmunity coincides with the Gulf War. The dramatic rise in adverse reactions after 1990—now so undeniably autoimmune that even the manufacturer had to admit it on its product insert—parallels the Army's decade-long effort to perfect its new anthrax vaccine by adding an oil proven by scientists the world over to induce autoimmunity. The vast discrepancy between the number of adverse reactions to anthrax vaccination reported by the Department of Defense and FDA on the one hand, and those documented by GAO on the other, emerged between September 1998 and September 2000, when anthrax vaccine lots containing dose-ranging dilutions of squalene were given to U.S. military personnel. It was during this time that the FDA, NIH and Department of Defense—not to mention the British government—all declared their intent to adopt the new vaccine as soon as possible. The British version also contained a squalene-based additive made by Ribi ImmunoChem Research—an updated version of the same one U.S. Army scientists had been using and then abandoned after the first Gulf War.[19] According to British scientists at Porton Down, the new vaccine combined with the Ribi adjuvant gave 100 percent protection in guinea pigs.[20] In contrast, guinea pigs given the new vaccine combined with alhydrogel—the only adjuvant licensed for human use in the United States and Britain—mostly died. Out of fourteen guinea pigs immunized with the new vaccine combined with alhydrogel, only one survived.[21] British scientists at Porton Down were sold on the new vaccine combined with squalene.

In the United States, the FDA, the agency that is supposed to regulate product safety, was actively participating in the Department of Defense effort to fast-track the new anthrax vaccine through the licensing gauntlet. When dose-ranging dilutions of squalene were found in anthrax vaccine, it was an FDA official, Dr. Mark Ellengold, who suggested to Congress that the "trace" amounts of squalene found in the vaccine were probably from the germ itself. FDA is supposed to be the watchdog agency that helps ensure the safety of vaccines. If it was now helping the Department of Defense create its new anthrax vaccine, then who was watching FDA? The answer was nobody.

"A Pattern of Deception"

Army scientists had been adding squalene to prototypes of its new anthrax vaccine since 1987, but when GAO investigators asked Department of Defense officials if they had used squalene before Operation Desert Shield in 1990, they denied it.[22] The officials insisted that military scientists had not conducted research with squalene until *after* the Gulf War.[23] Even then, they said, it was only added to vaccines being developed for malaria and HIV.[24]

These officials made no mention whatsoever of the Army's new anthrax vaccine. The GAO's November 1997 encounter with the Department of Defense on squalene was the first in a series of contentious exchanges that GAO investigators would later characterize as "a pattern of deception."[25] For the GAO it was a tedious, time-consuming and ultimately disillusioning game of cat and mouse: DOD officials would flatly deny using squalene; then GAO investigators would find evidence that they did. When GAO confronted these officials about the discrepancy, they then recalled how they used squalene after all. But what little these officials admitted to GAO was fragmentary and incomplete.

When it came to squalene, few scientists had memories more porous than the Army's chief adjuvant expert, the harshest critic of Tulane's findings, Col. Carl Alving of the Walter Reed Army Institute of Research. Alving told GAO investigators that he knew nothing about the vaccines used during Operations Desert Shield and Desert Storm. He was just a researcher, he said, not a decision-maker in the policy loop.[26] But the GAO investigators began to flatter Alving. Why wasn't a world-class expert such as himself consulted, they asked. Alving bit. Well, he admitted, someone at USAMRIID, he would not say who, asked him to develop a "new, more potent anthrax vaccine on a crash basis" for Operation Desert Shield.[27] Fort Detrick, he told the GAO, did not have the capability of making a new anthrax vaccine, but Walter Reed Army Institute of Research (where Alving worked) did.[28] If he made such a vaccine, he would have personally recommended using MF59, which contains squalene, because its manufacturer, Chiron, "had the manufacturing capacity and the desire to market it."[29] Alving was just getting warmed up. After he started working on a "new, more potent anthrax vaccine" for Desert Shield, he told the GAO,[30] someone at USAMRIID asked him to make at least one version of the new vaccine with his special adjuvant concoction, liposomes, which are made from squalene's oily molecular relative cholesterol.[31]

Then, having explained the advantages of using MF59 for the Army's new anthrax vaccine, Alving said he "doubted that a vaccine with squalene would produce a meaningful antibody response."[32] Wait a minute. Col. Alving had just told GAO that if he had been asked to make a "new, more potent anthrax vaccine" for Desert Shield, he would have recommended formulating it with MF59, which is made from what? It is made from water and . . . squalene.

Let's take another look at what Col. Alving said about squalene. GAO reported that "[Alving] doubted that a vaccine with squalene would produce a meaningful antibody response."[33] According to the GAO, Alving said this on April 6, 1998. But by 1998, it had already been ten years since the Army first started putting squalene into anthrax vaccine. After the Gulf War, when the Army decided that the squalene additives Tri-Mix and DeTox—put into its earliest prototypes of the second-generation vaccine—needed replacing, it switched over to MF59. MF59 was made from squalene and water. In other words, by 1998, squalene in one form or another had been a staple in the Army's second-generation anthrax vaccine for more than a decade. In 1998— the year that Britain decided to join the U.S. campaign to adopt the new vaccine—there was squalene in the British version, too. This was the year the NIH, the FDA and the Department of Defense formed the NIH Working Group to fast-track the new anthrax vaccine that contained squalene. It was also the year a near-perfect twofold dilution series of squalene appeared in five lots of anthrax vaccine given to U.S. military personnel. In other words, 1998 was *annus squalene*—the year of squalene in the Army's long march to develop a new anthrax vaccine. But the Army's chief adjuvant expert, Col. Carl Alving, the self-avowed "world's foremost expert on lipids," told the GAO investigators that he "doubted that a vaccine with squalene would produce a meaningful antibody response." That was after he said he would recommend MF59 for the new vaccine. Are you confused? Col. Alving appeared to be.

Apparently, Alving was also confused about the extent of his involvement with the Gulf War vaccinations. Remember, the GAO reported Alving disavowing all knowledge of vaccines used in Desert Shield and Desert Storm. He was, he insisted, just "a researcher, and an expert, but not in the policy loop."[34] Well, not exactly. According to Dr. Anna Johnson-Winegar, the Project Badger scientist in charge of finding a second source of anthrax vaccine for the war, Col. Alving advised the Project Badger team on adjuvants. He was, after all—as Johnson-Winegar took pains to point out—the Army's "in-house adjuvant expert."[35]

Alving's flip-flopping was apparently contagious. At first, Johnson-Winegar told GAO investigators that the Project Badger group barely discussed adjuvants. Then she said their discussions on adjuvants "were wide ranging and interesting."[36] Still, she pointed out, it was one thing to discuss adjuvants, and quite another to actually use them. After outing Col. Alving as Project Badger's adjuvant expert, Johnson-Winegar admitted, under pressure from GAO, that some Project Badger members were willing to *"jump out and use every-thing"* [italics mine].[37] But she refused to tell GAO who they were, just as Col. Alving refused to say who at USAMRIID asked him to make a "new, more potent anthrax vaccine" for Desert Shield. It was not a question of memory failure; GAO's notes say Alving simply declined to say who it was.

Dr. Peter Collis, a former chairman of Project Badger, dodged the GAO completely. He had lots of excuses. According to GAO investigators, Collis first said he could not meet with them unless he had the classified Project Badger summary; he needed it "to ensure his recall was accurate."[38] When GAO said it would provide the summary for Collis, Collis balked. Now he said that "as a civilian without clearance he could not look at the notes."[39] GAO then offered to obtain a temporary security clearance for Collis, allowing him to read the classified summaries.[40] No thank you, said Collis. Talking to him would be pointless, he said, because he "really didn't know much."[41] That was his third and final excuse. In this particular game of cat and mouse, the mouse was not going to play without a subpoena.

Caveat Emptor

No one in this saga has been more lavish in his criticism of Tulane's research than Alving. Alving has been relentless in his personal campaign to discredit Tulane's antibody data, starting with his comments at Dover Air Force base in May 1999 as a member of General Roadman's entourage. In addition to Alving, Roadman had been accompanied by Col. Arthur Friedlander—someone who not only oversaw the early development of the new vaccine but was named as a co-inventor (along with Dr. Bruce Ivins, Dr. Susan Welkos and others) in a patent awarded in May 2002.[42] The patent contains three ways of making the new vaccine, including one that is formulated with squalene and is a variant of the Ribi Adjuvant System first used by the Army prior to the Gulf War.[43] At the May 1999 meeting, Friedlander did not disclose this conflict of interest to the base commander, Col. Grieder, or any of the assembled pilots and air crew. What's more, Friedlander informed the men and women jammed into Dover's conference room that day that having tested anthrax strains from around the world, the Army had data that "suggests that the vaccine will protect against all these strains."

That was the most generous interpretation of the Army's research. In 1986, scientists at Fort Detrick identified nine anthrax strains that killed more than half the guinea pigs vaccinated with the old vaccine; by 2002 the Army had identified another twenty-four.[44] That brought the Army's total to thirty-three "wild" strains of B. anthracis that killed vaccinated guinea pigs. While the licensed vaccine gave "broad" protection against these strains in rabbits and monkeys, their ability to kill guinea pigs had been previously cited by Army scientists (in published papers) as grounds for replacing the old vaccine.[45] Fort Detrick routinely referred to some of these isolates, like Ames and New Hampshire, as "vaccine-resistant."[46] Neither Roadman nor Friedlander mentioned the new vaccine combined with squalene or the so-called vaccine-resistant strains that helped motivate the Army to pursue, what was at that point, a nineteen-year campaign to develop a better anthrax vaccine. Scientists like Tulane's Bob Garry and Pam Asa maintain that informing Dover's officers and enlisted men and women would have been preferable, if not necessary, in order to say that they had truly given their informed consent to anthrax vaccination.

Col. Alving kept mum about his connection to the new vaccine, too. Alving told Dover's pilots and air crew that Tulane had found antibodies to squalene in 65 percent of all healthy people tested. That was not even remotely correct. The inaccuracy of his attacks on Tulane's data set a tone. Garry and Asa found their exchanges with Alving increasingly petulant and inaccurate. His published attacks on their work, say Garry and Asa, have been rife with error, if not expedient invention.

Alving told Dover's personnel that everyone had naturally occurring antibodies to cholesterol, so he "wouldn't be a bit surprised if enormous numbers of people have antibodies to squalene." He said, "It will require further experimental work." At the time Alving made these remarks the Tulane paper had not been published yet. But what Alving omitted from the discussion at Dover that day was telling.

Antibodies to cholesterol were linked to potentially fatal disease. Alving knew this, because he had been saying so for more than ten years. In one of his early papers, titled "Antibodies to Cholesterol," published in the *Proceedings of the National Academy of Sciences* in 1988, Alving hypothesized that these antibodies could be related to the cause of atherosclerosis—a hardening of arteries due to a thickening of arterial walls and a loss in their elasticity.[47] When this occurs, it can raise blood pressure, lead to heart attacks and stroke.

Atherosclerotic disease is the leading cause of injury and death in America and most Western countries.[48] In 1986, just two years before Alving wrote his seminal paper on anticholesterol antibodies, almost a million Americans died of vascular disease—"twice as many as from cancer and 10 times as those from accidents."[49] So almost from the beginning, Alving drew a possible connection between antibodies to cholesterol and the No. 1 killer in America. That's not all. By the following year, Alving published his discovery of what he characterized in the title of his latest paper as: "Naturally Occurring Autoantibodies to Cholesterol in Humans." Alving reported that antibodies to cholesterol were linked to the activation of a cascade of human proteins called "complements."[50] If the immune system can be likened, quite loosely, to a shotgun, complement is like buckshot. It punches holes in the cell walls of invading microbes and other pathogens. The problem is when complement starts attacking your own cells. Alving suggested in his new paper that complement activation related to cholesterol antibodies might in fact be a cause of many vascular diseases, including atherosclerosis.[51]

In 1989, two notable things happened. Alving published Army data showing that miniature pigs injected with cholesterol-laden liposomes—Alving's own concoction—went into anaphylactoid shock, which can be fatal.[52] For the four miniature pigs that got a second infusion of Alving's cholesterol-laden liposomes, it was. They all died.[53] The pigs that survived this ordeal experienced a dangerous drop in blood pressure, what Alving characterized as "profound disturbances in cardiovascular" flow, and respiratory distress.[54] To corroborate his findings, Alving reported that other scientists observed similar reactions in a different animal. The University of California at San Francisco had administered cholesterol-based liposomes to sheep that then went into anaphylactoid shock like Alving's pigs.[55] So this deadly phenomenon was observed in more than one animal species. Yet, that very year, Alving traveled to a NATO-sponsored scientific meeting in Greece, and presented a paper advocating the use of cholesterol-laden liposomes in a prototype malaria vaccine. He made no reference at this meeting to his dead pigs, or the University of California's liposome-distressed sheep. He made no reference to the association he found between antibodies to cholesterol (induced by his liposomes) and atherosclerosis and other vascular diseases. Liposomes were good, he told everyone. "It is therefore logical," he wrote, "that liposomes should be proposed as carriers of antigens for vaccines."[56]

It is Alving's own research that perhaps poses the greatest challenge to the idea of using liposomes in vaccines. In 1992, he published even more self-damning data. Liposomes, he reported, also induced cross-reacting antibodies to phospholipids, DNA and cardiolipins.[57] "Cross-reacting" means the antibodies that form against the phospholipids in liposomes also bind to the body's *natural* phospholipids and cardiolipins. And what does that do? It can cause blood clots, which can lead to strokes and death. In women, antibodies to phospholipids, DNA and cardiolipins can cause spontaneous abortion. These antibodies are also associated with lupus.[58]

The meaning of autoimmune phenomena induced by liposomes seemed clear enough to Alving. There was no, on-the-one-hand this, and on-the-other-hand that in his published papers. No axe-grinding rival cited the dangers associated with liposomes. It was Alving who did. Not once, not twice, but many times. These are *his* observations. Alving pointed out the potential risks of injecting cholesterol-laden liposomes in virtually every paper he published on the subject in the 1980s to the mid-1990s—every paper, that is, except those in which he promoted the use of liposomes in vaccines. Given what Alving said about the possibility of cardiovascular disease resulting from cholesterol antibodies, it might have been reasonable to expect him to then look for a way to prevent their formation. Instead he did the opposite. He developed a vaccine to actually promote antibody production against cholesterol.[59]

That's when Col. Alving changed what he had to say about antibodies to cholesterol. In 1995, he dropped his previous warnings about these antibodies being harbingers if not actual agents of lethal vascular disease. Instead he began to declare that cholesterol antibodies might actually have a "beneficial effect"; the antibodies he had previously associated with potentially fatal disease might actually help lower cholesterol, he now said.[60] Never mind the dead miniature pigs or the anaphylactoid sheep or the antibodies induced by liposomes that other researchers have linked to atherosclerosis, vascular disease and lupus. After 1995, it is as if the pigs never died, the sheep never went into shock and he never said cholesterol antibodies could be bad for you. Why the about-face? Well, one possible incentive was money. Vascular disease is the biggest killer in America, and a fortune could be made from a vaccine that could actually reduce cholesterol. The same is true for a new adjuvant and Alving has attempted to capitalize on the demand for one. On August 29, 2000, Alving and two of his colleagues received a patent for a vaccine adjuvant containing liposomes emulsified in oil.[61] One of those oils was squalene.

So, when Col. Alving went to Dover in May 1999, he knew that antibodies to lipids like cholesterol, and possibly even squalene (if such antibodies really existed), could potentially kill you. Although he knew that antibodies to cholesterol could allegedly occur naturally, and maybe even anti-squalene antibodies could too, he also knew that one way to induce antibodies to a lipid was by injecting it. Inject cholesterol, and you got anticholesterol antibodies; maybe the same was true for squalene. In any case, both these lipids could stimulate a response from the immune system; Alving knew that better than anyone else at Dover Air Force Base that day. But he did not say this to anyone. He did not tell anyone that squalene was a component of the Army's new anthrax vaccine. He did not disclose that he had a financial conflict of interest in this matter. He was trying to develop an anticholesterol vaccine, using liposomes and squalene.

When Pam Asa, Yan Cao and Bob Garry finally published their first paper on antibodies to squalene in the journal *Experimental and Molecular Pathology*, Alving wrote a scathing review to the editor. Alving and his coauthor, the director of the Army's mandatory anthrax vaccination program, Col. John Grabenstein, attacked the validity of Tulane's assay to detect anti-squalene antibodies, mostly concentrating on various technical points that the authors had left out of the paper for brevity.[62] Alving and Grabenstein incorrectly assumed that certain things were left undone, as opposed to left unsaid, because, as their letter implied, the Tulane scientists were incompetent.

Asa and Garry's paper did in fact have at least one problem for which there was no simple solution. The issue concerned the two patients from the NIH herpes vaccine trial who served as the study's "positive controls." Both had been injected with MF59; Patient X got immunized with MF59 only. When both patients tested positive for the antibodies, Garry and Asa concluded that the antibody assay worked. After all, they knew the NIH patients had both been injected with squalene. Based on those patients alone, Asa and Garry could not be certain that the antibodies to squalene they detected were naturally occurring, or a consequence of immunization with squalene. To say the antibodies resulted from immunization, Garry and Asa would have had to have tested the two NIH patients before they were immunized with MF59 or any other squalene-based product. Alving and Grabenstein spotted this flaw: "the authors provide no preinjection results to establish that intentional injection of squalene led to antibodies to a substance already present in the body."[63]

Bob Garry and Pam Asa felt they had ruled out the possibility of a naturally occurring antibody to squalene, because with few exceptions, other patients who had not been immunized with squalene tested negative for the antibodies. Contrary to Alving's suggestion at Dover that everyone might have anti-squalene antibodies, most of the patients tested by Asa and Garry did not. The antibodies were strictly confined to sick military personnel experiencing symptoms consistent with autoimmunity. Healthy Gulf War veterans did not have these antibodies, nor did patients diagnosed with autoimmune diseases from unknown causes. The NIH patients injected with MF59, on the other hand, tested positive. If the assay did indeed work, and the antibodies did correlate with squalene injection, then it made sense that Patient X and the other NIH study volunteer were positive. But given the ramifications of these antibodies, that was not good enough to fend off the criticism. To have an airtight case, Asa and Garry would need before-and-after results from the same person: no squalene antibodies before injection, and antibodies after. If the NIH patients had been negative for the antibodies *prior* to injection with MF59, then tested positive *after* injection, it would have been a slam-dunk.

Alving and Grabenstein argued that Asa and Garry could have avoided this perception problem by first testing the antibody assay in animals; or, they suggested, Asa and Garry could get "comparable serum samples demonstrated to contain anti-squalene antibodies after injection with squalene."[64] Asa and Garry took "comparable" to mean *human* serum samples, and they were appalled at this suggestion. They wrote back that it would be "unethical to inject squalene, a substance that has a 25-year history of causing both autoimmune rheumatological disease and neurological disease into humans to see if we could raise antibodies to it."[65] That was the dilemma. It would be easy enough to get blood from people who had not been injected with squalene, but then what? If injecting squalene really did to people what Asa and Garry thought it did, they could not ethically put people's lives at risk. Few Catch–22s have ever presented choices so stark.

"Trust but Verify"

Serge Trullet read my article in *Vanity Fair,* and he did not want to believe it. Trullet was an Air Force Senior Master Sergeant close to retirement. He had spent nearly twenty years wearing the uniform of the United States Air Force; in 1999, he was with the 164th Tennessee Air National Guard in Memphis. A naturalized U.S. citizen, Trullet was unabashedly patriotic about his adopted country. Trullet fled his native Argentina during the time of the *desaparacidos,* "the disappeared," when casting a ballot against the country's despotic generals could get you thrown into prison, tortured, then tossed from a helicopter on some dark night over the Atlantic. He knew what it was like to be afraid of his own government. For Trullet, America meant freedom—a place where he could raise his family without fear. The very suggestion that the Department of Defense could be using its own troops as guinea pigs was anathema to him. Pam Asa and Gary Matsumoto must be wrong. But when Dover's commander, Felix Grieder, temporarily halted the immunizations, Trullet could not ignore the implication that something might really be wrong with the vaccine.

By then, the Air Force was circulating among its personnel a tape of General Roadman's presentation at Dover. Trullet popped it into his VCR and listened. "Let me say this as succinctly as I can," said General Roadman, ambling across the front of the conference room, "there is not, there never has been . . . squalene as an adjuvant in the anthrax immunization, period." As Trullet saw, the videotape of Roadman's briefing was like an Air Force infomercial with a three-star general as pitchman. Roadman, in his fractured syntax, started repeating his message over and over again. Trullet was getting a little bored. "I know that squalene is, in fact, a red herring," Roadman said. Trullet perked up again when Col. Alving chimed in, suggesting that the antibodies were nothing to worry about. "Everybody has naturally occurring antibodies to cholesterol," Alving said. "I wouldn't be a bit surprised if enormous numbers of people have naturally, unrelated to injection or disease or anything else like that . . . antibodies to squalene." Like his squadron mates at the 164th, Trullet wanted to believe the Air Force, not Dr. Asa. But he could not get out of his mind something his favorite president, Ronald Reagan, used to say, quoting an old Russian adage when negotiating arms control with the Soviets: "Trust but verify." That's what he resolved to do.

Dr. Asa lived in Memphis. He looked her up in the local phone book and called.

"She wouldn't tell me to refuse the shot," said Trullet. "That would be disobeying an order, and she wasn't going to tell anyone to do that. But she drew my blood." Asa drew two tubes of blood and shipped them to Tulane. It took a while to get his results. As days turned to weeks, he grew anxious. Every day he read some new email from someone complaining about getting sick from the shots. About a month later, Pam Asa called. He was negative. He exhaled as if he were purging himself of an entire month's tension and stale air. He took another breath, because he knew what he wanted to do next. Just to be sure, he wanted his blood drawn again. The wait did not feel as interminable this time, and he was reassured to hear that his results were again negative. Then in the fall of 1999, it was his turn to take the shot.

"I felt like I went against my conscience when I took it," says Trullet. "My arms swelled up a little, and you know, it felt a little bit more uncomfortable than any of the other shots that I've taken in twenty-some years in the military." But the pain went away quickly; so did the swelling. Two weeks later, Trullet got another shot. Nothing happened. Two weeks after that, he took his third shot. "I started having a rash, pretty much all over my body, but mainly on the back side of my forearms and my face. And my lips started to swell up. So did my eyelids." The swelling persisted. The rash did not go away either. Something was wrong. Trullet still trusted, but it was time to verify again. Trullet sent his blood to Tulane.

He was positive.

Two other members of the 164th did the same thing. They had Asa and Garry test their blood twice, and twice they were negative. After taking their anthrax shots, one of them turned positive like Trullet.

Another Air Force sergeant at Dover had the same idea. Ted Peifer did not know Trullet or anyone else at the 164th, but he knew that Earl Stauffer had been suffering from dizzy spells, memory loss and chronic ringing in his ears after his anthrax shots. He and Stauffer were both loadmasters on C-5 Galaxies, and like everyone else at the base, Peifer found it a little unnerving when Stauffer started having problems after his anthrax injections. Earl was no whiner; he never complained about much, and especially not about some shot. Peifer did not watch the Roadman tape. He did not have to; he had attended the briefing. Peifer decided he could not afford to take Col. Alving at his word when Alving said that everyone might have the antibodies. Before he took his shots, Peifer sent Pam Asa a blood sample. He did not have the antibodies. Then he got his shots. It did not take long for him to get ill. "Within a couple of weeks I start getting sick," he says, "and it seems like I'm getting sicker." After his shots, Peifer's leg muscles started seizing up on him so badly that at times he could not walk. This was no ordinary cramping. Peifer had never experienced pain like this in his life. The spasms were so severe that he sometimes had to lie on the floor of his kitchen for relief, tears streaming from his eyes. He asked Tulane to test his blood again. This time, he was positive— +3 on a scale of 1 to 4.

It would be another year before these men learned that the FDA had proven there was squalene in almost every jab they got. Trullet got three injections from Lot FAV043, confirmed by the FDA to contain a 40 parts per billion concentration of squalene. Peifer got a total of five injections. Among them was FAV008, confirmed by subsequent Army testing to contain a squalene concentration no greater than nine parts per billion.[66] After injection with anthrax vaccine containing squalene, Trullet developed arthritis and urticaria—a chronic hive-like rash that seems to occur randomly without any particular stimulus. Pam Asa says such hypersensitivities can be autoimmune. Trullet absorbs this information intently; he has never been allergic to anything in his life before. "Growing up in Argentina, things aren't as homogenized, pasteurized and everything else, as they are in the U.S.," he says. "So I guess I've built up some resistance to most things. I can practically pull poison oak or ivy by hand, just yank it off, and I don't get any kind of a reaction." Trullet continues to test negative for every known allergen. Peifer has been diagnosed with autoimmune thyroid disease and chronic muscle inflammation consistent with polymyositis—another autoimmune disease. But what bothers these men far more than their physical injuries was the knowledge that the FDA knew these vaccine lots contained squalene as far back in June 1999, and did nothing about it. "I felt betrayed by the very country—" Trullet starts to break down. "I'm sorry. I'm forty years old and I'm crying. I don't cry very easily."

"I was very disappointed, very hurt [and] upset," says Peifer, "that our own people would do that to us." Peifer is convinced that this was done as part of an intentional experiment, but as upsetting as that conclusion is to him, he tries to keep perspective on what happened. "To me, it's sorta like D-Day," he says. "They knew they were going to lose so many and they did it anyway. I just wish I wasn't one of 'em. I don't blame Uncle Sam for it. I blame a couple people somewhere along the line that did it."

"I don't know what to think about my commanders," Trullet says. "I think that they're just ignorant—you know, 'follow-the-leader' types that absolutely question nothing that their superiors tell them. I feel that some of them would have probably done the same things that the Nazis did to the Jews with the excuse that they were following orders." Trullet speaks less stoically than Peifer, and he is unapologetic about it. "I joined the military out of patriotic reasons," he says, "to serve the country that allowed my family to live in freedom and without the fear of persecution. Having grown up under a military dictatorship all my life, and believing in freedom and the Bill of Rights, the Constitution and everything this country was founded on, and then the very people that I serve do this to me and to others in my unit . . . this is not right."

This was the data that Alving considered necessary to even begin to give any credence to Tulane's assay. In the fall of 1999, four Air Force sergeants had their blood tested for the presence of anti-squalene antibodies before getting their shots. All four were negative. After injections from anthrax vaccine lots containing low concentrations of squalene, three out of four tested positive for the antibodies. The data from Tulane's second study was just about as black and white as it gets in immunology. *Before* getting immunized with anthrax vaccine lots containing squalene, these four Air Force sergeants *did not* have the antibodies. *After* injection, three of them *did*. The antibodies appeared following injection with anthrax vaccine from lots found by the FDA to contain squalene; so did the onset of Gulf War Syndrome–like problems, leading in some cases to fully diagnosed autoimmune diseases. So there was a direct correlation between squalene-positive vaccine lots and the antibodies. The same lots also correlated with disease. Here was the experiment that, for ethical reasons, Asa and Garry had refused to run on human subjects. Running it was not Asa and Garry's idea but the brainchild of the four Air Force sergeants, who came up with it on their own back in 1999—before *Experimental and Molecular Pathology* even published Asa and Garry's first paper, let alone Alving and Grabenstein's criticisms. Here was the very evidence that Alving and Grabenstein demanded before they would concede there was even limited validity to the Tulane study.

But Alving already knew the Tulane assay worked. He was the first scientist anywhere to corroborate in studies with mice that naturally occurring antibodies to squalene did *not* exist.[67] He was also the first to prove that antibodies unique to squalene existed in animals but only after they were injected with adjuvant formulations containing squalene.[68] And not just any formulation. Only two, in fact: one that contained his very own liposomes emulsified in squalene; and one made from components identical to the ones in Tri-Mix— the squalene emulsion that Fort Detrick scientists added to their second-generation anthrax vaccine prior to Desert Shield.[69] Alving already knew all about this when he sent his withering review of Asa and Garry's work to the editor of *Experimental and Molecular Pathology*. He had already submitted for publication his groundbreaking paper corroborating the existence of anti-squalene antibodies—induced by injection only—to another journal in April 2000[70]—one month before he sent his letter to *Experimental and Molecular Pathology* attacking Tulane.[71] Then, just a few months later, Alving received a patent for his cholesterol-laden liposomes combined with oils, including squalene.[72] These were the same liposomes that sent miniature pigs into anaphylactoid shock and killed some of them—and the same liposomes that Alving admits to adding to the "new, more potent anthrax vaccine" that he made for Operation Desert Shield (but did not put into production, he says).[73] Alving also admitted to GAO investigators that had anyone asked him (by his account, they did not), he would have recommended making an anthrax vaccine for Desert Shield using the squalene emulsion MF59.[74] So Col. Alving had been a proponent of the use of squalene in vaccines since the late 1980s; he has been an aggressive advocate for their use ever since. In his relentless campaign to discredit the Tulane research, Alving has never disclosed these conflicts of interest—not to Asa and Garry, not to the media, not even to the military personnel for whom he advocates squalene's use.

When I spoke to Col. Alving in 1999, he denied working with squalene. He told me that he only worked with liposomes that did not contain this oil. He made no mention of the patent application he had filed the year before—on May 28, 1998—for an adjuvant formulation containing liposomes and squalene.[75] When I tried to contact Alving again in 2004, he did not respond. I also tried to contact his principal coauthor on the papers concerning anti-squalene antibodies, Dr. Gary Matyas. Dr. Matyas did not respond to my letter either.

When I asked Fort Detrick's Freedom of Information Act officer, Mike Stitely, for copies of the Army's contracts with companies that made adjuvants containing squalene, he sent back its regrets. "We identified two contracts and fifteen purchase orders that most closely meet your request," he wrote. "Unfortunately, all have been destroyed."[76]

Mark Ammends would have appreciated knowing all this. Ammends is a quadriplegic so profoundly paralyzed with amyotrophic lateral sclerosis—ALS, better known as Lou Gehrig's disease—that he cannot even blink. He spends his days on a special bed in the living room of his home outside of Memphis;

the bed is mechanized to gently shift his body around on his mattress to prevent bed sores. His family bathes him, removes his waste . . . turns pages of books for him to read. His brain is alert. He just cannot use it to communicate with anyone, or to move his limbs, or even breathe. He is on a ventilator twenty-four hours a day, seven days a week. Some ALS sufferers in the disease's advanced stages can still move some parts of their bodies. Dr. Stephen Hawking can still move one thumb, which enables him to communicate via a computer keyboard. Mark Ammends can't even do that. Ammends's mind is trapped in a body that will not work. He was a fireman working part-time for the 164th Tennessee Air National Guard when he got orders to take his anthrax shots. He took three of them before starting to lose his equilibrium, like Jeff Rawls.

What is especially significant about Ammends's case to the larger discussion on Gulf War Syndrome is the disease from which he suffers. On December 10, 2001, the Secretary of Veterans' Affairs, the Honorable Anthony J. Principi, announced that Gulf War veterans who deployed to the Persian Gulf between August 1990 and July 1991 were two times more likely to develop ALS as veterans who did not.[77] "We found 40 cases of ALS among deployed veterans," said Principi, "almost twice as many as we would have expected compared to those who were on active duty during that period but did not serve in the Gulf.[78] About half are now deceased." NIH scientists working in cooperation with the Department of Defense carried out an epidemiological study involving 700,000 veterans who served in Southwest Asia, and an additional 1.8 million veterans who did not.[79] It was the largest investigation of its kind.

Omitted from this study was something only Pam Asa and Bob Garry knew. Two out of the forty Gulf War veterans who developed ALS had their blood tested by Tulane. Both were positive for anti-squalene antibodies. After Mark Ammends developed ALS, his wife, Mary, sent her husband's blood to Tulane. He turned up positive, too. Three U.S. military personnel with ALS—an Army medic, an Air Force pilot and an Air National Guard fireman—have had their blood tested by Tulane. All three have anti-squalene antibodies. That is three for three so far. Only two of these men deployed to the Persian Gulf in 1990–1991; Mark Ammends did not. If there was something in Southwest Asia that could have triggered ALS, Mark Ammends was not exposed to it, because he was not there. The main thing that all three ALS sufferers have in common are antibodies demonstrated in animals and humans to occur after injection with a vaccine additive the Army has been adding to its new anthrax vaccine since 1987. It is an additive that could possibly explain what happened to each of these men with ALS and the antibodies. In the late 1990s, scientists in Europe proved that injections with squalene induced severe neurological damage in rats.

"Oil adjuvants are the most insidious chemical weapon ever devised," says Pam Asa. "All sorts of factors like wind and rain, and even temperature, can affect whether or not you can deliver a lethal dose of nerve agent against your enemy," she says. "None of these factors come into play with an oil adjuvant; that's because you stick 'em right into somebody's veins."

Strictly speaking, it is not the injected oil that does the damage; it is the immune system's response to the oil. Squalene is a kind of trigger for the real biological weapon: the immune system. When the immune system's full repertoire of cells and antibodies start attacking the tissues they are supposed to protect, the results can be catastrophic—a fact that did not escape the notice of the Soviet Union.

A New Kind of Biological Weapon

By developing a range of squalene-based vaccine additives, the creators of what were supposed to be safe oil adjuvants ignored the inherent risk in immunizing people with a molecule found in their bodies. The Soviets understood exactly what this could do and with that concept in mind, they made a weapon.

In the 1980s, when the Iraqis were buying seed cultures for their biological weapons from the United States, the Soviets, possessors of the largest biological weapons program in the world, got an idea for their new weapon from American scientists. American molecular biologists had discovered that certain microbes might cause autoimmune disease because some of those microbes possessed amino acids that were very similar, if not identical, to those found in human beings. As disconcerting as it might seem, we *Homo sapiens* at the top of the food chain actually possess molecules with identical structures to those found in microbes at the bottom of that chain. If the immune system forms an antibody to one of these shared structures, called "epitopes," that antibody will attack that epitope wherever it is found—whether it is on a molecule that belongs to a virus or on one that belongs in your brain.

This phenomenon is called "molecular mimicry." An example of such mimicry is when a strep infection turns into rheumatic fever. The *Streptococcus* germ actually shares an amino acid sequence with cardiac myosin, a protein in the muscles and valves of your heart.[80] If the strep infection goes unchecked, an immune response to the strep germ can "cross-react" with cardiac myosin, initiating an autoimmune attack against these proteins in the heart. Because this link between strep and rheumatic fever is well known, doctors keep a special eye out for strep and treat an infection with antibiotics the minute they spot one. This has greatly reduced the incidence of rheumatic heart disease. If molecular biologists could catalogue the epitopes shared by other microbes and man, they might be able to pinpoint the origins of other autoimmune diseases and then devise ways to prevent them.

Molecular mimicry caught Dr. Sergei Popov's attention, but not because he was looking for ways to prevent autoimmune disease. Just the opposite. Popov wanted to *induce* autoimmunity. In the 1980s, having already stockpiled tons of old standbys like anthrax, Soviet bioweaponeers began looking for something new to work on. Making a silo-full of anthrax or plague did not pose an interesting enough challenge to the Soviet Union's newest generation of germ warriors. They were an almost cocky bunch—intent on creating something Mother Nature had not. "Designer disease," they would later call it. Popov was one of the Soviet Union's best young germ warriors, running highly classified research projects at The State Research Center for Applied Microbiology at Obolensk, just outside of Moscow, and another laboratory specializing in viruses called VECTOR, a thousand miles to the east in Koltsovo, Siberia. While at Obolensk, Popov supervised a program codenamed "FACTOR"—as in "pathogenic factors" or "virulence factors"—where he helped engineer designer germs resistant to antibiotics. That is when he got interested in U.S. research with myelin basic protein.

American molecular biologists had mapped out the entire amino acid sequence for myelin—one of the chief components of the insulation surrounding nerve endings.[81] Now they were hard at work trying to identify the epitopes on viruses that would cross-react with a special site on the myelin molecule to which an antibody might react and cause experimental allergic encephalomyelitis—the animal version of multiple sclerosis.[82] As the California-based scientists Robert Fujinami and Michael Oldstone explained in a landmark paper in *Science*: "during the cross-reacting immune response, virus may be cleared, but the components of the immune attack continue to assault self elements. The autoimmune response leads to tissue injury that, in turn, releases more self antigen, and the cycle continues."[83] Fujinami and Oldstone called the initial infection a "hit and run event." By this they meant the virus attacked, and though it didn't stick around, it left behind lasting damage. That is because the immune system continues to attack the molecule in the body that resembles the one in the germ, long after the immune system has gotten rid of that germ. Once this self-destructive process begins, it never stops, our bodies continue making the molecule the immune system is now trained to attack. If this new target for the immune system happened to be myelin, for example, the body would continue making this protein in order to replenish and repair the sheath around its nerve endings. But in the act of doing so, the body immunizes itself against itself, administering over and over again what amounts to a booster dose of something that the immune system now wants to get rid of. This vital constituent of your own body is now the enemy, and the immune system is now programmed to obliterate it in an endless loop of self-destruction. Popov saw real potential here.

He would not bother looking for a naturally occurring molecule that could trigger this process. He would make one. Popov spliced a fragment of myelin basic protein into legionella—the bacterium that causes Legionnaires' Disease—creating a "chimera," named for the mythical creature with a lion's head, goat's body and serpent's tail. Inside Popov's new constructed chimera was what amounted to a living "nano-bomb"—molecular contraband that could theoretically cause MS. When Popov infected guinea pigs with his chimera, the immune system cleared the legionella, and, just as he predicted, the myelin molecule smuggled into the guinea pigs inside of his microbial Trojan horse germ initiated a second wave of disease. This stealth germ caused experimental allergic encephalomyelitis, the animal version of MS. Popov felt as proud as a new parent. He could not wait to show "the client."

"The client" is what VECTOR scientists called the Soviet Army officers who commissioned their biological warfare research projects. "Their initial response was rather discouraging," says Popov, "because they did not see the fast onset of symptoms." What the generals were accustomed to seeing was a germ with an immediate and catastrophic effect, but when they came back a few weeks later and saw the guinea pigs crippled by MS, they recognized Popov's creation for what it was—a biological time bomb. Soviet scientists then constructed another one of these time bombs with a virus. They chose vaccinia, the non-lethal cousin of smallpox.[84] Popov, who is now living in America, believes the "final construct" for this viral time bomb was not vaccinia, but smallpox itself. In any case, it worked. "The client" had seen enough. The generals were sold on the idea. "The Russian Ministry of Defense wanted us to construct these designer germs, using myelin basic protein from monkeys and humans," says Popov. "That would create a human version of the disease."

Molecular mimicry, seen for its diabolical potential as a weapon by the Soviets as far back as the 1980s, also applies to squalene. But the real problem with using squalene, of course, is not that it mimics a molecule found in the body; it *is* the same molecule. So what American scientists conceived as a vaccine booster was another "nano-bomb," instigating chronic, unpredictable and debilitating disease. When the NIH argued that squalene would be safe because it is native to the body, just the opposite was true. Squalene's natural presence in the body made it one of the most dangerous molecules ever injected into man. When UCLA Medical School's Michael Whitehouse and Frances Beck injected squalene combined with other materials into rats and guinea pigs back in the 1970s, few oils were more effective at causing the animal versions of arthritis and multiple sclerosis.[85] By the late 1990s, Sweden's Karolinska Institute proved that injecting squalene all by itself could cause arthritis.[86] The Polish Academy of Sciences proved that squalene alone could cause severe neurological damage.[87] Now Tulane University Medical School and its ardent intellectual adversary—the Army's Col. Carl Alving—have both shown that the immune system makes antibodies to squalene, but only after it is injected.

For squalene's proponents in the U.S. Army and the NIH, this has been a relentless march towards an unpalatable truth. By adding squalene to their new anthrax vaccine, they did not make a better vaccine; they made a biological weapon. The anti-squalene antibodies in sick U.S. and British military personnel are evidence that military experiments may have caused more casualties with its new anthrax vaccine than have been caused by anthrax weapons since they were first used by the Japanese Army in the 1940s.

Chapter Twelve

Same Song, Third Verse

On June 15, 2004, around six in the evening at the Tulane University Health Science Center in New Orleans, several rows of cellulose strips began to change color. They were the size and shape of the litmus paper that you used to test the pH of liquids in your high school chemistry class. Each strip had been carefully sliced from a larger sheet of cellulose with what looked like a miniature bread cutter, and then soaked all day in various chemicals. Dr. Russell Wilson, who coauthored the second Tulane antibody paper with Asa and Garry, was running the Western Blot assay to detect antibodies to squalene in military personnel given anthrax vaccinations for Operation Iraqi Freedom. Garry, Asa and I were in the lab with him.

Wilson barely spoke. Running the assay required great concentration and he did not want to be distracted. It was tedious work, and the process of soaking the strips, then draining and washing them before adding the next chemical, had to be repeated several times. Each step had to be precisely executed; otherwise he would have to start over again. There were thirty-six serum samples in this particular run. Wilson applied several dabs of serum onto the cellulose with a Q-tip. Then he placed the strips into plastic trays with wells shaped like long grooves where they incubated in their chemical bath—about an hour for each chemical. With Garry and Asa assisting, Wilson had methodically worked his way through each step since eight in the morning. Every so often, Bob Garry took the odd moment to advise a doctoral student working in another part of the "Garry Lab." Apart from that—and a short break for lunch down the street at the

Arabesque Café where customers ate off paper plates and drank Cokes straight from the can—all three worked through the day without interruption. Around five o'clock in the afternoon, Wilson added the last chemical, an enzyme called horseradish peroxidase that acted like a photo developer. It would reveal the antibodies that until now had been invisible. In the presence of human antibodies, in this case against squalene, horseradish peroxidase would turn the strips varying shades of blue. The higher the concentration of antibodies, the deeper the blue. Wilson checked his watch. It was time. He and Asa walked over to the tray in which the strips were soaking. Garry was already standing nearby.

"Oh God," said Pam Asa.

"We've definitely got some positives here," said Garry.

"We'll let them dry overnight," said Russ Wilson, "then we'll score 'em in the morning. Bob, you got a drawer we can stick these in so nobody messes with them?"

"How 'bout this one," Garry said, pulling open an empty drawer.

They would wait till morning.

Bob Garry, pen and notepad in hand, stared down at the numbered strips, scoring each one with a notation next to the corresponding numbers on his notepad. "Plus/minus," he muttered to himself. This was a sample right on the margin of being weakly positive. Mostly, he stood there in silence, writing down his scores. Wilson would repeat the process later, without Garry present; the two would then compare scores and discuss those on which they differed. In the end, they would differ on only two.

Out of thirty-six samples, four came from control patients who had not been injected with anthrax vaccine. Twenty samples were positive. They came from service members at military bases across the country—Randolph Air Force Base in Texas, Westover Air Force Base in Massachusetts, Dover Air Force Base again, and the 164th Air National Guard in Memphis. Most had been injected with anthrax vaccine between 1998 and 2000 as part of the Defense Department's Anthrax Vaccine Immunization Program. Five had been injected expressly for deployment in Operation Iraqi Freedom.

The last time the United States fought Iraq, in 1990, the Armed Forces Epidemiological Board reminded military doctors and scientists that the deployment of large numbers of U.S. troops to a foreign battlefield would present "unique research opportunities." Project Badger scientists not only proposed using investigational new drugs, they wanted to run trials with them "in theater," because there was no better way to test how well these experimental products actually worked. "Thus we have the research requirement of determining true efficacy during times of actual deployment," wrote Project Badger's chairman during Operation Desert Shield.[1] In the "Garry Lab" at Tulane University in 2004, there was now stark evidence on five freshly cut strips of blue-black cellulose that gave evidence that the Army had once again turned the battlefield into a laboratory.

Under the circumstances, it was a wonder that the Department of Defense wasn't even harsher in its criticism of Tulane's squalene antibody data. But in connecting the illnesses and the antibodies with anthrax immunization, Asa and Garry were only doing what a team of Army investigators had done more than fifty years before under similar circumstances. When more than 51,000 Army soldiers were hospitalized with jaundice in 1942, epidemiologists were able to trace the source of the outbreak to an experimental yellow fever vaccine. Seven out of one hundred forty-one vaccine lots that had been contaminated with hepatitis B virus, affecting more than 330,000 troops in the Army's Western Defense Command.[2] If these circumstances sound familiar, it is because they were. They were, in fact, almost identical. The Army, fearing a biological warfare attack, resorted to using an experimental vaccine. In this instance, the epidemiologists investigating the outbreak for the Army could show a dose-response relationship between a specific pathogen, hepatitis B virus, and a known consequence of hepatitis infection—jaundice. They identified the problem lots by matching the jaundice cases with specific lot numbers. Seven out of one hundred forty-one lots were found to be contaminated with the virus.

Asa and Garry did the same thing those World War II Army scientists had done: they followed a serological trail. The path back to the source was in the blood of their patients. That is why Pam Asa requested that everyone submitting serum for testing supply the lot number of the anthrax vaccine they had received. At the end of each run, she would check those numbers. That is how she and Bob Garry spotted the pattern. Patients suffering from autoimmune disease, and testing positive for the antibodies, had been immunized with vaccine from the same lots. The antibody-positive troops were based all across the country. What linked them was immunization from the same lots.

Out of the six anthrax vaccine lots "contaminated" with squalene, Pam Asa had identified five *before* the FDA disclosed its results from the June 1999 tests. She had only missed one of them. An Army subcontractor confirmed that a sixth lot, FAV008, also contained squalene. Too few patients in the Tulane study had been injected with that lot to permit her to correlate it with disease.

Until the FDA disclosed its results, the antibodies were circumstantial evidence that U.S. and British troops had been injected with an experimental vaccine additive. The FDA data, then combined with results of the before-and-after experiment by the four Air Force sergeants, made the connection direct: troops turning up positive for anti-squalene antibodies had been given anthrax vaccine from squalene-positive lots. What's more, antibody-positive troops were experiencing symptoms that matched those listed in the Air Force case definition of Gulf War Syndrome—fatigue, rashes, short-term memory loss, headaches, joint and muscle pain, and dizziness. Many were getting diagnosed with lupus, multiple sclerosis and rheumatoid arthritis—all diseases induced in animals by squalene injection, and all diseases listed by BioPort on its new package insert after the FDA disclosed it found squalene in anthrax vaccine.

By cross-referencing the shot records of military personnel with the antibody data, Pam Asa succeeded in predicting which lots contained squalene and which ones probably didn't; the FDA did her the unintended courtesy of proving her correct. Now military personnel injected with other lots were testing positive. "Because of the antibody results, we have three new lots of vaccine that we believe contain squalene—FAV041, FAV070 and FAV071," says Pam Asa. In her experience, chronic sickness following a shot also has been a reliable predictor of the presence of squalene in anthrax vaccine. "I could almost peg which lots were 'hot,' because of the autoimmunity showing up in the people injected with them," says Asa. "It was one-for-one every time." She also thinks four other lots contain squalene because autoimmune disease has shown up in troops injected with them, but she can't begin to prove it without testing the sera from people injected with those lots only. "People immunized with these lots didn't just get sick," says Asa. "Some even died of diseases that were specifically autoimmune. Based on this unique pathology, I'm leery of four more anthrax vaccine lots—FAV017, FAV048, FAV066 and FAV073."

More evidence came from people who never intended to provide it. In a class action lawsuit filed by a New Jersey-based law firm against BioPort, attorneys for the plaintiffs drew up a list of their clients, their illnesses and the vaccine lots each received.[3] The attorneys, Alan Milstein and Derek Braslow—who specialize in litigation related to vaccines and clinical trials—cited the FDA complaints against BioPort, not squalene, as evidence that their clients had been recipients of an "adulterated" and "misbranded" drug. In July 2002, Milstein called Asa about his plaintiffs. As she has done since beginning her research, Asa declined to be involved in litigation, but she could not avoid noticing something about the client list Milstein sent her. There were sixty-five clients in the "class"; fifty-seven of them had a record of their vaccine lot numbers.[4] Of these fifty-seven plaintiffs, thirty-nine had been injected with vaccine lots confirmed by the FDA to contain squalene or lots that had been administered to troops who then developed the antibodies.[5] That meant *seven out of every ten* plaintiffs in Milstein's lawsuit complained of illness following injection with anthrax vaccine lots linked to squalene.

———

Not long afterward, something happened in England that telegraphed what would happen during the second Anglo-American foray into Iraq. In January 2003, vials of British anthrax vaccine starting washing up on a beach, near the village of West Bay, Dorset. Where these vials came from was a mystery, but geography offered a clue. West Bay was relatively close to the ports from which British warships have set sail for centuries, and troop ships had recently departed for Iraq. It didn't take long for suspicions to center on those ships. Like the Boston Tea Party—if the British will pardon the analogy—persons unknown in Her Majesty's Armed Forces may have dumped something overboard to send a message. Its meaning seemed clear enough to veterans of Operation Granby, the British code-name for the first Gulf War. Speaking to a reporter in London, a spokesman for Britain's National Gulf War Veterans and Families Association, Jim Moore, speculated that the vaccine might have been intentionally dumped.[6] "People say you accept the risks when you sign up to join the forces," said Moore. "That's true, but the risk you accept is one of an enemy bullet or a landmine. You don't accept the risk of being a guinea pig for a vaccine," he said. "All the same mistakes made in the Gulf War are being made again."

Moore had no idea how prescient his remarks were.

When the vaccine started to wash up on the beach, the British Ministry of Defence did its best to retrieve every vial. It didn't succeed. Asif Hasan, an investigative producer for the British news magazine show *Tonight with Trevor McDonald*, got his hands on some of the vials and had them tested at a lab in Manchester where his network, Granada Television, has its headquarters. Scientific Analyses Laboratories, Ltd. in Manchester is one of the most highly regarded laboratories in England. British corporations send materials to SAL to ensure their compliance with government regulations; sometime the British government itself will send samples there for testing. In a report dated 26 February 2003, SAL reported that it found a thirty-six nanogram per milliliter concentration of squalene in two lots of anthrax vaccine produced by Britain's Center for Applied Microbiological Research (CAMR) at Porton Down.[7] Scientists at CAMR had been experimenting with squalene-based additives since the late 1980s and had resumed their work with squalene following the British government's commitment in 1998 to adopt the U.S. Army-designed recombinant anthrax vaccine.

Thirty-six nanograms per milliliter was almost indistinguishable from the squalene concentration found in BioPort vaccine lot # FAV043, which contained 40 parts per billion (nanograms), according to the analysis done by the FDA's Center for Biologics Research and Evaluation. This amount was found in two vials of anthrax vaccine from a stockpile believed to be accompanying British troops on their way to Iraq.

The antibodies in Iraq-bound U.S. troops, and the presence of squalene in what may have been Iraq-bound British anthrax vaccine, were evidence of unfinished business. The new anthrax vaccine—now an Anglo-American project—needed more work. Here was forensic evidence that someone in the chain of command saw Operation Iraqi Freedom as another "unique research opportunity." Unknown to U.S. and British military personnel, the California-based corporation VaxGen and the Health Protection Agency (HPA) for England and Wales were about to negotiate a binding Letter of Intent to license Fort Detrick's new anthrax vaccine to HPA.[8] This agreement would give HPA the right to manufacture the new anthrax vaccine in England and possibly market it elsewhere. Recent declassified briefings on the new vaccine given by one of its patent holders, Col. Arthur Friedlander (U.S. Army, ret.), made it clear that prototypes of the new vaccine were still being formulated with additives containing squalene.[9] When the new vaccine, rPA102, was finally patented in 2002, Friedlander and his colleagues made sure that the patent included at least one version of their new invention that contained squalene.[10] When VaxGen commenced clinical trials with the new vaccine in 2004, it only contained alum, not squalene. Without squalene, the Army would be immunizing troops with something that hardly differed from the ineffective vaccine it had had since 1970, only made with the latest technology. Something happened between 2002 and 2004. The question is whether another disastrous trial on a distant battlefield had anything to do with it. There are reasons to suspect that it did.

Drowning in the Desert

In the spring and summer of 2003, nineteen American service members in Iraq developed pneumonia so severe they had to be put on ventilators to help them breathe; two of them died. Out in the desert, they were drowning in their own fluids. An Army medical spokesman, Col. Bob DeFraites, suggested that smoking had something to do with it.[11] "It's not a coincidence, the association with smoking," said DeFraites. "It's a known irritant for lungs and a known risk factor for pneumonia in general. It may be sensitizing the lungs for the pneumonia." When questioned about a possible vaccine connection, Col. John Grabenstein—Col. Alving's erstwhile coauthor and chief apologist for the Army's anthrax vaccine—said there was no evidence that anthrax vaccine or smallpox vaccine had anything to do with these pneumonias.

Perhaps that was little hasty. Of the nineteen documented pneumonia patients by September 2003, ten of them, including the two who died, had elevated counts of a specialized immune cell called eosinophils. "Levels of eosinophils in the ten soldiers ranged from three times to eleven times higher than normal," DeFraites said.[12] Elevated eosinophil counts can result from a number of different events, including parasitic infection or allergic reactions. Military doctors did not report the presence of parasites in these patients. The previous year, however, Navy doctors did report an allergic reaction to anthrax vaccine that resulted in pneumonia.[13] Clinical examination and laboratory testing ruled out a bacterial or viral infection in a 39-year-old, non-smoking marine with pneumonia in Florida. As his doctors at the Naval Hospital in Pensacola pointed out, this marine developed a severe rash after his first anthrax shot on his right arm. By the next morning, it had spread to his entire upper body. By the next week it had spread down his trunk, past his waist and onto both legs. The Allergy Clinic at Pensacola treated him with steroids and diagnosed him with vasculitis—an inflammation of the blood vessels, which is autoimmune.

Despite steroid therapy for his vasculitis, the patient's allergic response to anthrax vaccine advanced into his lungs. It created something called "ground glass opacities." In a black and white computerized tomography scan, his lungs appeared saturated with thousands of near-translucent speckles, as if the tissues had been impregnated with tiny fragments of glass. After the Navy doctors put the sick marine on a higher dosage of steroids, the ground glass speckles disappeared from his lungs. In their published paper discussing this case, Navy doctors reported that the sick marine received "two unknown vaccinations during the 1990–1991 Persian Gulf War while in the military theater of operation." This time his doctors knew exactly which vaccine he had been given—anthrax. It resulted in an allergic reaction severe enough for steroid therapy. The Navy doctors diagnosed "Hypersensitivity pneumonitis." If you read the package insert included with every dose of anthrax vaccine starting on January 31, 2002, it specifically lists as a reported consequence of immunization, "*Hypersensitivity* reactions."[14]

The nineteen non-infectious pneumonias seen in the first months of the war have a possible squalene connection, too. An Army Reserve Chaplain, Captain Dave Hodge, tested positive for antisqualene antibodies in 1997. He does not have records of the shots he received for the Persian Gulf War. In 1998, however, he received three shots of anthrax vaccine at Fort Lewis in Tacoma, Washington, that Hodge says were "progressively more debilitating." His muscles and joints ached. His head felt as though it would split. When he went to the aide station, he says, the brigade surgeon told him he had an "allergic" response to the anthrax shot and gave him medicine to counteract the reaction. When he felt well enough again, he went back to the surgeon to ask for a waiver from any more anthrax shots. "That's when she began yelling at me that she never said 'allergic reaction,'" says Hodge.[15] "Several medics that had been present that day were shocked enough to come outside and assure me she had said it ... This is what led the physician's assistant to write down the lot numbers in my shot records." Hodge says he got injections from lot #FAV030, one of the five squalene-positive lots. Later, he developed "ground glass opacities" in his lungs just like the marine at Pensacola. Doctors diagnosed Hodge with "hypersensitivity pneumonia." At age 52, he is recovering from colorectal cancer while suffering from Mixed Connective Tissue Disorder, which is a kind of autoimmune smorgasbord. MCTD has symptoms of lupus, rheumatoid arthritis and Sjögren's syndrome but cannot be narrowed down to any one of them. Hodge says his lung capacity is down to less than fifty-two percent.

So contrary to Col. Grabenstein, the illnesses afflicting Captain Hodge and the marine at Pensacola were documented examples of pneumonia associated with anthrax vaccination. The doctors making that association were all in the military. According to pathology textbooks, hypersensitivity pneumonia does not induce a heightened eosinophil count, but another type of non-infectious pneumonia does. It is called Churg-Strauss Syndrome, and it is autoimmune.[16] When vasculitis, an autoimmune inflammation of blood vessels, occurs in the lungs, fluids seep from the damaged pulmonary vessels, causing pneumonia. This particular syndrome is also associated with another autoimmune disease called polyarteritis nodosa.[17] If you look on page six of BioPort's January 2002 package insert for anthrax vaccine, there among the reported consequences of immunization is "Polyarteritis nodosa."[18]

If Grabenstein was unfamiliar with Captain Hodge's pneumonia and the Pensacola marine's, he should have known about Rachael Lacy's pneumonia, because he had to comment on her case in the news. Lacy was a 22-year-old African-American woman who died on April 4, 2003, barely a month after receiving vaccinations for anthrax and smallpox. A nurse in training at Fort McCoy in Wisconsin, Lacy received her shots in late February and early March 2003 for deployment to Kuwait.[19] Within days after her shots, she developed chronic muscle pain. Things got steadily worse. Her chills, fatigue and fever became so severe in March that an ambulance had to take her to a hospital, where doctors diagnosed her with pneumonia and admitted her for two to three days. She complained of increasing shortness of breath, chest pain and a persistent cough. All her blood cultures were negative—no viral or bacterial infection, no fungal growth. Lacy did not have any known drug allergies, and did not smoke. At the Franciscan Skemp Healthcare Medical Center in Lacrosse, Lacy experienced a "complex partial seizure" like the ones that used to leave Col. Herb Smith so dazed that he couldn't find his way home.[20] The medical center transferred her to the intensive care unit of Saint Mary's Hospital in Rochester, Minnesota, where she died a little over a month after she received her first anthrax shot. Dr. Eric Pfeifer, the pathologist performing Lacy's autopsy at the nearby Mayo Clinic, noted that she had severe damage in her lungs with "scattered eosinophils."[21] A reduced supply of oxygen had injured her brain. The fluid extracted from the sac enclosing her lungs showed signs of acute and chronic inflammation. Pfeifer concluded that the immediate cause of death was due to a "lupus-like autoimmune disorder."[22] Following immunization against anthrax and smallpox, Lacy developed pneumonia, some degree of eosinophilia, and an autoimmune disorder that Pfeifer characterized as "lupus-like." Let's go back to the new package insert for America's only licensed anthrax vaccine, BioThrax, which Grabenstein says is effective and safe. Listed among the myriad autoimmune diseases that recipients of this vaccine have reported is "Systemic lupus erythematosus."[23]

Rachael Lacy did not see her twenty-third birthday. The closest she got to Kuwait was the office that cut her orders to deploy there. She did not smoke. Like at least nineteen U.S. military personnel in the Persian Gulf, she developed pneumonia; like at least ten of those soldiers, her pneumonia was not caused by a germ and she had an elevated eosinophil count. Like Captain Hodge and the sick marine at Pensacola, Lacy had severe inflammation destroying her own tissues. The only thing all these service members had in common besides non-infectious pneumonia was anthrax vaccination. Hodge and the marine did not get vaccinated against smallpox. I suspect that the people who developed this strange and debilitating pneumonia may have had something else in common too. I don't think any of them were told that as of January 2002, the makers of anthrax vaccine admitted that among the adverse events known to have occurred after immunization with their product were "hypersensitivity reactions, polyarteritis nodosa and lupus." It appears that Lacy's doctors were unaware of this. They make no mention of it in her medical records. Had they known about the allergic reactions and the autoimmunity now associated with the vaccine, they might have been able to prescribe medicine that could have arrested the progress of the lupus-like disease that killed her.

According to the Army, the number of severe pneumonia cases in 2004 is running close to what it was in 2003. Many of these pneumonia patients have been on ventilators to help them breathe, and by the Army's count, eight of them have elevated eosinophil counts.[24] Unlike 2003, there have been no fatalities—a fact that the Army attributes to something it is doing different this year.

"Doctors are treating pneumonia patients earlier with steroids, which decreases the time they must spend in intensive care units and hospitals," says Col. Bruno Petruccelli, Director of Epidemiology and Disease Surveillance for the Army's Center for Health Promotion and Preventive Medicine (USACHPPM). What Petruccelli isn't saying is why military doctors are treating pneumonia patients in Iraq with steroids, which are not used for bacterial pneumonia. Among their many uses, steroid drugs are a standard treatment for inflammation due to allergic reactions and autoimmune diseases. On 10 February 2004, the Army Surgeon General, Lt. General James Peake, issued a memo for regional medical commanders advising them to "consider the possibility of autoimmune disease and appropriate treatments for such conditions."[25]

According to UPI's Mark Benjamin, the true number of cases of "pneumonia-like illnesses" may be much higher than military doctors are admitting.[26] Benjamin found other military personnel who developed these pneumonias who, like Lacy, did not smoke and did not actually serve in the Persian Gulf. Air Force Staff Sergeant Neal Erickson, who served in Turkey during Operation Iraqi Freedom, told Benjamin that doctors "thought he had blood clots or a heart attack," but then diagnosed him with "a type of pneumonia." The death toll from these pneumonias may be much higher than reported. Benjamin tracked down eight more soldiers—allegedly unacknowledged by the Pentagon investigation into this matter—who died after experiencing "pneumonia-like symptoms and breathing problems."

Erickson told Benjamin his problems started after his anthrax shots; the same thing happened to Army Pvt. Dennis Drew, who never left Texas. Drew said he started feeling sick three days after his first anthrax shot. When Drew checked into the hospital, doctors told him he had pneumonia and myocarditis—an inflammation in the heart. "It is like my immune system does not work anymore," said Drew. "When I first got to Fort Hood, the doctor there thought the mycocarditis might have been caused by the vaccine." That would have been a good guess. Myocarditis is listed on BioPort's package insert too.[27]

BioPort describes the reactions it started listing on its package insert in January 2002 as "infrequently reported serious adverse events" that occurred in people injected with BioThrax.[28] Patients reported these problems to the FDA's Vaccine Adverse Event Reporting System (VAERS) but BioPort says "the report of an adverse event to VAERS is not proof that a vaccine caused the event."

This is true. Simply reporting that these illnesses occurred following immunization does not prove cause and effect. The question is whether knowing that other people have developed bona fide cases of myocarditis, rheumatoid arthritis or lupus after anthrax immunization would have persuaded people to decline the shot. Even more important, would the knowledge that allergic and autoimmune problems sometimes follow anthrax shots help doctors choose an appropriate treatment for immunized patients before their symptoms become too severe? Could this knowledge have saved Rachael Lacy's life?

One Other Pneumonia

It was six A.M. on April 6, 2003. NBC News correspondent David Bloom had slept that night in the "Bloommobile." The Bloommobile was a pickup truck on steroids—a Ford F-450 with an extended cab and a jury-rigged satellite dome the size of a small asteroid sitting in the truck bed. It traveled with an M88A Tank Recovery vehicle, a squat bogey-wheeled monster on treads, courtesy of the Army, rigged up with a gyro-stabilized camera. Together, the two vehicles were a TV studio on wheels that gave NBC a clean television signal with barely a jiggle from the middle of the battlefield. Bloom liked to sleep inside the truck, if you could really call it sleep. He was up a lot of the time working; he had high-speed Internet access to read the news wires, and satellite phones to check in with the desk. Sometimes he'd call home and help one of his daughters with her homework from the other side of the world. That meant a lot to him.

So did this story. Bloom was embedded with the 3rd Armored Division, one of the units that would lead the assault on Baghdad. He anchored NBC's *Weekend Today* show, but whenever he could, Bloom liked to get out in front of big story. He was aggressive and had a knack for scooping the competition out of their Ralph Lauren socks. His cameraman, Craig White—the man whose brainchild was the Bloommobile—had just gotten up from his cot outside when David rolled down the window.

"Hey buddy! We're going to Baghdad! Tell the guys to pack it up," yelled Bloom. "We leave in an hour … I just got the news last night."

Bloom was happy. History was about to unfold in front of the 3rd Armored Division's big guns and he had the best seat in the house. White was checking in with his wife on one of the cordless phones when he caught a movement out of the corner of his eye. He turned around. Somebody was down in the dirt. White started walking over to the person. When he saw it was Bloom, he started running. Bloom was on his back, propped up on an elbow like he was trying to get up, but he couldn't. White could see he was dazed.

"Medic! Medic! MEDIIIC!" yelled White. He recalls Bloom lying there "like a fighter who'd just been knocked out trying to get up off the canvas, not knowing where he was." White thought Bloom had just hit his head on something—there were lots of sharp corners on the M88—or maybe he was dehydrated.

"David, you've just fainted," said White. "We've got a medic coming."

The medic got an IV into him, but Bloom's body wouldn't accept the fluids. It was shutting down. That's when the seizures started. Every minute or so, Bloom would go very red in the face and start trembling. This wasn't just dehydration. White ran to the battalion TOC (Tactical Operations Center).

"We need a Medivac right away for David! He's in bad shape ... we gotta get him outa here, now. Please, now ... work on it!"

The battalion couldn't land a helicopter near the Bloommobile: It was too dangerous for the chopper to land so close to the fighting. White and the other NBC staffers would have to drive Bloom in a Humvee more than a mile to the helicopter.

Bloom was on a stretcher now. White was holding his hand. "David, we're gonna Medivac you outa there, you understand that? You're gonna be okay!" Bloom's producer, Paul Nassar, would fly out on the chopper with him. "Paul is with you," White said to Bloom. White was speaking louder now, because he could sense Bloom was slipping away. "We'll get you help ... we're getting you to help!"

White stared into Bloom's eyes, the mesmerizing blue eyes that could dazzle in the harsh flat light of a TV studio. Bloom stared back. That's when White saw something he did not wish to see. In that brief moment before the Humvee pulled away White saw something change in Bloom's eyes. They were still staring, but they were no longer seeing. His pupils had dilated out and fixed. As the Humvee gunned its engine and pulled away, White knew it was already too late. His friend and colleague had died.

It has been nearly a year since Bloom's death. When White tells this story, he fights off his emotions. He is one of NBC's best cameramen, a square-jawed athletic man who is one of the Peacock web's go-to guys for tough as-signments. When NBC wanted to do a feature on a paraplegic climber at-tempting to scale Yosemite's El Capitan, Craig White was dangling from ropes and caribiners on a sheer rock face, shooting video. As tough as he is, his eyes are watering, though not quite spilling over. White is fighting it. It is difficult for him to speak about this. It is almost as difficult to hear.

"So tell me about your anthrax shots," I ask.

"Well, we joked when we got that last shot out in the field. It's a whopper of a shot," says White. "When you get that in your arm, if you're not ready for it, it's a surprise. Man, does your arm cramp up and get a big knot in it."

Then White tells me something peculiar. He got his jabs directly into the muscle. The FDA license calls for the shot to be administered subcuta-neously—just under the skin. That is the way the BioPort package insert says the shot should be given.[29]

"It wasn't subcutaneous," says White. "No."

"It was in the muscle?"

"Yeah, it was I-M. Definitely. I know the difference." White is surprised to learn that giving the anthrax shot intramuscularly is part of a current experi-ment organized by the Centers for Disease Control and the Walter Reed Army Institute of Research to see if changing the route of administration to "I-M" will reduce the soreness and swelling at the injection site that commonly oc-curs with the licensed vaccine. This study is also investigating the possibility that intramuscular injection will elicit better protection with fewer shots.[30] Interestingly, giving the shot intramuscularly also happens to be the way the Army's new rPA102 anthrax vaccine is supposed to be given. In fact, there is another clinical trial underway right now, sponsored by the DynPort Vaccine Company, that is called: "A New Anthrax Vaccine Administered by the *Intra-muscular (IM) Route* in Healthy Adults." [Italics mine] This trial is also being conducted at Walter Reed Army Institute of Research.[31] This study was scheduled to start in April 2003 (just a few weeks after Operation Iraqi Free-dom commenced), and was scheduled for completion in April 2004.

White has been on assignment in more than a hundred countries and has gotten a lot of jabs. So he knows the difference between subcutaneous and I-M, and he is certain that he got his anthrax shots directly into his muscle. "These were all done I-M," he assures me. "No doubt about it."

Something else happened to White. He developed pneumonia. An army doctor gave him antibiotics and it went away in just a couple of days—but anyone who has ever had pneumonia knows that a scant two days of antibiotics isn't enough to clear it. I tell him about Tulane's work and White decides to have his serum tested. For the helluvit, so did I.

———

White was +1. It was not an ambiguous result. Pam Asa had personally drawn White's blood, but Bob Garry scored all the samples without knowing the identities of any of the patients. I was negative. So far, the antibodies have been a reliable marker for anthrax vaccine lots containing squalene, as well as for autoimmune disease. Aseptic pneumonia has been associated with anthrax vaccination in many cases already—Hodge, Lacy, the Pensacola marine, Erickson and Drew. It is also associated with oil adjuvants. In the 1980s, scientists at the U.S. Department of Agriculture's Plum Island laboratory in New York wanted to study "interstitial lung disease," so they developed a way to induce pulmonary inflammation.[32] It had already been done in rodents.[33] The USDA scientists wanted to see if it could also be done in pigs. It could. They induced pneumonia with injections of Freund's Complete Adjuvant.

The question is whether injection with squalene could have been a factor in David Bloom's death. An autopsy performed at Dover Air Force Base by the Armed Forces Institute of Pathology attributed Bloom's death to natural causes. A thrombus or clot had lodged in his pulmonary artery and killed him. Otherwise he was a healthy and fit 39-year-old-man. Army pathologists found a gene called heterozygous Leiden Factor V in Bloom's blood, making him up to six times more susceptible than most of us to developing "deep vein thromboses" merely from sitting in a cramped position for long periods of time as he had done in Iraq.[34] Had Bloom been "homozygous," meaning that he had two copies of the abnormal gene instead of one normal and one abnormal, the Army autopsy report says he would have been fifty to a hundred times more susceptible to developing a DVT. An estimated five percent of all Caucasians carry the Factor V gene, but with or without this gene, it is possible to develop a clot that can kill you. The question is whether one can responsibly ask if something besides sitting around in the Bloommobile or the cramped interior of the M88 for long stretches killed David Bloom.

There are several reasons to raise this question. First, scientists at the University of Michigan and Harvard Medical Schools have recently published research showing that immune cells and inflammatory molecules accelerate the formation of clots.[35] Among rheumatologists, it is well known that autoimmune inflammatory processes can induce vascular disease and clotting. According to their medical records, both Hodge and the Pensacola marine suffered pulmonary damage due to vascular inflammation. Rachael Lacy's sera showed signs of "acute and chronic inflammation" following anthrax vaccination. The package insert for BioThrax contains a long list of autoimmune diseases reported by patients following anthrax injections—diseases like "inflammatory arthritis," "polyarteritis nodosa," and "myocarditis." All of these involve self-injury due to inflammation.

Out on the battlefield, David Bloom received an injection from the same aliquot of anthrax vaccine from which Craig White's inoculation was drawn. Following immunization with this vaccine lot—a lot originally designated for use by soldiers, not necessarily by embedded journalists—White developed anti-squalene antibodies and pneumonia. Although White has not suffered any further injury as a result of his anthrax vaccination, Jason Nietupski of Sunnyvale, California, another patient in the class action lawsuit filed by Alan Milstein, also suffered deep vein thromboses after being injected with anthrax vaccine from a lot that Tulane has identified as inducing anti-squalene antibodies. Unfortunately, this was not the worst of it for Nietupski. He also suffered liver damage and Stevens-Johnson Syndrome—an autoimmune affliction that results in the blistering and peeling of skin as though the patient had been scalded. According to the *Merck Manual*, the skin on Stevens-Johnson sufferers can peel off in large sheets with only gentle pulling or touching—think Scott Siefken.[36]

In 2003, the year Bloom developed deep vein thromboses following anthrax immunization, the same thing happened to Pfc. Terrell Fraser, the son of NBC News cameraman "Wolfy" Fraser. Terrell received two shots of anthrax vaccine—lots FAV074 and FAV075—at Fort Riley, Kansas, in July and August 2003. Within two months he developed severe pain in his right leg. "It felt like I had pulled muscle," says Fraser. "It got worse every day. I would soak it, massage it; it wouldn't go away. It got to the point where I couldn't walk. It was so bad I had to hop on one foot." Fraser finally had to admit that this was no ordinary muscle pull and visited a doctor, who discovered a blood clot behind Fraser's right knee. Although blood thinners eliminated the clot, he continued to suffer chronic pain in his leg, as well as chronic fatigue and memory problems. "My memory is not nearly as quick as it used to be," says

Fraser. Neither is his jump shot. Terrell Fraser was a point guard for Jackson State University—a man who could launch himself towards the basket with the ball cocked behind his head with both hands and bring it forward on his downward trajectory for a monster jam. Today, Terrell Fraser walks with a cane. "Hang time" is out of the question for him. Forget his game above the rim; Fraser doesn't play basketball at all anymore. In September 2004, Fraser says, doctors at Walter Reed Army Medical Center confirmed a second clot in his right leg, this time in his calf.

Finally, two Air Force Reserve pilots from Dover Air Force Base suffered strokes following anthrax immunization. One of them was landing a Fokker-100 passenger plane in January 2002 with around eighty passengers and crew at Chicago's O'Hare International Airport when he suffered an "embolic stroke"—a stroke from a blood clot in his brain. Descending to 13,000 feet and coming up fast on the runway, this pilot felt the fingers on one of his hands go numb. As copilot, he was talking to the O'Hare tower when he started to slur his words like he had just come out of a dentist's office with a mouth full of novocaine. The plane landed safely, but upon examination by doctors in Chicago, this pilot tested positive for antinuclear antibodies, which are antibodies that attack the nuclei of cells; these antibodies occur with a number of different autoimmune diseases. Military doctors, however, attributed this pilot's clot formation and subsequent stroke to a congenital heart defect. They disregarded his positive lab results for antinuclear antibodies as well as the fact that he had been injected four times with anthrax vaccine lots proven by the FDA to contain squalene (three shots from FAV030 and one shot from FAV047).[37] In 2004, a second Dover pilot suffered a stroke—this time a blood clot in the brain—following anthrax immunization. According to Lt. Col. Jay Lacklen, this young pilot first had a transient ischemic attack (TIA), which is a neurological event that can be a prelude to a full blown stroke.[38] The symptoms are sudden numbness and weakness that last for anywhere from two minutes to half an hour. Instead of admitting this man to a hospital, a doctor at Dover suggested that he take another anthrax shot, after which the pilot suffered a brain stem stroke that put him in a coma. He emerged from this coma paralyzed. This pilot received immunization from one of the lots newly suspected to contain squalene, as based on Tulane's antibody data.

Whether or not David Bloom received a vaccination containing squalene—and the antibodies in his cameraman indicate that he did—the BioPort package insert contains a long list of "adverse events" reported by recipients of anthrax vaccine, which include diseases known for acute inflammation. This connection between anthrax immunization and inflammatory disease has been reported by many patients receiving injections from vaccine lots proven to contain squalene. As an NBC News anchorman and correspondent who spent long hours jetting to remote locations to cover stories, Bloom had no previous history of DVT, despite his genetic predisposition. If recent reports linking smallpox vaccine to inflammation of heart muscle and the sac surrounding the heart are true, then David Bloom who was also immunized against smallpox, got a double whammy.[39] Anthrax vaccination, with its reported allergic and autoimmune sequelae, and now the possible induction of inflammatory disease from smallpox vaccine, as well, would have exposed Bloom to a heightened risk of blood clotting due to inflammation—the very thing that killed him.

Hidden in Plain Sight

On May 11, 1999, Lieutenant General Charles H. Roadman told the personnel at Dover Air Force Base that squalene was a red herring: "It is not, has never been, will not be in the immunization for anthrax."

On March 15, 2002, I downloaded the Pentagon's Facts on Squalene, written in question and answer form, from the website of the Secretary of Defense.[40] This is what the SECDEF's staff said:

3. Does the anthrax vaccine contain squalene?

Yes.

The Secretary of Defense, in short, did not agree with Lt. General Roadman. The two of them did agree that squalene was safe to inject. But that would put them both at odds with Aldrich Chemical Company—one of the chemical companies that sells squalene—which has this to say about the oil in its Material Safety Data Sheet:

————————TOXICOLOGICAL INFORMATION————————

May be harmful by inhalation, ingestion, or skin absorption.

Vapor or mist is irritating to the eyes, mucous membranes and upper respiratory tract.

Causes skin irritation.

To the best of our knowledge, the chemical, physical and toxicological properties have not been thoroughly investigated.[41]

The folks at Aldrich would not recommend inhaling squalene, let alone injecting it. Dr. Johnny Lorentzen, an immunologist on the faculty of the celebrated Karolinska Institute in Stockholm proved in 1999 that otherwise benign molecules like squalene can stimulate a self-destructive immune response even though they occur in the body. And what does Lorentzen say about injecting squalene into your veins? "I would not do it to myself," he says.

There are now data in more than two dozen peer-reviewed scientific papers—from ten different laboratories in the United States, Europe, Asia and Australia—documenting that squalene-based adjuvants can induce autoimmune diseases in animals. Scientists have observed this phenomenon in mice, rats, guinea pigs and rabbits. The Karolinska Institute has demonstrated that squalene alone can induce the animal version of rheumatoid arthritis. The Polish Academy of Sciences has shown that in animals, squalene alone can produce catastrophic injury to the nervous system and the brain. The University of Florida Medical School has proven that squalene alone can induce the production of antibodies specifically associated with systemic lupus erythematosus. What these labs have in common, besides evidence that squalene can cause crippling and incurable disease in animals, is this: none of them are selling anything. More to the point, none are selling squalene additives for vaccines.

These laboratories do not all agree, however, on how squalene causes injury. Scientists at the Karolinska Institute argue that it activates a self-destructive immune response to everything but itself. "When injecting these molecules, you create a chaos in the immune system," says Lorentzen. "You have an extremely powerful response, but you can ... I mean the end result is, of course, the arthritis that looks just like rheumatoid arthritis in humans."

Since 1999, the Karolinska researchers have published nearly half a dozen papers on squalene's destructive qualities, but they have remained aloof from the conflict over the anti-squalene antibodies in the United

States. Some at the Karolinska, like Dr. Lars Klareskog, have argued that squalene's ability to induce autoimmune disease in rats specifically bred to be susceptible to these diseases does not necessarily mean it will cause disease in humans. That view is challenged by the fact that scientists at the University of Florida Medical School have found that squalene can induce lupus-associated antibodies in mice that have no particular proclivity to developing autoimmune disease.

What is remarkable is the close match between the squalene-induced diseases in animals and those observed in humans injected with this oil: rheumatoid arthritis, multiple sclerosis and systemic lupus erythematosus. More autoimmune diseases have been associated with squalene injection in humans, but rheumatoid arthritis, MS and lupus are the three illnesses that this oil has been proven to cause in multiple species.

The scientific and arguably moral adversaries in this conflict—Tulane University Medical School and the Army's Walter Reed Army Institute of Research—have both proven that the immune system responds specifically to the squalene molecule. Squalene's pathway through the body has been tracked with a radioactive tracer in animals by none other than Chiron—the maker of the only squalene-based adjuvant licensed for human use anywhere in the world. What this all shows is that the immune system does in fact see squalene—an oil molecule native to the body—as an enemy to be attacked and eliminated. The key is "route of administration." As any immunologist will tell you, the way an antigen encounters the immune system makes all the difference. Studies in both animals and man show that injecting squalene will galvanize the immune system into attacking it, which can produce a self-destructive cross reaction against the same molecule in the places where it occurs naturally in the body—and where it is critical to the health of the nervous system.

Of da Vinci and Dollar Signs

There is one question I have been asked repeatedly over the years. If squalene is so manifestly bad to inject, why would anyone with two brain cells continue doing it? I have three answers. First, intelligence has nothing to do with it. Intelligent people, even geniuses, have been known to deny the obvious.

Boston University's noted philosopher of medicine, Alfred I. Tauber, likes to tell his students a story about Leonardo da Vinci and the way he drew the brain.[42] Da Vinci is well known for many things, not the least of which is his exquisite drawings of the human body, which were part science and part fine art. When Pope Sixtus IV granted permission in 1482 to take the bodies of legally executed criminals and dissect them, Leonardo began a series of studies that became celebrated for their unromantic depiction of the human body—sinew, bone and testicles all anatomically correct in an inglorious if not grisly way. Well, almost correct. Prejudice distorted the accuracy of some of his drawings. From the time of Aristotle, physicians and scientists understood the brain to be a tripartite structure performing sensory, cognitive and memory functions. So although Leonardo had pried open any number of skulls by 1489, and therefore should have seen the brain's two hemispheres, he nevertheless drew the brain as three connected bubble-like structures all in a line. He drew what he thought he should be seeing, not what was actually there. Another twenty years would pass before Leonardo finally took a wax cast of a human brain, something finally clicked, and he began to see—and draw—hemispheres.

Something similar has been happening with squalene and adjuvants. Scientists are supposed to be clear-eyed realists who see only what is there. As Richard Feynman put it, "Nature cannot be fooled." In truth, however, scientists are as vulnerable to bias as the next person. Where squalene is concerned, American scientists have become so deeply invested in the idea that this oil is safe to inject they have been unable to concede there is evidence to the contrary. For years, it was almost an article of faith in immunology that only big, complex molecules like proteins could elicit a response from the immune system; lipid molecules were too small. Yet even today, long after antiphospholipid antibodies became a routine diagnostic test for autoimmune diseases like lupus, there are scientists (outside of immunology) who are still unaware that lipid molecules, as small as they are, can interact with the immune system. The same is true for adjuvants. The idea that there were substances that could activate an immune response to everything but themselves was a concept formulated before the advent of molecular biology in the 1950s. There is now abundant evidence that the immune system is perfectly capable of making antibodies to just about anything anyone chooses to inject, however wisely or unwisely. After nearly thirty years of experimentation, there is now a significant body of data showing that squalene is disastrously unsafe as an immunization. If there is any such thing as an "oil adjuvant," an oil that stimulates the immune system to react to everything but itself, squalene clearly isn't it. But tellingly, most evidence has been published abroad.

The second answer is that scientists in the United States are now literally invested in squalene. The Army scientists who developed the second generation anthrax vaccine have reputations to protect, if not licensing fees to reap for the Army. The company awarded the license to manufacture the new anthrax vaccine, VaxGen, will pay USAMRIID an "execution fee, patent maintenance fees, anniversary fees, milestones and royalties" for the worldwide rights to develop and commercialize the new recombinant vaccine for anthrax.[43]

The National Institutes of Health has been supporting both animal and human research with squalene since the 1980s. Squalene has become perhaps the most ubiquitous oil adjuvant on the planet, which is something that should concern everyone. Many of the cutting edge vaccines currently in development by the NIH and its corporate partners contain squalene in one formulation of those vaccines or another. There is squalene in the prototype recombinant vaccines for HIV, malaria, herpes, influenza, cytomegalovirus and human papillomavirus. Some of these prototypes like HIV, malaria and influenza are intended for mass immunization around the globe.

Until scientists find an alternative to squalene adjuvants, it is hard to see how clinical investigators can develop viable recombinant DNA vaccines, which are uniformly weak. Abandoning squalene would be tantamount to flushing one of the most fashionable scientific ideas of the last three decades down the toilet, along with billions of research dollars. Such an investment makes it easier to relax safety standards and use immunologically active substances like oil adjuvants instead of saline as placebos, or to conveniently ignore the fact that autoimmune phenomena known to occur as a result of HIV infection could mask any causal link between the adjuvant and autoimmune disease when testing prototype HIV vaccines on infected patients.[44] What might not have appeared in an HIV-positive population could become painfully obvious in populations relatively free of HIV infections—like U.S. and British military personnel.

A third factor may have played a part in the military's willingness to assume a higher risk in using squalene: the risk/benefit calculation in public health. General Roadman actually talked about this at his May 1999 briefing at

Dover. "If there's a threat," said Roadman, "for me as Surgeon General, I would be guilty of malpractice, in my mind, not deploying [anthrax vaccine] because it is our number concern of bacteriological warfare." Roadman was talking about the old vaccine, of course. But the very same argument could be made for using the new vaccine. Army doctors and scientists have been arguing since the first Gulf War that the new vaccine is not only safe, it is supposedly better. When relying on a risk/benefit calculation to decide whether to use of a new vaccine without informed consent, the question is who benefits? How much are the decision-makers thinking about the safety of U.S. troops as opposed to safeguarding their own careers? "Let me tell yah," Roadman told Dover's pilots and aircrew, "that the recriminations if we are hit by it, and have not given the immunization ... will never end."

Through the Looking Glass

Because the information in this book opens doors that have rarely been opened before, it will be all the more shocking and polarizing for some people. Some will be tempted to equate all such experimentation with "Nazi medicine." That was, in fact, what the Nazi doctors tried to do at the Nuremberg Tribunal when they compared their malaria experiments on prisoners at the Dachau concentration camp with the research carried out by Dr. Alf S. Alving at Stateville Penitentiary in Illinois.[45] I would urge readers to resist that temptation. First, there is a clear difference between Dachau and Stateville. The prisoners at Stateville volunteered for those experiments, and they did so knowing that their sacrifice would help the war effort in the Pacific where malaria felled as many marines as bullets did. If birth of our Republic rested, in part, on General Washington's decision to use a controversial (there were no licenses in the 18th century) procedure, variolation, to keep the Continental Army from falling apart because of rampant smallpox infections, then it is difficult to dismiss the argument that there may be a time and place in which military doctors will have no other choice than to use experimental medicines to keep troops alive.

This would be an interesting question to put to Col. Carl Alving, were he willing to speak to me. Some might assume that in declining to give me an interview for this book, Alving has something to hide. On the contrary, he has been quite outspoken on this subject. He has published three papers about antisqualene antibodies. He wrote an *amicus curiae* brief on them for the 1999 court martial of a marine refusing to take anthrax vaccine, and he made his views about the antibodies plain at the Dover briefing. The Air Force was so pleased by what he had to say that it even circulated a videotape of Alving's Dover comments, along with those made by General Roadman, to bases across the country. There are copies of the tape everywhere; I have one myself. It could be that Alving's too busy to talk to me or is on vacation. Maybe he thinks, like his acquaintance, Dr. Spanggord of SRI, that I have such difficulty understanding the technicalities of this subject that talking to me would be a waste of time. I don't know.

I *do* know there are some things that still warrant clarification—like why Alving told GAO investigators that he "doubted that a vaccine with squalene would produce a meaningful antibody response," then to the same investigators on the very same day (April 6, 1998), he said if he were asked to develop and anthrax vaccine on a crash basis for Desert Shield that he "would have recommended MF59 for anthrax." If wouldn't work that well, why recommend it? Later, Alving admitted to the GAO that he did, in fact, work on a "new, more potent anthrax vaccine" for Desert Shield. Did he use the squalene-based MF59 as he would have recommended? In light of Dr. Anna Johnson-Winegar's admission to the GAO that there were members of Project Badger willing "to jump out and use everything," this line of inquiry seems worthy of follow-up. Congressman Metcalf certainly thought so—before he left office in the fall of 2000, he called for the cessation of mandatory anthrax vaccination in the military until the squalene issue got resolved.[46] It is not yet resolved.

Were he willing to talk, there is another subject I would like to discuss with Col. Alving. In his latest paper on antibodies to squalene, published in March 2004, he says he has now found "naturally occurring antibodies to squalene in humans and mice."[47] In his first two papers, which concerned animals only, he did not.[48] What changed? He says he's now found antibodies to squalene in humans too: There are at least two potential issues with that finding.

The first is Alving's patient groups. One group of volunteers he tested were retired employees of USAMRIID who were given "numerous doses" of anthrax vaccine through USAMRIID's "special immunization program."[49] Alving does not specify the vaccine lot numbers these retirees received when they were immunized against anthrax, and whether, through USAMRIID's special immunization program, any of the volunteers had been inoculated with the second generation anthrax vaccine containing squalene.

The second issue is the serum dilution that Alving used in this study. In order to ensure that an antibody being detected is specific for an antigen, in this case squalene, the serum dilution must be very high. Dilutions around 1:400 are fairly typical; this is what Tulane uses to detect antibodies to squalene in military personnel. What Alving and his colleagues at WRAIR used is exceptionally low—1:25 and 1:50. "That's considered non-specific," says Pam Asa. In other words, at that low dilution a lot of things will stick to the cellulose strip or the plastic tray—whatever you happen to be using in your assay—besides the antibody you're looking for. When Col. Alving first reported finding antibodies to squalene's molecular relative, cholesterol, he used a significantly higher dilution: 1:100.[50] In one study he did, he detected antibodies to cholesterol at a phenomenally high dilution of 1:31,250.[51] Now that is a specific antibody. "Serum is pretty thick, so 1:25, you've still got a pretty gummy dilution there," says Bob Garry. "There's lots of sticky things in blood, and that's why you get false positives with a low dilution." "A 1:25 or 1:50 dilution is not used in commercial assays, according to Garry, who helped develop the original antibody assay for HIV. "I don't know any commercial assay that is run at anything less than 1:100. Even that's considered pretty non-specific."

———

I have no whistleblower saying the experiments on military personnel described in this book took place. I have no copy of a memo ordering them to commence. There is hidden in plain sight, however, clinical and forensic scientific evidence that they were done. The two-fold serial dilution of squalene, Tulane's antibodies, the autoimmune diseases in troops that are known sequelae to injection with oil adjuvants, and the dramatic rise in adverse reactions to the vaccine in the 1990s—specifically allergic and autoimmune reactions—all point to an experiment with an oil adjuvant that the Army has been using in its new anthrax vaccine from 1987 to the present day.

For those who still resist the voluminous—I would say overwhelming—amount of data supporting these allegations, I have a joke. Lawyers tell this story to illustrate the danger of asking one question too many, but it also demonstrates the power of circumstantial evidence. A defense attorney is cross-examining a witness:

"So, Mr. Jones, you didn't actually *see* the defendant bite the victim's ear off in that fight?"

"No, sir."

"Then how do you know he did?"

"Because I saw him spit it out."

———

This book is about that ear.

———

If an anthrax vaccine is indeed vital to our nation's defenses, then it is clear from nearly fifty years of research that a new vaccine is necessary, but not if it's Vaccine A. Vaccine A—its original prototypes and all its descendants through rPA102—is the same design that Dr. Ralph Lincoln and Fort Detrick's best talents tried to reject as flawed and inadequate in the 1960s.[52] This is what they wrote:

> "...there is no experimental basis for selection or use of a single antigen for immunizing man, domestic, or experimental animals. Indeed all evidence is to the contrary to this practice for the "protective antigen" of Gladstone as well as later workers who use serum in the production or processing of the antigen was probably composed of all components of toxin."

Experiments run by U.S. and British military scientists over the past forty years have reached the same conclusions over and over again: a vaccine comprised of a single protein secreted by the anthrax germ, protective antigen, is at best inadequate. Here's what NIH scientists wrote in 2002: "Evidence that other antigens can contribute to immunity suggests that the most effective vaccines would contain multiple antigens."[53]

The act of refining protective antigen to an unprecedented purity succeeded in doing two things: it made a vaccine so weak that scientists had to resort to forbidden fruit—the oil adjuvants that have proven so harmful in the past century that some countries now consider their use in animals cruel and inhumane. It also created a vaccine that still will leave U.S. and British troops vulnerable to infection from super virulent strains.

If the new license holder for the second generation vaccine, VaxGen, is only adding alum to the new vaccine, then all America will have to show for nearly a quarter century's research is the same vaccine, made with the latest equipment and techniques, but based on the same design Fort Detrick's Ralph Lincoln et al. wanted to dump. This is why I now look with a jaundiced eye at the Army's claim that a protective antigen vaccine, a vaccine for which the FDA once required six shots to generate a reasonable level of protectiveness, will now work with three shots or less. If it is indeed purer, then it will have fewer anthrax epitopes to which the immune system will respond. By rights, it should be even weaker than the old vaccine. Fewer epitopes means less protection.

That is not just my assessment. A team of Russian scientists attending the International Workshop on Anthrax in 1995 announced that they had genetically engineered an anthrax strain that could overcome the Russian STI vaccine, which in test after test throughout the 1980s had generated much better protection than either U.S. or British protective antigen vaccines. The implication of this new Russian strain was not lost on Dr. Ken Alibek, the Soviet biopweaponeer who defected to the United States in the early 1990s. Alibek knew the scientists who engineered this new strain and had talked to them about it. "You know," he says, "I hate to say this, but I need to be truthful. I talked to some of these scientists. They say there was no question that this strain will defeat the American vaccine."[54] That is why the new vaccine was needed in the first place—to counter the threat from Russian anthrax, and any anthrax that the Russians might have helped the Iraqis create. "The United States had a perfect vaccine," says Alibek. "It's veterinary, but it's a perfect vaccine to vaccinate humans, offering much higher protection—say one hundred percent." On this point, Alibek is in accord with Joe Jemski. "If I thought we were really in danger of an attack with anthrax, I'd take one shot of the old protective antigen vaccine, and then follow it up with a single shot of the Sterne whole spore vaccine," he says.[55] "All the animal studies I did showed the protective antigen vaccine just didn't live up to its name—it didn't protect, at least not enough." All the Army has to show for twenty-five years of research, some of it with tragic consequences, is a high-tech retread.

In reviewing half a century of military medical research involving U.S. troops, the Senate Committee on Veterans' Affairs made this recommendation in December 1994:

The Feres Doctrine Should Not Be Applied For Military Personnel Who Are Harmed By Inappropriate Human Experimentation When Informed Consent Has Not Been Given.[56]

The Feres Doctrine is the rule that prohibits members of the Armed Forces from suing the military for any harm they suffer from negligence during their service. To safeguard these men and women, Congress should invoke this recommendation so that we may prevent a reprise of what I have documented in this book. In the past four years it has only become easier to experiment on U.S. military personnel. Following an executive order that President Bill Clinton signed in September 1999, all the Secretary of Defense need do now is make a persuasive case to the President that it is necessary to give troops experimental medicines without informed consent for their own good.[57] But the order lays out no criteria for making such a decision. And the FDA, the regulatory agency that is supposed to monitor these activities, has been cut out of the loop. Also cut out of the loop by these decisions are U.S. military personnel. They are not being given a say about what is put into their bodies. The question is whether they are being denied informed consent because it is logistically infeasible for military doctors to secure that consent, or because they already know what the answer is going to be. As Dr. Henry Beecher wrote in his landmark 1966 paper, *Ethics and Clinical Research*, "the usual patient will never agree to jeopardize seriously his health or his life for the sake of 'science.'"[58]

General Washington did indeed order the use of the 18th century equivalent of an investigational new drug, but there are two differences between then and now. The Continental Army troops getting variolated against smallpox knew what was happening to them. Someone couldn't slice open a soldier's arms and insert material from an active smallpox sore without that soldier knowing about it. One other thing. No one made money from it. No company planned to market variolation in the thirteen colonies if its safety were proven by giving it to Continental troops.

One hundred and twenty-three years after Louis Pasteur grandly demonstrated the effectiveness of a live spore anthrax vaccine at Pouilly-le-Fort, scientists at the Pasteur Institute in Paris—publishing research consistent with the data from Fort Detrick in the 1960s, Fort Detrick and Porton Down in the 1980s, and Russia's State Research Institute of Applied Microbiology at Obolensk in the 1990s—added killed anthrax spores to protective antigen, creating a vaccine that produced 100 percent immunity in guinea pigs.[59]

Fifty years after the Department of Defense first began conducting experiments on U.S. military personnel with oil adjuvants, and seventeen years after it began specific research with squalene in anthrax vaccine, there is still no oil adjuvant considered safe enough to license for human use in the United States or Britain.

Five years after my allegation in "Vanity Scare" that military personnel were developing antibodies to squalene and autoimmune disease following immunization with specific lots of anthrax vaccine, the Army insisted there was no squalene in the vaccine. When the FDA later found squalene in anthrax vaccine, the Army and the FDA then stated, in this order, that: (1) squalene in anthrax vaccine could come from vaccine antigens grown in eggs (remember, *Bacillus anthracis* is grown in a broth containing no eggs), (2) squalene could be a contaminant from the oil on someone's fingers (which would constitute a GMP violation), (3) squalene could be made by the organism itself. In five years, neither the Army nor the FDA has cited any peer reviewed data to support any of these assertions.

One year after BioPort released a new package insert disclosing that recipients of anthrax vaccine have developed autoimmune diseases like lupus and multiple sclerosis, the French—who in 1991 did not immunize their troops in the Persian Gulf against anthrax, or report any cases of Gulf War Syndrome afterwards—now suspect that Gulf War illness may be "a vaccine adjuvant-related syndrome," characterized by diffuse muscle pain and chronic fatigue, progressing in about a third of patients to full-blown autoimmune disease "such as multiple sclerosis." [60]

Although a squalene-containing vaccine, Chiron's influenza vaccine FLUAD, has now been licensed for use in the European Common Market, researchers at the University of Florida Medical School in 2004 demonstrated that some, but not all, hydrocarbon oils have the ability to induce "lupus autoantibodies" in mice. Among the oils that induce lupus autoantibodies is squalene, prompting these researchers to conclude that "caution should be exercised in the use of oil adjuvants in human and veterinary vaccines."[61]

Also in 2004, the same University of Florida scientists published new data showing that just one shot of squalene will induce in mice a "highly restricted subset of autoantibodies usually only associated with lupus. [62] They suggested that it would be "ideal" to conduct a "long-term observation of a large number of subjects like the one performed in army recruits who received influenza vaccine containing IFA."[63] The recruits to whom the Florida researchers refer are the U.S. Army soldiers at Fort Dix who were injected with Freund's Incomplete Adjuvant—light mineral oil and water—in Dr. Jonas Salk's 1951–53 experiment to develop a new and improved influenza vaccine.[64] Anyone looking for a large number of subjects injected with squalene for a long-term study now has a choice—more than five hundred thousand patients have been injected with FLUAD in Italy; and tens of thousands of U.S. and British military personnel, possibly hundreds of thousands, have now been injected with anthrax vaccine containing, by accident or by design, trace quantities of this oil.

It is conceivable that squalene in influenza vaccine may be safe in humans, but in light of recent studies in animals from the Karolinska Institute and the University of Florida, the question is whether it has been proven. As the University of Florida group points out, "the effects of vaccine components" can differ according to the dosage and how the components are injected—subcutaneously or intramuscularly.[65] They write that if autoimmune diseases have not been previously observed in some animal experiments with squalene or in Italian patients injected with FLUAD, it may be because "chemicals have long-term effects over many years, which may be difficult to evaluate in mice over two years." If two years are not enough to ensure that squalene is safe in mice, then it is reasonable to expect that seven days would not be enough in humans. Yet documentation of serious adverse reactions to FLUAD in Italy's biggest experiment with it—a nationwide Phase IV clinical trial—was limited to only those problems requiring a doctor's visit within seven days of immunization.[66] When the Army tested a flu vaccine with oil adjuvant on troops at Fort Dix, it conducted follow-up studies looking for a statistical spike in tumors and autoimmune disease for twenty-one years after that trial began. Despite subsequent epidemiological studies reporting that the oil adjuvant vaccine appeared to have been well tolerated, the FDA never licensed it. Responses to squalene in FLUAD may also be less severe due to differences in the vaccine antigen. In other words, squalene may be dangerous when added to anthrax protective antigen protein or herpes simplex virus, but safer when formulated with influenza virus. It is impossible to know for sure without more studies being done to establish the facts.

The Unknown

There is a lot more that scientists need to learn about the effects of injecting squalene. For instance, they do not yet know which "animal model" for squalene-induced autoimmune disease correlates most closely with the oil's effects in humans. They do not know the minimum amount of squalene required to stimulate an immune response. They do not know what percentage of people injected with squalene will develop autoimmunity. They do not know if there is a specific gene in humans that will predispose some individuals to an autoimmune reaction to squalene. They do not know if administering squalene subcutaneously as opposed to intramuscularly will alter its effects. If injecting squalene induces lupus autoantibodies in humans as it does in mice, scientists do not yet know how long after squalene vaccination that lupus might occur.

To discover these facts, University of Florida researchers suggest that "long-term observation of a large number of subjects" is needed.[67] There are now large numbers of U.S. military personnel who have been injected with anthrax vaccine containing squalene. Should they volunteer to be evaluated because of their *involuntary* immunization with trace amounts of this oil, the study might be done along the research guidelines for "toxicology, epidemiology and epistemology" proposed by The Environmental Disease Study Group of the American College of Rheumatology (ACR). The ACR proposes a four-stage process:[68]

STAGE 1—Proposing the association (as Garry and Asa have done at Tulane University Medical School);

STAGE 2—Testing the association (a process already begun by Tulane);

STAGE 3—Defining the disorder (also a process begun by Tulane);

STAGE 4—Refining the disorder.[69]

To shield such a study from bias, Tulane's Robert Garry and Russ Wilson of Autoimmune Technologies propose the creation of a broad, population-based epidemiological study like the one set up to study Vietnam veterans exposed to Agent Orange. During Operation Ranch Hand, which ran between 1962 and 1971, the United States Air Force sprayed an estimated eighteen million gallons of the organophosphate herbicide dioxin, aka Agent Orange, over large tracts of jungle in South Vietnam to defoliate it and deny cover to infiltrating enemy soldiers.[70] The Ranch Hand study was "insulated from bias as best as possible as a line item in the U.S. budget," says Wilson. "It was set up by President Carter because of the controversy over whether the military was obfuscating on the Agent Orange issue. To prevent bias with Gulf War Syndrome and squalene antibodies," says Wilson, "something similar should be set up." Wilson acknowledges that his company has licensed the anti-squalene antibody assay from Tulane for commercial use. "We all have bias," says Wilson, "but we need to reduce those as much as possible."

The Known

Here is what we know about injecting squalene. Beginning with UCLA Medical School's pioneering research with a squalene adjuvant in the early 1970s, laboratories around the world have demonstrated this oil's ability to induce autoimmune disease with severe neurological damage. Since NIH began administering squalene to patients in clinical trials in 1980s, ten university and government laboratories around the world have found that adjuvants containing squalene or squalene alone induced autoimmunity in four different species of animals. By injecting squalene, scientists have induced the animal version or "model" of at least four autoimmune diseases: rheumatoid arthritis, multiple sclerosis, autoimmune thyroiditis and systemic lupus erythematosus. All of these diseases have occurred in military personnel following injection with anthrax vaccine proven by the FDA to contain squalene. NIH-funded clinical trials have reported a possible association between immunization with squalene-adjuvanted vaccines and adverse reactions like chronic fatigue, rashes, and joint and muscle pain, which are all associated with autoimmunity. Tulane University Medical School has reported a *specific* association in humans between immunization with anthrax vaccine containing squalene and anti-squalene antibodies (a de facto autoimmune response), as well as autoimmune diseases like lupus, multiple sclerosis, ALS and rheumatoid arthritis.

Although scientists at the Karolinska Institute in Stockholm, Sweden, and the University of Florida Medical School attribute squalene's ability to induce autoimmune disease to "non-specific stimulation"—or as the Karolinska's Johnny Lorentzen puts it, "immunological chaos"—there is now clinical evidence from at least three laboratories that both the animal and human immune systems mount a highly specific immune response to this oil. Tulane has documented antibody production—one of the most highly specific biological responses known—in humans who have been injected with squalene. The Army's Carl Alving has also shown antibody production in animals injected with squalene. Chiron Corporation has described the specific interaction between injected squalene and various cells of the immune system. As demonstrated by Chiron's researchers in mice, upon injection with the corporation's squalene-based MF59 adjuvant, immune cells called macrophages ingested molecules of squalene and then transported them to the lymph nodes.[71] Once in the lymph nodes, macrophages "presented" squalene molecules, like runners passing the baton in a relay race, to another type of immune cell called dendritic cells for further processing as antigens.[72] This means squalene is not only an immunostimulant or "adjuvant," it is also, in immunological parlance, an "immunogen"—a substance capable of highly specific interactions with the immune system and its products. Because the immune system responds to squalene, injecting it can result in a dangerous cross-reaction to naturally occurring molecules of squalene found in many parts of the body, but especially in the nervous system. There appears to be a "tropism,"—an affinity or attraction—between oil molecules and neurological tissue. So it is not surprising that severe neurological damage has been observed in animals injected with squalene.

Ingested squalene is transported though the bloodstream in lipid vesicles that the body sees as a normal constituent. Scientists in Finland have documented in mice how ingested squalene molecules are absorbed through the gut and then "packaged" inside chylomicrons—a lipid membrane not unlike liposomes—and carried to different tissues in the body where they serve as building blocks for molecules like cholesterol.[73] This phenomenon is one reason some scientists thought the immune system would ignore injected squalene. The problem with this assumption, as any immunologist will tell you, is that an age-old issue, route of administration, can come into play. The means by which a molecule encounters the body will affect whether or not the immune system will respond to that molecule. So just because squalene is edible doesn't mean it's safe to inject. "The same is true of a peanut butter and jelly sandwich," says Pam Asa. "I'd eat one, but wouldn't inject one." In animals, squalene appears to be unsafe wherever it is injected. As Asa points out, "squalene has induced autoimmunity when injected subcutaneously, sub-dermally and intramuscularly at various points in the body, including the scalp, the tail, the hind limbs, the forelimbs, and in footpads."

The Wager

The FDA and the Army have disclosed the presence of squalene in some lots of anthrax vaccine administered to U.S. military personnel in the late 1990s. In 2003, a British laboratory found squalene in anthrax vaccine believed to be en route to Iraq for administration to British troops during Operation Iraqi Freedom. Based on Department of Defense and FDA data on people injected with anthrax vaccine in the 1990s (the overwhelming majority being military personnel), the licensed manufacturer of anthrax vaccine, BioPort, reports that recipients of its vaccine have developed rheumatoid arthritis, lupus and multiple sclerosis following immunization. This does not mean there is a proven cause-and-effect association between anthrax immunization and these diseases. There is not. But there is, in animals, a proven cause-and-effect association between squalene immunization and these diseases. The animal versions of rheumatoid arthritis and multiple sclerosis, and autoantibodies specifically associated with lupus, all have occurred in animals injected with squalene.

Somewhere between half a million and a million people have been injected with FLUAD—an influenza vaccine containing the squalene-based adjuvant MF59—in Italy, Spain and Germany. The papers published by Chiron scientists working in conjunction with university researchers in Italy make no mention of the animal studies documenting the occurrence of autoimmune diseases in animals injected with the oil. Investigators conducting clinical trials with FLUAD also have *not* recorded the occurrence of autoimmunity in elderly Italian patients receiving one shot (per year) of FLUAD. However, Italian clinical investigators also do not report whether they analyzed the sera from these patients for autoimmune responses—like antinuclear antibodies, anti-double stranded DNA antibodies, and complement levels. Italian researchers did record more unpleasant reactions at the injection site—i.e., soreness, redness and swelling—experienced by patients immunized with FLUAD than with those who received another of Chiron's influenza vaccines, Agrippal S1, which does not contain MF59.[74] Systemic reactions like chills, malaise, muscle pain and headaches were more commonly reported in patients after their first immunization with FLUAD than after their first shot of Agrippal S1.[75] These complaints could have any number of different causes, including one too many glasses of vino. Perhaps only coincidentally, however, patients suffering from the Air Force case definition of Gulf War Syndrome as well as fully diagnosed autoimmune diseases, complain of chills, malaise, muscle pain and headaches.

Based on the dramatic jump in serious adverse reactions observed in military personnel injected with anthrax vaccine after 1990, the GAO called for an "active surveillance program" to monitor adverse events "associated with each anthrax immunization."[76] By "active" surveillance, the GAO meant investigators should take the initiative and monitor inoculated patients, even clinically evaluate them, instead of depending on the "passive" surveillance of the FDA's VAERS system, which relies solely on self-reported data from patients, who, as the GAO has taken pains to point out, often do not know that such a system even exists.[77] GAO investigators report that Defense Department officials rejected this recommendation, citing a statement in a report from the Institute of Medicine saying that the "committee observes no data that indicate the need for the continuation of special monitoring programs for anthrax vaccine have emerged."[78] In rebuttal to DOD officials, GAO investigators point out that the IOM did, in fact, recommend that individuals immunized with anthrax vaccine lots produced after BioPort's 1990 renovations should be monitored for "possible acute or chronic events of immediate or later onset."[79]

Lt. Col. Jay Lacklen, the former chief pilot in the reserve squadron at Dover Air Force Base, who has anti-squalene antibodies and has tested positive for rheumatoid factor—an antibody associated with rheumatoid arthritis—and Col. Felix Grieder, Dover's former commander, are just two retired senior Air Force officers who think they should have been informed about *all the above*—but especially the animal studies on the induction of autoimmune disease in animals injected with squalene, as well as the fact that various prototypes of the Army's second generation anthrax vaccine have contained squalene since 1987. "I see parallels in this tragedy and the [Air Force] Academy sexual assault cover-up and the Abu Ghraib scandal," says Col. Grieder. "Military leaders who fail to identify problems and who do not take action to resolve problems once they become aware of them are irresponsible, or worse. I actually had a senior officer advise me (while I was at the Pentagon to meet with the AF Chief of Staff) to 'not rock the boat, Felix.' Unfortunately, that is the mindset of too many senior officers."

It's worth remembering that the U.S. Army has tested an experimental oil adjuvant in troops before, beginning at Fort Dix in 1951; the Armed Forces Epidemiological Board even recommended in the 1960s that the adjuvant be injected into every man and woman serving in the military—license or no license. During World War II, in response to a perceived biological warfare threat, the Army also injected an experimental vaccine into hundreds of thousands of American troops, landing more than fifty thousand of them in the hospital. The antibodies to squalene, and Fort Detrick's declassified documents and scientific papers, are evidence that the military has done both again with tragic results.

Is the danger of injecting squalene into humans proven beyond all reasonable doubt? No. But humans injected with squalene in the 1990s and in the new century have been developing autoimmune diseases that are identical to the ones proven to occur in animals injected with it. These are facts that doctors and scientists working for the U.S. military medical command have omitted from their public comments on squalene in anthrax vaccine. These facts are also absent from the papers published by Chiron on FLUAD and MF59. Anyone reading this book, having now been informed of these facts, faces a wager should they be presented with the choice of whether to be immunized with a vaccine containing squalene. This is an especially pressing issue in Europe, where one such vaccine is now licensed.

A number of different, as yet unidentified factors may affect who develops autoimmunity as a result of injection with squalene and who does not. Most immunologists would agree that an individual's genetic makeup is at least one such factor. In fact, NIH scientists have demonstrated that animals injected with an adjuvant, in this case Freund's Complete Adjuvant, developed different autoimmune diseases—including insulin-dependent diabetes, thyroiditis, and experimental autoimmune uveitis—depending on the animal's immune response genes.[80] So the question for a person considering taking FLUAD in Europe, or any experimental vaccine with squalene in the United States, is whether to take this risk. Should a patient agree to immunization with squalene knowing these facts, that patient can be said to have given his or her "informed consent."

U.S. and British military personnel injected with squalene in anthrax vaccines, who have not been privy to this information, cannot be said to have given informed consent. If a patient in Europe does not want to take a flu shot that contains squalene, he or she has several choices. Chiron Corporation alone makes three other influenza vaccines that do not contain this oil.[81] Here in the United States, the FDA's list of vaccines licensed for human use includes three squalene-free influenza vaccines made by manufacturers other than Chiron.[82]

For military personnel facing mandatory immunization with anthrax vaccine, there is no such selection or freedom of choice. While the Department of the Defense vehemently denies adding squalene to its licensed anthrax vaccine, DOD does admit there are small amounts of squalene in certain lots. Military doctors and scientists, as well officials with the FDA, say these "trace amounts" could come from the organism itself. As I have documented, there are a number of reasons to challenge this assertion, not least of which is the unanswered question of why, if squalene does in fact come from *Bacillus anthracis*, is it only in some lots of vaccine and not all of them. But even if one accepts the unproven allegation that the squalene comes from the germ, military personnel face a disconcerting wager: will they get immunized with a vaccine lot that for some unexplained reason contains squalene?

Millions of U.S. civilians now face the same wager. President Bush has purchased seventy-five million doses of the Army's new anthrax vaccine to create an emergency stockpile sufficiently large to inoculate twenty-five million people, all of them civilians, in case of a biological attack. These civilians are to be immunized whether the vaccine is licensed or not. Right now it is not. As the second-generation anthrax vaccine is formulated by its appointed developer, VaxGen, it contains alum, not squalene. But if, as Army and FDA scientists maintain, trace quantities of squalene—a proven immunostimulant and inducer of autoimmune disease in animals—come from *Bacillus anthracis* itself, then anyone taking either the old vaccine or the new one is faced with a potentially lethal and debilitating game of Russian roulette. Not with a gun, but with a hypodermic needle.

Acknowledgments

Finishing this book has been the single most difficult task of my professional life and there have been many times when I've thought about quitting. Leveling allegations of this magnitude against two of the most powerful bureaucracies in the world—the U.S. Department of Defense and the Department of Health and Human Services—is not for the fainthearted. But if some of my more secular-minded friends will pardon my lapse into the quasi-theological, I have to say that whenever I have faltered, I have always received help. I didn't find it; it found me. And so I kept going.

Finding the wherewithal to continue would not have been possible without the support of some people braver and smarter than I am, chief among them, Dr. Pamela Asa and Dr. Kevin Asa. Without their help I could not have written this book. It was Pam and Kevin Asa who diagnosed autoimmune diseases in Gulf War veterans as early as 1995. It was Pam Asa who first suspected that many of these diseases were due to vaccination with an oil adjuvant, and along with Dr. Robert F. Garry of Tulane University Medical School, came up with a way to put this hypothesis to the test. Later, Dr. Russell Wilson joined in this work. All of them graciously schooled me over a period of many years in the arcana of immunology and molecular biology. Dr. Garry has been especially gracious in allowing me to spend time in his busy laboratory at Tulane to do research for my book. Coming to terms with the ramifications of their data has not been easy for any of them, yet they stayed the course—without, I might add, any prospect of financial recompense. They have charged no fees for their testing and have received no grants from the government to support their research.

Although I did not receive direct help from the General Accounting Office, I relied heavily on reports the agency published on anti-squalene antibodies and anthrax vaccine. The GAO pursued these matters when no other agency of government would. GAO investigators encountered such resistance to their efforts that they later characterized the Defense Department's conduct as "stonewalling and obfuscation." Yet in the face of such opposition, the GAO still managed to generate critical information in an effort to safeguard the health and well being of U.S. military personnel.

Next to the antibodies, the most important forensic evidence to emerge so far has been the squalene concentrations detected in anthrax vaccine by the FDA. That data not only verified the presence of squalene in the vaccine, it helped establish a "dose-response" relationship between squalene-contaminated lots of anthrax vaccine and autoimmune disease. The FDA's tests were provoked by my 1999 *Vanity Fair* article commissioned by the magazine's editor, Graydon Carter and the Senior Articles Editor Douglas Stumpf. We are in their debt.

For help and guidance in immunology, I am also indebted to Dr. Johnny Lorentzen of the Karolinska Institute, Dr. Dorothy Lewis of Baylor University College of Medicine, Dr. Julius Cruse of the University of Mississippi Medical Center, Dr. Michael Whitehouse of the University of Queensland, Dr. Frances W. J. Beck of Wayne State Medical School, Dr. Douglas R. Shanklin of the University of Tennessee Health Science Center, Drs. Morris Reichlin and Paul W. Kincade of the Oklahoma Medical Research Foundation.

For general help and guidance in microbiology and biological warfare, I would like to thank Dr. Richard O. Spertzel, Dr. Frank B. Engley, Dr. Jack Melling, Dr. Hugh Tresselt, Dr. Martin Hugh-Jones of Louisiana States University, Dr. Peter C.B. Turnbull, Drs. Ken Alibek and Sergei Popov of George Mason University, Dr. Joseph V. Jemski, Dr. Alexis Shelokov, Mr. William C. Patrick III, Orley Bourland, Edgar "Bud" Larson, William P. Walter, the late J.R.E. Smith, Robert "Bud" Zentner, Donald B. Schattenberg, George Hedstrom, Col. David R. Franz D.V.M., Dr. Paul J. Jackson of Los Alamos National Laboratory and Dr. Alan Zelicoff of Sandia National Laboratories.

For various mathematical calculations, I am grateful to immunopathologist Doug Shanklin who is also a member of the American Mathematical Society. Russ Wilson, Kevin Asa and Dr. John Petrovic of Los Alamos National Laboratory also did some of the most important calculations used in this book.

For general help and guidance in pharmacology and chemistry, I would like to thank Dr. Lewis B. Sheiner of the University of California at San Francisco and Dr. Paul Leitman of Johns Hopkins School of Medicine and Dr. Malcolm Hooper, emeritus Professor of Medicinal Chemistry at Britain's Sunderland University.

For assistance in understanding the Byzantine politics of the Department of Defense I am particularly indebted to Lt. Col. Roger Charles (USMC ret.) an investigator for CBS *60 Minutes*, Col. David Hackworth (U.S. Army ret.), military correspondent and columnist extraordinaire as well as tireless champion for the men and women in the U.S. military; and Emmy-winning investigative reporter and producer Scott Malone.

For legal advice and assistance in securing critical documentation, I would like to thank James B. Goodale, Edwin G. Schallert of Debevoise and Plimpton and their former associate Winsome Gayle, and for the legal review of my manuscript, Damion K. Stodola of Coudert Brothers.

The research I conducted in Russia on the 1979 anthrax outbreak at Sverdlovsk would not have been possible without the generous help of Dr. Olga Veniaminovna Yampolskaya of Moscow's Botkin Hospital, Ms. Elena Groznaya candidate at Ural State University in Yekaterinburg, and the irrepressible Dr. Faina Afanasyevna Abramova—former Associate Professor of Pathology at the Svedlovski Gosudarstveny Medicinsky Institut and consultant in pathology at Sverdlovsk Hospital 40. Despite her advanced years, Dr. Abramova kindly spent many days with me recounting the details of the Sverdlovsk outbreak and the critical role she played in it. Her physical and intellectual vigor is extraordinary. She is a living treasure. While I mainly relied on the eyewitness accounts from Dr. Abramova and Dr. Yamposkaya for my description of what happened to Boris Georgievich Romanov and the other victims of the Sverdlovsk outbreak, I also benefited greatly from the recollections of Dr. Martin Hugh-Jones and Dr. Alexis Shelokov who in 1993 went to Sverdlovsk to investigate the incident as members of a scientific team led by Dr. Matthew Meselson of Harvard University. I also relied on the wonderful book that resulted from that research, *Anthrax: The Investigation of a Deadly Outbreak* by another member of the Meselson team, his wife, sociologist Dr. Jeanne Giullmain of Boston College. I also consulted the book *Plague Wars: The Terrifying Reality of Biological Warfare*, by Tom Mangold and Jeff Goldberg and Dr. Alibek's autobiography, *Biohazard*, another terrific book, which he co-wrote with Stephen Handelman, an old acquaintance of mine from the years we both worked in London. For anyone interested in reading more about the Sverdlovsk incident or about anthrax in general, I highly recommend all these books.

I am grateful for help received from the librarians of the Augustus C. Long Health Sciences Library at Columbia University, the New York Academy of Medicine, the National Library of Medicine, the National Archives and Regenstein Library of the University of Chicago.

For their unswerving support and at times indispensable insights, I would like to thank the people on whom I relied most in the researching and writing of this manuscript—Greg Hunter of ABC News and his wife Betty Williams, Lt. Col. Roger Charles, Pam Asa, Bob Garry, Julius Cruse, Frances Beck, Lori Greenleaf, Col. John R. Brownlee M.D. (USAF ret.), William Stacey Cowles III, publisher of the *Spokesman Review* newspaper, my parents Alice and Kimitsu Matsumoto, my brother Kim who did research for me at the University of Chicago, my uncle Lt. Col. Shigeshi Madokoro (U.S. Army, ret.), and my daughter Helen, whose opinions matter.

A book's readability has a lot to do with its appearance. Unfortunately, we *do* judge our books by their covers. For organizing critical eleventh-hour changes into an aesthetically pleasing text that is much "cleaner" than it has right to be, I owe a great deal to my indefatigable project manager, Christine Marra, who runs a very tight ship, and to poet and copy editor Norman MacAfee.

There are some people I cannot acknowledge by name in order to shield them from possible reprisal for having assisted me in writing this book. You know who you are and I thank you.

For my literary agent, Susan Rabiner, and my editor at Basic Books, William Frucht, I owe very special thanks for shepherding this book into fruition. As much as I appreciate your editorial savvy, which is formidable, I think I appreciate even more the moral commitment that you each made to this book. Your hearts were always in the right place—with the military personnel who have suffered a great injustice. To you I say *domo arigato*, which is generally translated from the Japanese as a simple "thank you." I can't verify this because I don't speak the language, but my parents tell me that *domo arigato* is more accurately translated as "without you, it would not be possible." I am going to take my parent's word on that. Bill, Susan … *domo arigato*.

Finally, for all the men and women who serve in military, I think you deserve a better hand than you've been dealt, which is why this book exists.

Notes

Chapter One

1. Boris Georgeievich Romanov was the "index patient" in the Sverdlovsk anthrax outbreak—not the first patient to contract anthrax, but the first one to be diagnosed with it by Dr. Faina Afanasyevna Abramova. My account of what happened to Romanov was reconstructed from interviews with Dr. Abramova in Ekaterinburg (formerly Sverdlovsk) between February 15–17, 2004, interviews with Dr. Olga Yampolskaya between February 14–19, 2004 in Ekaterinburg and Moscow, and further interviews with both of them over the telephone after I returned to the United States. For information about some of the other victims who died in the 1979 Sverdlovsk outbreak, I relied on three books—Dr. Jeanne Guillemin's *Anthrax: The Investigation of a Deadly Outbreak*, Dr. Ken Alibek's *Biohazard* and Tom Mangold and Jeff Goldberg's *Plague Wars: The Terrifying Reality of Biological Warfare*. Details about the city's weather in April and May 1979 came from newspaper accounts in the *Vercherny Sverdlovsk* (Evening Sverdlovsk) kept in the archives of Ekaterinburg's main library. The account of how Romanov's anthrax infection probably progressed came from the interviews with Dr. Abramova and from the case histories written by her protégé, Dr. Lev Grinberg, who was recuperating from a heart attack when I was in Ekaterinburg and consequently unavailable for an interview. My description of Romanov's physical appearance was drawn from the photograph of him on his gravestone in Ekaterinburg's Vostochniy Cemetery and from Dr. Abramova's recollection of what he looked like when she supervised his autopsy. The depiction of life in Sverdlovsk in April 1979 was based on newspaper articles (mainly on the front page), listings for cultural events, newspaper advertisements and TV and radio guides published in the paper (on the day Boris Romanov fell ill and later on the day he died). References to pop culture were based on interviews with local residents, including the parents of my Russian researcher, Ms. Elena Groznaya, and comments from my driver.

2. Guillemin J, *ANTHRAX: The Investigation of a Deadly Outbreak*, University of California Press, Berkeley and Los Angeles, 1999, pg. 105. Guillemin reports that Vinogradov's neighbor, a "Mrs. T," recalled that "he fell down in the street and died in the

.e body was returned home for the funeral. But at night the police came and
/. He worked at the ceramics factory. He was a big, healthy man."

collected by the parents of Elena Groznaya, a doctoral student in International Relations at Ural State University in Ekaterinburg who gave me and Dr. Yampolskaya a personal tour of the city in January 2004, then conducted research for me after my return to New York.

4. Interview with Dr. Olga Yampolskaya, a member of the Moscow team who, along with Dr. Nikiforov, was an infectious disease specialist from Moscow's Botkin Hospital (Dr. Yampolskaya accompanied me to Ekaterinburg and acted as my interpreter with Dr. Abramova).

5. Guillemin, pg. 105.

6. Ibid., pg. 87. Guillemin interviewed Anna Komina's son, Yuriy Komin. From that interview, Guillemin reported the following: "For five days, her body was held at the hospital, which prevented her relatives from performing the usual Russian washing and dressing rituals and from holding a wake. In the interim, public health workers came and gave tetracycline pills to Komin and his wife, but not to their son, who was only an infant. On the fifth day, Anna's coffin was transported by truck directly from the hospital to the cemetery and buried in Sector 13. The family, on a tip from the hospital staff, went to the cemetery but was not allowed inside the gate. There were police, Komin says, but no soldiers, and certainly none with weapons (as some newspaper reports had claimed)."

7. Ibid., pg. 90. "At the cemetery, a policeman guarded the special coffin; the city, not the family members, paid for it."

8. Ibid., pg. 132. Some of the earliest victims may have been buried in another cemetery called "Isetsk," but it is impossible to tell. It is believed the first victims to die of anthrax succumbed on April 4th, but Dr. Abramova did not identify the disease as anthrax until she supervised the Romanov autopsy on April 10th.

9. Mangold T, Goldberg J, *Plague Wars: The Terrifying Reality of Biological Warfare*, St. Martin's Griffin, New York, 1999, pg. 71. Guillemin, pg. 132, Dr. Margarita Ilyenko told Guillemin that four or five bodies were buried in another cemetery called Isetsk, and that "the coffins were doused in lime."

10. Interview with Dr. Faina Abramova (01/16/04).

11. Ibid.

12. Ibid.

13. Interview with Dr. Faina Abramova (01/15/04).

14. Ibid.

15. Interviews with Dr. Faina Abramova (01/15/04 and 01/17/04).

16. Interview with Abramova (01/16/04).

17. Drs. Abramova and Yampolskaya both provided detailed descriptions of the symptoms of inhalation anthrax.

18. Dr. Abramova discussed the autopsy of Boris Romanov on all three days I interviewed her, but she provided the most extensive account on the second day (01/16/04).

19. To augment Dr. Abramova's description of brain structures I consulted medical textbooks, principally: Moore KL, Dalley AF, *Clinically Oriented Anatomy*, Fourth

Edition, Lippincott Williams and Wilkins, Baltimore and Philadelphia, 1999, pgs. 887–888.

20. The equivalent of three or four tablespoons.

21. Interviews with both Dr. Abramova and Dr. Yampolskaya (01/17/04).

22. Ibid.

23. The National Security Archive, The George Washington University, *Volume V: Anthrax at Sverdlovsk, 1979, U.S. Intelligence on the Deadliest Modern Outbreak*, National Security Archive, Electronic Briefing Book, No. 61, edited by Robert A. Wampler and Thomas S. Blanton, 15 November, 2001. Editor's Note: "This cable also reports on information obtained from a Soviet emigré about an accident in May 1979 at the Soviet biological warfare institute in Sverdlovsk, resulting in 40 to 60 deaths. Other reports of a quarantine imposed by the military in the city in mid-May tend to support these rumors, but there is no evidence that the events were linked to BW storage activities. As with the CIA report (Document 1), this cable says there is no conclusive evidence that a Soviet BW accident caused these deaths."

24. This account is drawn from a series of interviews with Col. Richard O. Spertzel, Ph.D., in February 2004. These interviews were conducted in person and over the telephone.

Chapter Two

1. A History of Medicine, Louis Pasteur, *http://www.historylearningsite.co.uk/louis_pasteur.htm.*

2. Lehrer S, *Explorers of the Body*, Doubleday, New York, 1979, also online at *http://stevenlehrer.com/explorers/chapter_chapter 6.2,htm.*

3. Pasteur L (with the collaboration of Mr. Chamberland and Mr. Roux, Summary Report of the Experiments Conducted at Pouilly-le-Fort, near Melun, on the Anthrax Vaccination, *Comptes Rendus de l'Académie des Sciences*, 13 June 1881 (92): 1378–1383 [Translated by Tina Dasgupta, Yale School of Medicine, Original Contributions Editor, Yale Journal of Biology and Medicine. [*Yale Journal of Biology and Medicine*, 2002 (75): pg. 61].

Pasteur initially agreed to expose twenty-five vaccinated sheep and twenty-five unvaccinated sheep (a control group) to anthrax. As Pasteur points out in his report to the French Academy of Sciences, the Agricultural Society of Melun (Hippolyte Rossignol's farm at Pouilly-le-Fort was located outside of Melun) requested changes to the original protocol. Two sheep would be replaced with goats, and various cattle would be included in the experiment, including eight cows, an ox and a bull. A total of thirty-one animals were thus immunized with Pasteur's anthrax vaccine.

4. Ibid.

5. Ibid.

6. Ibid.

7. Ibid.

8. Ibid.

9. Lehrer *http://stevenlehrer.com/explorers/chapter_chapter 6.2,htm*, pg. 9.

10. Ibid.

11. http://www.historylearningsite.co.uk/louis_pasteur.htm.

12. Pasteur (Yale), pg. 60.

13. Koch R, Die Aetiologie der MilzbrandKrankheit begrundet auf die Entwicklungsgeschichte des Bacillus Anthracis (The Etiology of Anthrax, Based on the Ontogeny of the Anthrax Bacillus), *Beitrage zer Biologie der Pflanzen*, 1877, Vol. 2, No. 2, pgs. 277–310 (Re-published in *Medical Classics*, Williams and Wilkins, 1937, Baltimore, pgs. 787–820).

14. Lehrer, pg. 10.

15. Turnbull PC, Anthrax vaccines: past, present and future, *Vaccine*, 1991 Aug;9(8): pg. 533; Hambleton P, Carman JA, Melling J, Anthrax: the disease in relation to vaccines, *Vaccine*, 1984 Jun;2(2): pg. 127.

16. Sterne M, Nichol J, Lambrechts MC, The Effect of Large Scale Active Immunization Against Anthrax, *Journal of the South African Veterinary Medical Association*, 1942;13: pgs. 53–63; Sterne M, The Effects of Different Carbon Dioxide Concentrations on the Growth of Virulent Anthrax Strains. Pathogenicity and Immunity Tests on Guinea-pigs and Sheep with Anthrax Variants Derived from Virulent Strains, *Onderstepoort Journal of Veterinary Science and Animal Industry*, 1937, Volume 9: pgs. 49–67.

17. Sterne M, Variation in *Bacillus anthracis, Onderstepoort Journal of Veterinary Science and Animal Industry,* April 1937, Vol. 8(2): pgs. 271–350; Turnbull, pg. 534.

18. Ivins BE, Welkos SL, Little SF, Knudson GB, Cloned Protective Activity and Progress in Development of Improved Anthrax Vaccines, *Salisbury Medical Bulletin* (Proceedings of the International Workshop on Anthrax, Winchester, England, April 11–13), 1989, pg. 87; Turnbull PC, Anthrax vaccines: past, present and future, *Vaccine*, 1991 Aug;9(8): pg. 534; Little SF, Knudson GB, Comparative efficacy of *Bacillus anthracis* in live spore vaccine and protective antigen vaccine against anthrax in the guinea pig, *Infection Immunity*, 1986 May;52(2): pgs. 509–512; Turnbull PCB, Broster MG, Carman JA, Manchee RJ, Melling J, Development of Antibodies to Protective Antigen and Lethal Factor Components of Anthrax Toxin in Humans and Guinea Pigs and Their Relevance to Protective Immunity, *Infection and Immunity*, May 1986;52(2): pgs. 356–363.

19. Harris SH, *Factories of Death: Japanese Biological Warfare, 1932–45, and the American Cover-Up*, Routledge (1994), pg. 69.

20. Ibid., pg. 77.

21. Ibid., pg. 48.

22. Ibid.

23. Ibid., pg. 156; Mangold T, Goldberg J, *Plague Wars: The Terrifying Reality of Biological Warfare*, St. Martin's Griffin, New York, 1999, pg. 29.

24. Regis, pgs. 15–16.

25. Institute of Medicine and National Research Council, pg. 146.

26. Ibid.

27. Ibid.

28. Sawyer WA, Meyer KF, Eaton MD, Bauer JH, Putnam P, Schwentker FF, Jaundice in Army personnel in the western region of the United States and its relation to vaccination against yellow fever, *American Journal of Hygiene*, 1944, (39): pgs. 337–430; Sawyer W, et al., Jaundice in Army personnel in the western region of the United States and its relation to vaccination against yellow fever, *American Journal of Hygiene*, 1944, (40): pgs. 35–107; Walker DW, Some epidemiological aspects of infectious hepatitis in the U.S. Army, *American Journal of Tropical Medicine*, 1945, (25): pgs. 75–82; Havens WP Jr., Viral Hepatitis. In: Andersen RS, ed., *Internal medicine in World War II. Vol. 3. Infectious disease and general medicine*, Washington DC: Government Printing Office, 1968: pgs. 331–384.

29. Seeff LB, Beebe GW, Hoofnagle JH, Norman JE, Buskell-Bales Z, Waggoner JG, Kaplowitz N, Koff RS, Petrini JL, Schiff ER, Shorey J, Stanley MM, A Serologic Follow-up of the 1942 Epidemic of Post-Vaccination Hepatitis in the United States Army, *The New England Journal of Medicine*, 16 April 1987, 316;(16): pgs. 965–966. Norman JE, Beebe GW, Hoofnagle JH, Seeff LB, Mortality Follow-up of the 1942 Epidemic of Hepatitis B in the U.S. Army, *Hepatology*, 1993, 15;(4): pgs. 790–791.

30. MilitaryHistoryOnline.com, *http://www.militaryhistoryonline.com/wwii/usarmy/infantry.aspx*.

31. Lincoln RE, Hodges DR, Klein F, Mahlandt BG, Jones WI Jr., Haines BW, Rhian MA, Walker JS, Role of Lymphatics in the Pathogenesis of Anthrax, *Journal of Infectious Diseases*, 1965 Dec, 115(5): pgs. 481–494.

32. Bail O, Pettersson A, Untersuchungen über natürliche und künstliche Milzbrandimmunität, *Centralblatt für Bakteriologie, Parasitenkunde, Infektionskrankheiten und Hygiene*, 1904, XXXIV, No. 8, pgs. 247–259; Hambleton et al., pg. 127.

33. Bloom WL, Watson DW, Cromartie WJ, Freed M, Studies on Infection with *Bacillus Anthracis* IV. Preparation and Characterization of an Anthracidal Substance from Various Animal Tissues, *Journal of Infectious Diseases*, 1947, (80): pgs. 41–52.

34. Cromartie WJ, Watson DW, Bloom WL, Heckly RJ, Studies on Infection with *Bacillus Anthracis* II. The Immunological and Tissue Damaging Properties of Extracts Prepared from Lesions of *B. Anthracis* Infection, *Journal of Infectious Diseases*, 1947;(80): pg. 14; Cromartie WJ, Watson DW, Bloom WL, Kegeles G, Heckly RJ, Studies on Infection with *Bacillus Anthracis* III. Chemical and Immunological Properties of the Protective Antigen in Crude Extracts of Skin Lesions of *B. Anthracis*, *Journal of Infectious Diseases*, 1947;(80): pg. 28.

35. Gladstone GP, Immunity to Anthrax: Protective Antigen Present in Cell-Free Culture Filtrates, *British Journal of Experiment Pathology*, 1946, (27): pgs. 394–410.

36. Tresselt HB, Boor AK, An Antigen Prepared in Vitro Effective for Immunization Against Anthrax, III. Immunization for Monkeys Against Anthrax, *Journal of Infectious Diseases*, 1955, Sept-Oct;97(2): pg. 209.

37. Boor AK, An Antigen Prepared in Vitro Effective for Immunization Against Anthrax, I. Preparation and Evaluation of the Crude Protective Antigen, *Journal of Infectious Diseases*, 1955, Sept-Oct;97(2): pg. 195; Cohn EJ, Strong LE, Hughes WL, Mulford DJ, Ashworth JN, Melin M, Taylor HL, Preparation and Properties of Serum and Plasma Proteins. IV. A System for the Separation into Fractions of the Protein and Lipoprotein Components of Biological Tissues and Fluids, *Journal of the American Chemical Society*, 1946 March (68): pgs. 459–474.

38. Wright GG, Hedberg MA, Slein JB, Studies on Immunity in Anthrax. III. Elaboration of Protective Antigen in a Chemically-Defined Non-Protein Medium, *Journal of Immunology*, 1954 April;72(4): pg. 264.

39. Belton FC, Strange RE, Studies on a Protective Antigen Produced in Vitro from Bacillus Anthracis: Medium and Methods of Production, *British Journal of Pathology*, 1954, (35): pgs. 144–152.

40. The numbers vary. According to a U.S. Public Health Service article in the British medical journal the *Lancet* (published on June 25, 1955), the Salk polio vaccine caused 168 cases of polio and six deaths among vaccinated patients and an additional 149 polio infections and six deaths among people who contracted from vaccinated patients who were then contagious. Six manufacturers of the Salk vaccine tested their products and found fully virulent polio virus in their products. One manufacturer found fully virulent polio in four out of six lots of vaccine.

41. Smith, pg. 869.

42. Ibid.

43. Stanley JL, Smith H, The Three Factors of Anthrax Toxin: Their Immunogenicity and Lack of Demonstrable Enzymic Activity, *Journal of General Microbiology*, 1963;(31): pg. 336.

44. Mahlandt, pg. 733.

45. Klein F, Dearmon IA Jr., Lincoln RE, Mahlandt BG, Fernelius AL, Immunological studies of anthrax. II. Levels of immunity against *Bacillus anthracis* obtained with protective antigen and live vaccine, *Journal of Immunology*, 1961 Jan(88): pg. 18: "To realize maximal immunity against anthrax infection antibodies against spores, vegetative cells, and toxin may be necessary. Perhaps only partial antibody activity is formed against the protective antigen and complete antibody activity is formed as a result of *in vivo* growth of the live vaccine. This could explain why antigen alone caused only partial immunity in the host and protective antigen in combination with live vaccine produced a synergistic effect, stimulating complete antibody activity with an enhanced immunogenic effect"; Mahlandt et al., pg. 733: "The antigen used to immunize man and animals should contain all the toxin components for maximum efficiency." Mahlandt BG, Klein F, Lincoln RE, Haines BW, Jones WI Jr. Friedman RH, Immunologic Studies of Anthrax IV. Evaluation of the Immunogenicity of Three Components of Anthrax Toxin, *The Journal of Immunology*, 1966 Apr;96(4): pg. 733: "The antigen used to immunize man and animals should contain all the toxin components for maximum efficiency."

46. Coggins CH, Weapons of Mass Destruction, *Military Review*, 1963, (42): pgs. 43–50.

47. Alexandrov NI and Gefen NYe, *Aktivnaya Spersifcheskaya Profilaktika Infektsionnykh Zabolevaniy i Puti yeye Usovershenstvovaniya*, Moscow (Translation number JPRS 16,793. *Active specific prophylaxis of infectious diseases and its improvement*. U.S. Department of Commerce, Office of Technical Service, Joint Publications Research Service, Washington, DC); Shylakhov EN, Rubinstein E, Human live anthrax vaccine in the former USSR, *Vaccine*, June 1994, 12(8): pgs. 727–730.

48. Ibid., p. 728; Alexandrov NI, Gefan NE, Garin NS, Gapochko KG, Sergeev VM, Smirnov MS, et al., Experience in massive aerogenic vaccination of humans against anthrax, *Voenno-Meditsinskii Zhurnal*, 1959(8): pgs. 27–32.

49. Klein, pg. 19.

50. Ibid.

51. Ibid.

52. Ibid.

53. Lincoln RE, Walker JS, Klein F, Haines BW, Anthrax, *Advances in Veterinary Science*, 1964, (9): pg. 353; Norman PS, Roy JG, Brachman PS, Plotkin SA, Pagano JS, Serologic testing for anthrax antibodies in workers in goat hair processing mill, *American Journal of Hygiene*, 1960;(72): pgs. 32–37; Brachman PS, Gold H, Plotkin SA, Fekety FR, Werrin M, Ingraham NR, Field evaluation of a human anthrax vaccine, *American Journal of Public Health*, 1962;(52): pgs. 632–645.

54. Mahlandt et al., pg. 732.

55. Ibid.

56. The Sterne whole-spore vaccine, and the Soviet whole-spore vaccine (which is called STI) contain slightly different strains. This may account for reported differences in their virulence.

57. CDC traveler's advisory for Southeast Asia.

58. Ibid., Chapter 8 (End of an Era), pg. 4.

59. Personal interviews with Dr. Joseph V. Jemski in Frederick, Maryland on 03/01/04 and 03/04/04.

60. Jemski JV and Phillips GB, Chapter 8, "Aerosol Challenge of Animals" in *Methods of Animal Experimentation*, Volume 1, edited by William Gray, Academic Press, 1965, pgs. 274–341.

61. A lethal dose was never an absolute number; it was a curve—a morbid parabola measured in an average of cc's and spore counts. Jemski worked with these averages. He could find an average number that would kill *half* of them. This is called an LD_{50}, which stands for "lethal dose, fifty"—a dose that kills fifty percent of any given animal species.

62. Fact Sheet, *Project Whitecoat/Medical Research Volunteer Subject Program*, Department of the Army Headquarters, U.S. Army Medical Research Institute of Infectious Disease, Fort Detrick, Frederick, Maryland 21701, pg. 4.

63. Plotkin SA, Brachman PS, Utell M, Bumford FH, Atchison MM, An Epidemic of Inhalation Anthrax: The First in the Twentieth Century, II. Epidemiology, *American Journal of Medicine*, December 1960;(29): pg. 7.

64. Ward MK, McGann VG, Hogge AL, Huff ML, Kanode RG, Roberts EO, Studies on Anthrax Infections in Immunized Guinea Pigs, *Journal of Infectious Diseases*, 1965;(115): pg. 61.

65. Ibid.

66. Little, pg. 510.

67. Ibid.

68. Ibid.

69. Ibid., pg. 511.

70. Turnbull PC, Broster MG, Carman JA, Manchee RJ, Melling J, Development of Antibodies to Protective Antigen and Lethal Factor Components of Anthrax Toxin in Humans and Guinea Pigs and Their Relevance to Protective Immunity, *Infection and Immunity*, May 1986;52(2): pg. 360.

71. Ibid.

72. Personal interview with Dr. Jack Melling in New York City, 02/18/04.

73. Phillips AP, Martin KL, Investigation of spore surface antigens in the genus Bacillus by the use of polyclonal antibodies in immunofluorescence tests, *Journal of Applied Bacteriology*, 1988, Jan;64(1); pgs. 47–55; Ezzell JW Jr., Abshire TG, Immunological analysis of cell-associated antigens of Bacillus anthracis, *Infection and Immunity*, 1988 Feb;56(2): pgs. 349–356.

74. Ibid., pg. 356.

75. Interview with Dr. Jack Melling, 3 March 2004, Stroudsburg, PA.

76. Ibid.

77. CIA, 713761, REPORT CLASS SECRET, October 1987, SUBJ: IRAQI DEVELOPMENT OF BIOLOGICAL AGENT FOR MILITARY PURPOSES, pg. 3.

78. Background Paper for Under Secretary of Defense for Strategy and Resources, SUBJECT: Iraqi Biological Warfare (BW) Agents and Their Effects, Section 2, Subheading a, Paragraph 1, *file://E:\IRAQ, BOTOX &SILICA (DIA).html*.

79. Ibid., Section 2, Subheading a, Paragraph 4. Memo, FROM: DIRAFMIC FTDETRICKRD, TO: CG THIRD FSSG, *SUBJ: IRAQI BW CAPABILITIES*. Section 6: "Delivery of biological toxins or infectious agents bound to a silica matrix capable of penetrating permeable protective suits may be within Iraqi capability. It is possible that such an agent could work its way through the-fabric [sic] of protective clothing and become imbedded in the skin."

80. Gordon MR, Trainor BE, *The General's War: The Inside Story of the Conflict in the Gulf*, Little, Brown and Company, 1995, New York, pg. 44; Cheney RB, Memorandum, FY 1992–1997, Defense Planning Guidance, 24 January 1990, Classified: SECRET, "The Secretary has increased the relative priority of Southwest Asia by making explicit that the region ranks above South America and Africa in terms of global peacetime prior-

ities and by outlining an initial theater strategy," he wrote in a memo to the service secretaries and the Joint Chiefs.

81. Gordon et al., pg. 44.

82. Ivins BE, Welkos S, Recent Advances in the Development of an Improved Anthrax Vaccine, *European Journal of Epidemiology*, 1988 Mar;4(1): pg. 13.

83. Gulf Veterans' Illnesses, Background to the Use of Medical Countermeasures to Protect British Forces During the Gulf War (Operation Granby), *Ministry of Defense, Gulf Veterans' Illnesses Home Page*, pg. 8, Section 42, *http://www.mod.uk/policu/gulfwar/info/mcm.htm*.

Chapter Three

1. Leenaars PP, Koedam MA, Ester PW, Baumans V, Claassen E, Hendriksen CF [National Institute of Public Health and Environmental Protection (RIVM), P.O. Box 1, 3720 BA, Bilthoven, The Netherlands], Assessment of side effects induced by injection of different adjuvant/antigen combinations in rabbits and mice, *Laboratory Animals* (1998) Oct;32(4): pgs. 387–406.

2. Ibid.; Leenaars PP, Hendriksen CF, Angulo AF, Koedam MA, Claasen E [National Institute of Public Health and Environmental Protection (RIVM), P.O. Box 1, 3720 BA, Bilthoven, The Netherlands], Evaluation of several adjuvants as alternatives to the use of Freund's adjuvant in rabbits, *Veterinary Immunology and Immunopathology*, (1994) Mar;40(3): pgs. 225–241; Leenaars M, Koedam MA, Hendriksen CF, Claassen E [National Institute of Public Health and Environmental Protection (RIVM), Bilthoven, The Netherlands], Immune responses and side effects of five different oil-based adjuvants in mice, *Veterinary Immunology and Immunopathology*, (1998) Feb 27;61(2–4): pgs. 291–304.

3. Freund J, The Mode of Action of Immunologic Adjuvants, *Advances in Tuberculosis Research*, 1956, 7: pgs. 134–136.

4. Beebe GW, Simon AH, Vivona S, Long-Term Mortality Follow-Up of Army Recruits Who Received Adjuvant Influenza Virus Vaccine in 1951–1953, *American Journal of Epidemiology*, 1972 Apr; 95(4): pgs. 337–46. *N.B.* Twenty-one years after the Fort Dix experiment with an experimental influenza vaccine augmented with Freund's Incomplete Adjuvant (FIA), in addition to clincal trials at other bases, HHS did not license the oil adjuvant for use in humans.

5. Salk JE, Contakos M, Laurent AM, Sorensen M, Rapalski Col. AJ, Simmons Col. IH, Sandberg, Lt. J, Use of Adjuvants in Studies on Influenza Immunization; 3. Degree of Persistence of Antibody in Subjects Two Years After Vaccination, *Journal of the American Medical Association*, 4 April 1953, pg. 1169.

6. Salk JE, Bailey ML, Laurent AM, The Use of Adjuvants in Studies on Influenza Immunization; II. Increased Antibody Formation in Human Subjects Inoculated with Influenza Virus Vaccine in a Water-in-Oil Emulsion, *American Journal of Hygiene*, 1952, (55): pg. 455.

7. *Grant nos. DA-MEDDH–61–20 and DA-MD–49–193–63 G72.*

8. Beebe GW, Simon AH, Vivona S, Follow-Up Study on Army Personnel Who Received Adjuvant Influenza Virus Vaccine 1951–1953, *The American Journal of the Medical Sciences*, April 1964, pg. 385.

9. Davenport FM, Seventeen Years' Experience with Mineral Oil Adjuvant Influenza Virus Vaccines, *Annals of Allergy*, 1968 June;26(6): pgs. 288–292.

10. Op cit., Beebe (1972), pg. 337.

11. USAMRDC *Contract no. DCDA17-C–8147.*

12. Moseley Col. CH (MC), Memorandum for: The Surgeon General, Department of the Army; The Surgeon General, Department of the Navy, The Surgeon General, Department of the Air Force, *SUBJECT: AFEB Recommendations on Influenza Vaccine Formula for FY 1964*, 14 December 1962; Moseley Col. CH (MC), Memorandum for: The Surgeon General, Department of the Army; The Surgeon General, Department of the Navy, The Surgeon General, Department of the Air Force, *SUBJECT: Mineral Oil Adjuvant Vaccines*, 26 December 1962.

13. Beebe, 1964, pgs. 387–388.

14. Beebe, 1972, pg. 343.

15. Ibid.

16. Little SF, Knudson GB, Comparative efficacy of Bacillus anthracis live spore vaccine and protective antigen vaccine against anthrax in the guinea pig, *Infection and Immunity*, 1986 May;52(2): pg. 510.

17. Ibid., pg. 511.

18. Ibid.

19. Ivins BE, Welkos SL, Little SF, Knudson GB, Cloned Protective Activity and Progress in Development of Improved Anthrax Vaccines, *Salisbury Medical Bulletin (Proceedings of the International Workshop on Anthrax, Winchester, England, April 11–13)*, 1989, pg. 88.

20. Byars NE, Allison AC, Adjuvant formulation for use in vaccines to elicit both cell-mediated and humoral immunity, *Vaccine*, 1987 Sept;5(3): pgs. 223, 227.

21. Geerligs HJ, Weijer GW, Welling GW, Welling-Wester S, The influence of different adjuvants on the immune response to a synthetic peptide comprising amino acid reside 9–21 of herpes simplex virus type 1 glycoprotein D, *Journal of Immunological Methods*, 1989, 124: pg. 97; Diano M, Le Bivic A, Hirn HA, Method for Production of Highly Specific Polyclonal Antibodies, *Analytical Biochemistry*, 1987, 166: pgs. 224–29; Johnston BA, Eisen H, Fry D, An Evaluation of Several Adjuvant Emulsion Regimens for the Production of Polyclonal Antisera in Rabbits, *Laboratory Animal Science*, 1991 Jan;41(1): pg. 15; personal communications with the Corixa Corporation, which bought out Ribi Immunochem Research.

22. Ivins BE, Welkos S, Recent Advances in the Development of an Improved Anthrax Vaccine, *European Journal of Epidemiology*, 1988 Mar;4(1): pg. 13.

23. After faxing me a copy of his landmark paper in 1999, Dr. Bruce Ivins has refused every one of my requests for an interview.

24. Telephone interview with Dr. Michael Whitehouse (01/28/02).

25. Whitehouse MW, Orr KJ, Beck FW, Pearson CM, Freund's adjuvants: relationship of arthritogenicity and adjuvanticity in rats to vehicle composition, *Immunology*, 1974 Aug;27(2): pg. 319.

26. Ibid.

27. Interview with Dr. Michael Whitehouse (01/28/02).

28. Ibid., pg. 314 ["+ = either irregular incidence of disease, or a consistent minimal incidence of lesions on non-injected feet, but enduring and prominent swelling of adjuvant-inoculated foot: ++ = consistent mild disease affecting non-injected feet (but causing only modest swelling thereof) in 75 per cent of the inoculated animals; +++ = normal consistent severe disease, affecting all limbs (day 14) and often the tail (day 17) with frequent ear lesions; ++++ = gross swelling of all extremities, inflamed scrotum, prominent ear lesions, frequent balinitis, but never lethal].

29. Ibid., pg. 318.

30. Ibid.

31. Beck FW, Whitehouse MW, Pearson CM, Improvements for consistently inducing experimental allergic encephalomyelitis (EAE) in rats: I. Without using mycobacterium, II. Inoculating encephalitogen into the ear, *Proceedings of the Society for Experimental Biology and Medicine*, 1976 March; 151(3): pgs. 615–622; personal communication with Frances W. Beck, 2001.

32. Yarkoni E, Rapp HJ, Tumor regression after intralesional injection of mycobacterial components emulsified in 2,6,10,15,19,23,-hexamethyl–2,6,10,14,18,22-tetracosahexaene (squalene), 2,6,10,15,19,23-hexamethyltetracosane (squalane), peanut oil, or mineral oil, *Cancer Research*, 1979 May; 39(5): pgs. 1518–1520.

33. Ibid., pg. 1519.

34. Acquired Immunodeficiency Syndrome (AIDS), *Weekly Surveillance Report (United States)*, AIDS Activity, Center for Infectious Diseases, Centers for Disease Control, 22 December 1983.

35. Acquired Immunodeficiency Syndrome (AIDS), *Weekly Surveillance Report (United States)*, AIDS Activity, Center for Infectious Diseases, Centers for Disease Control, January 1989.

36. Dertzbaugh MT, Genetically Engineered Vaccines: An Overview, *Plasmid*, 1998;39(2): pg. 110.

37. Alibek K, *Biohazard*, Random House, New York, 1999, pg. 138.

38. Author interview with Jack Melling, New York, 18 February 2004.

39. Loktev NA, Pilipenko VG, Basilova GI, Shchedrin VI, Lunina EA, Jet immunization with polyvalent vaccines against plague, tularemia and anthrax, *Zhurnal Mikrobiologii Epidemiologii Immunobiologii*, 1980 June, (6): pgs. 109–110; Stepanov AV, Marinin LI, Vorob'ev AA, Aerosol Vaccination Against Dangerous Infectious Diseases, *Vestnik Rossiiskoi Akademii Meditsinskih Nauk*, 1999, (8): pgs. 47–54.

40. I count four because I do not include Bruce Ivins's "aro-mutants"; because they were streptomycin-resistant, they were never viable candidates. The Army had also

cloned the PA gene into *E. coli,* but I do not include that either. *E. coli* would have been too problematic to inject into people.

41. Turnbull PC, Anthrax vaccines: past, present and future, *Vaccine,* 1991 Aug;9(8): pg. 537.

42. Ibid.

Chapter Four

1. *The United States Dual-Use Exports to Iraq and Their Impact on the Health of the Persian Gulf War Veterans*, United States Senate Committee on Banking, Housing, and Urban Affairs, United States Senate, 103rd Congress, U.S. Government Printing Office, Washington, D.C. 25 May 1994, pgs. 39, 40, 44.

2. Ibid., pgs. 41, 47.

3. Power S, *A Problem from Hell,* Basic Books, New York, 2002, pg. 178.

4. Director of Central Intelligence, *Impact and Implications of Chemical Weapons Use in the Iran-Iraq War,* CIA, declassified, pg. 19.

5. Brown RJ, *U.S. Marines in the Persian Gulf, 1990–1991: With Marine Forces Afloat in Desert Shield and Desert Storm,* U.S. Marine Corps, History and Museums Division, Washington, DC, 1998.

6. Staff of U.S. News and World Report, *Triumph Without Victory: The Unreported History of the Persian Gulf War,* Times Books, Random House, New York, 1992, pg. 11.

7. Ibid., pg. 14.

8. Smyth RADM JP, J4—Medical Readiness Officer, Joint Chief of Staff, *Biodefense Log (08/08/90–02/92)* (Declassified 1 November 1996): pg. 1.

9. Klenke Maj, *Secret Working Papers: Medical Biological Defense (07/12//88–02/07/92)*; DASG-HCD: pg. 1.

10. Ibid.

11. Ibid., pg. 2.

12. Ibid.

13. Rammelkamp CH Jr., *Annual Report to the Commission on Streptococcal Diseases of the Armed Forces Epidemiological Board*, AFEB Research Contract No. DA–49–007-MD–380, Studies Conducted at the Streptococcal Disease Laboratory, Frances E. Warren Air Force Base, Wyoming, pg. 3.

14. Ibid., pg. 1.

15. Ibid., pg. 6.

16. Ibid.

17. Ibid., Table 2 and pg. 7.

18. Jones JH, *Bad Blood: The Tuskegee Syphilis Experiment, New and Expanded Edition*, The Free Press, New York, 1993, pg. 8.

19. Gaydos Col. JC, *Adenovirus Vaccines in the United States Military*, U.S. Army Center for Health Promotion and Preventative Medicine, Aberdeen Proving Ground, Briefing, 25 February 1995, pg. 3.

20. Mieklejohn G, *Viral Respiratory Disease at Lowry Air Force Base in Denver*, 1952–1982, Division of Infectious Diseases, Department of Medicine, University of Colorado School of Medicine; Gaydos, pg. 1; Fletcher GF, Fogelman Col. VL (USAF), Memorandum for the Assistant Secretary of Defense (Health Affairs), The Surgeon General, Department of the Army; The Surgeon General, Department of the Navy, The Surgeon General, Department of the Air Force, *SUBJECT: Recommendation for the Use of Adenovirus Vaccine*, 9 January 1998, pg. 1.

21. Mieklejohn, pg. 10.

22. Britten Capt. SA (USN), Memorandum for the Assistant Secretary of Defense (Health Affairs), The Surgeon General, Department of the Army; The Surgeon General, Department of the Navy, The Surgeon General, Department of the Air Force, *SUBJECT: Live Type 4 Adenovirus Vaccine*, 2 June 1965.

23. Prior Col. BW (USAF), Memorandum for the Assistant Secretary of Defense (Health Affairs), The Surgeon General, Department of the Army; The Surgeon General, Department of the Navy, The Surgeon General, Department of the Air Force, *SUBJECT: Use of Adenovirus Vaccines and Need for Research*, 2 June 1970.

24. Department of Defense contracts *DAMD 17–82 C 2024* and *DAMD 17–82 C 2023*.

25. Britten Capt. SA (USN), Memorandum for the Assistant Secretary of Defense (Health Affairs), The Surgeon General, Department of the Army; The Surgeon General, Department of the Navy, The Surgeon General, Department of the Air Force, *SUBJECT: Interim Use of Trivalent Inactivated Adenovirus Vaccine*, 2 June 1965.

26. Ibid.

27. Ibid., pg. 9.

28. Jones, pg. 7.

29. Dr. John D. Millar quoted in *Birmingham News*, 27 July 1972, pgs. 1, 4; *Atlanta Journal*, 27 July 1972, pg. 2; Jones, pg. 7.

30. Advisory Committee on Human Radiation Experiments, *ACHRE Report*, Chapter 3, The Development of Human Subject Research Policy DHEW.

31. Ibid.; Armed Forces Epidemiological Board, *Minutes: 24 May 1957*, ACHRE No. NARA–032495-B.

32. Frederick L. Ehrman Medical Archives Exhibit, NYU School of Medicine, http://library.med.nyu.edu/library/eresources/featuredcollections/krugman/index/html; Woodward TE, *The Armed Forces Epidemiological Board: Its First Fifty Years*, Office of the Surgeon General, Borden Institute, Walter Reed Army Medical Center, Washington, D.C., 1940–1990, pg. 102.

33. ACHRE Report, Chapter 3, Footnote 41.

34. Beecher HK, Ethics and Clinical Research, *The New England Journal of Medicine*, 16 June 1966, 274(24): pg. 1354.

35. Ibid., pg. 1356.

36. Takafuji ET, Russell PK, Military Immunizations: Past, Present and Future Prospects, *Infectious Disease Clinics of North America*, 1 March 1990, 4(1): pg. 145; Top

FH Jr., Grossman RA, Bartelloni PJ, Segal HE, Dudding BA, Russell PK, Buescher EL, I. Immunization with live types 7 and 4 vaccines. I. Safety, infectivity, antigenicity, and potency of adenovirus type 7 vaccine in humans, *Journal of Infectious Diseases*, 1971, 124(2): pgs. 148–154.

37. Benenson A, Immunization and Military Medicine, *Reviews of Infectious Diseases*, 1984 January-February, 6(1): pg. 2.

38. Ibid.

39. Takafuji, pg. 144; Gillett MC, The Army Medical Department, 1775–1818, *Center of Military History* (Washington, DC), U.S. Army, 1981, pg. 75.

40. Ibid., pg. 803.

41. Appel HL, Medicine and War (Letter to the Editor), *The New England Journal of Medicine*, 8 October 1992, 327(15): pg. 1096.

42. Ibid.

43. Ibid., pg. 156.

44. Barry J, The *Great Influenza: The Epic Story of the Deadliest Plague in History*, Viking, New York, 2004, pg. 95.

45. Howe EG, Ethical Issues Regarding Mixed Agency of Military Physicians, *Social Science and Medicine*, 1986(23)8: pgs. 803-15.

46. Mintz M, Cohen JS, Human guinea pigs, *Progressive*, 1976, (40), pg. 36.

47. Annas, G, Chapter 7 by Dr. Michael Grodin, M.D. (Boston University Schools of Medicine and Public Health), pg. 137.

48. Carl R. Alving is the second son of Dr. Alf S. Alving, M.D. Confirmation of this can be found in the Special Collections Research Center, Regenstein Library, University of Chicago.

49. Biographical Sketch for Dr. Alf Sven Alving, The University of Chicago, 1 March 1964.

50. Ibid., pg. 98.

51. Ibid., pgs. 204, 218.

52. Harris SH, *Factories of Death: Japanese Biological Warfare, 1932–45, and the American Cover-Up*, Routledge, London, 1994, pg. 207.

53. Annas, pg. 106.

54. Ibid., pg. 107.

55. Ibid., pg. 217.

56. Ibid.

57. Between 1946 and 1953, seventy-four boys from the Walter E. Fernald State School in Waltham, Massachusetts, were fed oatmeal mixed with trace amounts of radioactive calcium and iron.

58. Welsome E, *The Plutonium Files*, The Dial Press, Random House, New York, September 1999, pg. 214.

59. Ibid.

60. 39 *Federal Register 18914*, 30 May 1974.

61. 45 *CFR part 46; 40 Federal Regulations 33526, Section 46.102 (a)*, 8 August 1975.

62. Tyler HR Jr., Carlson NA, *H.R. 3603: Use of Federal Prisoners in Medical Research Projects*, 2 October 1975; Cohn V, "Medical Research on Prisoners, Poor Defended, Hit"; Hornblum, AM, *Acres of Skin: Human Experiments at Holmesburg Prison; A True Story of Abuse and Exploitation in the Name of Medical Science*, Routledge, NY, 1988, pg. 112.

63. Valdes-Depena P, *"What's it pay to be a soldier?"* CNNmoney, 28 March 2003.

64. Furmanski M, Unlicensed Vaccines and Bioweapon Defense in World War II, *Journal of the American Medical Association* (Letter), 1 September 1999, 282(9): pg. 822.

65. Brown D, Severe Vaccine Shortages Termed Unprecedented, *The Washington Post,* 20 April 2002, pg. A01.

66. U.S. Supreme Court, FERES v. UNITED STATES, 340 U.S. 135 (1950), *FERES, EXECUTRIX v. UNITED STATES*, CERTIORARI TO THE UNITED STATES COURT OF APPEALS FOR THE SECOND CIRCUIT, No. 9, Argued 12 October 1950, Decided 4 December 1950, pgs. 136–146.

67. Department of Health and Human Services, *Rules and Regulations for the Protection of Human Research Subjects, Code of Federal Regulations 45 (1983): sec. 46.101–46.409.*

68. Ibid., Section III, Subheading C, pg. 3.

69. *Hepatitis A Vaccines: Assessment of Strategies for Prevention of Hepatitis A in Saudi Arabia*, Document Identification Number 00878167.002 A L, 5 December 1990, Enclosure 1, Subheading 1, pgs. 2; The Salk Institute, *Project Title: Hepatitis A Vaccine*, Project Order No. 14–88-P, Contract No. DAMD17–88-C–8082, 1 April 1988.

70. Document Identification Number 00878167.002 A L, pg. 1.

71. Ibid.

72. Ibid., pg. 2.

73. Woodward, pg. 183.

Chapter Five

1. The highest number of troops deployed was around 550,000 troops in 1968.

2. United States Army Medical Research and Development Command, *Briefing on Project Badger*, Classification: SECRET, undated.

3. Klenke Maj, *Secret Working Papers: Medical Biological Defense (07/12//88–02/07/92)*; DASG-HCD, pg. 11.

4. Prepared by a Tri-Service Task Force in Response to a Tasking from the Secretary of Defense Given on 3 October 1990, *Short Term Production of Anthrax Vaccine* (S), Classification: SECRET, declassified 13 May 1999, U.S. Army Medical Research and Development Command, Fort Detrick, Frederick, Maryland 21702–5012, 12 November 1990, pg. 2.

5. Johnson-Winegar A, *INFORMATION PAPER: Guinea Pig Potency Testing for Anthrax Vaccine*, SGRD-PLA, 7 January 1991, pg. 1.

6. Ibid.

7. Ibid.

8. Ibid.

9. Ibid.

10. Tri-Service Task Force, pg. 4.

11. Ibid.

12. Ibid.

13. Ibid., pg. 5.

14. Ibid., pg. 5, Appendix C.

15. Ibid., pg. 6.

16. Prepared by a Tri-Service Task Force in Response to a Tasking from the Secretary of Defense Given on 3 October 1990, *Long Term Expansion of Production Capability for Medical Defense Against Biological Warfare Agents (S)*, Classification: SECRET, declassified 13 May 1999, U.S. Army Medical Research and Development Command, Fort Detrick, Frederick, Maryland, 21702–5012, 15 January 1991, pg. 7.

17. "BL" stands for "Biosafety Level." There are four such levels. Your average high-school biology lab would be a BL–1. BL–2 is fairly tame stuff too. Meeting BL–2 standards requires minimal precautions—basically, you close the doors and wear gloves and a lab coat; most pharmaceutical labs qualify as BL–2. BL–3 is the level where some people's sphincters start to pucker. Hazardous organisms require BL–3 containment; in a BL–3 laboratory, workers wear protective clothing and handle the microbes inside of glass-partitioned cabinets. These "biological safety cabinets" have portals through which a technician can insert his or her hands up to the elbows directly into a pair of long gloves attached to the inside of the cabinet. Exhaust air from a BL–3 lab is vented to the outdoors. BL–3 also prohibits "the re-use of equipment for purposes other than the growth of spore-forming microorganisms," which means valuable equipment must, in essence, become disposable. Biosafety Level 4 is the most onerous—it is the ultimate in containment, the only place safe enough to handle killer pathogens like smallpox and Ebola. In BL–4, workers wear "moon suits"; they are covered from head to toe and breathe "supplied air" delivered by hose to their suits. There is negative air pressure in a BL–4 suite—the ventilation system blows air back into the lab area to prevent germs from escaping into the environment.

18. Tri-Service Task Force, *Long Term Expansion of Production Capability for Medical Defense Against Biological Warfare Agents*.

19. Ibid., Appendix E, pg. E2.

20. Ibid., pg. E1.

21. Tramont Col. EC, *SUBJECT: Tri-Service Task Force (Appendix A)*, SGRD-UWZ-H, 7 December 1990.

22. Ibid.

23. Ibid.

24. World Medical Association, *Declaration of Helsinki IV*, 41st World Medical Assembly, Hong Kong, September 1989, Section II, Medical Research Combined with Professional Care (Clinical Research), Subheading 1.

25. Ibid., Section III, Non-Therapeutic Biomedical Research Involving Human Subjects (Non-clinical biomedical research), Subheading 4.

26. Wilson CE, *Memorandum for the Secretary of the Army, Secretary of the Navy, Secretary of the Air Force, SUBJECT: Use of Human Volunteers in Experimental Research*, Classification: TOP SECRET, Section 2, Subheading a. (1), 26 February 1953, (Downgraded to UNCLASSIFIED, 22 August 1975).

27. Ibid.

28. Tramont Col. EC, Tri-Service Vaccine Task Force, *(Appendix A)*, Classification: CONFIDENTIAL, 7 December 1990 (Declassified); Taylor Lt. Col. D, MEMORANDUM FOR: Head, Tri-Service Vaccine Task Force, *SUBJECT: Vaccines to Prevent Diarrhea and Typhoid Fever in Operation Desert Shield (Appendix B)*, Classification: CONFIDENTIAL, 7 December 1990 (Declassified); Sadoff Col. G, MEMORANDUM FOR: Head, Tri-Service Vaccine Task Force, *SUBJECT: Use of specific human immune globulin monoclonal antibody or anti-septic vaccines in Operation Desert Shield (Appendix D)*, Classification: CONFIDENTIAL, 7 December 1990, (Declassified); *Desert Shield Medical Issues Review and Ad Hoc Working Group, 28 Dec 1990, Agenda*, Classification: SECRET, (Declassified: 17 October 1996).

29. Berman Col. J, MEMORANDUM FOR: INTERESTED PARTIES, *SUBJECT: OPERATION DESERT SHIELD AND LEISHMANIASIS: MEMORANDUM OF FOURTH USAMRDC LEISHMANIASIS STEERING COMMITTEE MEETING*, SGRD-UWZ-P, 14 September 1990, Section 4, Subheading b., pg. 2.

30. Ibid., Section 2, pg. 1.

31. Ibid., Section 3, pg. 1.

32. Ibid., Section 2, pg. 1.

33. Ibid., Section 4, Subheading b., pg. 3.

34. Ibid.

35. Ibid.

36. Ibid., Section 4, Subheading b., pg. 2.

37. Ibid.

38. Informed Consent for Human Drugs and Biologics, *Determination that Informed Consent Is Not Feasible*, 55 Fed. Reg. 52,814, 52814 (21 December 1990) (codified at 21 C.F. R. pt. 50).

39. Exceptions from General Requirements, 21 C.F.R. § 50.23.(d), 18 December 1990.

40. Ibid., Section 4.

41. Klenke *[Secret Working Papers: Medical Biological Defense (07/12//88–02/07/92), DASG-HCD]*, pg. 23; *The Washington Post*, "FDA Consents to Use of Unapproved Drugs on U.S. Desert Troops," 22 December 1990.

42. *The New York Times*, "The Ethics of Troops Vaccination," 16 January 1991, at A22, col. 1 (editorial).

43. Klenke, pg. 18; Schwarzkopf Gen HN, *MSG 061400Z Dec 90, UNCINCENT/ CCC/, SUBJECT: Personal For* (06 December 1990, 2 p.m. Greenwich Mean Time).

44. Smyth *(J–4 Biodefense Log)*, pg. 17: "Eyes Only" message from CINC to CJCS expressing concern about "who" and "when" to immunize.

45. Ibid.

46. Ibid., pg. 20—"J5 received Department of State issued paper, 'Managing Fall-out from British BW Inoculations.' Paper highlights courses of action available to U.S. which range from consultation with other governments and press lines, dealing with other coalition armies, stockpiling medicines for use by civilian, surplus British Anthrax [sic] vaccine, and protection for children."

47. Klenke, pg. 7; Smyth (J–4 Biodefense Log), pg. 13.

48. Klenke, pg. 18.

49. Ibid.

50. Smyth (J–4 Biodefense Log), pg. 12.

51. Ibid., pg. 17.

52. Defense Intelligence Agency Memorandum, *Results and Analysis of Iraqi Serum Samples*; Klenke, pg. 21.

53. Ministry of Defence, *Background to the Use of Medical Countermeasures to Protect British Forces During the Gulf War (Operation Granby)*, Section 42, pg. 8, http://www.mod.uk/policy/gulfwar/inro/mcm.htm. There is some conflict over how long "full immunity is conferred with the licensed U.K. anthrax vaccine. Although the Ministry of Defence background paper states in several places that full immunity occurs only after '32 weeks' Annex A says the fourth dose is administered at 6 months."

54. Smyth, pg. 9—"Chairman expressed concern about timing requirements to vaccinate in-theater US forces as soon as Anthrax vaccine quantities permit". (17 October 1990)

55. Klenke, pg. 19—"BW defense issues raised by Gen Powell to President, but no feedback provided."

56. Dr. Jack Melling, formerly of Britain's Center for Applied Microbiological Research, says Iraq tried to acquire the Ames strain from CAMR prior to the war. Melling says he turned them down.

57. *Operation Desert Shield: Response to the Biological Warfare (BW) Threat*, Draft Document, 20 August 1990, Distribution Limited, Section V, pg. 6—"As with all vaccines, the degree of protection is proportional to the challenge dose; vaccine-induced protection is undoubtedly overwhelmed by extremely high spore challenge"; Tomlinson Col. P. Eng Maj. R., *Information Paper, SUBJECT: Medical Defense Against Anthrax (U)*, 28 October 1990, SGPS-PSP, Classification: SECRET—"There is a Food and Drug Administration (FDA) licensed vaccine for AX. [Redacted] Side effects are similar to but less severe than a typhoid shot. This protection *can be overcome with a large exposure to AX* such as near the source of dissemination" [italics mine].

58. Interview with Dr. Edmund Tramont (U.S. Army Colonel retired and former Chairman of Project Badger), 1999.

59. Johnson-Winegar A, Department of the Army, U.S. Army Medical Research and Development Command, Fort Detrick, Maryland 21702–5012, *MEMORANDUM FOR RECORD, SUBJECT: Trip Report to England (U)*, Section 1, subheading a., 30 January 1991—"The [redacted] started administration of anthrax vaccine in AOR (Area of Re-

sponsibility) the week of 4 January 1991. Vaccine is being given simultaneously with per-tussis vaccine." The sole U.K.-licensed manufacture, Wellcome could only provide 80,000 doses. For this war, Britain would have to bend its health regulations too. To cover the shortfall, the Ministry of Defence would procure another 50,000 doses of the French-made pertussis vaccine, Vaxicoq Adsorbé, from Institut Merieux in Lyon.

60. Johnson-Winegar A, *Letter to Dr. Peter C. B. Turnbull*, PHLS Centre for Applied Microbiological Research, Division of Biologics, Porton Down, Salisbury. United Kingdom, dated 26 November 1990. Johnson-Winegar A, MEMORANDUM FOR RECORD, SUBJECT: Trip Report to England, SGRD-PLA, Department of the Army, U.S. Army Medical Research Development Command, Fort Detrick, Frederick, Maryland 21702–5012, 30 January 1991, pg. 1.

61. Johnson-Winegar A, *Letter to Dr. Peter C. B. Turnbull*.

62. Turnbull PCB, Quinn CP, Hewson R, Stockbridge MC, Melling J, Protection conferred by microbially-supplemented UK and purified PA vaccines, *Salisbury Medical Bulletin: Proceedings of the International Workshop on ANTHRAX*, Winchester, England, April 11–13, 1989, pg. 90.

63. Ibid.

64. Ibid., pgs. 90, 91.

65. Ibid.

66. Ivins BE, Welkos S, Little SF, Knudson GM, Cloned Protective Activity and Progress in Development of Improved Anthrax Vaccines, *Salisbury Medical Bulletin: Proceedings of the International Workshop on ANTHRAX*, Winchester, England, April 11–13, 1989, pgs. 86–88.

67. Ibid., pg. 88.

68. Ibid. "Three doses of MDPH-PA, or one or two doses of Tri-Mix + PA provided complete protection."

69. Ibid.

70. Kussman Col. MJ, *SUBJECT: Minutes of the Operation Desert Shield Medical Issues Working Group*, SGPS-CP, 27 December 1990, Office of the Surgeon General, Room 691, pg. 2.

71. Ibid. "3. Recommendations: b. Pursue Typhoid TY21A vaccines for its long term viability but do not pursue for use in Operation Desert Shield. c. Research availability and cost of Hepatitis A vaccine. Continue to rely on ISG in Saudi Arabia. When available and efficacy demonstrated, use Hepatitis A for predeployment (2 doses) and for recruits."

72. Ibid. "3. a. Research availability, shelf life, etc. on the oral cholera vaccine and present to BG Blanck and TSG."

73. Ibid. "3. Use centoxin for prophylaxis as recommended by tri-service committee."

74. Brandt WE, MEMORANDUM FOR Commander, U.S. Army Medical Research and Development Command, ATTN: SGRD-ZB, Fort Detrick, Maryland, Frederick, Maryland 21702–5012, *SUBJECT: Return of Unused Vaccine and Investigational New*

Drugs from Saudi Arabia, 1 April 1991—"1. Supplies of Anthrax Vaccine and Investigational New Drugs (INDs) Botulinal Toxoid (Pentavalent), BB-IND 3723, Botulism Antitoxin f(ab')2, BB-IND 3703, Centoxin, BB-IND 3747, and Ribavirin, BB-IND 16,666, were escorted to the 47th MEDSOM in Saudi Arabia and are currently stored under controlled refrigerated conditions. The IND products were sent to Saudi Arabia for administration under IND protocols."

75. Kussman, pg. 2.

76. Klenke, pg. 25. "Anthrax immunization starts."

77. Johnson-Winegar, Letter to Dr. P. C. B. Turnbull, 26 November 1990.

Chapter Six

1. From an initial series of interviews with Dr. Gregory V. Dubay (U.S. Army Reserves, ret.) in the spring of 1999.

2. Interview with Dubay, 7 June 2004.

3. From Dubay Letter to Author dated 10 June 2004. The italics and underline beneath the word "secret" are Dubay's.

4. Interviews with Dubay, spring 1999.

5. Ibid.

6. Dubay, Gregory V, Compensation and Pension Exam Report, Tuskegee, Final, For MENTAL DISORDERS Exam, VA Form 2507, August 10, 1995, Examining Provider: Del Castillo, MD.

7. Ibid.

8. Interview with Dubay, 7 June 2004.

9. Interview with Dubay, 10 June 2004.

10. *MEMORANDUM TO THE UNIT COMMANDERS, SUBJECT: INFLUENZA/ISG VACCINE*, Major Sharee Smith, Headquarters 62nd Medical Group, APO, New York 09657; there were at least seven clinics immunizing troops in the Dharhan/Dammam area: Cement City Clinic; White Hospital Clinic; Batar Clinic; Dragon Base Clinic; Expo Center Clinic; Sunshine (Rainier) Clinic; Guardian City Clinic.

11. *DEPARTMENT OF THE ARMY, MEDICAL GROUP (PROVISIONAL), APO NY 09616, AFFL-HQ; SUBJECT: DOCUMENTATION GUIDELINES FOR ANTHRAX IMMUNIZATION, 9 JUL 91*: "1. Soldiers in the Southwest Asia Theater of Operations during the time frame 1 January through 16 February 1991 were ordered to receive the anthrax immunization *which was the only "secret" immunization given in theater* [italics mine]. Some soldiers received one immunization; others received a second injection (A1, A2)."

12. Rudicell's recollections are consistent with the declassified biomedical defense documents from Desert Storm; these documents, such as the one referenced in the previous footnote, number "xi," only refer to plans to give soldiers a maximum of two shots. Giving only one or two shots also is consistent with Greg Dubay's account of being told

he was giving out a "new vaccine," which was the "best the Army had available." Bruce Ivins and his Fort Detrick colleagues alleged that they were getting as much protection in guinea pigs with one shot as they got with three shots of the licensed vaccine. Some have reported plans to give troops a third anthrax shot; this was not done according to these accounts because there was insufficient time to do this before the war ended. In some cases, there was plenty of time. The licensed anthrax vaccine protocol called for boosters administered at two-week intervals. For those soldiers who received their initial shot in the first week of January there was more than enough time to get the third booster before the end of the hostilities ceased on February 28, 1991. In still other cases, such as Major Greg Dubay's, the shot intervals were way off; according to the entries in his WHO immunization card, the interval between his two shots was six weeks (A1–01/13/91 and A2–02/27/91).

13. *Certificate of Release or Discharge from Active Duty* for "RUDICELL, JAMES PATRICK," DD Form 214, Nov. 88, Section 18: "SERVICE IN QUWAIT [*sic*] DATES GIVEN 910415–910416 (1991 April 15th to 1991 April 16th), 910421–910502, 910525–910601, 910704–910706 // NOTHING FOLLOWS."

14. Berkow R, Editor-in-Chief, *The Merck Manual of Diagnosis and Therapy, Sixteenth Edition*, Merck Research Laboratories, Merck & Co., Inc., Rahway, NJ, 1992, pg. 1318.

15. Ibid.

16. Ibid.

17. Ibid., pg. 1319.

18. Cotran R, et al., *Robbins Pathologic Basis of Disease, 5th Edition*, W. B. Saunders Company, A Division of Harcourt Brace, Philadelphia, 1994, pg. 199.

19. Ibid.

20. Ibid.

21. Hardegree Dr. MC, Director, Officer of Vaccines Research and Review, Center for Biologics Evaluation and Research, *LETTER TO: Mr. Thomas S. Clement, Organon Teknika Corporation, Durham, North Carolina*, 21 August 1998; The Department of Health and Human Services licensed the first BCG vaccine to Organon Teknika Corporation in 1990. You can get this information from the FDA or from the website of the National Network for Immunization Information at *www.immunizationinfo/org/vaccine-Info/vaccine_detail.cfv?id=18*

22. Email from Lt. Mary Jones (USN ret.), 07:32:07, 1 June 2004: Mary discusses this with her mother again, who, through a fog of chemo and radiation treatments, starts to remember a bit more about the circumstances in which she was immunized with BCG vaccine. "She told me that when she received the shots it was a controlled study," says Mary. "They were divided into three groups. Some got the shots, some got a placebo."

23. Email from Lt. Mary Jones (USN ret.), 08:42:16, 1 June 2004; Mary Jones answer my question in email later—the day that I asked it on the phone. "I knew nothing about experimental vaccines [in the Persian Gulf]," she wrote.

24. Berkow et al., pg. 2437.

25. Interview with Ardie Siefken, June 2004.

26. Asa, Dr. D. K., *LETTER TO: Maj. Michel J. Roy, M.D., Clinical Director, GWHC, WRAMC, RE: Col. Herbert J. Smith*, 1 November 1995.

27. Ibid.

28. Strickland R, *Chronological Record of Medical Care for Col. Herbert J. Smith*, Walter Reed Army Medical Center, 13-23 September 1991.

29. *MEDICAL EVALUTION FOR COL. HERBERT SMITH*, USA, AUGUST 1, 1995, MAJ Michael J. Roy MD, MPH, Clinical Director GWHC, WRAMC, pg. 1: "Col. Smith requests a medical board at this time, having down the CCEP (Comprehensive Clinical Evaluation Program for Persian Gulf War Veterans) last year. He is now 55 years old. Diagnoses rendered during the CCEP were: 1. Somatization Disorder; 2. Seborrheic dermatitis; 3. Seborrheic keratosis." American Psychiatric Association: *Diagnostic and Statistical Manual of Mental Disorders, Fourth Edition,* Text Revision (DSM-IV-TR). Washington, DC: American Psychiatric Association, 2000, pgs. 486–489.

30. Op. Cit., Asa Letter, pg. 2.

31. Ibid.

32. Ibid.

33. Cotran, pg. 202; "Low levels of serum complement and immunoglobulins in the glomeruli further support the immune complex nature of the disease [systemic lupus erythematosus]." Kelley WN, Harris ED, Ruddy S, Sledge C, *Textbook of Rheumatology,* 4th *Edition, Volume I,* W. B. Saunders, Philadelphia, 1993, pg. 197; Under the Heading: SYSTEMIC LUPUS ERYTHEMATOSUS: "Depressions of complement levels are associated with increased severity of disease, especially renal disease. Serial observations often reveal decreased levels preceding clinical exacerbations; reductions in C4 occur before reductions of C3, other components, and total hemolytic complement activity. Authors of studies with more detailed clinical characterizations of patients and longer follow-ups tend to conclude that complement determinations are useful adjuncts for management of patients with known SLE and that they are useful tools in the diagnosis of this disease."

34. Kuby J, *Immunology (Third Edition),* W. H. Freeman and Company, New York, 1997, pg. 335; Virella G (Editor), *Medical Immunology, Fifth Edition, Revised and Expanded,* Marcel Dekker, Inc., New York, 2001, pgs. 135–160.

35. Kuby, pg. 342.

36. Task Force on DSM-IV, *Diagnostic and Statistical Manual of Mental Disorders, Fourth Edition, Text Revision, DSM-IV-TR,* American Psychiatric Association, Washington, DC, 2000, pg. 487; at the time of Roy's diagnosis, he would have been consulting the DSM-III (third edition).

37. Berkow, pg. 1590.

38. Ibid., pg. 488.

39. Ibid., pg. 486.

40. Ibid.

41. Asa DK, Letter addressed TO WHOM IT MAY CONCERN, 1 November 1995.

42. Chin BB, Lin K, *Consultation Report, The Johns Hopkins Hospital, Department of Radiology and Radiological Science, 2190 BRAIN PERFUSION – SPECT*, 24 June 1997, pg. 1.

43. Wear JD, Adjudication Officer, *Rating Decision, VA For 22–5490*, Department of Veterans Affairs, Regional Office, Federal Building, 31 Hopkins Plaza, Baltimore, MD 21201.

44. Dey HM, *Nuclear Medicine Report*, West Haven VA Medical Center, 5/23/95; "The patient is a 55 YO man with suspected multiple chemical toxicity syndrome and progressive neurologic dysfunction."

45. Rating Decision for Herbert J. Smith, Department of Veterans Affairs, Baltimore Regional Office, 09/02/97, pg. 1.

Chapter Seven

1. Brandt WE, *MEMORANDUM FOR RECORD, SUBJECT: Second Generation Anthrax Vaccine for Advanced Development*, 19 April 1991.

2. Ibid.; "1. Meeting in USAMRIID Commander's office chaired by COL. Williams, and attended by COL Friedlander, Dr. Dalrymple, and Dr. Brandt (USAMMDA). The purpose of the meeting was to determine the best candidate new anthrax vaccine that was ready for scale-up production in a GMP facility (Salk)."

3. *QUARTERLY REPORT, CONTRACT NO. DAMD17–88-C–8082, Project Order No.: 52–91-T Baculo/Anthrax Expression*, Principal Investigator, Alexis Shelokov, M.D., 1 October 1991, pg. 24.

4. *ACTION SUMMARY SHEET, Anthrax Contract, PRI, 28 August 1991*; "USAMRD [*sic*] requires a statement from us stating that funds are programmed in FY92 and FY93 in order to process the $15.4M contract with Program Resources, Inc. for the anthrax vaccine"; Department of Defense contract # *DAMD17-C–91–1086*.

5. Pentagon "TANK" briefing, Brigadier General Ronald R. Blanck, 13 September 1991, STATUS: Declassified.

6. Ibid.
"2. *NATIONAL CANCER INSTITUTE/PROGRAM RESOURCES, INC.*
CONTRACT FOR 'BEST EFFORT' FOR TWO YEARS
PROJECT 2 – [Redacted]
REQUIRES SEPARATE CONTRACT WITH MICHIGAN FOR POTENCY TEST, BOTTLING, LABELLING, AND STORAGE"

7. Ibid.
"*PROJECTED AVAILABILITY IN NEAR TERM*
(<FIVE YEARS)
RECOMBINANT ANTHRAX VACCINE"

8. Johnson-Winegar A, DEPARTMENT OF THE ARMY, U.S. Army Medical Research and Development Command, Fort Detrick, Frederick, MD 21702–5012, *MEMORANDUM FOR COMMANDER, U.S. Army Medical Materiel Development Activity, ATTN: SGRD-UMB (Dr. Brandt)*, Fort Detrick, Frederick, MD 21702–5009, *SUBJECT: Second Generation Anthrax Vaccine for Advanced Development*, 28 February 1992.

9. Ibid.

10. Personal communication with confidential U.S. government source.

11. Fumento M, "Operation Illness: Gulf War Syndrome," *Priorities Magazine*, 1994.

12. Ibid.

13. Schlesinger N, Baker DG, Schumacher Hr Jr., Persian Gulf War myalgia syndrome, *Journal of Rheumatology*, 1997 May;24(5): pg. 1019.

14. Berkow R, et al., *The Merck Manual*, Sixteenth Edition, Merck Research Laboratories, Rahway, N.J. 1992, pg. 1525.

15. *Fed Reg 1990;55:52*, pgs. 814–817; "Informed consent for human drugs and biologics; determination that informed consent is not feasible."

16. *Doe v. Sullivan, 756 F Supp. 12* (D.D.C. 1991); *Doe v. Sullivan, 938 F.2d 1370* (D.C. Cir. 1991).

17. Committee on Veterans' Affairs, United States Senate, 103rd Congress, 2nd Session, *Is Military Research Hazardous to Veterans' Health? Lessons Spanning Half a Century*, U.S. Government Printing Office, Washington, DC, 8 December 1994, pg. 35.

18. Ibid.

19. Committee on Banking, Housing, and Urban Affairs With Respect to Export Administration, 103rd Congress, 2nd Session, *U.S. Chemical and Biological Warfare-Related Dual Use Exports to Iraq and Their Possible Impact on the Health Consequences of the Persian Gulf War*, U.S. Government Printing Office, Washington, DC, 25 May 1995, pg. 135.

20. Kark P, *New Patient Evaluation – Second Opinion*, North Medical Center, Suite 4-J, 5100 West Taft Road, Liverpool, NY 13088, pg. 3; "Gait is spastic, and he is unable to tandem gait."

21. Factor SO, *Letter to Dr. Joseph Booth, M.D. from Dr. Stewart A. Factor*, Associate Professor of Neurology, The Riley Family Chair in Parkinson's Disease, The Albany Medical College, Department of Neurology, the Neil Hellman Medical Research Building, 47 New Scotland Avenue, Albany, NY 12208–3479, 9 May 1996.

22. Honnorat J, Trouillas P, Thivolet C, Aguera M, Belin MF, Autoantibodies to glutamate decarboxylase in a patient with cerebellar cortical atrophy, peripheral neuropathy, and slow eye movements, *Archives of Neurology*, 1995 May;52(5): pgs. 462–468.

23. In the four months I spent in Saudi Arabia and Iraq as a reporter with NBC News, I had not seen a single soldier, sailor, airman or marine wear a flea collar.

24. Straus SE et al., *Re: Subject Information, To: Subjects enrolled 93–1–0141, V5P13 vaccine trial*, Department of Health and Human Services, National Institutes of Health, Bethesda, MD 20892, 02/23/95, one page only.

25. Ibid.

26. Myers ML, Asbill, Junkin and Myers Chtd., 1615 New Hampshire Avenue, NW, Washington, DC 20009, Interrogatories, *Attachment to Claim for Damage, Injury or Death, Answer to No. 8 – Basis of Claim*, No Date, pg. 2.

27. Straus et al.

28. Myers, pg. 4; *SURGICAL PATHOLOGY REPORT & ADDENDUM [for Patient X]*, GEORGETOWN UNIVERSITY HOSPITAL, Department of Pathology, 3900 Reservoir Road, NW, Washington, DC 20007, 14 August 1997.

29. Beck FW, Whitehouse MW, Pearson CM, Improvements for consistently inducing experimental allergic encephalomyelitis (EAE) in rats: I. Without using mycobacterium, II. Inoculating encephalitogen into the ear, *Proceedings of the Society for Experimental Biology and Medicine*, 1976 March; 151(3): pgs. 615–622.

30. Yarkoni E, Rapp HJ, Tumor regression after intralesional injection of mycobacterial components emulsified in 2,6,10,15,19,23,-hexamethyl–2,6,10,14,18,22-tetracosahexaene (squalene), 2,6,10,15,19,23-hexamethyltetracosane (squalane), peanut oil, or mineral oil, *Cancer Research*, 1979 May; 39(5): pgs. 1518–1520.

31. Pyle S, Morein B, Bess JW, Jr., et al., Immune response to immunostimulatory complexes (ISCOMS) prepared from human immunodeficiency type virus type I (HIV–1) or the HIV –1 external envelope glycoprotein (gp120), *Vaccine*, 7, 1989, pgs. 465–473.

32. Edelman R, Tacket CO, Adjuvants, *International Reviews of Immunology*, 7(1): pg. 62; "In summary, HIV vaccine studies described have generally not been designed to measure the effect of the adjuvant or to make comparisons between adjuvants."

33. Salk J, Prospects for the control of AIDS by immunizing seropositive individuals, *Nature*, 1987 Jun 11–17;327(6122): pgs. 473–476; Redfield RR, Birx DL, Ketter N, Tramont E, Polonis V, Davis C, Brundage JF, Smith G, Johnson S, Fowler A, et al., A phase I evaluation of the safety and immunogenicity of vaccination with the recombinant gp 160 in patients with early human immunodeficiency virus infections, *The New England Journal of Medicine*, 1991 Jun 13;234(24): pgs. 1677–1684.

34. Straus SE, Corey L, Burke RL, Savarese B, Barnum G, Krause PR, Kost RG, Meier FL, Sekulovich R, Adair SF, Dekker CL, Placebo-controlled trial of vaccination with recombinant glycoprotein D of herpes simplex virus type 2 for Immunotherapy of genital herpes, *Lancet*, 1994 Jun 11;343(8911): pgs. 1460–1463.

35. Ibid., pg. 1463.

36. Lipman NS, Trudel LJ, Murphy JC, Sahali Y, Comparison of immune response potentiation and in vivo inflammatory effects of Freund's and Ribi adjuvants in mice, *Laboratory Animal Science*, 1992 April; 42(2): pg. 196; "Gross lesions were present in all mice immunized with an adjuvant but not with saline. The characteristics of the lesions were similar; however there were differences in severity (Table 2). Lesions were detectable at all time points in both adjuvant treatment groups. Distinction in severity over time could not be assessed as the number of animals euthanized at each time point was small. Lesions consisted of white plaques approximately 1 to 3 mm in diameter located on the peritoneal surface of the abdominal wall, diaphragm, and abdominal organs. Fi-

brous adhesions were present which adhered abdominal organs to one another and the body wall. Gross lesions were more severe in the Freund's immunized mice as compared with mice immunized with Ribi. Histologically, the Ribi and Freund's immunized mice had lesions consisting of multiple foci of granulomatous inflammation. Lesions were restricted to the serosal surface of abdominal organs, diaphragm, peritoneal lining, and mesentery with minimal parenchymal involvement. The lesions were characterized by the accumulation of lipid vacuoles of various sizes surrounded by an infiltrate composed predominately of mononuclear cells consisting of lymphocytes, macrophages, and small clusters of polymorphonuclear leukocytes. Fibrous connective tissue was interspersed in the inflammatory lesions resulting in adhesions. No gross lesions were present in the mice immunized with saline and immunogen only and histologic lesions were mild."

37. For a more technical discussion of granulomas you can consult the following publications, or any other textbook on pathology or immunology of your choice:

Cotran R, et al., *Robbins Pathologic Basis of Disease,* 5th *Edition*, W. B. Saunders Company, A Division of Harcourt Brace, Philadelphia, 1994, pgs. 80–84; and

Cruse JM, Lewis RE, *Illustrated Dictionary of Immunology*, CRC Press, New York, 1995, pg. 124.

38. Lipman et al., pg. 196.

39. Leenaars PP, Hendriksen CF, Angula AF, Koedam MA, Claasen E, Evaluation of several adjuvants as alternatives to the use of Freund's adjuvants in rabbits, *Veterinary Immunology and Immunopathology*, 1991 March 4;40(3): pg. 226.

40. Ibid.

41. Ibid., pg. 236.

42. Ibid., pg. 240.

43. Yoshino S, Yoshino J, Recruitment of Pathogenic T Cells to Synovial Tissues of Rats Injected Intraarticularly with Nonspecific Agents, *Cellular Immunology*, 1994 Oct 15;158(2): pgs. 305, 307.

44. Keitel W, Couch R, Bond N, Adair S, Van Nest G, Dekker C, Pilot evaluation of influenza virus vaccine (IVV) combined with adjuvant, *Vaccine*, 1993;11(9): pg. 913.

45. Ibid.

46. Ibid.

47. Ibid., pg. 910.

48. Ibid.

49. Ibid.

50. Ibid.

51. Ibid., pg. 912, "ACKNOWLEDGEMENTS, Computational assistance was provided by the Clinfo project, funded by the Division of Research Resources of the NIH under grant no. RR03350."

52. Ibid., pg. 909. Letter to C. Dekker, M.D., Medical Director of Chiron Corporation, from Stephen E. Straus, M.D., Chief, Laboratory of Clinical Investigation, NIAID, dated 5 May 1992.

53. Bennett B, Check IJ, Olsen MR, Hunter RL, A comparison of commercially available adjuvants for use in research, *Journal of Immunological Methods*, 1992 Aug 30;153(1–2): pg. 40.

54. Letter from Dr. Stephen E. Straus, M.D. to Dr. Michael Sneller, M.D., Chairman NIAID CRS, Through: Dr. H. Clifford Lane, Clinical Director NIAID, Subject: Change in Consent Form, 6 July 1993.

55. Straus et al., *Memo RE: Subject Information*.

56. Myers, pg. 3.

57. Straus et al., *Lancet*, pg. 1462.

58. Ibid.

59. Ivins B, Fellows P, Pitt L, Estep J, Farchaus J, Friedlander A, Gibbs P, Experimental anthrax vaccines: efficacy of adjuvants combined with protective antigen against an aerosol Bacillus anthracis spore challenge in guinea pigs, *Vaccine*, 1995 Dec;13(18): pg. 1780.

Chapter Eight

1. Michael Burdette, Dr. Pamela Asa's nephew, eventually decided not to accept an appointment to the Air Force Academy.

2. The two officers were Major Craig W. Hendrix, Director of the Air Force HIV Program, and Lt. Col. R. Neal Boswell, Associate Chief of the Division of Medicine whose comments were quoted by officials with the Public Citizen Research Group to the Maryland State Legislature.

3. Peter Lurie, Sidney Wolfe: *Statement to the Maryland State Legislature*, Dec. 14, 1995.

4. Ibid.

5. The United States General Accounting Office, Report to the Honorable Jack Metcalf, House of Representatives, *GULF WAR ILLNESSES, Questions About the Presence of Squalene Antibodies in Veterans Can Be Resolved*, GAO/NSAID–99–5, March 1999, pg. 3.

6. Ibid., pg. 5.

7. Ibid.

8. Ibid., pg. 3.

9. There were five candidate adjuvants: (1) Ribi Adjuvant System (RAS), which contains squalene, (2) MF59, (3) QS21, (4) Alum and (5) Walter Reed Liposomes.

10. Mazzuchi JF, *OFFICE OF THE SECRETARY OF DEFENSE, HEALTH AFFAIRS, Washington D.C. 20301–1200, LETTER TO: Dr. Pamela B. Asa, P.O. Box 38151, Memphis, TN 38183, 8 February 1996*; "The investigation team, USAMRMD, and the independent experiment's findings concluded that the theory of Persian Gulf War Veterans' illnesses relationship to human adjuvant disease is generally unsupported."

11. Brandt WE, *SAIC REPORT TO: Commander, U.S. Army Medical Research and Material Command, ATTN: MCMR-PLD (Dr. Anna Johnson-Winegar), Fort Detrick,*

Frederick, MD 21702–5012, Subject: "Report on Gulf War Syndrome" by Dr. Pamela Asa, 27 November 1995.

12. Ibid.

13. Personal communication with Lieutenant General Ronald R. Blanck (U.S. Army ret.).

14. That is strictly a ballpark estimate from the Army sources. Some of the recombinant protein would be used in prototype vaccines, they said, and some in a special immunoassay to determine if someone had been exposed to *B. anthracis;* or if a person had been vaccinated against anthrax, it would help measure more precisely the level of antibody in that person's serum to protective antigen.

15. Asa PB, *Report on Gulf War Syndrome,* Personal Communication with Col. Edward Koenigsburg, M.D. (U.S.A.F.), 1995, pg. 4.

Keitel W, Couch R, Bond N, Adair S, Van Nest G, Dekker C, Pilot Evaluation of influenza virus vaccine (IVV) combined with adjuvant, *Vaccine,* 1993;11(9): pgs. 909–913.

Inselburg J, Bathurst IC, Kansopon J, Barr PJ, Rossan R, Protective immunity induced in Aotus monkeys by recombinant SERA protein of Plasmodium falciparum: further studies using SERA 1 and MF75.2 adjuvant, *Infection and Immunity,* 1993 May;61(5): pgs. 2048–2052.

Burke RL, Goldbeck C, Ng P, Stanberry L, Ott G, Van Nest G, The influence of adjuvant on the therapeutic efficacy of a recombinant genital herpes vaccine, *Journal of Infectious Diseases,* 1994 Nov;170(5): pgs. 1110–1119.

Haigwood N, Nara PL, Brooks E, Van Nest GA, Ott G, Higgins KW, Dunlop N, Scandella CJ, Eichberg JW, Steimer KS, Native but not denatured recombinant human immunodeficiency virus type I gp120 generate broad-spectrum neutralizing antibodies in baboons, *Journal of Virology,* 1992 Jan; 66(1): pgs. 172–182.

Valensi JP, Carlson JR, Van Nest GA, Systemic cytokine profiles in BALB/C mice immunized with trivalent influenza vaccine containing MF59 oil emulsion and other advanced adjuvants, *Journal of Immunology,* 1994;153(9): pgs. 4029–4039.

Choo QL, Quo G, Ralston R, Weiner A, Chien D, Van Nest G, Han J, Berger K, Thudium K, Kuo C, Kansopon J, McFarland J, Tabrizi A, Ching K, Moss B, Cummins LB, Houghton M, Muchmore E, Vaccination of chimpanzees against infection by the hepatitis C virus, *Proceedings of the National Academy of Sciences,* 1994 Feb 15;91(4): pgs. 1294–1298.

Kahn JO, Sinangil F, Baenziger J, Murcar N, Wynne D, Coleman RL, Steimer KS, Dekker CL, Chernoff D, Clinical and immunological responses to human immunodeficiency virus (HIV) Type 1SF2 gp120 subunit vaccine combined with MF59 adjuvant with or without muramyl tripeptide dipalmitoyl phosphatidylethanolamine in non-HIV-infected human volunteers, *Journal of Infectious Diseases,* 1994 Nov;170(5): pgs. 1288–1291.

Haigwood N, et al., Mechanisms for the generation of homologous and heterologous neutralizing antibodies in primates immunized with recombinant HIV SF2 gp120, *Vaccines,* 1992;92: pgs. 143.

Van Nest G, et al., Advanced adjuvant formulations for use with recombinant subunit vaccines, *Vaccines*, 1992;92: pgs. 57.

16. Ibid.

17. Ibid.

18. Weissburg RP, Berman PW, Cleland JL, Eastman D, Farina F, Frie S, Lim A, Mordenti J, Nguyen TT, Peterson MR, Characterization of the MN gp120 HIV-1 vaccine: antigen binding to alum, *Pharmaceutical Research*, 1995 Oct;12(10): pgs. 1439–1446.

19. Committee on Banking, Housing, and Urban Affairs With Respect to Export Administration, 103rd Congress, 2nd Session, *U.S. Chemical and Biological Warfare-Related Dual Use Exports to Iraq and Their Possible Impact on the Health Consequences of the Persian Gulf War*, U.S. Government Printing Office, Washington, D.C., 25 May 1994, pg. 1.

20. Ibid.

21. Ibid.

22. Ibid., pg. 5.

23. Ibid., pg. 2.

24. Haley RW, Kurt TL, Self-reported exposure to neurotoxic chemical combinations in the Gulf War. A cross-sectional epidemiologic study, *JAMA*, 1997 Jan 15;277(3): pgs. 231–237.

25. Walpole RD, Rostker B, *Modeling the Chemical Warfare Agent Release at the Khamisiyah Pit (U)*, Central Intelligence Agency, Department of Defense, 4 September 1997, pg. 2; *http://www.cia.gov/cia/reports/gulfwar/555/425055597.html*.

26. Ibid., pg. 17.

27. Committee on Government Reform and Oversight, 105th Congress, 1st Session, *GULF WAR VETERANS' ILLNESSES: VA, DOD CONTINUE TO RESIST STRONG EVIDENCE LINKING TOXIC CAUSES TO CHRONIC HEALTH EFFECTS*, 7 November 1997.

28. Fumento M, Gulf Lore Syndrome, Why are the Gulf War vets getting sick? You won't find out by reading The New York Times or USA Today, *Reason Magazine*, March 1997.

29. CBWInfo.com.

30. "Subclinical" refers to dosages that do not cause observable symptoms of disease or injury.

31. *http://www.cnn.com/SPECIALS/2001/gulf.war/facts/gulfwar/*

32. Fukuda K, Nisenbaum R, Stewart G, Thompson WW, Robin K, Washko RM, Noah DL, Barrett DH, Randall B, Herwaldt BL, Mawle AC, Reeves WC, Chronic multisymptom illness affecting Air Force veterans of the Gulf War, *JAMA*, 1998 Sept 16;280(11): pgs. 981–988.

33. Defense Intelligence Agency, *SUBJ; IIR 6 807 0058 94/Belgian Sailors Show No Signs of Persian Gulf Syndrome*, Department of Defense, 18 December 2003, pgs. 1–3.

34. The Staff of U.S. News and World Report, *Triumph Without Victory: The Unreported History of the Persian Gulf war*, Times Books, a Division of Random House, Inc., New York, 1992, Map on pg. 289.

35. Ibid.

36. Defense Intelligence Agency (DIA), *Gulf War Syndrome as an Intelligence Question*, filename: 0191pgv.00d.

37. One Army private received a Bronze Star and a Purple Heart for experiencing burns when he searched certain bunkers. This injury was the only one consistent with chemical weapons exposure; in this case, a "blister" agent (e.g., dusty mustard), as opposed to nerve agent. The DIA report notes, however, that "advanced laboratory analysis of his flak jacket, shirt, the swab used to clean his wound, subsequent urinalysis, and a subsequent reexamination of the bunker, all cast considerable doubt that the burns were the results of contact with a CW agent."

38. Fukuda, 981-988.

39. Ibid., pg. 981.

40. Ibid., pg. 985.

41. CDC, Department of Health and Human Services, Emergency Preparedness & Control, *NIOSH Emergency Response Card, Nerve Agent: Sarin, http://www.bt.cdc.gov/ agent/sarin/erc107–44–8.asp.*

42. Ibid.

43. Ibid.

44. DIA, *Gulf War Syndrome as an Intelligence Question.*

45. Sekijima Y, Morita H, Shindo M, Okudera H, Shibata T, Rinsho Shinkeigaku, [A case of severe sarin poisoning in the sarin attack in Matsumoto—one-year follow-up of clinical findings, and laboratory data], *Rinsho Shinkeigaku*, 1995 Nov;35(110): pgs. 1241–1245. Yokoyama K, Yamada A, Mimura N, Clinical profiles of patients with sarin poisoning after the Tokyo subway attack, *American Journal of Medicine*, 1996 May;100(5): pg. 586. Okumura T, Takasu N, Ishimatsu S, Miyanoki S, Mitsuhashi A, Kumada K, Tanaka K, Hinohara S, Report on 640 victims of the Tokyo subway sarin attack, *Annals of Emergency Medicine*, 1996 Aug;28(2): pgs. 223–224. Nakajima T, Ohta S, Morita H, Midorikawa Y, Mimura S, Yanagisawa N, Epidemiological study of sarin poisoning in Matsumoto City, Japan, *Journal of Epidemiology*, 1998 Mar;8(1): pgs. 33–41.

46. Morita H, Yanagisawa N, Nakajima T, Shimizu M, Hirabayashi H, Okudera H, Nohara M, Midorikawa Y, Mimura S, Sarin poisoning in Matsumoto, Japan, *Lancet*, 1995 Jul 29;346(8970): pgs. 290–293. Ohbu S, Yamashina A, Takasu N, Yamaguchi T, Murai T, Nakano K, Matsui Y, Mikami R, Sakurai K, Hinohara S, Sarin poisoning on Tokyo subway, *Southern Medical Journal*, 1997 Jun;90(6): pgs. 587–593. Suzuki J, Kohno T, Tsukagosi M, Furuhata T, Yamazaki K, Eighteen cases exposed to sarin in Matsumoto, Japan, *Internal Medicine*, 1997 Jul;36(7): pgs. 466–470. Nakajima T, Ohta S, Fukushima Y, Yanagisawa N, Sequelae of sarin toxicity at one and three years after exposure in Matsumoto, Japan, *Journal of Epidemiology*, 1999 Nov;9(5): pgs. 337–343.

47. DIA, *Gulf War Syndrome as an Intelligence Question.* Nasiriyah is approximately 100 miles northwest of Kuwait's northern border.

48. DIA, *Gulf War Syndrome as an Intelligence Question.*

49. Defense Intelligence Agency, *SUBJECT: Gulf War Health Issue; Evidence against use of chemical or biological warfare (CBW) during Desert Storm*, PURPOSE: To provide the Secretary of Defense the basis of DIA's assessment that no chemical or biological weapons were used during Desert Storm, and are therefore not the cause of the Gulf War Mystery Illness, Filename: 0614rpt.00.

50. Committee on Veterans' Affairs, United States Senate, 103rd Congress, 2nd Session, *Is Military Research Hazardous to Veterans' Health? Lessons Spanning Half a Century*, U.S. Government Printing Office, Washington, D.C., 8 December 1994, pg. 35.

51. Landsteiner K, *The Specificity of Serological Reactions*, Revised Edition, Harvard University Press, Cambridge, MA, 1946, pgs. 156–174.

52. Beck FW, Whitehouse MW, Pearson CM, Improvements for consistently inducing experimental allergic encephalomyelitis (EAE) in rats: I. Without using mycobacterium. II. Inoculating encephalitogen into the ear, *Proceedings for the Society of Experimental Biology and Medicine*, 1976 Mar;151(3): pgs. 615–622. Smialek M, Gajkowska B, Ostrowski RP, Piotrowski P, Experimental squalene encephaloneuropathy in the rat, *Folia Neuropathologica*, 1997;35(4), pgs. 262–264. Gajkowska B, Smialek M, Ostrowski RP, Piotrowski P, Frontzcak-Baniewicz M, The experimental squalene encephaloneuropathy in the rat, *Experimental and Toxicologic Pathology*, 1991 Jan;51(1): pgs. 75–80.

53. Tenenbaum SA, Rice JC, Espinoza LR, Cuellar ML, Plymale DR, Sander DM, Williamson LL, Haislip AM, Gluck OS, Tesser JR, Nogy L, Stribrny KM, Bevan JA, and Garry RF, Use of Antipolymer Antibody Assay in Recipients of Silicone Breast Implants, the *Lancet*, 1997 Feb 15;349 (9050): pgs. 449–454.

54. Garry RF, Witte MS, Gottlieb AA, Elvin-Lewis M, Gottlieb MS, Witte CL, Alexander SS, Cole WR, Drake WL Jr., Documentation of an AIDS Virus Infection in the United States in 1968, *JAMA*, 1988 Oct. 14;260(14), pg. 2085–2087.

55. Ibid., pg. 2086.

56. Alving CR, Wassef NM, Potter M, Antibodies to cholesterol: biological implication of antibodies to lipids, *Current Topics in Microbiology and Immunology*, 1996;210: pgs. 181–186.

57. Angella M: *Letter to the Lancet*, 1997 April 19;vol. 349, 1171–1172.

58. Edlavitch SA et al: *Letters to the Lancet*, 1997 April 19;vol. 349, 1170–1173.

59. Author interview with Dr. Robert F. Garry. Tenenbaum SA, Rice JC, Espinoza LR, Garry RF, Author's Reply, the *Lancet*, 1997 April 19;349, pgs. 1172–1173.

60. Asa PB, Cao Y, Garry RF [Department of Microbiology and Immunology, Tulane Medical School, 1430 Tulane Avenue, New Orleans, La. 70112], Antibodies to Squalene in Gulf War Syndrome, *Experimental and Molecular Pathology*, 2000 Feb;68(1): pg. 60.

61. Ibid.

62. Ibid.

63. Squalene's proven link to lupus would not be established until 2003 by the University of Florida School of Medicine in Gainesville. Satoh M, Kuroda Y, Yoshida H,

Behney KM, Mizutani A, Akaogi J, Nacionales DC, Lorenson TD, Rosenbauer RJ, Reeves WH (Division of Rheumatology and Clinical Rheumatology, Department of Medicine, University of Florida, Gainesville), Induction of lupus autoantibodies by adjuvants, *Journal of Autoimmunity*, 2003 Aug;21(1): pgs. 1–9. Kuroda Y, Akaogi J, Nacionales DC, Wasdo SC, Szabo NJ, Reeves WH, Satoh M (Division of Rheumatology and Clinical Immunology, Department of Medicine, University of Florida, Gainesville), Distinctive Patterns of Autoimmune Response Induced by Different Types of Mineral Oil, *Toxicological Sciences*, 2004 Apr;78(2): pgs. 222–228. Kuroda Y, Akaogi J, Nacionales DC, Wasdo SC, Szabo NJ, Reeves WH, Satoh M (Division of Rheumatology and Clinical Immunology, Department of Medicine, University of Florida, Gainesville), Distinctive Patterns of Autoimmune Response Induced by Different Types of Mineral Oil, *Toxicological Sciences*, 2004 Apr;78(2): pgs. 222–228. Carlson BC, Jannson AM, Larsson A, Bucht A, Lorentzen JC [Department of Medicine, Karolinska Institutet, Stockholm, Sweden], The endogenous adjuvant squalene can induce a chronic T-cell-mediated arthritis in rats, *American Journal of Pathology*, 2000 Jun;156(6): pgs. 2057–2065. Beck FW, Whitehouse MW, Pearson CM [Division of Rheumatology, Department of Medicine, University of California School of Medicine, Los Angeles, California], Improvements for consistently inducing experimental allergic encelphalomyelitis (EAE) in rats: I. without using mycobacterium. II. inoculating encephalitogen into the ear, *Proceedings of the Society for Experimental Biology and Medicine* (1976) Mar;151(3): pgs. 615–622.

Chapter Nine

1. Rodriguez P, Anti-HIV Mix Found in Gulf Veterans, *The Washington Times*, August 8, 1997.

2. Rodriguez P, Sickness and Secrecy, *Insight on the News*, August 25, 1997.

3. Ibid.

4. Rodriguez P, Gulf War Mystery and HIV, *Insight on the News*, October 16, 1997.

5. The Department of Defense has declassified many of its biomedical-defense documents from Desert Shield/Desert Storm and they can be found at the following web address: *http://www.gulflink.osd.mil/*; *MEMORANDUM FROM: CDRFORSCOM, Fort McPherson, Georgia, TO: AIG 757, AIG 7473, AIG 9169, AIG 9879, AMRF//SUBJ: MEDICAL RECORDS AND ROSTERS RELATED TO VACCINATION AGAINST BIOLOGICAL WARFARE (BW) AGENTS//*, 19 June 1991, pg. 2; "For anthrax vaccine, medical personnel may have recorded the shot as quote: Anthrax, A Vaccination, A-Vacc, A-Vax (Unquote) or something similar." Bussey FN (Major General U.S. Army Medical Command, Deputy Surgeon General), Department of the Army, Office of the Surgeon General, 5109 Leesburg Pike, Falls Church, VA 22081–3288, SGPA-PSP (40), *MEMORANDUM FOR: SEE DISTRIBUTION, SUBJECT: Medical Records and Rosters Related To Vaccination Against Biological Warfare Agents*, 21 May 1991, pg. 1, Section 5, "5. For the anthrax vaccine, medical personnel

may have records of it as 'Anthrax', 'A Vaccination', 'A-Vacc', 'A-Vax' or something similar." O'Brien T (CPT, MS), Department of the Army, 428th Medical Supply, Optical Maintenance Battalion, APT New York 09698, *MEMORANDUM FOR COMMANDER 332ND MED BDE, ATTN: CAPT. RICHARDS, APT NY, SUBJECT: Apple Vaccine*, 29 May 1991, "1 A list of the soldiers who received the Apple Vaccine on February 22, 1991 is enclosed."

6. Dubay G, WHO immunization card.

7. Smith HJ, WHO immunization card.

8. Czerwinski J, WHO immunization card. The date of alleged conversation with Brig. General Thomas Sikora: 8 January 1991.

9. These symptoms are listed for patients in the special log kept by Captain Richard Rovet while at Dover AFB. Rovet called this log "The Matrix."

10. Stauffer EC, *Clinical Summary*, Walter Reed Regional Vaccine Healthcare Center, 16 November 2001, pg. 1.

11. Ibid.

12. Ibid., pg. 2.

13. An official Air Force tape of General Roadman's presentation was once available on both VHS and CD-Rom. Since the discovery of squalene in the vaccine, Col. Lacklen says the Air Force has been trying to retrieve all the copies.

14. May JC: Memo to Neil Goldman, Ph.D., *Chemical Test Results for Michigan Department of Public Health, Anthrax Vaccine Adsorbed, Lots FAV020 AND FAV030*, FDA Center for Biologics Evaluation and Research, June 25, 1999.

15. Friedlander A, *rPA Anthrax Vaccine Candidate, Briefing to RADM Clinton*, United States Army Medical Research Institute of Infectious Diseases, USAMRMC, 22 May 2000, pg. 5.

16. Friedlander A, *Next Generation Anthrax Vaccine Candidate, Briefing to IPT*, United States Army Medical Research Institute of Infectious Diseases, USAMRMC, 28 June 2000, pg. 2; Ivins B, Fellows P, Pitt L, Estep J, Farchaus J, Friedlander A, Gibbs P, Experimental anthrax vaccines: efficacy of adjuvants combined with protective antigen against an aerosol Bacillus anthracis spore challenge in guinea pigs, *Vaccine*, 1995 Dec;13(18): pg. 1780; Ivins BE, Pitt ML, Fellows PF, Farchaus JW, Benner GE, Waag DM, Little SF, Anderson GW Jr., Biggs PH, Friedlander AM, Comparative efficacy of experimental anthrax vaccine candidates against inhalation anthrax in rhesus macaques, *Vaccine*, 1998 Jul;16(11–12): pg. 1142.

17. Friedlander, pg. 8.

18. McBride BW, Mogg A, Telfer JL, Lever MS, Miller J, Turnbull PC, Baillie L, Protective efficacy of a recombinant protective antigen *Bacillus anthracis* challenge and assessment of immunological markers, *Vaccine*, 1998 May;16(8), pg. 811.

19. Johnson-Winegar A., Deputy Assistant to the Secretary of Defense for Chemical and Biological Defense, *Anthrax and Other Vaccines: Use in the U.S. Military, Joint Statistical Meeting 2001: Anthrax and Other Vaccines: Just the Stats*, sponsored by the Committee on Statisticians in Defense and National Security, Atlanta, 5 August 2001, pg. 15.

20. Yoshino S, Yoshino J [Rheumatology Unit, Royal Adelaide Hospital, Adelaide, SA5000, Australia], Recruitment of pathogenic T cells to synovial tissues of rats injected intraarticularly with nonspecific agents, *Cellular Immunology*, 1994 October 15;158(2): pgs. 305–313; Lorentzen JC [Department of Medicine, Karolinska Hospital, Karolinska Institutet, Stockholm, Sweden], Identification of arthritogenic adjuvants of self and foreign origin, *Scandinavian Journal of Immunology*, 1999 Jan;49(1): pgs. 45–50.

21. Beck FW, Whitehouse MW, Pearson CM [Division of Rheumatology, Department of Medicine, University of California School of Medicine, Los Angeles, California], Improvements for consistently inducing experimental allergic encephalomyelitis (EAE) in rats: I. without using mycobacterium. II. inoculating encephalitogen into the ear, *Proceedings of the Society for Experimental Biology and Medicine*, 1976 Mar;151(3): pgs. 615–622; Smialek M, Gajkowska B, Ostrowski RP, Piotrowski P [Department of Neuropathology and Laboratory of the Ultrastructure of the Nervous System, Medical Research Centre, Polish Academy of Sciences, Warszawa, Poland], Experimental squalene encephaloneuropathy in the rat, *Folia Neuropathologica*, 1997;35(4): pgs. 262–264; Gajkowska B, Smialek M, Ostrowski RP, Piotrowski P, Frontczak-Baniewicz M [The Laboratory of the Ultrastructure of the Nervous System, Medical Research Centre, Polish Academy of Sciences, 5 Pawinskiego Street, 02–106 Warsaw, Poland], The experimental squalene encephaloneuropathy in the rat, *Experimental and Toxicologic Pathology*, 1999 January; 5: pgs. 75–80.

22. Leenaars PP, Hendriksen CF, Angulo AF, Koedam MA, Claasen E [National Institute of Public Health and Environmental Protection (RIVM), P.O. Box 1, 3720 BA, Bilthoven, The Netherlands], Evaluation of several adjuvants as alternatives to the use of Freund's adjuvant in rabbits, *Veterinary Immunology and Immunopathology*, 1994 Mar;40(3): pgs. 225–241; Leenaars M, Koedam MA, Hendriksen CF, Claassen E [National Institute of Public Health and Environmental Protection (RIVM), Bilthoven, The Netherlands], Immune responses and side effects of five different oil-based adjuvants in mice, *Veterinary Immunology and Immunopathology*, 1998 Feb 27;61(2–4): pgs. 291–304; Leenaars PP, Koedam MA, Ester PW, Baumans V, Claassen E, Hendriksen CF [National Institute of Public Health and Environmental Protection (RIVM), P.O. Box 1, 3720 BA, Bilthoven, The Netherlands], Assessment of side effects induced by injection of different adjuvant/antigen combinations in rabbits and mice, *Laboratory Animals*, 1998 Oct;32(4): pgs. 387–406.

23. Keitel W, Couch R, Bond N., Adair S, Van Nest G, Dekker C [Baylor College of Medicine, Department of Microbiology and Immunology, One Baylor Plaza, Houston, TX 77030], Pilot evaluation of influenza virus vaccine (IVV) combined with adjuvant, *Vaccine* (1993);11(9): pgs. 909–913.

24. SRI stands for Stanford Research Institute. SRI International is a non-profit organization.

25. Prepared by a Tri-Service Task Force In Response to a Tasking from the Secretary of Defense Given on 3 October 1990, *Short Term Production of Anthrax Vaccine (S)*, Classification: SECRET, declassified 13 May 1999, U.S. Army Medical Research and

Development Command, Fort Detrick, Frederick, MD 21702–5012, 12 November 1990, pg. 2.

26. Lim P, Spanggord RJ, *LETTER TO: William Y. Ellis, Chief, Department of Chemical Information, Division of Experimental Therapeutics, Walter Reed Army Institute of Research*, Washington, DC, 7 May 1999, "The method sensitivity is ~0.7 nanogm squalene/10 microL injection, based on squalene in 2-propanol. . . We find no measurable amount of squalene in the vials. If any squalene were present, it would be less than 70 nanogrm per 0.5. milliL vaccine preparation, which volume is the label dose"; 0.5 milliL is the amount of anthrax vaccine in one dose.

27. May JC, Chief LAC, DMPQ, Del Grosso AV, Swartz L, Progar JJ, Department of Health and Human Services, Food and Drug Administration, DBER/OCBQ/DMPQ/LAC, HFM–673, 1401 Rockville Pike, Rockville, MD 20852, TO: Neil Goldman, HFM020, *SUBJECT: Chemical Test Results for Michigan Department of Public Health, Anthrax Vaccine Adsorbed, Lots FAV020 and FAV030*, 25 June 1999; Spanggord RJ, Wu B, Sun M, Lim P, Ellis WY, Development and application of an analytical method for the determination of squalene in formulations of anthrax vaccine adsorbed, *Journal of Pharmaceutical and Biomedical Analysis*, 2002 Jun;29(1–2): pgs. 183–193; SRI's newly stated detection limit was 140 parts per billion per 0.5 milliL of vaccine.

28. Sulpice JC, Ferezou J, Squalene isolation by JPLC and quantitative comparison by HPLC and GC, *Lipids*, 1984 Aug;19(8): pgs. 631–635.

29. The Senate Veterans' Affairs Committee's Special Investigation Unit began its inquiries into squalene in July 1997, which was before the appearance of the first article by Paul Rodriguez on squalene in the August 8, 1997 edition of *The Washington Times*. The Senate inquiry, then, was based on Pam Asa's direct contact with the Senate Veterans' Affairs Committee.

30. Committee on Veterans' Affairs, *United States Senate, Report of the Special Investigation Unit on Gulf War Illnesses*, One Hundred Fifth Congress, S. PRT. 105–39, Part I, Arlen Specter, Chairman, U.S. Government Printing Office, 1998, pg. 123.

31. Ibid.; SIU staff communication with the Food and Drug Administration, July 23, 1997.

32. Ivins BE, Welkos S, Recent Advances in the Development of an Improved Anthrax Vaccine, *European Journal of Epidemiology*, 1988 Mar;4(1): pg. 13: "There are several drawbacks to the human vaccine, however, including the need for numerous boosters, the apparent inability to protect guinea pigs against certain virulent strains of anthrax, and occasional local reactogenicity"; Little S, Knudson GB, Comparative Efficacy of *Bacillus anthracis* Live Spore Vaccine and Protective Antigen Vaccine against Anthrax in the Guinea Pig, *Infection and Immunity*, May 1986, 52 (2): pg. 510.

33. Ivins, pg. 1146: "Results of recent studies show that anthrax vaccines vary in their efficacy among different species. . . . A study in rhesus macaques demonstrated that immunization with AVA (Anthrax Vaccine Adsorbed) at 0 and 2 weeks protected them against an aerosol anthrax spore challenge for at least two years"; Ivins BE, Fellows PF, Pitt MLM., Estep JE, Welkos SL, Worsham PL, Friedlander AM, Efficacy of

a standard human anthrax vaccine against Bacillus anthracis aerosol spore challenge in rhesus monkeys, *Proceedings of the International Workshop on Anthrax, 19–21 September 1995, Winchester U.K., Salisbury Medical Bulletin, Special Suppl. No. 68,* 1990, pg. 89–91.

34. Chan KC, Gulf War Illnesses, Report to the Honorable Jack Metcalf, House of Representatives, *The Question About the Presence of Squalene Antibodies in Gulf War Veterans Can Be Resolved.* United States General Accounting Office, National Security and International Affairs Division, 29 March 1999, pgs. 1–25.

35. Ibid., pg. 5.

36. Friedlander, pg. 5, below is an excerpt from Col. Arthur Friedlander's briefing to RADM Clinton, regarding the NIH Working Group. NB: the dates:

NIH Working Group

NIH Meeting – Jan 1998

NIH Working Group formed Oct 1998 – NIH, FDA, and USAMRIID

Fast Track moving rPA into clinical trials

NIH collaboration with USAMRIID to manufacture pilot GMP lot of rPA

– NIH/USAMRIID Interagency Agreement, Sep 1999

– NBC-FCRDC Production Facility, fast track contract, Sep 1999

– Production to commence, summer 2000

37. Ivins, pg. 1146: "However, there were no data from non-human primates [read humans] that compared AVA with other anthrax vaccine candidates. The data from this study show that rhesus macaques are protected from a single immunization with either AVA, PA + Alhydrogel (Alum), Pa + QS–21 or PA + MPL (Monophosphoryl lipid A) in SLT (Squalene, Lecithin, Tween 80)."

38. Testimony of Lieutenant Richard Rovet before the Committee on Government Reform, House of Representatives, Subcommittee on National Security, Veterans Affairs, and International Relations, 106th Congress, First Session, *ANTHRAX VACCINE ADVERSE REACTIONS, Serial No. 106–131,* pg. 17.

39. Testimony of Captain Michele L. Piel before the Committee on Government Reform, House of Representatives, Subcommittee on National Security, Veterans Affairs, and International Relations, 106th Congress, First Session, *ANTHRAX VACCINE ADVERSE REACTIONS, Serial No. 106–131,* pg. 7.

40. Ibid., pg. 31.

41. Ibid., pg. 32.

42. Details of this incident were provided in 1999 by Captain Bill Law and in several subsequent interviews with Lt. Colonel Jay Lacklen.

43. Newcomb Col. EW, *III/DASG-ZH/DSN 223–5820, UNCLASSIFIED EXECUTIVE SUMMARY, (U) POSSIBLE ANTHRAX VACCINE RELATED REACTION (U) (DASG-ZH):*

"The Navy recently reported a possible adverse reaction to an anthrax vaccination. A 24-year old white male serving aboard the USS John F. McCain (DDG–56) in SWA received his 3rd anthrax vaccination on 17 May 1998. Within 24 hours, he began to develop generalized weakness progressing to the point where he was unable to walk up stairs within 48 hours. He was evacuated to Bahrain International Hospital where, following a series of tests, a diagnosis of Guillain-Barré Syndrome was made. He was treated appropriately and was subsequently evacuated to the Naval Medial Center San Diego, CA on 7 June 1998, where he continues to improve and is expected to make a full recovery and return to his ship. Guillain-Barré Syndrome (GBS) is an acute, sporadic, relatively rare disease wherein the body's own immune system is stimulated by an outside agent to attack the nervous system, specifically the myelin sheaths of nerves. Agents known to be associated with GBS include influenza vaccine (especially Swine flu), and have rarely been reported with other vaccines such as polio, rabies, typhoid and tetanus. It has not previously been reported with anthrax vaccine. In about two thirds of the cases, a mild infection (upper respiratory of G.I.) precedes the onset of GBS by 1–3 weeks. GBS is characterized by a rapid, symmetrical paralysis, to include respiratory paralysis, which typically resolves over a period of weeks but may persist for much longer times. Approximately 85% of patients make a full recovery, however, there is a mortality rate of 3–4%. I n this case, in the absence of any known preexisting infection or condition, the anthrax vaccine can not be ruled out as a possible cause of this sailor's disease. Because this is an isolated case and the first reportable adverse reaction in the 29-year history of the anthrax vaccine, it is recommended to continue with the DOD Anthrax Immunization Program and remain vigilant for any other reports of adverse reactions."

44. Martin-Allaire RJ, *Written Statement, Congressional Hearings, Anthrax Vaccine Immunization Program, House Government Reform and Oversight Committee, Chairman Shays Presiding,* 29 April 1999, pg. 1.

45. Ibid.

46. Plaisier MK, Associated Commission for Legislation, Food and Drug Administration, *LETTER TO: The Honorable Jack Metcalf, House of Representatives, Washington D.C., 20 March 2000,* pg. 2: "After an article appears in the May 1999 issue of Vanity Fair entitled 'The Pentagon's Toxic Secret,' CBER tested in its laboratories the two lots mentioned in the article (FAV020 and FAV030) for squalene. Three other anthrax lots (FAV038, FAV043, FAV047) and two other lots of bacterial vaccines (Wyeth Diphtheria and Connaught Tetanus) containing alum adjuvants were randomly selected for comparative purposes. Due to the inability to detect trace amounts of squalene parts per million, CBER developed a test to detect the substance in parts per billion. The trace amounts of squalene were determined by gas chromatography with flame ionization detection. The squalene content of the lots was determined to be in the low parts-per-billion and was comparable to levels determined in three other lots of anthrax vaccine and the other biological products that were tested."

47. Garrett L, Healthy Shot of Distrust/Military's Disclosures, decree on anthrax vaccine sparks criticism, *Newsday,* 4 May 1999.

48. Wallberg M, Weffer J, Harris RA, Vaccination with myelin oligodendrocyte glycoprotein adsorbed to alum effectively protects DBA/1 mice from experimental autoimmune encephalomyelitis, *European Journal of Immunology*, 2003 Jun;33(6): pgs. 1539–1547.

49. Butterworth T, *Anthrax Vaccine and Gulf War Syndrome, Vanity Scare*, STATS at George Mason University.

50. Straus SE, Corey L, Burke RL, Savarese B, Barnum G, Krause PR, Kost RG, Meier FL, Sekulovich R, Adair SF, Dekker CL, Placebo-controlled trial of vaccination with recombinant glycoprotein D of herpes simplex virus type 2 for immunotherapy of genital herpes, *Lancet*, 1994 Jun 11;343(8911): pgs. 1460–1463.

51. In February 1999, Dr. Lundberg was abruptly fired after serving as JAMA's editor for 17 years. Lundberg had published a survey the previous month that showed the majority of American college students did not regard oral-genital contacts as "sex." This article appeared in the midst of the national furor over whether or not President Clinton had had sex with White House intern Monica Lewinsky. In a highly criticized move, AMA Vice-President E. Anderson Ratcliffe Jr. accused Lundberg of "inappropriately and inexcusably interjecting *JAMA* into a major political debate [Clinton's impeachment trial] that has nothing to do with science or medicine."

Chapter Ten

1. Showalter E, *Hystories*, Columbia University Press, New York, 1997.

2. Office of Public Affairs News Service, *Illnesses of Gulf War Veterans, VA Fact Sheet*, Department of Veterans Affairs, Washington, DC 20420, April 2000, www.va.gov, pg. 1.

3. Ibid.

4. Ibid.

5. Straus SE, Bridging the gulf in war syndromes, the *Lancet*, 1999 Jan 16;353(9148): pg. 176.

6. CDC, Unexplained illness among Persian Gulf War veterans in an Air National Guard unit: August 1990-March 1995, *MMWR (Morbidity and Mortality Weekly Report)*, 1995;44: pgs. 443–447; Fukuda K, Nisenbaum R, Stewart G, Thompson WW, Robin L, Washko RM, Noah DL, Barrett DH, Randall B, Herwaldt BL, Mawle AC, Reeves WC,Chronic multisymptom illness affecting Air Force veterans of the Gulf War, *Journal of the American Medical Association*, 1998;280: pgs. 981–988.

7. Unwin C, Blatchley N, Coker W, Ferry S, Hotopf M, Hull L, Ismail K, Palmer I, David A, Wessely S, Health of UK servicemen who served in Persian Gulf War, the *Lancet*, 1999 Jan 16;353(9148); pg. 177.

8. Ibid.

9. Goss Gilroy, Inc., *Health Study of Canadian forces personnel involved in the 1991 conflict in the Persian Gulf, Vol. 1*, Prepared for Gulf War Illness Advisory Committee, Department of National Defence, Ottawa, Canada: Department of National Defence, 1998; (http://www.dnd.ca/menu/press/Reports/Health/healthy_study_e_vol1_TOC.htm).

10. Hotopf M, David A, Hull L, Ismail K, Unwin C, Wessely S, Role of vaccinations as risk factors for ill health in veterans of the Gulf war: cross sectional study, *BMJ (British Medical Journal)*, 2000 May 20;320(7246): pgs. 1363–1367.

11. Steele L, Prevalence and patterns of Gulf War illness in Kansas veterans: association of symptoms with characteristics of person, place, and time of military service, *American Journal of Epidemiology*, 2000, No. 15;152(10): pgs. 992, 999.

12. Ibid., pg. 992.

13. At least one British veteran was vaccinated against tularemia.

14. Melinda K. Plaisier, Associate Commissioner of Legislation, Food and Drug Administration, *Letter to the Honorable Jack Metcalf*, House of Representatives, March 20, 2000.

15. Personal communication with Norma Smith.

16. Mark Ellengold, *Testimony to the House Government Reform Committee*, 3 October 2000.

17. *Personal Communication* with Monica Revelle, FDA Spokesperson, 3 October 2000.

18. Powell MF, Newman MJ, *Vaccine Design, The Subunit and Adjuvant Approach*, Plenum Press, New York, 1995, pg. 285.

19. Ott G, Barchfield GL, Chernoff D, Radhakrishnan R, van Hoogevest P, Van Nest G, MF59, Design and evaluation of a safe and potent adjuvant for human vaccines, *Pharmaceutical Biotechnology*, 1995; pgs. 6:277–296.

20. Ibid., pg. 284.

21. Ibid., 285.

22. http://pmep.cce.cornell.edu/profiles/extoxnet/TIB/ppm.html.

23. BioPort, *Vaccine Lot Inventory for Anthrax Vaccine Adsorbed*, CONFIDENTIAL communication, 23 October 1998; the information in the confidential BioPort inventory conflicts with recent information published by researchers at USAMRIID, which states FAV008 was first filled and potency tested in March 1991, and was therefore not administered to U.S. personnel during Operation Desert Storm/Desert Shield. You can read the Fort Detrick reference to FAV008 in the following paper:

Hart MK, Del Giudice RA, Korch Jr. GW, Absence of Mycoplasma Contamination in Anthrax Vaccine, *Emerging Infectious Diseases*, 2002 Jan;8(1): pg. 94.

24. Personal communication from Dr. John Petrovic, Los Alamos National Laboratory, *Molar concentration problem*, 23 August 2001; Personal communication from Dr. Russell B. Wilson, Autoimmune Technologies, *Calculations*; I received about five different calculations on the number of squalene molecules in a concentration of 10 ppb squalene per 0.5 ml of anthrax vaccine. I used the two calculations that agreed with each other. The smallest number of molecules calculated to be in a 10 ppb/0.5 ml. concentration of squalene was 1.67×10^{12} molecules or 1.67 trillion, which is still a significant dose of molecules. This calculation was made by Dr. Douglas Shanklin, an M.D. and Ph.D. pathologist who is also a member of the American Mathematical Society.

25. "Think about the body as a bathtub," says Dr. Lewis Sheiner, "and the dose is the size of the . . . mass that you put in, then you can dilute it out. So the concentration can

be nanograms per mil, but since the body is liters, nanograms per mil is micrograms per liter, and then if you have a widely distributed drug, let's just say a 100 liters worth—so then it becomes in the order of hundreds of micrograms, total, and that's a, you know, a fraction of a milligram. So it's not a lot, but it's not a trivial amount."

26. Mowat AM, Donachie AM, Jagewell S, Schon K, Lowenadler B, Dalsgaard K, Kaastrup P, Lycke N, CTA1-DD-immune stimulating complexes: a novel, rationally designed combined mucosal vaccine adjuvant effective with nanogram doses of antigen, *Journal of Immunology*, 2001 Sept 15;167(6): pgs. 3398–3405.

27. http://www.isconova.se/text_press_eu.htm.

28. Zoon KC, Vaccines, pharmaceutical products, and bioterrorism: challenges for the U.S. Food and Drug Administration, *Emerging Infectious Diseases*, 1999 Jul-Aug;5(4): pg. 536. In this paper on vaccines and bioterrorism, Zoon discussed the current studies of "new anthrax vaccine products." She recommended that "Comparisons of immune responses in human cohorts receiving new or licensed vaccines should be performed."

29. Russell PK, Vaccines in Civilian Biodefense Against Bioterrorism, *Emerging Infectious Diseases*, 1999 Jul-Aug;5(4): pg. 533.

30. Committee on R&D Needs for Improving Civilian Medical Response to Chemical and Biological Terrorism Incident, Institute of Medicine and Board on Environmental Studies and Toxicology, Commission on Life Sciences, National Research Council, *National Academy Press*, Washington, DC, 1999, pg. 136; "8–15 A vigorous national effort is needed to develop, manufacture, and stockpile an improved anthrax vaccine. This will both benefit the armed forces and enhance the ability to protect population. The ongoing DoD effort should be supported and accelerated by a well-coordinated complementary DHHS program."

31. LaForce FM, Diniega BM, Memorandum for the Assistant Secretary of Defense (Health Affairs), The Surgeon General, Department of the Army, The Surgeon General, Department of the Navy, The Surgeon General, Department of the Air Force, *SUBJECT: Armed Forces Epidemiological Board Recommendations Regarding the Anthrax Vaccine Immunization Program*, DEPARTMENT OF DEFENSE, Armed Forces Epidemiological Board, 5109 Leesburg Pike, Falls Church, VA 22041–3258, AFEB (15–1a) 00–1, 29 March 2000, pg. 2.

32. LaForce FM., Diniega BM, Memorandum for the Assistant Secretary of Defense (Health Affairs), The Surgeon General, Department of the Army, The Surgeon General, Department of the Navy, The Surgeon General, Department of the Air Force, *SUBJECT: Armed Forces Epidemiological Board (AFEB) Comments and Recommendations Concerning the JCS BW Threat List for 2000*, DEPARTMENT OF DEFENSE, Armed Forces Epidemiological Board, 5109 Leesburg Pike, Falls Church, VA 22041–3258, AFEB (15–1a) 00–7, 03 August 2000, pg. 1.

33. LaForce FM, Diniega BM, Memorandum for the Assistant Secretary of Defense (Health Affairs), The Surgeon General, Department of the Army, The Surgeon General, Department of the Navy, The Surgeon General, Department of the Air Force,

SUBJECT: *Armed Forces Epidemiological Board (AFEB) Recommendations Regarding Review of the Paper, "Antibodies to Squalene in Gulf War Syndrome" by P. B. Asa, Y. Cao and R.F. Garry,* DEPARTMENT OF DEFENSE, Armed Forces Epidemiological Board, 5109 Leesburg Pike, Falls Church, VA 22041–3258, AFEB (15–1a) 00–6, 11 July 2000, pg. 1.

34. *Inspection Report, U.S. Food and Drug Administration, Period of Inspection 2/4 – 20/1998, C.F. Number 1873886,* Name of Individual to Whom Report Issued: Robert C. Myers, DVM, Michigan Biologic Products Institute, 3500 N. Martin Luther King Jr. Boulevard, Lansing, MI 43902.

35. Berkow R, Fletcher AJ, Beers MH, et al., *The Merck Manual,* Sixteenth Edition, Merck Research Laboratories, Rahway, NJ, 1992, pg. 690.

36. Hart MK, Del Giudice RA, Korch Jr. GW, Absence of Mycoplasma Contamination in Anthrax Vaccine, *Emerging Infectious Diseases,* 2002 Jan;8(1), pg. 95.

37. Ibid.

38. Johannes L, McGinley L, Search for Better Anthrax Vaccine Expands; Clinical Trials Are Expected, *The Wall Street Journal,* October 19, 2001.

39. Ibid.

40. Allison AC, Squalene and Squalane emulsions as adjuvants, *Methods,* 1999 Sept;19(1): pg. 88.

41. Ibid.

42. Christian MS, Final Report on the Safety Assessment of Squalane and Squalene, *Journal of the American College of Toxicology,* 1982;1(2): pgs. 37–56.

43. Institute of Medicine, The Anthrax Vaccine: Is It Safe? Does It Work? *National Academy Press,* 2002, pg. 97.

44. These are the six papers:

Minutello M, Senatore F, Cecchinelli G, Bianchi M, Andreani T, Podda A, Crovari P, Safety and immunogenicity of an inactivated subunit influenza virus vaccine combined with MF50 adjuvant emulsion in elderly subjects, immunized for three consecutive influenza seasons, *Vaccine,* 1999 Jan;17(2): pgs. 99–104.

De Donato S, Granoff D, Minutello M, Lecchi G, Faccini M, Agnello M, Senatore F, Verweij P, Fritzell B, Podda A, Safety and immunogenicity of MF59-adjuvanted influenza vaccine in the elderly, *Vaccine,* 1999 Aug 6;17(23–24): pgs. 3094–3101.

Podda A, The adjuvanted influenza vaccines with novel adjuvants: experience with the MF59-adjuvanted vaccine, *Vaccine,* 2001 Mar 21;19(17–19): pgs. 2673–2680.

Squarcione S, Sgricia S, Biasio LR, Perinetti E, Comparison of the reactogenicity and immunogenicity of a split and a subunit-adjuvanted influenza vaccine in elderly subjects, *Vaccine,* 2003 Mar 7;21(11–12): pgs. 1268–1274.

Iorio AM, Francisci D, Camilloni B, Stagni G, De Martino M, Toneatto D, Bugarini R, Neri M, Podda A, Comparison of the safety, tolerability, and immunogenicity of a MF59-adjuvanted influenza vaccine and a non-adjuvanted influenza vaccine in non-elderly adults, *Vaccine,* 2003 Oct 1;21(27–30): pgs. 4234–4237.

Frey S, Poland G, Percell S, Podda A, Comparison of the safety, tolerability, and immunogenicity of an MF59-adjuvanted influenza vaccine and a non-adjuvenated influenza vaccine in non-elderly adults, *Vaccine*, 2003 Oct 1;21(27–30): pgs. 4234–4237.

45. Minutello M, Senatore F, Cecchinelli G, Bianchi M, Andreani T, Podda A, Crovari P, Safety and immunogenicity of an inactivated subunit influenza virus vaccine combined with MF50 adjuvant emulsion in elderly subjects, immunized for three consecutive influenza seasons, *Vaccine*, 1999 Jan;17(2): pg. 101: "All enrolled subjects were white. Their mean age was 71.5 (range 65–81) for the Fluad group and 73.4 years (range 65–90) for Aggripal S1 group."

46. Podda A, The adjuvanted influenza vaccines with novel adjuvants: experience with the MF59-adjuvanted vaccine, *Vaccine*, 2001 Mar 21;19(17–19): pg. 2676: "A large phase IV trial was not included in the safety meta-analysis because the safety follow-up did not include the assessment of common post-immunisation reactions, but only that of adverse events leading to a physician visit within 7 days of immunisation."

47. Gasparini R, Pozzi T, Montomoli E, Fragapane E, Senatore F, Minutello M, Podda A, Increased immunogenicity of the MF59-adjuvanted influenza vaccine compared to a conventional subunit vaccine in elderly subjects, *European Journal of Epidemiology*, 2001;17(2): pg. 136: "During the study days 28–180, only hospitalisations and deaths were collected and recorded as serious adverse events."

48. Ibid.

49. Letter from Howard H. Pien, Chiron President and Chief Executive Officer, 4 March 2004, Chiron 2003 Annual Report, www.chiron.com/investors/shareholder/2003_AR/letter.html.

50. The makers of the TiterMax squalene adjuvant explicitly state on their website that their adjuvant is meant for research in animals only.

51. (1) University of California School of Medicine, Los Angeles; (2) Karolinska Institute in Sweden; (3) Immunology Unit, Department of Endocrinology, Lund University, also in Sweden; (4) Division of Rheumatology and Clinical Immunology at the University of Florida Medical School at Gainesville; (5) Rheumatology Unit at the Royal Adelaide Hospital in Australia; (6) University of Queensland in Brisbane (7) National Institute of Public Health and the Environment (RIVM) in the Netherlands and (8) Department of Neuropathology and Laboratory for the Ultrastructure of the Nervous System at the Polish Academy of Sciences.

52. Kuroda Y, Nacionales DC, Akaogi J, Reeves WH, Satoh M [Division of Rheumatology and Clinical Immunology, Department of Medicine, University of Florida, Gainesville], Autoimmunity induced by adjuvant hydrocarbon oil components of vaccine, *Biomedicine & Pharmacotherapy*, 2004 Jun(58)5: pg. 325.

53. Satoh M, Kuroda Y, Yoshida H, Behney KM, Mizutani A, Akaogi J, Nacionales DC, Lorenson TD, Rosenbauer RJ, Reeves WH [Division of Rheumatology and Clinical Immunology, Department of Medicine, University of Florida, Gainesville], Induction of lupus autoantibodies by adjuvants, *Journal of Autoimmunity*, 2003 Aug;21(1): pg. 8.

54. Formerly available at: http://www.anthrax.osd.mil/Site_Files/qna/SQUALENE-FACTS.HTM (2000). An updated and condensed version of the information formerly available in SQUALENEFACTS is available at http://www.anthrax.osd.mil/resource/qna/myths_facts.asp.

55. Ibid., pg. 1.

56. Ibid., pg. 2.

57. Depuis M, Denis-Mize K, LaBarbara A, Peters W, Charo IF, McDonald DM, Ott G, Immunization with the adjuvant MF59 induces macrophage trafficking and apoptosis, *European Journal of Immunology*, 2001 Oct;31(10): pg. 2915.

58. Lewis DE, Baylor College of Medicine, Department of Immunology, One Baylor Plaza, BCMM-M929, Houston, TX, *LETTER TO: Congressman Jack Metcalf*, 2930 Wetmore Avenue, Suite 9-E, Everett, WA 98201, 22 September 2000.

59. Asa PB, Wilson RB, Garry RF, Antibodies to Squalene in Recipients of Anthrax Vaccine, *Experimental and Molecular Pathology*, 2002 Aug;73(1); pg. 23; Cannon PR, Antibody production and the anamnestic reaction, *The Journal of Laboratory and Clinical Medicine*, 28, pgs. 127–139.

60. Kaneda T, Fatty acids in the genus Bacillus. II. Similarity in the fatty acid compositions of Bacillus thuringiensis, Bacillus anthracis, and Bacillus cereus, *Journal of Bacteriology*, 1968 June;95(6): pgs. 2210, 2212 (Table 2), 2214 (Table 4).

61. Goldfine H, Comparative aspects of bacterial lipids, *Advances in Microbial Physiology*, 1972;8: pg. 2.

Chapter Eleven

1. BioPort Corporation, *Package Insert for BioThrax™*, 31 January 2002, pg. 4.

2. Myths and Facts About Anthrax Vaccine, Anthrax Vaccine Immunization Program, http://www.anthrax.osd.mil/resource/qna/myths_facts.asp.

3. Op cit., BioPort Corporation, pg. 4.

4. Michigan Department of Public Health, *Package Insert for Anthrax Vaccine Adsorbed*, ADVERSE REACTIONS, U.S. Licensed No. 99,Auth.: Act 368, 1978, pg. 2.

5. Kingsbury NR, United States General Accounting Office, Anthrax Vaccine, GAO's *Survey of Guard and Reserve Pilots and Aircrew*, GAO-02-445, September 2002, pg.18.

6. Ibid., pg. 19.

7. Ibid., pg. 21.

8. Ibid.pg. 21.

9. Ibid. pg. 21.

10. Ibid., pg. 23.

11. Kingsbury N, *Anthrax Vaccine: Changes to the Manufacturing Process*, GAO, United States General Accounting Office, Testimony Before the Subcommittee on National Security, Veterans' Affairs, and International Relations, Committee on Government Reform, House of Representatives, GAO–02–181T, October, 23, 2001.

12. Ibid., pg. 3. The producer of anthrax vaccine at the time, Michigan Department of Public Health, switched from ceramic filters to nylon ones.

13. BioPort Corporation (new insert), pgs. 5–6.

14. Kerrison JB, Lounsbury D, Thirkill CE, Lane RG, Schatz MP, Engler RM, Optic neuritis after anthrax vaccination, *Ophthalmology*, 2002 Jan;109(1):99–104.

15. Berkow R, et al., *The Merck Manual*, Sixteenth Edition, Merck Research Laboratories, Merck & Co., Rahway, NJ, 1992, pg. 2392.

16. Op cit., Kerrison.

17. Op cit., Kerrison.

18. Op cit., BioPort Corporation (new insert), pg. 6.

19. Miller J, McBride BW, Manchee RJ, Moore P, Baillie LW, Production and purification of recombinant protective antigen and protective efficacy against *Bacillus anthracis*, *Letters in Applied Microbiology*, 1998 Jan;26(1): pg. 58.

20. Ibid., pgs. 58–59.

21. Ibid., pg. 59.

22. Congressman Jack Metcalf, *Metcalf Report on the Potential Role of Squalene in Gulf War Illnesses*, Prepared by the office of Congressman Jack Metcalf, Submitted to Subcommittee on National Security, Veterans Affairs and International Relations, September 27, 2000, pg. 2.

23. Ibid.

24. Ibid.

25. Ibid.

26. Ibid., pg. 3.

27. Ibid., pg. 4.

28. Ibid., pg. 3.

29. Ibid.

30. Ibid., pg. 4.

31. Ibid.

32. Ibid.

33. Ibid.

34. Ibid., pg. 3.

35. Ibid., pg. 4.

36. Ibid.

37. Ibid., pg. 5.

38. Ibid., pg. 6.

39. Ibid.

40. Ibid.

41. Ibid.

42. United States Patent 6,387,665, *Method of making a vaccine for anthrax*, Assignee: The United States of America as represented by the Secretary of the Army, 14 May 2002, pg. 1.

43. Ibid., pgs., 3, 10.

44. Little SF, Knudson GB, Comparative efficacy of Bacillus anthracis live spore vaccine and protective antigen vaccine against anthrax in the guinea pig, *Infection and Immunity*, 1986 May;52(2): pg. 510. Fellows PF, Linscott MK, Ivins BE, Pitt MLM, Rossi CA, Gibbs PH, Friedlander AM, Efficacy of a human anthrax vaccine in guinea pigs, rabbits and rhesus macaques against challenge by Bacillus anthracis isolates of diverse geographical origin, *Vaccine*, 2001 Nov 12;20(3–4), pg. 3244.

45. Ivins BE, Welkos S, Recent Advances in the Development of an Improved Anthrax Vaccine, *European Journal of Epidemiology*, 1988 Mar;4(1): pg. 13.

46. Ivins BE, Fellows PF, Nelson GO, Efficacy of a standard human anthrax vaccine against *Bacillus anthracis* spore challenge in guinea pigs, *Vaccine*, 1994 Aug;12(10): pg. 872. Fellows, pg. 3243.

47. Swartz GM Jr., Gentry MK, Amende LM, Blanchette-Mackie EJ, Alving CR, Antibodies to cholesterol, *Proceedings of the National Academy of Sciences*, 1988, Mar;5(6): pg. 1906. Berkow, pg. 409.

48. Ibid.

49. Ibid.

50. Alving CR, Swartz GM Jr., Wassef NM, Naturally occurring autoantibodies to cholesterol in humans, *Biochemical Society Transactions*, 1989 Aug;17(4): pg. 638.

51. Ibid.

52. Wassef NM, Johnson SH, Graeber GM, Swartz GM Jr., Schultz CL, Hailey JR, Johnson AJ, Taylor DG, Ridgway RL, Alving CR, Anaphylactoid reactions mediated by autoantibodies to cholesterol in miniature pigs, *Journal of Immunology*, 1989 Nov. 1;143(9), pg. 2992.

53. Ibid., pg. 2993.

54. Ibid., pg. 2992.

55. Miyamoto K, Schultz E, Heath T, Mitchell MD, Albertine KH, Staub NC, Pulmonary intravascular macrophages and hemodynamic effects of liposomes in sheep, *Journal of Applied Physiology*, 1988 Mar;64(3): pgs. 1143–1152.

56. Alving CR, Richards RL, Hayre MD, Hockmeyer WT, Wirtz RA, Liposomes as carriers of vaccines: development of a liposomal malaria vaccine, *Immunological Adjuvants and Vaccines*, ed. Gregory Gregoriadis, Anthony C. Allison, George Poste, Plenum Press and NATO Scientific Affairs Division, New York and London, 1989, pg. 125.

57. Alving CR, Immunological aspects of liposomes: presentation and processing of liposomal protein and phospholipids antigens, *Biochimica et Biophysica Acta [International Journal of Biochemistry and Biophysics]*, 1992 Dec 11;1113(3–4), pgs. 307–322.

58. Berkow, pgs. 1318–1319.

59. Alving CR, Wassef NM, Potter M, Antibodies to cholesterol: biological implications of antibodies to lipids, *Current Topics Microbiology and Immunology*, 1996;210: pg. 182.

60. Alving CR, Swartz GM Jr, Wassef NM, Herderick EE, Virmani R, Kolodigie FD, Matyas GR, Ribas JL, Kenner JR, Cornhill JF, Vaccination against cholesterol: immunologic modulation of diet-induced hypercholesterolemia and atherosclerosis, In: Wood-

ford P, Davignon J, Sniderman A (eds), *Atherosclerosis X*, 1995a, Elsevier Science BV, Amsterdam pgs. 944–948.

61. United States Patent 6,110,492, *Immunogenic compositions*, Inventors: Alving CR, Muderhwa JM, Lynn E, Assignee: Jenner Biotherapies, Inc., August 29, 2000.

62. Alving CR, Grabenstein JD, Re: Antibodies to squalene in Gulf War syndrome, *Experimental and Molecular Pathology*, 2000 Jun;68(3): pgs. 196–198. Asa PB, Cao Y, Garry RF, Asa PB, Reply, *Experimental and Molecular Pathology*, 2000 Jun;68(3), pgs. 197–198.

63. Alving, pg. 196.

64. Ibid.

65. Asa, pg. 197.

66. *FACTS ON SQUALENE*, U.S. Department of Defense, Health Affairs, pg. 3; http://www.anthrax.osd.mil/Site_files/qna/SQUALENEFACTS.HTM.

67. Matyas GR, Wassef NM, Rao M, Alving CR, Induction and detection of antibodies to squalene, *Journal of Immunological Methods*, 2000 Nov 1;245(1–2), pgs. 5, 7.

68. Ibid.

69. Ibid., pg. 5.

70. Ibid., pg. 1.

71. Ibid. Personal communication with Dr. Julius Cruse, M.D., Editor-in-Chief, *Experimental and Molecular Pathology*.

72. United States Patent 6,110,492, pg. 1.

73. Metcalf, pg. 4.

74. Ibid.

75. United States Patent 6,110,492, pg. 1.

76. Michael D. Stitely, Deputy Director, Freedom of Information Act Officer, Department of the Army, U.S. Army Medical Research Acquisition Activity, *Letter to Gary Matsumoto*, February 28, 2001.

77. Press Conference: Anthony J. Principi, Secretary for Veterans' Affairs, Washington, DC, December 10, 2001.

78. Ibid.

79. Horner RD, Kamins KG, Feussner JR, Grambow SC, Hoff-Lindquist J, Harati Y, Mitsumoto H, Pascuzzi R, Spencer PS, Tim R, Howard D, Smith TC, Ryan MA, Coffman CJ, Kasarskis EJ, Occurrence of amyotrophic lateral sclerosis among Gulf War veterans, *Neurology*, 2003 Sep 23;61(6): pgs. 742–749.

80. Virella G (ed.), *Medical Immunology, Fifth Edition, Revised and Expanded*, Marcel Dekker, Inc., New York, 2001, pg. 331.

81. Dunkley PR, Carnegie PR, Amino acid sequence of the smaller basic protein from rat brain myelin, *The Biochemical Journal*, 1974 Jul;141(1):243–255.

82. Sheremata W, Wood DD, Moscarello MA, Antimyelin basic protein antibodies and cellular hypersensitivity in multiple sclerosis, *Transactions of the American Neurological Association*, 1976;101: pgs. 291–294. Fujinami RS, Oldstone MB, Amino acid ho-

mology between the encephalitogenic site of myelin basic protein and virus: mechanism for autoimmunity, *Science*, 1985 Nov 29;230(4729): pgs. 1043–1045.

83. Fujinami, pg. 1045.

84. Shchelkunov SN, Stavitskii SB, Batenko LI, Gashnikov PV, Shchelkunova GA, Kostyrev OA, Sandakhchiev LS, Viral chimeric protein including a determinant of myelin basic protein is capable of inducing allergic encephalomyelitis in guinea pigs, *Biomedical Science*, 1991;2(5): pgs. 493–497.

85. Whitehouse MW, Orr KJ, Beck FW, Pearson CM, Freund's Adjuvants: Relationship of Arthritogenicity and Adjuvanticity in Rats to Vehicle Composition, *Immunology*, 1974 Aug;27(2): pgs. 311–330.

86. Lorentzen JC, Identification of arthritogenic adjuvants of self and foreign origin, *Scandinavian Journal of Immunology*, 1999 Jan;49(1): pgs. 45–50.

87. Gajkowska B, Smialek M, Ostrowski RP, Piotrowski P, Frontczak-Baniewicz M, The experimental squalene encephaloneuropathy in the rat, *Experimental and Toxicologic Pathology*, 1999 January; 5: pgs. 75–80.

Chapter 12

1. Tramont Col. EC, *SUBJECT: Tri-Service Task Force (Appendix A)*, SGRD-UWZ-H, 7 December 1990.

2. Sawyer WA, Meyer KF, Eaton MD, Bauer JH, Putnam P, Schwentker FF, Jaundice in Army personnel in the western region of the United States and its relation to vaccination against yellow fever, *American Journal of Hygiene*, 1944, (39): pg. 337–430. Sawyer W, et al., Jaundice in Army personnel in the western region of the United States and its relation to vaccination against yellow fever, *American Journal of Hygiene*, 1944, (40): pgs. 35–107. Walker DW, Some epidemiological aspects of infectious hepatitis in the U.S. Army, *American Journal of Tropical Medicine*, 1945, (25): pgs. 75–82. Havens WP Jr., Viral Hepatitis. In: Andersen RS, ed., *Internal medicine in World War II. Vol. 3. Infectious disease and general medicine*, Washington D.C.: Government Printing Office, 1968: pgs. 331–384. Seeff LB, Beebe GW, Hoofnagle JH, Norman JE, Buskell-Bales Z, Waggoner JG, Kaplowitz N, Koff RS, Petrini JL, Schiff ER, Shorey J, Stanley MM, A Serologic Follow-up of the 1942 Epidemic of Post-Vaccination Hepatitis in the United States Army, *The New England Journal of Medicine*, 16 April 1987, 316;(16): pgs. 965–966. Norman JE, Beebe GW, Hoofnagle JH, Seeff LB, Mortality Follow-up of the 1942 Epidemic of Hepatitis B in the U.S. Army, *Hepatology*, 1993, 15;(4): pgs. 790–791.

3. Ammend et al., Plaintiffs, v. BioPort et al., Defendants, Case No. 5.03-CV-031, Honorable Gordon J. Quist, United States District Court for the Western District of Michigan, Southern Division.

4. Eventually, attorneys Alan C. Milstein and Derek T. Braslow (of the New Jersey firm Sherman, Silverstein, Kohl, Rose and Podolsky) represented a total of 71 plaintiffs in Ammend et al.

5. Client list for Ammend et al., Plaintiffs, v. BioPort et al., Defendants, Case No. 5.03-CV-031, Honorable Gordon J. Quist, United States District Court for the Western District of Michigan, Southern Division, 16 July 2002.

6. Wendling M, Anthrax Vaccine May Have Been Thrown Overboard, Vets Say, http://www.crosswalk.com/news/1182299.html.

7. Wood D, The Determination of Squalene in a Vaccine Sample, *Scientific Analysis Laboratories Ltd.*, 26 February 2003, pg. 3. Anthrax Vaccine Lots 81236/391; SAL Ltd. had combined the two lots to make one composite sample for testing.

8. VaxGen, VaxGen and Britain's Health Protection Agency Sign Preliminary Pact to Deploy Anthrax Vaccine in U.K., http://vaxgen.com/pressroom/index.html, News Events, Press Releases, 3 September 2003.

9. Friedlander A, *rPA Anthrax Vaccine Candidate, Briefing to RADM Clinton*, United States Army Medical Research Institute of Infectious Diseases, USAMRMC, 22 May 2000, pg. 5. Friedlander A, *Next Generation Anthrax Vaccine Candidate, Briefing to IPT*, United States Army Medical Research Institute of Infectious Diseases, USAMRMC, 28 June 2000, pg. 2.

10. United States Patent 6,387,665, *Method of making a vaccine for anthrax*, Assignee: The United States of America as represented by the Secretary of the Army, 14 May 2002, pg. 1.

11. Kelly M, Soldiers' pneumonia blamed on smoking, *Associated Press*, 10 September 2003.

12. Ibid.

13. Timmer SJ, Amundson DE, Malone JD, Hypersensitivity Pneumonitis Following Anthrax Vaccination, *Chest*, 2002 Aug;122(2): pg. 741–745.

14. BioPort package insert for Anthrax Vaccine Adsorbed (BioThrax(tm)), 31 January 2002, pg. 6.

15. Email from Captain David Hodge, 31 May 2002, pg. 1.

16. Giullevin L, Cohen P, Gayraud M, Lhote F, Jarrouse B, Casassus P, Churg-Strauss Syndrome (Clinical Study and Long-Term Follow-Up of 96 Patients, *Medicine*, 1999;78(1), pg. 26–37. Val-Bernal JF, Mayorga M, Garcia-Alberdi E, Pozueta JA, Churg-Strauss syndrome and sudden cardiac death, *Cadiovascular Pathology*, 2003;12: pgs. 94–97.

17. Op cit., Giullevin et al., pg. 26.

18. Op cit., BioPort, pg. 6.

19. Skobic M, *Transfer Summary*, MR #32067, Franciscan Skemp Healthcare Medical Center, La Crosse Campus, 4 April 2003, pg. 1.

20. Ibid.

21. Pfeifer EA, *Autopsy Report*, Rachael A. Lacy, Mayo Clinic - Rochester, 4 April 2003, pg. 1,

22. Ibid.

23. Op cit., BioPort, pg. 6.

24. Jontz S, Pneumonia again hits troops in Middle East, The Stars and Stripes, European edition, 10 July 2004.

25. Peak JG, MEMORANDUM FOR Commanders, Regional Medical Commands, SUBJECT: learning from Adverse Events After Vaccination—ACTION MEMORANDUM, Department of the Army, Headquarters, United States Army Medical Command, 2050 Worth Road, Fort Sam Houston, Texas 78234-6000, 10 February 2004.

26. Benjamin M, Mystery Pneumonia Toll May Be Much Higher, United Press International, 17 September 2003.

27. Op cit., BioPort, pg. 6.

28. Ibid, pg. 5.

29. Op Cit., BioPort, pg. 6.

30 http://www.wrairclinicaltrials.com/Study_AVA_Active.shtml.

31 http://www.clinicaltrials.gov/ct/gui/show/NCT00057525.

32. Edwards JF, Slauson DO, Complete Freund's Adjuvant-induced Pneumonia in Swine: A Model of Interstitial Lung Disease, Journal of Comparative Pathology, 1983 July;93(3), pgs. 353–361.

33. Brooks RE, Betz RD, Moore RD, Injury and repair of the lung: response to intravenous Freund's adjuvant, Journal of Pathology, 1978 Apr;124(4), pgs. 205–217. Fisher MV, Morrow PE, Yuele CL, Effect of Freund's complete adjuvant upon clearance of iron-59 oxide from rat lungs, Journal of Reticuloendothelial Society, 1973 Jun;13(6), pgs. 536–56.

34. Taubenberger JK, Molecular diagnostics # 2003-812, Patient Name: Bloom, David, AFIP Molecular Diagnostics Laboratory Report, 28 April 2003.

35. Myers DD, Hawley AE, Farris DM, Wroblski SK, Thanaporn P, Schaub RG, Wagner DD, Kumar A, Wakefield TW, P-selectin and leukocyte microparticles are associated with venous thrombogenesis, Journal of Vascular Surgery, 2003 Nov;38(5): pgs.1075–89.

36. Berkow R, The Merck Manual of Diagnosis and Therapy, Sixteenth Edition, Merck Research Laboratories, Rahway, N.J. 1992, pg. 2441.

37. Author interview with pilot.

38. Ibid, pg. 1452.

39. Klotter J, Vaccine-induced heart problems; Smallpox vaccinations and anthrax vaccine, Townsend Letter for Doctors and Patients, Gale Group Inc. and The Townsend Letter Group, August 1, 2004.

40. FACTS ON SQUALENE, U.S. Department of Defense, Health Affairs, pg. 1, formerly found at the following web address, http://www.anthrax.osd.mil/Site_files/qna/SQUALENEFACTS.HTM.

41. Aldrich Chemical Co., Inc., 1001 West St. Paul, Milwaukee, WI 53233, MATERIAL SAFETY DATA SHEET, pg. 2, wyswyg://96/http://infonew.sigma-aldrich...i-bin/gx.cgi/Applogic+MSDSInfo.ReturnMSDA.

42. Tauber AI, The Immune Self (Theory or metaphor?), Cambridge University Press, New York, 1997, pg. 1–2.

43. *VaxGen Finalizes Commercial Rights to Anthrax Vaccine Candidate*, http://www. biospace.com/news_story.cfm?StoryID=14022220&full=1.

44. Silvestris F, Williams RC Jr, Dammacco F, Autoreactivity in HIV-1 infection: the role of molecular mimicry, *Clinical Immunology Immunopathology*, 1995 Jun;75(3): pgs. 197–205.

45. Hornblum AM, Acres of Skin, Routledge, New York, 1998, pg. 81.

46. *Metcalf Report on the Potential Role of Squalene in Gulf War Illness*, 27 September 2000, pg. 12.

47. Matyas GR, Rao M, Pittman PR, Burge R, Robbins IE, Wassef NM, Thivierge B, Alving CR, Detection of Antibodies to Squalene III. Naturally occurring Antibodies to Squalene in Humans and Mice, *Journal of Immunological Methods*, 2004;286: pg. 47-67.

48. Matyas GR, Wassef NM, Rao M, Alving CR, Induction and detection of antibodies to squalene, *Journal of Immunological Methods*, 2000 Nov 1;245(1–2):1–14. Matyas G, Rao M, Alving C, Induction and detection of antibodies to squalene. II. Optimization of the assay for murine antibodies, *Journal of Immunological Methods*, 2002 Sep 15; 267(2):119.

49. Op cit., Matyas, 2004, pg. 50.

50. Alving CR, Swartz GM, Wassef NM, Naturally occurring autoantibodies to cholesterol in humans, Biochemical Society Transactions, 1989 Aug;17(4): pg. 637.

51. Alving CR, Wassef NM, Potter M, Antibodies to cholesterol: biological implications of antibodies to lipids, *Current Topics Microbiology and Immunology*, 1996;210: pg. 182.

52. Mahlandt BG, Klein F, Lincoln RE, Haines BW, Jones WI Jr. Friedman RH, Immunologic Studies of Anthrax IV. Evaluation of the Immunogenicity of Three Components of Anthrax Toxin, *The Journal of Immunology*, 196 Apr;96(4): pg. 732.

53. Leppla SH, Robbins JB, Schneerson R, Shiloach J, Development of an improved vaccine for anthrax, *The Journal of Clinical Investigation*, 2002 Jul;110(2), pg. 143.

54. Author interview with Dr. Ken Alibek, 19 October 2001.

55. Author interview with Dr. Joseph Jemski, 10 March 2004.

56. Staff Report Prepared for the Committee On Veterans' Affairs, United States Senate, 103rd Congress, 2nd Session, *Is Military Research Hazardous to Veterans' Health? Lessons Spanning Half a Century*, U.S. Government Printing Office, Washington D.C., 8 December 1994, pg. 44.

57. President William J. Clinton, Executive Order, The White House, Office of the Press Secretary, 30 September 1999, pg. 1.

58. Beecher HK, ETHICS AND CLINICAL RESEARCH, *The New England Journal of Medicine*, 1966 Jun 16;274(24): pg. 1355.

59. Op cit., Mahlandt, pg. 732; Jemski JV, Anthrax, Professional Staff Meeting to be Presented by Aerobiology Division, [USAMRIID],Thursday, 25 March 1982, 1430 Hours, Main Conference Room., pg. 11; Little SF, Knudson GB, Comparative efficacy of Bacillus anthracis live spore vaccine and protective antigen vaccine against anthrax in the guinea pig, *Infection and Immunity*, 1986 May;52(2) pg 509–12;

Turnbull PC, Broster MG, Carman JA, Manchee RJ, Melling J, Development of antibodies to protective antigen and lethal factor components of anthrax toxin in humans and guinea pigs and their relevance to protective immunity, *Infection and Immunity*, 1986 May 52(2) pg. 356–63; Stepanov AV, Marinin LI, Pomerantsev AP, Staritsin NA, Development of novel vaccines against anthrax in man, *Journal of Biotechnology*, 1996 Jan 26;44(1–3): pgs. 155–60.

60. Gherardi RK, [Lessons from macrophagic myofasciitis: towards definition of a vaccine adjuvant-related syndrome], *Revue Neurologique*, 2003 Feb;159(2): pgs. 162–4.

61. Satoh M, Kuroda Y, Yoshida H, Behney KM, Mizutani A, Akaogi J, Nacionales DC, Lorenson TD, Rosenbauer RJ, Reeves WH, Induction of lupus autoantibodies by adjuvants, *Journal of Autoimmunity*, 2003 Aug;21(1): pg. 9.

62. Kuroda Y, Nacionales DC, Akaogi J, Reeves WH, Satoh M, Autoimmunity induced by adjuvant hydrocarbon oil components of vaccine, *Biomedicine & Pharmacotherapy*, 2004 Jun;58(5): pg. 337.

63. Ibid.

64. Beebe GW, Simon, HA, Vivona S, Follow-up study on Army Personnel Who Received Adjuvant Influenza Virus Vaccine 1951–1953, *The American Journal of the Medical Sciences*, 1964 April; 247: pgs.385–406; Beebe GW, Simon AH, Vivona S, Long-term mortality follow-up of Army recruits who received adjuvant influenza virus vaccine in 1951–1953, *American Journal Epidemiology*, 1972 Apr;95(4):337–46.

65. Op cit., Kuroda, pg. 9.

66. Podda A, The adjuvanted influenza vaccines with novel adjuvants: experience with the MF59-adjuvanted vaccine, *Vaccine*, 2001 Mar 21;19(17–19): pg. 2676. "A large phase IV trial was no included in the safety meta-analysis because the safety follow-up did not include the assessment of common post-immunisation reactions, but only that of adverse events leading to a physician visit within 7 days of immunisation."

67. Op cit, Kuroda, pg. 335.

68. Miller FW, Hess EV, Clauw DJ, Hertzman PA, Pincus T, Silver RM, Mayes MD, Varga J, Medsger TA Jr, Love LA, Approaches for identifying and defining environmentally associated rheumatic disorders, *Arthritis and Rheumatism*, 2000 Feb;43(2): pgs. 243–9.

69. Ibid.

70. http://www.vietnam-war.info/battles/operation_ranch_hand.php.

71. Depuis M, Denis-Mize K, LaBarbara A, Peters W, Charo IF, McDonald DM, Ott G [*Cardiovascular Research Institute and Department of Anatomy, University of California, San Francisco, CA 94143*], Immunization with the adjuvant MF59 induces macrophage trafficking and apoptosis, *European Journal of Immunology*, 2001 Oct;31(10: pgs. 2910–8; Depuis M, McDonald DM, Ott G [*Cardiovascular Research Institute, University of California, San Francisco, CA 94143*], Distribution of adjuvant MF59 and antigen gD2 after intramuscular injection in mice, *Vaccine*, 1999 Oct 14;18(5–6): pgs. 434–9.

72. Depuis M, Murphy TJ, Higgins D, Ugozzoli M, Van Nest G, Ott G, McDonald DM [*Cardiovascular Research Institute, University of California, San Francisco, CA*

94143], Dendritic cells internalize vaccine adjuvant after intramuscular injection, *Cellular Immunology*, 1998 May 25;186(1): pgs. 18–27.

73. Tilvis RS, Miettinen TA [*Department of Medicine, University of Helsinki, Helsinki, Finland*], Absorption and metabolic fate of dietary 3H-squalene in the rat, *Lipids*, 1983 Mar;18(3): pgs. 233–8; Gylling H, Miettinen TA [*Second Department of Medicine, University of Helsinki, Helsinki, Finland*], Postabsorptive metabolism of dietary squalene, *Atherosclerosis*, 1994 April;106(2): pgs. 169–78; Relas H, Gylling H, Miettinen TA [*Department of Medicine, University of Helsinki, Helsinki, Finland*], Effect of stanol ester on postabsorptive squalene and retinyl palmitate, *Metabolism*, 2000 April;49(4): pgs. 473–8.

74. Minutello M, Senatore F, Cecchinelli G, Bianchi M, Andreani T, Podda A, Crovari P, Safety and immunogenicity of an inactivated subunit influenza virus vaccine combined with MF59 adjuvant emulsion in elderly subjects, immunized for three consecutive influenza seasons, *Vaccine*, 1999 Jan;17(2): pgs. 99–104.

75. Ibid, pg. 101.

76. Kingsbury NR, Anthrax Vaccine: GAO's Survey of Guards and Reserve Air Crew, United States Accounting Office Report to Congressional Requesters, *GAO–02–445*, pgs. 24–25.

77. Kingsbury NR, Anthrax Vaccine: GAO's Survey of Guards and Reserve Air Crew, United States Accounting Office Report to Congressional Requesters, *GAO–02–445*, pgs. 24–25.

78. Institute of Medicine, The Anthrax Vaccine: Is It Safe? Does It Work?, *National Academy Press*, Washington D.C., 2002.

79. Ibid, pg. 25.

80. Kawahito Y, Cannon GW, Gulko PS, Remmers EF, Longman RE, Reese VR, Wang J, Griffiths MM, Wilder RL, Localization of quantitative trait loci regulating adjuvant-induced arthritis in rats: evidence for genetic factors common to multiple autoimmune diseases, *Journal of Immunology*, 1998 Oct 15;161(8): pgs. 4411–9.

81. http://www.chiron.com/products/vaccines/fluvaccines/index.html.

82. http://www.fda.gov/cber/vaccine/licvacc.htm.

Squalene References

Squalene Induces Autoimmune Disease in Animals

1. Whitehouse MW, Orr KJ, Beck FW, Pearson CM [Division of Rheumatology, Department of Medicine, University of California School of Medicine, Los Angeles, California], "Freund's Adjuvants: Relationship of Arthritogenicity and Adjuvanticity in Rats to Vehicle Composition," *Immunology*, (1974) Aug;27(2)311-30.
2. Beck FW, Whitehouse MW, Pearson CM [Division of Rheumatology, Department of Medicine, University of California School of Medicine, Los Angeles, California], "Improvements for consistently inducing experimental allergic encelphalomyelitis (EAE) in rats: I. without using mycobacterium. II. inoculating encephalitogen into the ear," *Proceedings of the Society for Experimental Biology and Medicine*, (1976) Mar;151(3):615-22.
3. Kohashi O, Pearson CM [Division of Rheumatology, Department of Medicine, University of California School of Medicine, Los Angeles, California], "Arthritogenicity of Mycobacterium smegmatis subfractions, related to different oil vehicle and different composition," *International Archives of Allergy Applied Immunology*, (1976);51(4):462-70.
4. Beck FW, Whitehouse MW [Division of Rheumatology, Department of Medicine, University of California School of Medicine, Los Angeles, California and Department of Experimental Pathology, John Curtin School of Medical Research, The Australian National University, Canberra A.C.T. 2600, Australia], "Modifications in the Establishment of Allergic Encephalomyelitis (EAE) in Rats; an Improved Assay for Immunosuppressant Drugs," *Agents Actions*, (1976) July;6(4):460-7.
5. Zamma T [Department of Oral Surgery, School of Medicine, Nagoya University, Showa-Ku, Nagoya, 466 Japan], "Adjuvant-Induced Arthritis in the Temporomandibular Joint of Rats," *Infection and Immunity*, March 1983;39(3), pg. 1291-1299.

6. Johnston BA, Eisen H, Fry D [Fred Hutchinson Cancer Research Center, Seattle, Washington], "An Evaluation of Several Adjuvant Emulsion Regimens for the Production of Polyclonal Antisera in Rabbits," *Laboratory Animal Science*, (1991) Jan;41(1):15-21.

7. Lipman NS, Trudel LJ, Murphy JC, Sahali Y [Division of Comparative Medicine, Massachusetts Institute of Technology, Cambridge, MA 02139], "Comparison of Immune Response Potentiation and In Vivo Inflammatory Effects of Freund's and Ribi Adjuvants in Mice," *Laboratory Animal Science*, (1992) April;42(2):193-7.

8. Leenaars PP, Hendriksen CF, Angulo AF, Koedam MA, Claasen E [National Institute of Public Health and Environmental Protection (RIVM), P.O. Box 1, 3720 BA, Bilthoven, The Netherlands], "Evaluation of several adjuvants as alternatives to the use of Freund's adjuvant in rabbits" *Veterinary Immunology and Immunopathology*, (1994) Mar;40(3):225-41.

9. Leenaars M, Koedam MA, Hendriksen CF, Claassen E [National Institute of Public Health and Environmental Protection (RIVM), Bilthoven, The Netherlands], "Immune responses and side effects of five different oil-based adjuvants in mice," *Veterinary Immunology and Immunopathology*, (1998) Feb 27;61(2-4):291-304.

10. Leenaars PP, Koedam MA, Ester PW, Baumans V, Claassen E, Hendriksen CF [National Institute of Public Health and Environmental Protection (RIVM), P.O. Box 1, 3720 BA, Bilthoven, The Netherlands], "Assessment of side effects induced by injection of different adjuvant/antigen combinations in rabbits and mice," *Laboratory Animals* (1998) Oct;32(4):387-406.

11. Kleinau S, Erlandsson H, Klareskog L [Department of Clinical Immunology, University Hospital, Uppsala, Sweden], "Percutaneous exposure of adjuvant oil causes arthritis in DA rats," *Clinical Experimental Immunology*, (1994) May;96(2):281-4. (*Refers to olive oil, which contains squalene).

12. Yoshino S, Yoshino J [Rheumatology Unit, Royal Adelaide Hospital, Adelaide, SA5000, Australia], "Recruitment of pathogenic T cells to synovial tissues of rats injected intraarticularly with nonspecific agents," *Cellular Immunology*, (1994) October 15;158(2):305-13.

13. Smialek M, Gajkowska B, Ostrowski RP, Piotrowski P [Department of Neuropathology and Laboratory of the Ultrastructure of the Nervous System, Medical Research Centre, Polish Academy of Sciences, Warszawa, Poland], "Experimental squalene encephaloneuropathy in the rat," *Folia Neuropathologica*, (1997);35(4):262-4.

14. Gajkowska B, Smialek M, Ostrowski RP, Piotrowski P, Frontczak-Baniewicz M [The Laboratory of the Ultrastructure of the Nervous System, Medical Research Centre, Polish Academy of Sciences, 5 Pawinskiego Street, 02-106 Warsaw, Poland], "The experimental squalene encephaloneuropathy in the rat," *Experimental and Toxicologic Pathology*, (1999) January; 5:75-80.

15. Lorentzen JC [Department of Medicine, Karolinska Hospital, Karolinska Institutet, Stockholm, Sweden]," Identification of arthritogenic adjuvants of self and foreign origin," *Scandinavian Journal of Immunology*, (1999) Jan;49(1):45-50.

16. Carlson BC, Jannson AM, Larsson A, Bucht A, Lorentzen JC [Department of Med-icinee, Karolinska Institutet, Stockholm, Sweden], "The endogenous adjuvant squa-lene can induce a chronic T-cell-mediated arthritis in rats," *American Journal of Pathology*, (2000) Jun:156(6):2057-65.

17. Holm BC, Zu HW, Jacobsson L, Larson A, Luthman H, Lorentzen JC [Center for Molecular Medicine, Department of Medicine, Unit of Rheumatology, Karolinska Institutet, S-17176 Stockholm, Sweden], "Rats made congenic for Oia3 on chromo-some 10 become susceptible to squalene-induced arthritis," *Human Molecular Ge-netics*, (2001) Mar 215;10(6):565-72.

18. Holmdahl R, Lorentzen JC, Lu S, Olofsson P, Wester L., Holmberg J, Pettersson U, [Section of Medical Inflammation Research, Lund University, Sweden]. "Arthritis induced in rats with nonimmunogenic adjuvants as models for rheumatoid arthritis" *Immunological Reviews*, (2001) Dec;184:184-202.

19. Holm BC, Svelander L, Bucht A, Lorentzen JC [Department of Medicine, Unit of Rheumatology, Karolinska Institutet, Stockholm and Department of Medical Coun-termeasures, Division of NBC Defense, Defense Research Agency, Umea, Swe-den], "The arthritogenic adjuvant squalene does not accumulate in joints, but gives rise to pathogenic cells in both draining and non-draining lymph nodes," *Clinical and Experimental Immunology*, (2002) Mar;127(3):430-5.

20. Whitehouse MW, Beck FWJ, Matsumoto G [Department of Medicine, University of Queensland, Princess Alexandra Hospital, Queensland, Australia; Wayne States University Medical Center, Detroit, Michigan, U.S.A.], "Squalene is an Auto Toxi-cant Inducing Polyarthritis in Rats and Immunopathies in Man, Abstract," *The Aus-tralian Health and Medical Congress*, 2002, no. 1143.

21. Gherardi RK [Groupe Nerf-Muscle, Departement de Pathologie, Hopital Henri Mondor, Creteil], "Lessons from macrophagic myofasciitis: towards definition of a vaccine adjuvant-related syndrome," *Revue Neurologique* (Paris), (2003) Feb;159(2):162-4.

22. Backdahl L, Ribbihammar U, Lorentzen JC [Center for Molecular Medicine, Karolinska Institutet, Stockholm], "Mapping and functional characterization of rat chromosome 4 regions that regulate arthritis models and phenotypes in congenic strains," *Arthritis and Rheumatism*, (2003) Feb;48(2):551-9.

23. Satoh M, Kuroda Y, Yoshida H, Behney KM, Mizutani A, Akaogi J, Nacionales DC, Lorenson TD, Rosenbauer RJ, Reeves WH [Division of Rheumatology and Clinical Immunology, Department of Medicine, University of Florida, Gainesville], "Induc-tion of lupus autoantibodies by adjuvants," *Journal of Autoimmunity*, (2003) Aug;21(1):1-9.

24. Kuroda Y, Akaogi J, Nacionales DC, Wasdo SC, Szabo NJ, Reeves WH, Satoh M [Division of Rheumatology and Clinical Immunology, Department of Medicine, University of Florida, Gainesville], "Distinctive Patterns of Autoimmune Response Induced by Different Types of Mineral Oil," *Toxicological Sciences*, (2004) Apr;78(2):222-8.

25. Kuroda Y, Nacionales DC, Akaogi J, Reeves WH, Satoh M [Division of Rheumatology and Clinical Immunology, Department of Medicine, University of Florida, Gainesville], "Autoimmunity induced by adjuvant hydrocarbon oil components of vaccine," *Biomedicine & Pharmacotherapy*, (2004), Jun;(58)5:325-37.

26. Holm BC, Lorentzen JC, Bucht A [Diabetes Research, Immunology Unit, Department of Endocrinology, Lund University, Malmo University Hospital, Stockholm], "Adjuvant oil induces waves of arthritogenic lymph node cells prior to arthritis onset," *Clinical and Experimental Immunology*, (2004) Jul;137(1):59-64.

Adverse Reactions in Humans to Experimental Vaccines Containing Squalene

27. Keitel W, Couch R, Bond N., Adair S, Van Nest G, Dekker C [Baylor College of Medicine, Department of Microbiology and Immunology, One Baylor Plaza, Houston, Texas 77030], "Pilot evaluation of influenza virus vaccine (IVV) combined with adjuvant," *Vaccine*, (1993);11(9):909-913; *[See also Nos. 27 & 31];

Squalene Stimulates the Immune System

28. Ott G, Barchfield GL, Chernoff D, Radhakrishnan R, van Hoogevest P, Van Nest G [Chiron Corporation, Emeryville, California 94608], "MF59. Design and evaluation of a safe and potent adjuvant for human vaccines," *Pharm Biotechnol*, (1995);6:277-96.

29. Ott G, Barchfield GL, Chernoff D, Radhakrishnan R, van Hoogevest P, Van Nest G [Chiron Corporation, Emeryville, CA 94608], "MF59. Design and Evaluation of a Safe and Potent Adjuvant for Human Vaccines," *Vaccine Design: The Subunit and Adjuvant Approach* (Monograph), (1995) Chapter 10:277-311.

30. Ott G, Barchfield GL, Van Nest G [Chiron Corporation, Emeryville, CA 94608], "Enhancement of humoral response against human influenza vaccine with the simple submicron oil/water emulsion adjuvant MF59," *Vaccine*, (1995) Nov; 13(16):1557-62.

31. O'Hagan DT, Ott GS, Van Nest G [Chiron Corporation, Emeryville, CA 94704], "Recent advances in vaccine adjuvants: the development of MF59 emulsion and polymeric microparticles," *Molecular Medicine Today*, (1997) Feb; 3(2):69-75.

32. Allison AC [Suromed Corporation, 1060 East Meadow Circle, Palo Alto, California 94303], "Squalene and squalane emulsions as adjuvants," *Methods* (1999) Sept;19(1):87-93.

How the Immune System Processes Squalene

33. Depuis M, Murphy TJ, Higgins D, Ugozzoli M, Van Nest G, Ott G, McDonald DM [Cardiovascular Research Institute, University of California, San Francisco, CA

94143], "Dendritic cells internalize vaccine adjuvant after intramuscular injection," *Cellular Immunology*, (1998) May 25;186(1):18-27.

34. Depuis M, McDonald DM, Ott G [Cardiovascular Research Institute, University of California, San Francisco, CA 94143], "Distribution of adjuvant MF59 and antigen gD2 after intramuscular injection in mice," *Vaccine*, (1999) Oct 14;18(5-6):434-9.

35. Depuis M, Denis-Mize K, LaBarbara A, Peters W, Charo IF, McDonald DM, Ott G [Cardiovascular Research Institute and Department of Anatomy, University of California, San Francisco, CA 94143], "Immunization with the adjuvant MF59 induces macrophage trafficking and apoptosis," *European Journal of Immunology*, (2001) Oct;31(10):2910-8.

Specificity of Antibody Response to Squalene

36. Asa PB, Cao Y, Garry RF [Department of Microbiology and Immunology, Tulane Medical School, 1430 Tulane Avenue, New Orleans, Louisiana 70112], "Antibodies to Squalene in Gulf War Syndrome," *Experimental and Molecular Pathology* (2000) Feb;68(1):55-64.

37. Matyas GR, Wasseff NM, Rao M, Alving CR [Department of Membrane Biochemistry, Walter Reed Army Institute of Research, 20910-7500, Silver Spring, MD], "Induction and detection of antibodies to squalene," *Journal of Immunological Methods* (2000) Nov 1;245(1-2):1-14.

38. Alving CR, Grabenstein JD [Walter Reed Army Institute of Research and Anthrax Vaccine Immunization Program Office], "RE: Antibodies to squalene in Gulf War Syndrome," *Experimental and Molecular Pathology* (2000) Jun;68(3):196-8.

39. Asa PB, Cao Y, Garry RF [Department of Microbiology and Immunology, Tulane Medical School, 1430 Tulane Avenue, New Orleans, Louisiana 70112], "Reply," *Experimental and Molecular Pathology* (2000) Jun;68(3):197-8.

40. Asa PB, Wilson RB, Garry RF [Department of Microbiology and Immunology, Tulane Medical School, 1430 Tulane Avenue, New Orleans, Louisiana 70112], "Antibodies to Squalene in recipients of anthrax vaccine," *Experimental and Molecular Pathology* (2002) Aug;73(1):19-27.

41. Matyas G, Rao M, Alving C [Department of Membrane Biochemistry, Walter Reed Army Institute of Research, 503 Robert Grant Avenue, 20910-7500, Silver Spring, MD, USA], "Induction and detection of antibodies to squalene. II. Optimization of the assay for murine antibodies," *Journal of Immunological Methods* (2002) Sep 15; 267(2):119.

42. Matyas GR, Rao M, Pittman PR, Burge R, Robbins IE, Wassef NM, Thivierge B, Alving CR [Department of Membrane Biochemistry, Walter Reed Army Institute of Research], "Detection of antibodies to squalene: III. Naturally occurring antibodies to squalene in humans and mice," *Journal of Immunological Methods*, (2004) Mar;286(102):47-67.

Ingested Squalene Is Processed Differently from Injected Squalene

43. Tilvis RS, Miettinen TA [Department of Medicine, University of Helsinki, Helsinki, Finland], "Absorption and metabolic fate of dietary 3H-squalene in the rat," *Lipids*, (1983) Mar;18(3):233-8.

44. Gylling H, Miettinen TA [Second Department of Medicine, University of Helsinki, Helsinki, Finland], "Postabsorptive metabolism of dietary squalene," *Atherosclerosis*, (1994) April;106(2):169-78.

45. Relas H, Gylling H, Miettinen TA [Department of Medicine, University of Helsinki, Helsinki, Finland], "Effect of stanol ester on postabsorptive squalene and retinyl palmitate," *Metabolism*, (2000) April;49(4):473-8.

Detecting Squalene in Anthrax Vaccine Adsorbed [BioThrax] and U.K. Anthrax Vaccine

46. Spangood RJ, Wu B, Sun M, Lim P, Ellis WY [SRI International, 333 Ravenswood Avenue, Menlo Park, CA 94025], "Development and application of an analytical method for the determination of squalene in formulations of anthrax vaccine adsorbed," *Journal of Pharmaceutical and Biomedical Analysis* (2002) June 20;29(1-2):183-93.

47. May JC, Del Grosso A, Swartz L, Progar JJ, "Chemical Test Results for Michigan Department of Public Health, Anthrax Vaccine Adsorbed, Lots FAV020 and FAV 030," *Department of Health and Human Services*, Food and Drug Administration, CBER, Lab Report, Personal Communication to Neil Goldman, Ph.D., 25 June 1999, pg. 1-6.

48. Wood D [Scientific Analysis Laboratories Ltd., Medlock House, New Elm Road, Manchester M3 4JH, United Kingdom], "The Determination of Squalene in a Vaccine Sample, Scientific Analysis Laboratories, SAL Report 3412OE," *Scientific Analysis Laboratories Ltd.*, Lab Report, Personal Communication to Asif Hasan, Granada Television, 26 February 2003, pg. 1-6;.

Index

Porton Down's Center for Applied
  Microbiological Research (CAMR),
  41
Porton International, 77
Potency test failure, 207
Powell, Colin
  anthrax vaccines/Gulf War, 82, 84
  Persian Gulf oil protection, 42
Powers, Francis Gary, 17
Presidential Action Committee, 154
Presidential Advisory Committee, 195
Primaquine, 69
Principi, Anthony J., 240
*Proceedings of the National Academy of
  Sciences*, 231
Programs Resources, Inc. (PRI), 114
Project Badger, 77–78, 80, 81, 85, 86,
  247
Protective antigen
  in early anthrax vaccine, 23, 32, 33,
    34–35
  in new anthrax vaccine, 40, 45, 51, 58,
    114, 115, 175
  purity/weakness of, 33, 38, 41, 45,
    51–52, 53, 271
Publications
  snobbery about, 130–131
  on squalene antibodies, 193, 205, 216,
    233
  on squalene/autoimmune disease, 129,
    132, 178, 261–263, 264
  on squalene toxicity, 126–127,
    128–131, 132
Pulmonary anthrax, 5–7, 10, 16–22
Pyridostigmine bromide pills, 82,
  116–117

Q fever, 36

Radioactivity experiments, 70
Rapp, Herbert, 56
Rawls, Carol, 120, 123
Rawls, Don, 120, 121, 122–123
Rawls, Jeff, 119–124, 152, 162, 240
Reactogenicity, 41

Reagan, Ronald, 235
Recombinant DNA technology
  anthrax vaccine (Desert Shield), 41,
    45, 58, 78, 91, 113, 117
  anthrax vaccine (early use), 45, 51–52
  anthrax vaccine (post–Gulf War), 113,
    114, 175, 192, 204
  description/uses of, 41
Redfield, Robert, 139, 164
Restriction endonucleases, 41
"Reversion" of anthrax, 31
Ribaviran, 80, 88
Ribi adjuvant, 128–129, 212, 229
Richter, John, 183, 186
Ricin, 83
Roadman, Charles H., 173–174, 176, 178,
  179, 181, 190, 229, 230, 235, 262
Robbins, John, 208
Rodriguez, Paul, 167–168
Rogers, Bernard, 20
Romanov, Boris Georgievich
  anthrax symptoms in, 1–2, 3–5, 14
  autopsy of, 8, 10–13
  death of, 5, 7–8
  hospital care, 4–5
Rose, Gerhard, 68–69
Rossignol, Hippolyte, 25, 26
Roux, Emile, 25
Rovet, Richard, 183–185
Roy, Michael J., 102–103, 106–107,
  108–109, 110, 111
Rudicell, James Patrick, 92–95, 105, 118,
  162, 163
Russell, Phillip K., 188, 204

Sabin, Albert, 71
Saddam Hussein
  biological/chemical weapons and, ix–x,
    xiv–xv, 146–147, 151–152
  Iraq-Iran War and, 42, 59
  as U.S. ally, 42, 59
SAF-1 adjuvant, 52, 53, 209
SAIC
  squalene vaccines and, 142
  test of Asa's theory, 176